Other books by Valerie Lawson

Connie Sweetheart: The Story of Connie Robertson
The Allens Affair

Mary Poppins, She Wrote

THE LIFE OF P. L. TRAVERS

Valerie Lawson

SIMON & SCHUSTER PAPERBACKS

NEW YORK   LONDON   TORONTO   SYDNEY   NEW DELHI

Simon & Schuster Paperbacks
1230 Avenue of the Americas
New York, NY 10020

This Simon & Schuster trade paperback edition December 2013

SIMON & SCHUSTER PAPERBACKS and colophon are registered
trademarks of Simon & Schuster, Inc.

For information about special discounts for bulk purchases,
please contact Simon & Schuster Special Sales at 1-866-506-1949
or business@simonandschuster.com.

The Simon & Schuster Speakers Bureau can bring authors to your live event.
For more information or to book an event contact the Simon & Schuster Speakers
Bureau at 1-866-248-3049 or visit our website at www.simonspeakers.com.

Interior design by Carla J. Little

Manufactured in the United States of America

10   9   8   7   6   5   4   3   2   1

The Library of Congress has cataloged the hardcover edition as follows:
Lawson, Valerie.
    [Out of the sky she came]
    Mary Poppins she wrote : the life of P. L. Travers / Valerie Lawson.—
1st Simon & Schuster ed.
        p. cm.
    "Mary Poppins she wrote" was previously published in London by Aurum, 2005.
    It was originally published by Hodder in 1999 under title: Out of the sky she came.
    Includes bibliographical references and index.
    1. Travers, P. L. (Pamela Lyndon), 1899–1996. 2. Authors, English—20th century—
Biography. 3. Authors, Australian—20th century—Biography. 4. Australians—
England—Biography. 5. Poppins, Mary (Fictitious character). I. Title.
    PR6039.R32Z74 2006   823'.912—dc22   [B]   2006050062

ISBN 978-0-7432-9816-2
ISBN 978-1-4767-6292-0 (pbk)
ISBN 978-1-4165-4246-9 (ebook)

For Lucy and Annie

Contents

List of Illustrations

What we call the beginning is often the end
And to make an end is to make a beginning.
The end is where we start from. And every phrase
And sentence that is right (where every word is at home,
Taking its place to support the others,
The word neither diffident nor ostentatious,
An easy commerce of the old and the new,
The common word exact without vulgarity,
The formal word precise but not pedantic,
The complete consort dancing together)
Every phrase and every sentence is an end and a beginning,
Every poem an epitaph. And any action
Is a step to the block, to the fire, down the sea's throat
Or to an illegible stone: and that is where we start...

We shall not cease from exploration
And the end of all our exploring
Will be to arrive where we started
And know the place for the first time.

T. S. Eliot,
"Little Gidding,"
Four Quartets

Mary Poppins, She Wrote

Preface

When the poet Ted Hughes was sent a collection of Mary Poppins books, he wrote in a note of thanks to the publisher, Collins:

I'm sorry my wife, Sylvia Plath, could not see these because Mary Poppins was the fairy godmother of her childhood. She spoke of her a great deal.[1]

As Plath instinctively knew, Mary Poppins was not so much a plain old nanny as a good mother from a fairy tale. Hiding behind the facade of a British nanny pushing a pram in Kensington, Poppins was more magical than Cinderella's godmother, more mysterious than the good fairy of "The Sleeping Beauty." But Poppins had yet another aspect. Something sinister lay behind the blue button eyes and flowerpot hat. As P. L. (Pamela) Travers, the creator of Mary Poppins, wrote, every good fairy has her evil counterpart, the necessary antagonist.[2]

In Mary Poppins, Travers created more than the saccharine image we know from the Walt Disney movie of the 1960s. Poppins has lasted because she is as peculiar as she is kind, as threatening as she is comforting, as stern as she is sensual, as elusive as she is matter of fact. Where did she come from, where did she go? The Banks children, her charges, knew only one thing: out of the sky she came, and back to the sky she would go.

Since the first book was published in 1934, Mary Poppins has become imprinted in the popular culture of many countries, almost a cartoon character, reinforced by the Walt Disney movie of 1964, its rereleases in 1973 and 1980, then the movie's release on video and DVD. The six Poppins books are still in print and have been translated into more than a dozen languages. The words "Mary Poppins" have become a catchphrase, a slogan, for an idealized woman. Most recently, the nanny made a reappearance in *The Simpsons,* transformed into Sherry Bobbins, who tried, but failed, to make order of the chaos in that household. Even that treatment did not destroy her. Instead, it enhanced her.

The image of Mary Poppins with her umbrella flying over the rooftops of London is indelible, but the concept of Mary Poppins is even stronger, implying a secure childhood and an answer to women's perennial problem: how to balance their lives between their needs and their family's demands.

Mary Poppins flew into a 1930s household where the mother did not work. (In the movie Mrs. Banks became a silly suffragette, an interesting change of perspective which represented Walt Disney's response to the dawn of the new age of feminism.) By the end of the twentieth century, most women did work and most mothers need child care. If they can afford it, they hire a nanny; if not, the "nanny" is a worker in a child care center or a family day-care home. Whoever the caregiver is, the mother and father are ambivalent about the surrogate parent.

The parents want to believe the best but often they sense, or imagine, a bad witch's face behind the good. The mother feels anxious that the nanny will steal either her child or her husband. (In popular culture the nanny is often portrayed as a bimbo, marking time while she lures a husband, like Fran Fine, the pretty Jewish nanny with the fabulous clothes in the TV series.)

Parents' anxieties are reinforced by the vivid accounts of real-life nannies who kill by shaking a helpless baby to death. As they leave the law courts, the nannies look like freshly scrubbed angels, their blond hair held back by an Alice band, their hands clasping a handbag, their body enclosed in a neat little suit.

Hammer Studios understood all this very well. In 1965, a year after the film *Mary Poppins* was released, the English company which specialized in horror movies released *The Nanny,* in which Bette Davis in the title role is referred to as "Mary Poppins." Davis plays a really scary crone. Those bug eyes perform their usual Davis magic under sinister black slashes of eyebrows. By night, this nanny braids her hair into a Poppins-ish plait.

In the first household scene, we see the mother in hysterics. Her young son is due home from a mental institution where his chilly father and hapless mother had sent him. The boy had refused to eat or sleep, claiming the nanny planned to poison him or drown him in his bath. It is clear that something awful has happened to his little sister. Davis's nanny creates a sense of unease and distrust as she infantilizes the incompetent mother. She alternates between spoon-feeding her mistress and calling her "Modom." Toward the end of the movie, when we realize the nanny is a psychopath, Davis says: "Being a nanny is based on trust."

The Nanny represents the negative image of the positive *Mary Poppins*, black to white, evil to goodness, the Wicked Fairy to the Good Fairy. *The Nanny* has come to kill. *Mary Poppins* has come to repair, to make order from disorder, to create unity from disunity. Once she has done so, Mary can leave for a secret place in the heavens.

Pamela Travers once said: "A Zen priest with whom I studied told me that Mary Poppins was full of Zen, that in every Zen story there is a single object which contains a secret. Sometimes the secret is revealed, sometimes not. It doesn't matter, but it is always present."[3]

The same can be said of Travers's own life. Almost everyone has heard of Mary Poppins but hardly anyone knows of Pamela Lyndon Travers. "I don't want to be labeled. I've got a distaste for it," she once told an interviewer.[4] She stipulated that she did not want a biography written about her after her death. Like Oscar Wilde, perhaps, who called biographers "body-snatchers," she deeply resented anyone prying into her personal life. "I don't let people dig around in my life...I don't wear my private life on my sleeve," she boasted to a friend.[5]

No, she placed it in labeled boxes instead. If Travers had been serious in her wish for privacy, she would have destroyed all her personal letters, all her notes, all the audiotapes made of her lectures, formal and informal, and her collection of photographs. Instead she sold her papers, including private papers, to the Mitchell Library in Sydney, where access to the material is unrestricted. Each photograph and letter and poem and haphazard thought was carefully preserved and even annotated for future readers. But perhaps by leaving such a large treasure trove Travers was trying to label her own life rather than have anyone else interpret it.

Despite her wish that no biography be written, I believe her death meant the ground rules changed. I took the same point of view as the biographer Michael Holroyd, who has said

"I discriminate between the rights of the living and the dead...
When we are living we need all our sentimentalities, our
evasions, our half-truths and our white lies, to get through
life. When we are dead different rules apply."[6]

For me, Travers became more fascinating the more I learned
of her mystery. That was what intrigued me most, not her subject matter, although I liked *Mary Poppins* as a child, and
understood the feelings of both comfort and fear of having a
nanny. Our nanny was "Hendy"—Mrs. Henderson, from next
door—who baked Afghan biscuits and was proper, fair, and
gruff. She had such a different manner from my mother, who
looked softer, but was just as determined. My mother
worked—an unusual thing for a New Zealand woman in the
1950s. I loved Hendy yet I sometimes feared her.

My search for Pamela Travers began with the discovery that
she was an Australian. Like myself, she had been a dancer,
actress and writer. Going on "the Pamela hunt" became a five-
year journey of discovery that took me down unexpected
paths, both geographically and emotionally. The most marvelous part of the journey was the setting out, knowing little.
I wrote to her agent. Travers replied. The blue aerogram was
dated August 22, 1994.

Dear Miss Lawson,
I don't like personal publicity but I'm willing to talk about
my work any way you like.

Her letter went on to say she had broken her shoulder and,
with this, had broken some of her memory as well. Had I read
her newest book, *What the Bee Knows*? The letter ended: "We've
been having such violently hot weather that I often long to
meet a southerly buster[7] at evening!" Dictated to a person with
simple, childish handwriting, the letter was signed P. L. Travers in a wavering script.

From an obscure Californian publisher I ordered a copy of *What the Bee Knows,* a book I quickly cast aside...I had no time then for Travers's mythological references and search for heroes.

One morning eighteen months later I woke knowing this was the right time of my life to write the book. Something Travers had written had taken hold. I understood what she meant about the three phases of a woman's life—"nymph, mother, crone"[8]—because they were all part of me, coexisting, just as a baby girl has all the eggs in her body for her own future babies.

The serious journey began in the Dixson Reading Room of the Mitchell Library in Sydney, a place of contemplation and peace, where Travers's life unfurled as I unwrapped each of her old letters or stories from its tissue paper and white ribbon packaging.

In 1996 I wrote again to her literary agent to ask if I could meet Travers in London in early May. Her agent replied that Travers was extremely ill. The day after that letter arrived, Travers died. I wrote her obituary for the *Sydney Morning Herald*. The next week I went to London anyway, to cover a court case that was to be a coda to a book I had written about a scandal in a law firm. The case was settled. It was definitely time to move on. I walked down the street—Shawfield Street, Chelsea—where Travers had lived for more than thirty years, with a feeling made up of one-third fear, one-third sadness and one-third excitement.

I thought about Pamela's own journey in 1924 from Sydney to London, about her wistful memory that "as a child I always had a strong wish, that I think I was born with, of wanting to get to England and Ireland. I built the whole of my life to it."[9]

Shawfield Street is a short street. It seemed shorter that day. I reached Pamela's pink front door too soon and rang the bell, hoping no one would answer. No one did. In the time it took to reach the Kings Road, everything jelled: the passage of time, journeys taken or not taken, and how this story was now imperative.

The next three years spent searching for the truth about Pamela became an end in itself, the search as important as the conclusion. At the end of 1997 I traveled through New Mexico, to Washington, New York and Boston, then through County Donegal to London, where I met Pamela's son, Camillus Travers. He was living at 29 Shawfield Street, as familiar to me as an old photo although I had never seen inside. Upstairs was her studio. He led the way. Up there her writing desk seemed untouched since her death.

It wasn't right to leave London then. The studio was lodged in my mind, the book impossible to write without returning.

Nine months later, I flew back to London. All day I sat at her desk, tidying as I went, combing through each drawer, pulling out yellowing photos, the remains of a diary, scraps of paper, making rough order, placing paper clips and rubber bands in piles. I was all alone. Camillus left early and came home after I had gone.

One day I discovered her old long-playing records of music composed for exercises created by her guru Gurdjieff, and lowered one onto the turntable. The piano music was more soothing than I had expected. Pamela's spirit returned to the room that morning. Near the end of the first week, late one morning, a wind suddenly slammed the studio door closed. Again, Pamela's presence was strong in the studio. The hairs on the nape of my neck stood up.

Each evening at twilight I walked down the Kings Road, past the string of makeup shops and the high street fashions, around this twisty road and that to South Kensington, notes tucked in a folder, a life in bits, not yet codified. Pamela Travers seemed all around me.

• • •

Travers said all happy books are based on sadness. She must have had her own in mind. Pamela Travers, too, was full of sorrow. As she knew, "the cup of sorrow is always full. For a grown-up it's a flagon, for the child, it's a thimble, but it's never less than full."[10]

She thought "we are all looking for magic. We all need to feel we are under a spell and one day a wand will be waved and the princes that we truly feel ourselves to be will start forth at last from the tattered shapeless smocks. But indeed we have to wave the wand for ourself. If only we could refrain from endlessly repairing our defenses. To be naked and defenseless. Oh we need it."[11]

She needed that but didn't find it, creating more defenses and masks with age. The writer Salman Rushdie summarized such a life—and so many of our lives—in his comment to an interviewer: "We live in a world of disappointment. You begin with high hopes and the beautiful innocence of childhood but you discover that the world isn't good enough, nor are our lives and nor are we. But there are moments in life when we can have an experience of transcendence, feel part of something larger, or simply our hearts burst inside."[12]

Travers experienced that marvelous transcendence more than most, I believe. It came unexpectedly, as it always does, in the pleasure of her search for a pattern and meaning in her life. As she told one of her favorite writers, Jonathan Cott: "There's a wonderful line in a poem by Theodore Roethke which says 'you learn by going where you have to go.' You can't learn before you set out, can you? You go along the road and learn as you go."[13]

Her life was much more than I ever imagined. My life expanded in the writing of hers.

Valerie Lawson

I

The Nymph

1899–1934

"The moment between day and dark...

"Come inside Lyndon...Lyndon, can you hear me? It's late, it's almost dark. I need you to help with the baby."

Lyndon heard. She was going to squeeze every last moment from the twilight, here in the field of weeds next to the big house. Lyndon lay on her back and stared into the heavens. The prickles jabbed into her bare shoulders. She wanted more and more and more to let the canopy of sky fall over her, as soft as the clean sheet Kate Clancy shook onto her high wooden bed on Saturdays.

There was Venus already up. On one side of the arc above she could see the Southern Cross, on the other, the seven stars of the constellation of the Pleiades. Johnny the stable boy had told her the stars were once women, the seven sisters of Atlas.

Lyndon felt as if she could fly into the blueness of the half hemisphere above her. Mummy said if she wasn't careful her hair could catch in the stars. She half wanted to believe it, but then her mother had such silly stories.

Lyndon never told anyone she could hear the stars humming. She loved the Pleiades most. What if one of the seven sisters shook herself free and flew down to earth, even right into her house with mother and father, Kate Clancy, and her little sisters, Barbara and baby Moya? She hoped it would be Maia, the most magical sister.

when anything can happen."[1]

If Lyndon lay still long enough, the trees might forget her and keep on whispering. The gossips! Lyndon knew that their chattering stopped as soon as they saw her.

"Lyndon!" She stood up and brushed down her cotton pinafore. The house glowed with candlelight and oil lamps. Lyndon could almost smell bathtime, see the big cake of Sunlight Soap. Her mother would be dressed in her camisole, the baby dribbling onto the blue ribbon tying the neckline. When Moya stopped crying as she latched onto Mummy's breast, and the water stopped splashing, and the horses were asleep in their stables, Lyndon would listen to the house. At night, it was full of crackles and creaks and sighs.

Lyndon had hidden a threepenny piece in her apron pocket all day. Just before bed she went to her father's room and showed him the coin. In the morning, she promised, she would buy him some pears.

"Pears! Just what I need!" Travers Robert Goff took the threepence and slipped it under his pillow.

Next morning, Lyndon awoke to find her mother, Margaret, already up, half sitting, half lying on the sofa in the drawing room. "Father has gone to God."

1

The Real Mr. Banks

Helen Lyndon Goff had two fathers. One was real. The other she imagined. The traces of both men can be found in a third father, the completely fictional George Banks, the melancholy head of the household in the adventures of Mary Poppins. Mr. Banks was a banker, but he represented more than a pillar of the City of London with bowler and furled umbrella, grumbling about his personal finances and the chaos of his Chelsea household. Mr. Banks hired Mary Poppins to create order from that chaos, and, though he never went with her on one of her heavenly adventures, he knew instinctively that Mary Poppins was magic.

Helen Lyndon Goff said she invented both George Banks and the practically perfect Mary Poppins "mainly to please myself." Mr. Banks fulfilled many roles. He was the father, and lover, Lyndon wished she had, this whimsical bank manager who lives with his family at 17 Cherry Tree Lane, London, where, one fantastic day, Mary Poppins flew in with the East Wind.

But instead of Mr. Banks, Helen Lyndon had Travers Robert Goff. He was nowhere near good enough. Lyndon took the best of him, though—what she remembered from her childhood—and enhanced the rest. The result was a composite Irish hero: glamorous, languid and charming, a father she later described to others as the handsome supervisor of a sugarcane plantation in far away, subtropical Australia, "the deep country," as she called it. Born in Ireland, this idealized, imagined father strode the cane fields of northern Queensland in a white silk suit, floppy white hat, gold earrings and scarlet cummerbund, surrounded by faithful servants and with a barn stocked with every sort of conveyance: a four-wheeler, hansom cab, old howdah, and an elegant sledge along with carts, wagons and sulkies.[1]

In truth, her father was a bank manager before he was demoted to bank clerk. He died in his early forties, his life unfulfilled, his family left destitute and forced onto the charity of rich but emotionally chilly relatives. Travers Robert Goff drank too much and wanted too much that he never attained. His legacy was establishing in his daughter's mind the idea that she was not Australian at all, but a misfit in the Antipodes, a woman destined to spend her life in search of the fairy tales, poetry and romance of her father's Irish fantasies. She even took his first name as her surname. As a journalist, writer and actress she used the pseudonym Pamela Lyndon Travers.

Travers Goff was a bamboozler. The tales he told his family and friends grew more romantic the more he drank. He liked to boast that his life was drenched in the Celtic Twilight, in the land of Yeats and George William Russell. But as much as he admired the poets and dramatists of the nineteenth century, he was most in love with the myths of ancient Ireland, and of the fictional personification of Ireland, immortalized in a play by William Butler Yeats, *Cathleen ni Houlihan*. Fairies, pixies and elves meant everything. The Great Serpent of his adopted land meant nothing. Even in Australia "he had Ireland round him like a cloak very much the way James Joyce wrapped Dublin around him even when he was in Paris."[2]

Helen Lyndon Goff followed Mary Poppins's greatest precept: Never Explain. She certainly never explained why she favored the cane-field version of her father's life. It may have been a case of simple snobbery. Lyndon preferred to be the daughter of a gentleman farmer in the tropical outback than the daughter of a pen-pusher in the back office of a provincial bank. Whatever the reason, false versions of her father and her own early years in Australia shadowed her through life, and even after her death. Her obituary in *The New York Times* claimed that she was the daughter of a sugar planter, while the *Guardian*'s obituary writer believed she was the granddaughter of the premier of Queensland, who was also the founder of one of Australia's biggest companies, Colonial Sugar Refining.

The confusion was understandable, considering Goff's own reluctance to reveal his origins, even to his wife. She told the doctor who signed his death certificate that he was born in County Wexford, Ireland. Lyndon herself said, "My father came from a very old Irish family, Irish gentry, what we call landed people...He was a younger son, and younger sons were sent to explore the world...what made him go to Australia I don't know. He was Anglo Irish, and the Irish are great wanderers."[3]

Goff was born at home in Queens Road, Deptford, London, in December 1863, the second son of a shipping agent, Henry Lyndon Bradish Goff, and his wife Charlotte Cecilia. He did have Irish connections, though, with relatives whose surname was Davis-Goff, who lived in both County Wexford and near Galway, in the west of Ireland.

As a young man, not yet twenty, Travers Goff sailed from London to Ceylon, where he took up tea planting before drifting on to Australia. He settled in New South Wales, and then, in about 1891, moved to the colony of Queensland. It is possible he was an overseer on a sugarcane farm at some time before his marriage. A portrait dated 1896, taken in a Sydney photographer's studio, shows him with a droopy, oversized handlebar mustache, posed stiffly in a white suit, white shoes and pith helmet. There are similarities in the costume to photographs of sugar plantation overseers in the 1880s. But his outfit could also be a nostalgic acknowledgment of the clothes he wore in Ceylon.

Whatever his original Australian occupation, Goff did not remain long in any town. His name does not appear in any residential directory of New South Wales or Queensland from the 1880s. But by July 23, 1898, he had settled in Maryborough, where he joined the Australian Joint Stock Bank. As branch manager, he earned a salary of £250 a year as well as a servants allowance of £50.[4]

For a single man, there were worse places to be than the pretty subtropical town of Maryborough, a river port about 250 kilometers north of Brisbane, named after the Mary River, which flows through it. Like many of the coastal towns of Queensland, Maryborough looked a little like colonial Ceylon, with its wooden buildings—lacy, delicate—built to withstand the worst of the sweltering summer months. Maryborough was proud of its town hall, and Queens Park, laid out in the London manner with ornamental trees. A gun recovered from a shipwreck in the Torres Strait was fired each day at one o'clock. By the 1880s, Maryborough's diversions included an Orchestra Society, band concerts held in the cool of the night, circuses, vaudeville, and moonlight excursions on the river. Just before Goff arrived, in the year of Queen Victoria's Jubilee, motion pictures came to town.

Maryborough lived on two industries: timber and sugar. In the decade to 1880, the sugar industry boomed with more than forty juice mills and sugar mills in the district. But the boom gave way to a drought that saw planters forced to mortgage their properties and unable to pay off their loans. Bankers, such as the directors of Goff's bank, fretted over the low price of sugar and the worrying outlook for the industry. They began to foreclose, to cut plantations into farming blocks and offer them for sale.

Australian banks were badly hung over from the 1880s boom, and the Australian Joint Stock Bank was no exception. By the time Goff joined in 1898, it claimed to be the third-biggest bank in New South Wales and Queensland, but a crisis of the early 1890s was still fresh in the minds of its directors. The AJS Bank relied heavily on London for its deposits. Bank problems in England in the early 1890s led directly to the AJS Bank closing its doors in April 1893, reopening two months later under a scheme of reconstruction.[5]

The roller-coaster ride of Australian banks in the 1890s continued to affect Travers Goff, professionally and personally, until his death. Lyndon's father's experiences, combined with bank problems involving her mother's family, remained in her mind for life. Both spilled over into her portrait of George Banks, whose personality was as ambivalent as her father's. In Mr. Banks, Lyndon created a worrier who dreamed of the stars, but had to go to his bank every day except Sundays and bank holidays. There he sat in a big chair at a big desk and made money. The Banks children, perhaps like little Helen Lyndon, thought he manufactured the coins himself, cutting out pennies and shillings and half-crowns and threepences, and bringing them home in his black Gladstone bag. Sometimes, when George Banks had no money for the children, he would say "The bank is broken." The two oldest Banks children, Jane and Michael, counted their money carefully into their money boxes, prudent like father: "Sixpence and four pennies—that's tenpence, and a halfpenny and a threepenny bit."[6]

In much the same way, Lyndon as an adult scrutinized her investments, asking bankers, lawyers and agents to constantly check the balances, never thinking she had enough. Her fears came not just from her father's problems, but from the foolish investments of her mother's uncle, Boyd Morehead, son of a dour, careful Scot. Boyd was the black sheep of the canny Moreheads, a Scottish family described by Lyndon as "very rich." She boasted that her mother, Margaret Morehead, was "educated in London and Paris and, until she married, always had her own maid."[7] From her mother's family came Lyndon's innate snobbery and prudence. Unlike the Goffs—elusive and difficult to pinpoint in their origins—the Moreheads' story is a wide open book, set out in dictionaries of biography and the records of some of Australia's oldest companies.

The first Morehead to settle in Australia was Robert Archibald Alison Morehead, the third son of the Episcopal dean of Edinburgh. Morehead, a manufacturer of shawls and cloth in Scotland, decided to move to a warmer climate when he feared he had tuberculosis. Late in 1840 he was appointed manager of the Scottish Australian Company, and with his wife, Helen Buchanan Dunlop, arrived in Sydney the following year. He was twenty-eight. Soon after, two sons were born, Robert Charles in 1842 and Boyd Dunlop a year later. The family moved to 1 O'Connell Street in the heart of the city. There, the Morehead family dining room opened up right into the Scottish Australian Company's office. Soon to move nearby were two Sydney institutions, the Australian Club (for men only), and the *Sydney Morning Herald*. At O'Connell Street, Helen Morehead gave birth to two more babies: Helen Christina, and the youngest, Jane Katherine.

The Moreheads traveled often, and in style. P&O liners carried the whole family back and forth from England. The boys were educated in Scotland and at Sydney Grammar, but the girls were taught at home by governesses. Life on O'Connell Street left its imprint on the fictional home of the Banks family, 17 Cherry Tree Lane. Lyndon was told as a child how the four Morehead children lunched with their parents but took their evening meal in the schoolroom with the governess. The servants included a cook, laundress, housemaid and parlormaid. The natural good humor of the children upset their father; they liked to shock him by sliding down the banisters and by singing in bed early in the evening when the bank clerks could hear the racket, downstairs in the office.

In 1861 Helen Morehead died, in her forties, leaving her husband to raise their four children, now in their teens. The youngest, Jane, just thirteen, was sent to boarding school at Carthona in Darling Point. Her big sister Helen learned how to become the matriarch and mothering nanny of the family. "At fifteen," she later wrote, "I had to take up housekeeping. I was terrified at having to order servants about and I am afraid I was not much of a housekeeper but I did my best for father and he helped me all he could."[8] She never married, unlike all her siblings. Robert was the first of the children to leave home, marrying Maria Jacobs in 1867. Five years later, Jane married the Englishman William Rose. The last to marry was Boyd in 1873. He and his bride, Annabella Ranken, moved to Brisbane. Some of these nineteenth-century Moreheads later appeared in different guises in Mary Poppins books. Two of the Banks children were Jane and Annabel, named after Jane Morehead and Annabella Morehead.

The Moreheads' comfortable early life was funded by their father's wise decisions. Robert Archibald Alison Morehead had arrived in Sydney with about £30,000 to invest for the Scottish Australian Company and had quickly moved into the moneylending business. He bought up mortgages and lent at the high interest rate of 12.5 percent. "Reaping the harvest of mortgages," he called it. In this way, he was able to buy property in Sydney, Melbourne and the country. Morehead also moved into the commission and agency business and advanced money against produce, especially wool. He developed coal-mining interests in Newcastle and bought pastoral land in Queensland and in the Gulf country, including the huge property Bowen Downs.

He retired in 1884, having built up a business empire embracing pastoral holdings, city property and productive coal mines.[9] But Morehead's private life was sadly out of kilter. Not only had his wife died, but his eldest child, Robert Charles, also died before him. Robert, a clerk in his father's business, was only thirty-two when he died of tuberculosis in 1874. (As an adult, Lyndon continually but mistakenly believed she had contracted tuberculosis and traveled the world in search of warm, tranquil places, dying a hundred deaths in fear of its grip.)

Because of Robert Charles Morehead's early death, and the subsequent remarriage of his widow, Maria, their daughter, Margaret, was left in the care of her spinster aunt. This unplanned outcome, involving two Morehead wills, affected Margaret deeply. It also affected the upbringing of her daughter, Lyndon, and meant both women came into the orbit of a woman who was the prototype for the character of Mary Poppins.

Robert Charles Morehead knew he was dying. Four days before his death, he signed a will appointing his father as trustee of his estate. He left £700 in trust for his wife Maria and his baby daughter Margaret. At the same time, his father, Robert Archibald Alison Morehead, changed his will. His trustees were to set aside £3,000 to be invested by his son, Boyd, and son-in-law, William Rose. The two men were to be trustees for Maria and Margaret.

Six years later, in 1870, Maria remarried, much to the anger
of the old man. That year, in another codicil, Robert Archibald
Alison Morehead directed that Maria was to get just £500 from
his estate on condition that she surrender "entirely all control
over Margaret Agnes Morehead. Failing such surrender, the
£500...is to pass into my general estate." Little Margaret went
into his own custody, the victim of very tense relations
between her mother and grandfather. She lived with her
maiden aunt Helen, and her grandfather, until he died in 1885.

Just before old man Morehead died he added a final codicil to his will, giving Helen the right to bequeath her share
of his estate, which amounted to £15,000, in whatever way
she wanted. With his death, she "assumed the position and
privileges of the head of the family...she retained them until
she herself followed him to the vault."[10]

After Morehead's death, Margaret Morehead remained in
the care of her Aunt Helen and her servants in Woollahra, one
of the most desirable suburbs in Sydney. From then on, Margaret was raised by this substitute mother whom she called
"Aunt Ellie." Aunt Ellie gave her the rules for life, as well as
her values, mannerisms and sayings. Margaret passed them on
to her own daughter, Lyndon, who in turn gave them to Mary
Poppins. But while Margaret grew up in a secure and wealthy
household, she was totally dependent on her Aunt Helen after
her Uncle Boyd squandered her trust funds.

While old man Morehead was prudent and slow, Boyd was
a wild boy, impatient and ambitious. Too eager for experience
to finish university, Boyd tried gold mining before working for
the Bank of New South Wales, until he was sacked for insub-
ordination. Father came to the rescue and Boyd went onto the
land, managing the Scottish Australian property, Bowen
Downs. After his marriage, he settled down to become a
member of the Queensland Legislative Assembly, and set up a
stock and station agency and mercantile business, B. D. More-

head and Co. Boyd became embroiled in a land sales scandal, yet rose to become the colonial secretary of Queensland, then premier for two years from the end of 1888.

In the grand house Cintra, at Bowen Hills in Brisbane, he lived in style with his wife and seven daughters, touring his country properties and tending his city businesses, which included, from 1876, his directorship of the Queensland National Bank.[11] This was no ordinary bank; it was more like a cross between the Bank of England and the opulent palace of a London bank which appeared in the film version of *Mary Poppins*. The Queensland National Bank was run by Edward Drury, an associate of Sir Thomas McIlwraith, who became Queensland premier in 1879. As premier, he transferred the government's account to the Queensland National Bank.

The Queensland National Bank was more than just the government banker. While it raised money for Queensland in London, it was also a plaything—a money box—for the businesses of government members. Its shareholders included eighteen members of the Legislative Council and Legislative Assembly. In 1891 the Queensland government and the Bank of England fell out with one another over a loan the government tried to raise in London. The tension undermined London's confidence in both the government and the Queensland National Bank, which had to be propped up with government deposits. English investors in the bank started to withdraw their deposits and the bank's shares fell well below par.

As a director of the bank, Boyd was deeply involved in the crisis. He and his fellow directors took out an account to purchase the bank's own shares. Over the years, Boyd had invested much of his own inheritance and much of his niece Margaret's in bank shares and deposits. In May 1893, the bank closed its doors while it tried to restructure. It reopened for business late the same year, but its most damaging secrets were not revealed until three years later when the general manager died, and an investigation revealed that the bank was insolvent. By 1898, Morehead and other directors of the bank were cleared of charges of negligence. The bank was restructured again but many depositors were unable to withdraw their funds for years.

For the Morehead clan, it had all been too close a call for comfort. Lyndon later told a trusted friend that her mother's uncle invested his money and Margaret's without due care, and so by the time her mother was married, she had very little of her own inheritance left.[12]

Margaret had grown into a timid, pretty woman in her early twenties when she met Travers Robert Goff in Sydney, before he took up his banking job. He must have seemed safe, steady—reliable enough to provide an income for life. Not only that, he would have appeared sophisticated, a traveler who told her tales of Ceylon and how he dressed every night for dinner, a sahib with servants around him. From Queensland, he wooed her with witty, lighthearted letters, many written in simple verse. They chose to marry in Boyd Morehead's hometown, Brisbane, on November 9, 1898, in the pretty Anglican Church of All Saints. Boyd gave the bride away.

Exactly nine months later, on August 9, 1899, Helen Lyndon Goff was born in Maryborough, in the residence attached to the AJS Bank. She was named Helen after both her maternal great-grandmother and her great aunt. But no one ever called her Helen, preferring Lyndon, an Irish name much used in her father's family for boys and girls alike. It was shortened to Lindy or Ginty. It pleased her that the name was Gaelic, meaning water and stone.[13]

Lyndon was never, in her own mind, an Australian, always an Irishwoman with a Scots mother. In her middle age, she found something slightly shameful about being born in Australia, explaining that her birth there came about "almost by chance." She regarded Australia as the "southern wild" and herself as a woman displaced. In a speech to the U.S. Library of Congress in the 1960s, Lyndon told the audience: "You remember [William] Blake's 'Little Black Boy'?...my mother bore me in the southern wild....In that sense I was a little black boy too, born in the subtropics."[14]

From this sense of misplaced birth, Lyndon felt a compulsion to travel away from the southern sun to the mists of Europe. That drive was fueled by her father's romantic ideas of Ireland. But, like every child, her personality was set long before she made her escape in her twenties. Lyndon was formed by a combination of three adults—her parents and her Great Aunt Ellie—and by the interconnections of those three. None of the three was direct with her, none supported and nurtured her wholeheartedly.

Lyndon made the first journey in her lifetime of restless journeys as a baby in her mother's arms. They traveled by train from Maryborough to Sydney, where Lyndon first encountered her Great Aunt Ellie. In the next decade Ellie was to represent a fixed, reliable support for Lyndon, whose father was the first of several men whose drinking almost ruined her life. Lyndon later believed that her mother realized early in her marriage that Travers Goff drank far too much. The habit of "deep drinking" he had learned in Ceylon increased over the years and "cast such a shadow on our lives."[15]

In 1900, with his wife and baby tucked away at Aunt Ellie's, Travers Goff became sentimental for his courting days. In his affectionate letters sent to Margaret in Sydney, he wanted to take "a peep at you both and the aunts and Emily and Eliza [the maids] fussing over her. Fancy a baby being at No. 2 Albert Street, what a difference that must make! I am delighted the aunts have taken to the wee one. Mrs. Goff, your offspring does you proud. Good old Margaret, pat yourself on the back for me. What do they call her, Baby or Lyndon? It was good of the aunt to give you such an expensive frock. You may give her my love if you like. Poor you having your hair done up, but as you say, it's best to please the Aunt."[16]

Goff clearly deferred to "the Aunt" who had always provided money and a second home to his wife and daughter. From her earliest years, Lyndon was often dispatched, alone, to Aunt Ellie or to another relative when either her mother or father went away. The separations helped create in Lyndon a form of self-sufficiency and stimulated her idiosyncratic form of fantasy life. Once, when Margaret left home for a long holiday, her father wrote to his wife of Lyndon's "great game." From the age of four, she pretended to be one of the household's hens, sitting on her eggs and brooding. These birds were not ordinary fowls, but friends of the family, named after the Goffs' neighbors and friends, Mrs. McKenzie, for example, or Mrs. Starke. Goff wrote, "It starts when she wakes in the morning, goes on til it's time for me to go to the office, and recommences as soon as I get home again and lasts til bedtime."

For most of her childhood, Lyndon was absorbed by the experience of being a bird, brooding, busy, purposeful. She sat for hours, her arms clasped tightly around her body.[17] "She can't come in, she's laying," her family and friends would say. Often her mother would drag her from her nest, but instead of squashing her little girl's fantasy with ridicule, she sometimes played the game as well. "I've told you once, I've told you a hundred times, no laying at lunchtime."[18]

The vision of herself as a mother hen suited Lyndon's theory that to write, one must brood, and to be a real woman, one must be a mother. When interviewers spoke to her of inspiration, she often said "I hate the word creative. Brooders. That's the word. I would say there are brooders in life. That's why I've always had this attachment to hens and nests, not because of the eggs, but the quiet brooding, pondering." In the kitchen of her last home in London, the dresser was covered with pottery hens.[19]

Lyndon's brooding was not just a product of her loneliness, but a protection against a certain coolness in her parents. Travers and Margaret Goff were typical of their own time and place. Smalltown parents of the early twentieth century taught their children self-sufficiency and subservience. But more than that, Travers and Margaret were also caught up in their own self-importance. If parents are "a child's first gods and responsible for many seeds of fate," as Lyndon later wrote, then the Goffs planted too many seeds of doubt and mystery. They left clues, but they were too simple, too rudimentary to be of much help. Lyndon fell back on her parents' proverbs, rules and random lines from poems, as well as their books, to elaborate, fantasize and help create sense.

She came to believe that her mother and father lived in a state that W. B. Yeats called, in his 1919 poem "A Prayer for My Daughter," "radical innocence." "In our family life, if there were moods to be respected, it was not ours." Her parents were absorbed in "their own existence, busy, contained, important" and that left the children of the marriage "free for ours." "I was allowed to grow in the darkness, unknown, unnoticed, under the earth like a seed." She could never remember that her father or anyone else explained anything. If Lyndon cried, Travers Goff would say, "Let her weep, we need the rain." She saw her mother, a woman with a passive face, as benign and generous, with doelike, soft eyes, yet she used to wonder, as a child, "if she was more like a doe or a serpent."[20]

Margaret Goff did not really want to know what Lyndon was doing. Rather, she issued instructions, "her voice full of clocks and water heaters." Lyndon told interviewers that her parents weren't scholars, but loved life, which meant "they left you to yourself a great deal." Her great sorrow was that both her grandmothers had died before she was born. These wise old women, as she called them, "carriers of tradition," might have answered who she was, why she was born, how did she get born—ordinary childhood questions but important ones. "I wanted the important answers, but the grown-ups around me were disappointing in their answers... I used to feel if only I had a grandmother she would know these things."[21]

The Goffs' life in Maryborough was simple, not indulgent, not centered around possessions. Lyndon had few toys or personal treasures. Each week her parents gave her a penny; Lyndon had no way of knowing the value of the mysterious object called a sovereign, encased in a small square contraption on her father's watch chain. Her mother might buy her little things, a roll of blue ribbon, or a delicate fan with shining pink roses. Her dolls were made of wooden spoons, dressed up, but they lived adventurous lives. In any case, it was not things, but words, that stirred Lyndon—the stories, ballads, and old wives' tales shared among widely scattered neighbors.

Her mother was forever casting around in her pool of maxims, which were passed on to Mary Poppins. Margaret liked to say "anything worth doing is worth doing well." Lyndon didn't believe it as a child. Her father was the greater force in her life, or rather the memory of her father. Although she liked to recall the cane fields father, the bright and witty poet drenched in Ireland, the real Goff could be maudlin and difficult, especially when drunk and reminiscing about his "homeland." "I had been brought up by a father who was a very poetic Irishman. It seemed nothing but Ireland would do, everything round you was Irish, if we had a horse it had an Irish name, and an Irish pedigree, the lace for our clothes was brought from Ireland, and I grew up and was nurtured on the Celtic Twilight, Yeats and all. Therefore Australia never seemed to be the place where I wanted to be. My body ran around in the southern sunlight but my inner world had subtler colors... the numberless greens of Ireland, which seemed to me inhabited solely by poets plucking harps, heroes...cutting off each other's heads, and veiled ladies sitting on the ground keening."22

In time Lyndon came to see him as a man who was full of Irish dissatisfaction, who never quite found his heart's desire. He was "proud and haughty, terribly gay and terribly amusing and poetic and always singing and quoting poems and weeping over them. But I've come to know he was melancholy and sad and that he needed someone to understand him. His melancholy was the other side of his Irish gaiety," inheritable and catching. "Whenever he had taken a glass he would grieve over the sack of Drogheda in 1649 [the scene of Cromwell's infamous massacre of civilians] until everyone round him felt personally guilty. He was Irish and determined in argument to have the last word even or perhaps specially with children."

Lyndon's refuge was books. She claimed she could read at the age of three. The alphabet was gradually revealed to her through household packaging, Sunlight Soap (Mary Poppins's favorite), which was used to wash "floors, clothes and children," letters stamped on flour bags, labels on boxes of Beecham's Pills, or the words "Jumble Today" on the church noticeboard. She even tried to decipher the stencils on tea chests, embossed with Chinese ideograms.23

Now that she could read, Lyndon finally understood that "grims" were not just fantastic stories told by the Goffs' washerwoman, Matilda. She had been "notorious throughout the district for telling these grims," which Lyndon thought was "a generic term for narrative, tarradiddle." Now she realized that Grimms' were fairy tales bound in two volumes, "squat, red, sturdy volumes, coarse of paper, close of print, discovered in my father's bookcase."24

Lyndon left Maryborough when she was three. Forever after, she remembered the town she wished it had been. From the Goffs' two-story home near the Mary River, she could see the Maryborough sugar factory. She imagined the factory for the rest of her life as a cane field, even transposing it to a dry, high, inland wheat town. "We lived by a lake," she once recalled, "by a sugar plantation....At night, when the moon was shining, there was a small bright lake beyond the cane fields, the tin roof of the sugar mill absorbed the light of the moon and stars and set off a whitish shimmer, so our house and the mill roof appeared to be flush with the land."[25]

Within this fairyland cane field, she later wove semi-autobiographical books around two servants, including Ah Wong, named after a Chinese cook who worked for the Goffs (at the time, it was customary to have Chinese cooks on sugar plantations) and Johnny Delaney, named in honor of their hunchbacked Irish groom, stable boy and carpenter. Johnny Delaney was so important, Lyndon wrote, that "when we were young we thought we had three parents: mother, father, and Johnny." He taught them how to hide from Kate Clancy, "our gorgon nurse."

Only much later, and only to trusted interviewers, did she confess that these stories were an amalgam of her childhood memories and that not everything she said should be taken for granted.

Early in 1902, Travers Goff was transferred—demoted, Lyndon later believed—to a new job with the AJS Bank in Brisbane. The Goffs traveled south early in the year. As an employee, but not the boss of the bank branch, Travers Goff's annual salary was shaved by £50, and he had no servants allowance.[26] The family lived on Brisbane Street, Ipswich, where their second daughter, Barbara Ierne (known as Biddy), was born in April that year. This was the start of a great deal of ferment and change in the Goff household. Travers Goff was soon forced into the disruptive job of standing in for other employees when they were on leave, first at Clifton on the Darling Downs near Toowoomba during August 1903, then during May 1905 at the bank's branch at Killarney, northwest of Brisbane. By then Margaret Goff was heavily pregnant with their third child. The family lived at "Heytor," Lisson Grove, Wooloowin, and Travers was officially a mere "bank clerk."[27]

Before the birth of the Goffs' third daughter, Cicely Margaret (Moya), in July 1905, Helen Lyndon, then five, was sent to Sydney to stay once again with Aunt Ellie. She never quite knew why she was sent away to her aunt. She thought it might have been a treat just for herself. In any case, that was how she decided to take it.

The journey from Brisbane to Sydney lasted all night. The guard lifted the five-year-old onto a makeshift bed in the luggage rack of his van. Lyndon heard the train's whistle as the carriages slid through the darkness, watched lighted windows in the little settlements along the way before drifting to sleep. The train was an iron thread, a fiery necklace, linking Mother in Brisbane with Aunt Ellie in Sydney. She liked to think that Ellie had sent the train herself. It was her own carriage taking her to the haven of a fairy godmother.[28] Many children would have clung to their mothers, the separation too much to bear. Helen Lyndon, though, was an adventurer even then.

2

Ellie and Allora

There she stood on the platform. Tall and gaunt, lips pursed tight. Her hat was almost airborne, its two pigeon wings bracketing the crown. Aunt Ellie leant on an ivory-and-ebony walking stick. "Hurrumph! Here you are at last!" The train was two minutes late. That greeting again! Lyndon had heard it before. Ellie's contralto never changed. Lyndon thought she sounded like Father Bear when he saw someone had been eating his porridge.

The driver ushered Aunt Ellie, her maid Elizabeth and the little blond girl into the carriage, and drove to Number 2 Albert Street. Lyndon vaguely remembered the special wallpaper—"one of the best *you're* likely to see"—the rows of photographs in close military formation on the piano, on the table tops and the mantelpieces, the way Miss Elizabeth grumbled about her "daily burden" as she scrubbed Lyndon's face until it burned and bundled her into frilled dresses and fur-collared coats. And how Aunt Ellie's mustache prickled her when she stooped to kiss her good night.

Aunt Ellie, a bulldog with a sentimental core, remained fixed in Lyndon's adult memory even more vividly than her parents. In a little book about Aunt Ellie's life, she described her as stern and tender, secret and proud, anonymous and loving. Her great aunt "stalked with her silent feet" through the pages of *Mary Poppins*.[1] Ellie lent her mannerisms to more than one woman in the Mary Poppins adventures. Not only did she live again in the starched and bustling figure of Mary Poppins herself, but she could also be found in the fearsome Miss Andrew—the nanny of Mr. Banks—and in Miss Lark, the Banks's arrogant yet romantic neighbor. Miss Andrew and Miss Lark—two fictional women of a certain age, neither burdened by husbands—represented the two sides of Aunt Ellie's character, bossy and benign.

Like Miss Lark, Ellie had two dogs, or rather a succession of dogs, always called Tinker and Badger. Although a child might be dismissed into thin air with a word, Ellie would dissolve into sentimentality over "anything with four legs, a patch of fur, a tail or a bark." And while the pet was often placed in the best spare bedroom, the child would be sent to a cot in the attic.

When Ellie was in one of her generous, indulgent moods, she gave Lyndon presents more extravagant and special than any little trinket her parents could afford. For her third birthday, Ellie presented Lyndon with a precious gift, a Royal Doulton bowl, with three little boys playing horses. The bowl later appeared in "Bad Wednesday," a story in *Mary Poppins*

Comes Back, as a christening gift given to Mrs. Banks by her Great Aunt Caroline.

Aunt Ellie was said to be disappointed in love, having fallen for one of her cousins, a member of Parliament, whom she felt she could not marry. After that, she never found the right man, but instead embraced in her fold many nieces and nephews, acting as the central pole of a familial merry-go-round, controlling all.

The old woman and Lyndon ate lunch together every day. The little girl was shocked by how much her aunt devoured, perhaps a dozen peaches at a sitting *and* most of the stew, leaving only what looked like a bundle of bones. She knew Ellie more intimately than her other great aunt, Jane. But both, in her adult memory, were forever linked as a pair of crows—much as she had seen herself as a hen—perched on a fence or outlined against the horizon, with an air of "terrible conviction, assurance and an unassailable knowledge that they were right," as she wrote in an unpublished article. As Lyndon became a specialist on the meaning and origin of legends, she would know by the time she wrote those words that a crow is usually an omen, a warning of bad luck, but can also be a fairy in disguise, usually a fairy with trouble in mind.

She decided the great aunts were to blame for "my never being able to endure authoritarianism of any kind." They were "huge cloudy presences...watching everything that transpired....I vowed when I grew up never to be like that. They are the authoritarian figures which have stayed with me...they were cruel, they wanted the world for themselves."[2] When she was told that Aunt Jane lived on her capital, Lyndon imagined her secretly living on her own person, gnawing at a finger or toe, or wolfing down an organ.

Aunt Ellie was not merely conjured up out of Lyndon's imagination as a powerful woman. She really did have position and power in Sydney society. Ellie lived to a great age, surviving into her nineties, an independent woman who never leant on a man other than her father for financial support. She carefully nurtured a social network and took care not to fossilize; Ellie often visited the Goffs in Queensland and traveled to and from England more than fifteen times.

In her will, Ellie revealed the essence of both her character and her social circle. She listed thirty separate bequests, explained in exquisitely intricate detail. Her most loved possessions were to be shared by her sister, nieces, nephews, grandnieces, grandnephews and friends, who included the founding family of the Colonial Sugar Refining Company, the Knoxes, who lived near Albert Street in the mansion Fiona.

These bequests, which might have come from Mary Poppins's carpetbag, included a traveling clock, travel hold-all and travel rug, silver table napkin ring, sugar sifter, teapot, tea caddy and spoon, teaspoons and sugar tongs, a Danish china tea set, framed photographs, two large cameo brooches, a tantalus, letter weight scales, cream-and-gold Wedgwood, a cut-glass and silver smelling-salts bottle and a silver-topped scent bottle, both engraved HCM, silverplate cutlery, all with the Morehead crest, a copper preserving pan and ladle, candelabra, a Russian commemorative mug, Worcester vases, and a gold thimble in its own case.

Ellie left shares, as well, including stock in the Australian Gas Light Company and the Colonial Sugar Refining Company which had earned her a £150 annual dividend. The shares were divided between Lyndon, her sister Cicely Margaret (Moya), and other nieces and grand nieces. The Goff girls eventually received Ellie's shares in the Commercial Banking Company of Sydney as well.

• • •

Lyndon celebrated her fifth birthday at Albert Street with Ellie, documenting for her parents the gifts she received in letters written in wobbly but careful penciled handwriting. The letters are eloquent with the silent presence of Ellie at her shoulder, supervising the five-year-old's first attempts at composing a letter. She asked her mama if the new baby had blue eyes and curly hair (as she did herself), whether the baby cried when she was christened, and how much Biddy liked her new sister, who was known as Moya from her earliest days.

Lyndon's father and mother had already told her they might call the baby Moya, which they said was Irish for Mary. Travers Goff was clearly hoping for a boy, whom he planned to call Brian Travers Goff. He wrote back to his little girl that he had heard from Aunt Ellie that Lyndon had grown "very fat. Why, little woman, you will be like a prize pig when you get home again. Never mind, we will all be delighted to see you home again after your nice long holiday. As you will be back so soon we are not going to send your birthday present to you but you will get it when you return."[3]

Back home, the "fat" girl had only just opened her present when her mother told her she must stay with friends until things settled down. Baby Moya needed all her attention. Lyndon later wrote that she always suffered from being the eldest of three girls.

Three months after the baby was born, Travers Goff was transferred again, to the Australian Joint Stock Bank branch in Allora, a small inland town on the Darling Downs, eighty kilometers from Toowoomba in southern Queensland. He started work as the bank manager on October 16, 1905. The next eighteen months were the most critical of Lyndon's early years. Most of her childhood memories came from that time and place, high up in the Darling Downs, where a sudden catastrophe was to change the direction of her life. She lived those days in Allora with the kind of intensity that often precedes either a triumph or deep disappointment.

Allora was a perfect place for dreaming. Quiet, far from anywhere, the town was bitingly cold in winter and intensely hot in summer—extremes that helped her imagination take flight as she sat before the fire and gazed into its flames or lay on the grass and looked at the heavens after summer's late sunsets. Lyndon felt a sense of emptiness and loneliness in Allora, whose melodious name hid its more prosaic origins—the Aboriginal word *gnallarah,* meaning "the place of the swamp."

The Australian Joint Stock Bank had maintained a branch in Allora for almost thirty years, its double-doored banking chamber opening onto the wide main street of the town, Herbert Street. The manager and his family lived in a residence attached to the bank, the whole surrounded by a veranda in the generously deep Queensland style. In summer, the sun wrinkled and burned the Allora townsfolk deep brown. Verandas and umbrellas provided the only shade. In winter, though, the wind swept through the bank manager's house. The winds bit more deeply than they did on the coast; the maids did their best to keep fires burning in all the high-ceilinged oblong rooms leading off the wide, cool hallway.

The two older Goff girls liked to play in the warm kitchen, or in summer, in the big weedy paddock out in back. At dusk, their friends would drift home, calling to one another in fainter and fainter voices as they parted and ran home across the gardens and fields. As they climbed into bed, the two girls still called to one another until they began to fall asleep.

Before her eyes closed, Lyndon watched the shadows climb the wall, bend in half and slip along the ceiling. What was that tapping on the wall, that rustling, creaking, groaning? She feared that an ancient mariner or cruel army captain was hidden behind her bedroom door, scraping the wall with a pencil. He wore red breeches, a blue jacket and tattered epaulets, his knees were bent in pain, the result of an old bullet wound.[4] Her mother reassured her the tapping was simply the wooden house "stretching itself luxuriously after the heat of the day." "See," she would say, flinging the door open, "he's not there and you know it!" The trouble was, Mother was speaking of a *real* captain. Lyndon's captain was inside her head, and her head was a door her mother could not open.[5] She found she could conjure up from her own mind the most fearsome monsters as well as a host of fairy-tale creatures. Fairies, giants and djinns stalked the earth, as close as her shadow.[6]

In the garden and paddock beyond, she made tiny parks for poor people. The Lilliputians sat on blades of grass and took tea. She thought she might look like a giant cloud to these dwarves. Her finger would be as big and scary as a lion.[7] The park became a story, "The Park in the Park," in the fourth Mary Poppins book, *Mary Poppins in the Park,* in which Jane Banks makes a tiny park for poor people. There, everybody is happy and no one ever quarrels. Flowers were trees, twigs were benches, and plasticine men lived in the houses and played at the funfair. "I had a passion for making these miniature clearings, no more than a foot square, all over our garden."[8] A grown-up foot could blot out the whole fantasy at any moment.

Lyndon was much closer to animals than people; she took care not to step on an ant or a beetle. They might be princes in disguise. She also was close to an imaginary friend, a child her own age and size. That Friend, she called him. She loved the big paddock with its spare, sunbaked trees and its slip fence. This paddock was later transformed into the Chelsea park visited so often by the Banks children and Mary Poppins. There, the slip fence became an elegant iron railing, the lean grass of the paddock a juicy lawn to be watered, and the kookaburras dissolved into nightingales. The horse mushrooms in the middle of the paddock grew into a merry-go-round.[9]

Lyndon felt surrounded by the spirits of the trees, by the grass and stone, but most of all by the stars. In Allora, the stars in the night sky seemed closer than in Brisbane, so close Lyndon thought she could hear them humming.[10] One of her father's odd-job men, Johnny Delaney, taught Lyndon basic lessons about the constellations until she "knew the southern sky at night like a book."[11] The heavens seemed "a celestial suburb...inhabited by a circle of friends," among them the two pointers of the Southern Cross, Berenice's Hair, Venus, and Orion with his studded belt.[12] Her favorite star was Hesperus or Venus.

She liked to imagine a great community at play in the sky. Friends and families must be circling, meeting and dancing. She knew Castor and Pollux, brothers and heroes, had been made into twin stars so they could be close forever. Lyndon hoped that might happen to her parents.[13] The heroes and creatures from ancient Greece who gave their names to the constellations were her first lesson in mythology, which grew to become a comfort, then an obsession in her later life.

The view of the heavens by night was both friendly and all-enveloping, but before the dark blue washed over the sky, there was that hour or more to be endured. Twilight. Dusk. For Lyndon, this was a time of melancholy and sometimes panic, when the "long rays of the sun lay across the earth like stripes on the back of a zebra."[14] "Will the sun come up tomorrow?" was one of the many questions her parents brushed off. "Of course . . ." "If someone knew and understood how anxious I was about the sun, what a help it would have been to me."[15] She would flee into the lighted house for comfort.[16]

How much of this anguish was created in retrospect is hard to know. It certainly sounded a romantic idea. As an adult, Lyndon wrote of twilight as the prime hour of childhood when anything can, and indeed *does* happen, when the game passes and the child sets out alone on the "glowing tide of dusk, a feeling of melancholy and sweetness possessing his spirit."[17] The feeling was reinforced by the poem she loved by the Irish writer George William Russell, who imagined a child playing at dusk, the moment when the grown-ups call him in from his dream.

> *Call not thy wanderer home as yet,*
> *Though it be late.*
> *Now is the first assailing of*
> *The invisible gate*
> *Be still through that light knocking,*
> *The hour is thronged with fate.*

Such dreams, she wrote, could be smuggled into the house and kept alive in some secret cupboard. Her father, too, was intrigued by the dusk. He stood by her, head tipped back, searching the sky for the first star.[18] At such a moment, the child was making her plans for life, while the romance was twice as fabulous for a Lyndon, a future writer, who was "building a storehouse from which she could draw her treasures."[19] But Lyndon went even further along this romantic path. She claimed her own journey and search for meaning arose from these moments at twilight.[20]

The night sky and the sunset grew into a ribbonlike theme in her articles and books. The tales of Mary Poppins are studded with stories of the Banks children playing in the stars, Poppins descending from the stars and ascending in a trail of stardust, and the various children in her articles puzzling over the moon—what was on the other side? Why was the moon broken when it was not a full moon?

Lyndon said she was happiest living in houses where she could actually see the sun set,[21] and she felt she wrote best at twilight. She often quoted other writers as having similar thoughts, including Georges Simenon, who said his children feared sunset, and the children's writer who later became her literary heroine, Beatrix Potter. The fascination with and fear of the dark remained with her into old age. She even panicked at blackouts in theatres.[22]

Lyndon also dwelt on the feelings of melancholy that washed over her at twilight, feelings that anticipated how an adult might feel at the frustration over a day lost, or much worse, a life wasted. At each sunset, she thought there must be something else.[23] Lyndon did not know what this *something* was, but..."as far as the wind blows and the sky is blue, I would go and find it...I seized on any opportunity that would set me on my way."[24]

At first, her escape route might have come with the gypsies. Lyndon had heard they walked the world and stole children. Her story, frequently told, never varied: a miragelike group of tall men in blue gowns and their veiled women, perhaps Mohammedans, were camped in peaked tents near her home. She stood nearby, hoping to be picked up like an item from a bargain counter, as she said. Lyndon offered the most stately man one of her sandals. He inspected it, but quietly returned it to her foot and directed her back to the road. Whether fantasy or reality, the dreamy quality of the story gives it a sexual undertone, as if the man were inspecting the young girl's wares, but found them wanting. "They didn't take me!" she told her parents. "Not surprising," scoffed Margaret and Travers.

Instead, the path to escape came through books. One of her Morehead relatives in England sent her a special issue of the *Children's Encyclopedia,* along with a letter from a certain Mr. Arthur Mee soliciting further book sales. The letter, apparently handwritten, was addressed "Dear Child." It was, she thought, her first love letter. The grown-ups, however, rudely assured her that the handwriting was done by some sort of machine and that thousands of children had received the same letter. Lyndon did not believe them. A friend would not betray her. She wrote to Mr. Mee, explaining who she was, and asking him to send her the fare to England. "The answer was long in coming, and when it came, unsatisfactory. I was reprimanded for bothering that dear Mr. Mee."[25]

Lyndon had already read all the fairy stories, "the great set pieces, to be wept over and doted on," about the Snow Queen, the Little Mermaid, the Sleeping Beauty, Cinderella, all full of nymphs, crones and strong mother figures. These Grimms' tales curdled her blood with delight and horror, as the women dispensed justice or found romance. Lyndon preferred the maidens who were brave rather than ciphers, like the Goose Girl and the fearless Sleeping Beauty. All the villains, dwarves, giants and stepmothers, wicked fairies, dragons and witches stayed with her for life. She liked the wickedest women most. Her mother wondered why Lyndon preferred "Rumpelstilt-skin" when "The Miller's Daughter" was "so much nicer." Much nicer, yes, but much less interesting. She was fascinated by the evil forces of the stories, the black sheep, the wicked fairy. The Grimms' tales were black, in contrast to the blander, saccharine whiteness of Hans Christian Andersen's fairy stories. She did wonder sometimes if she, too, were a wicked witch, one of the "devil's party," as Blake said of Milton.[26]

Once she had devoured the Grimms', she rummaged through every book in her parents' library, the hodgepodge of Dickens and Scott, Shakespeare, Tennyson and the Irish poets. Through the children's stories of Beatrix Potter, *Alice in Wonderland* and Kingsley's *Heroes*. There was just one Australian author there on the shelves: Ethel Turner, who wrote *Seven Little Australians*.

Most of all, she loved the little books she bought for a penny at the local store in Herbert Street. The fairy tales were printed in green binding; the story of Buffalo Bill came within red and blue covers. On the backs of the penny books were marvelous advertisements for alarm clocks and air rifles.

Lyndon planned to buy both, but never quite managed to save enough for either.

One of her favorite books from her father's collection was *Twelve Deathbed Scenes,* which she read so often she knew it by heart. Lyndon thought how pleasant it would be to die—if only she could come back. From her mother's bookshelves, she read *Home Chat* magazine with its store of recipes, knitting patterns and colic remedies. But her best, most secret, pleasure was to read her mother's library books, when Margaret took her half-hour siesta. Though the characters in the romances seemed like waxworks, she loved those stolen half-hours as a drunk loves his secret hoard of liquor.[27]

She was puzzled by the meaning of concubines. Father and daughter discussed the word but Travers was so evasive she thought concubines must mean servants. At this childish mistake, Travers stormed out of the room. She talked of Esau and Jacob with her mother. Lyndon preferred the bad son. Margaret explained that Esau was the black sheep of the family. Oh, Lyndon understood this—she always liked the black sheep: Dan in *Jo's Boys,* Peter Rabbit and her Uncle Cecil who had married a lady her mother described as "some sort of Hindoo."

Lyndon was fascinated by the Bible, the blackness of it, and its air of something forbidden. She relished what she called the "enormous terrible facts" of the Bible, its potent brew mixing in her mind with fairy tales and myths. The Goffs were pious churchgoers, worshiping each Sunday at St. David's Church of England. There, Travers wore his white suit, boomed out the old hymns in his best baritone and solemnly carried the collection plate up to the altar. To the children, God seemed to live nearby, not just in the town but right at home, in Herbert Street. Lyndon nagged her father about God. Why didn't he have a title, Duke God, say, or Mr. God? And why did he call God "Harry"? "I do not!" said her father. "You do... you say 'by the Lord God Harry.'"[28]

God, she believed, must be working among them all the time, playing the organ on Sundays, creeping through the fields, listening at windows and keyholes. She picked a sunflower and explained to her parents that this, too, must be God. Nonsense, they replied, no one could pick God and if they could, they would not.[29] So who *was* God? Did he reside in her favorite song "Green Grow the Rushes-oh"? She brooded for years on the line "One is one and all alone, and ever more shall be so." Who was One, was it God or herself?[30] She liked the idea so much she kept it in her mind for all her life, writing the line into her book *Mary Poppins in Cherry Tree Lane,* published in the 1980s.

Lyndon's first experience of compassion came one hot Sunday afternoon. The blinds were half down, shading the bedroom where Margaret read aloud the story of the crucifixion from *Peep of Day,* a collection of Bible stories. Lyndon began weeping uncontrollably for Jesus. She was drowning in sorrow. Her mother, not amused, not pitying, was merely annoyed. "I take the trouble to read to you and all you do is cry and feel sorry...dry your eyes, it was a long time ago."[31]

Lyndon liked to count the silver and notes falling into the collection plate at church. She wondered what God did with it all. Once, she tried to hold on to the sixpence that she was given to drop into the plate but her father, all-seeing, sang the warning "time like an ever rolling stream...put in that sixpence *now!*"[32]

To make the sermon go faster, Lyndon scanned the congregation for the ugliest faces and decided to kill the worst. Boom! "Mr. Ebb is dead." Bang! "Mrs. Haig is dead." Her mother, eyebrows raised at the fierce expression on Lyndon's face, whispered "What?" "Murdering," replied Lyndon. "Not in church," said her mother.[33]

The restless children were often sent from the pews before the sermon had ended. The Goff girls played among the gravestones, moving glass bowls of metal roses onto graves that had none. They imagined plucking long-dead babies from their graves, and passing them from lap to lap, comforting little Lucinda or Lizzie or Jack. They scurried past freshly dug graves, with their burden of fading lilies; there were people down there, they knew. The bodies were not beautiful, as their parents had promised, but ugly and frightening. Lyndon knew she would live forever. Maybe.[34]

In this world where nobody ever explained, Lyndon turned to imagination and poetry. In retrospect, she could never remember a time when she was not writing. She saw writing as a reporter might, as "listening and putting down what she heard. No one was pleased or proud." That, though, was good, because "I was never made to feel that I was anything special."[35] Her poems were hardly discussed—certainly no one thought they had a genius in the family. She recalled taking the verses to her mother, who was more concerned with burning the sausages than reading the poetry. "Another time, dear..." And when her mother did show them to Travers Goff, he sighed, "Hardly Yeats!"[36]

Her mother, softer, more imaginative, might make a real picnic breakfast for her daughter, or prepare a pretend picnic on the floor at home. But she, too, could be fearsome and full of anger, never more so than one evening when she tidied the children's rooms, placing their toys in cupboards. Unlike Mary Poppins, who wiggled her nose to make the toys tidy themselves, Margaret grew irritated with the chore, and finally became fiercely cross. She seized Lyndon's favorite doll with a serene china face, tossed it across the room and yelled at her to put it away herself. The doll's face struck the iron bedstead and broke. "Mother, you've killed her!" cried Lyndon, feeling the crack in her own body. Margaret gathered the pieces and slumped onto the bed, weeping "Forgive me."

Travers was just as likely to fly into a rage, but just as quick to forgive. One rainy night, a couple of rag dolls he had christened Lord Nelson and Lady Hamilton were abandoned in the garden. Lyndon was so fearful of his anger that she lied. It wasn't her, she would never leave the dollies outside. He bellowed, "You told me a lie!" but then, seeing her pinched face, softened the assault—"and let them catch their death of a cold."[37]

For one year, 1906, Lyndon and her sister Biddy attended the Allora Public School, where Biddy once found a brooch lost by a teacher. She handed it back. Her two-shilling reward seemed wealth beyond measure. Travers Goff, all bluster, all bank manager, insisted it must be returned at once. The girls could not bring themselves to do so. Lyndon and Biddy spent it on marzipan lollies in a packet, Simpsons Sugar Smokes.[38]

Lyndon was never sure whether her father would respond to her mishaps with a joke or an explosion. But she knew he might do something worse: dismiss her with ridicule. She admired a maid's parrot-headed umbrella so much that she decided to save to buy one. With the umbrella swinging by her side, the maid was far more elegant, Lyndon thought, than her mother. Lyndon was deeply hurt to hear her mother say she "wouldn't be seen dead" with one. But more embarrassing was her father's reaction to the maid's umbrella, which she often wrapped lovingly in tissue paper on her return from a day out: "We could put it in a cage and teach it to say 'Pretty Polly.'"[39]

Lyndon often daydreamed about the maid's journeys. When she came home, the girl would never quite say what she had done. She hinted. Full of stories about her widespread family, she would say—No, she could not really tell, the adventures were beyond the ears of children.[40]

Subdued by her cool yet conventional parents, though loving them deeply, and with a soaring imagination nurtured with books, Lyndon grew up thriving on what was difficult.

She had to become, she thought, "my own planet." She always longed to be *good,* to be better, but felt she was touched by the bad. Always, she wanted to be something larger than herself. She suspected she was not her mother's favorite—that was the beautiful Biddy. Lyndon's role was to be the lover, not the loved. The loved, she knew, could "sit in the lap of time" while the lover had to watch and pray, and grind his own grain.[41]

Yet she felt, hoped, she was her father's most loved. As the oldest and most perceptive child, Lyndon felt sharply the effects of his drinking, although, as she later wrote, "I did not know what it was I suffered from."[42] The drinking was not just a family secret but known to his employers. Late in January 1907, Goff believed he was about to be demoted once more at the bank. He became ill after he returned home from a day spent riding in a downpour.[43] For three days, Goff had a dangerously high temperature. One night, Lyndon tried to cheer him with a threepenny piece from her apron pocket. She was baffled by his face, as white as his pillows. Here was the man she knew as a Zeus, now diminished. Lyndon felt as all children do when they see their parents weakened and quiet. Panic surged up in her chest and gut.[44]

The local newspaper reported that Goff died that Thursday night. Margaret cannot have been with him, for she did not call a doctor during the night but later, after she found him dead in the morning. Dr. Francis Pain pronounced him dead on Friday, February 8. The cause of death was epileptic seizure delirium. When Margaret told Lyndon that morning that Daddy had gone to God, Lyndon felt a sense of shame quickly followed by disbelief. That couldn't be *right*. God didn't need him. He had all those angels.

Lyndon was seven and a half years old. For the next few months she wore mourning, a white dress with a black sash. It was six years before she accepted that her father had died.

As she grew into a young woman, Lyndon talked to her dead father, finally coming to the resolution that she should comfort him: "It's all right, it's all right, you don't have to be so unhappy." No one comforted her. As an adult, Lyndon believed that her father died because he could not face what was in store for him at the bank—that he allowed pneumonia to kill him instead. But while a seizure might have been the immediate cause of death, she always believed the underlying cause was sustained heavy drinking.[45]

After the doctor left that Friday morning, Margaret appeared to have a surge of energy. The funeral was arranged immediately. She sent a telegram to Aunt Ellie, and placed an advertisement in the local paper for the sale by auction of the household furniture and effects. There was to be no future here. She had no parents, her Great Uncle Boyd had died two years before, the bank owned the house.

Travers's funeral was held at the Allora Cemetery that Friday afternoon, the vicar from St. David's officiating. Ellie telegrammed back from Sydney that she would travel to Allora by train, without delay. A messenger was sent to meet her at the station. She greeted her niece in the cool hallway. It smelt of lilies. "Meg!" There was nothing more to say. Margaret merely leant her head against Aunt Ellie's bony shoulder. "You and the children will come to stay with me!" Ellie declared. Margaret began to pack. After the furniture, horse and sulky were sold on February 16, Ellie, Margaret and the three little girls said good-bye to the maid at the station.

The hours seemed to turn more and more slowly as they approached Sydney. "Is this New South Wales, is this the city?" Only Moya, just eighteen months old, remained passive as she was handed back and forth between the arms of Ellie and Margaret.

Back home, Ellie resumed her martinet pose. The dispirited little family was ushered into her hall at Albert Street.

"Watch out for that!" The object nestling in the shadows was a bust of Sir Walter Scott, given to her "by your great, great grandfather!" Margaret and the girls sat down to lunch with Ellie. First the soup, then the meat, the pudding, the fruit plate. It was February, a sweltering month in Sydney. Ellie monopolized the conversation, of course, remarking on the children's manners and prospects for the future. Biddy broke down first, then Margaret left the room, with Moya in her arms. Ellie scooped up a bunch of black-red cherries. Only Lyndon remained with her at the table. Her eyes were misty. Would she cry too? "No, I won't, you old beast. I am not crying, it's only my eyes." No one spoke. "Here," Ellie said at last, "take the cherries to your mother and say I'm a bitter old woman. I didn't mean a word." Lyndon picked up the cherries, folded her little hands over their roundness and looked into the eyes of her great aunt. Ellie, sixty-one, and Lyndon, seven, recognized in one another the soul of a woman who does not step back.[46]

3

Old England in Australia

Ivy, Myrtle, Holly, Elm, Daphne, Shepherd. The street names of Bowral contained the essence of the English countryside. The toy town set high on the southern tablelands of New South Wales was swathed in the transplanted trees and flowers of England: poplars, willows and peach blossom. From a distance, Bowral was a patchwork of every shade of green, from jade to apple. Unlike the coastal towns, sweating through endless summers, the town enjoyed real seasons, with snow and copper-colored leaves, tulips and daffodils.

The town, two hundred kilometers south of Sydney, resembled a hill station in colonial India, a place where homesick Englishmen and -women could retreat from the heat of the coast. Bowral was sleepy in winter then rambunctious in summer with city folk down for the views and the country air.[1]

The living was cheap in this little town. Margaret and her three girls moved there in 1907; Aunt Ellie had enrolled Lyndon and Biddy in the new Bowral branch of Sydney Church of England Girls Grammar School, founded a year earlier. The Goffs rented a wooden cottage, one of about four in Holly Street, then a dirt road. Aunt Ellie paid the rent. A willow drooped near a brown stream that ran through a paddock, fronting the garden. Here Lyndon grew from child to young woman, to the time of secrecy, when a girl knows her parents know *nothing*. She studied her mother, as all girls do, with a kind of gradual insight. Why, when she had known birth, love and grief, did her mother seem to understand so little?

Lyndon was eight when she moved to Bowral, the age when girls retreat into private games played with their "very best friend forever," when a passerby might hear confidences whispered between them, or between a little girl and her invisible companion. She daydreamed by the willow tree, which took on astounding forms: a princess running from an ogre, the arms of a prince, or a horse that carried her to victory. Another day it became a ship, red and black funneled, on which she sailed to a land of fairies. Later, by the age of eleven, Lyndon knew that men looked at her another way, with a speculative glance at her tiny breasts, like the man in the fruit shop who leant over the counter and asked her to be "my little girl."[2]

Many of these Bowral neighbors and shopkeepers were reborn years later in Lyndon's books and articles, among them "Uncle" Dodger Woods and his daughter Nellie Rubina, Miss Quigley, and Mrs. Corry, who lurked within the general store in the main street, bullying her gigantic daughters Annie and Fannie. Miss Quigley's heart had been broken, the Goff girls knew that much from crumbs of chatter overheard at tea parties, just outside the door, when the grown-ups asked the children to go and play. The girls were more interested in conquering Miss Quigley's garden, with its store of tempting apple trees. Like Eve, they might have come to grief over the apples they stole in the orchard, stashed under their sailor blouses and in the elastic legs of their bloomers. But Miss Quigley outsmarted them instead.

"Children, how lovely, have you come to pay me a visit?" Miss Quigley, drifting through her garden, called them down from the trees and into her front room, where she opened a gorgeous music box inlaid with silver and mother of pearl. Its long gilt cylinder tinkled "Brahms' Lullaby," "Barbara Allen" and "The Blue Danube." Miss Quigley waltzed around the jardiniere, holding her arms curved before her, and the children picked up the waltz. "Oh children!" She whispered to them of the Danube, the river "blue as an eye, blue as heaven, blue blue…"—who would *they* marry, tinker, tailor, poet?—and as they waltzed, the apples fell from their bloomers, of no use, of no meaning now.[3]

They had learned the art of advanced tree climbing from Uncle Dodger, who rescued them when they were too high in the branches to descend without panic. Dodger had a way with children and birds. Kookaburras, sparrows and parrots flocked to his call and sat on his head. His niece Nellie Rubina, then about eight years old, was a stolid, rosy, wooden child who lived across the field from the Goffs. She fished sticky conversation lollies from her pockets and offered them with a deep, expressive glance. The sugary pink-and-green tablets were inscribed with enigmatic messages: "Wait Till Tomorrow," "Help Yourself." Nellie Rubina wandered the dirt lanes, a string bag containing just one bun looped over an arm. She called out to Lyndon, "What's your name, Back Lane?" and refused to share the bread.

Nellie Rubina and Uncle Dodger appear in the second Mary Poppins book, *Mary Poppins Comes Back,* in a story called simply "Nellie Rubina." The title character sweeps away the snow by bringing spring to the world. An adult, not a child, who resembles a wooden doll, Nellie lives with her uncle in a wooden ark with a hinged top. She may be the daughter of God. Nellie and her uncle share conversation lollies with Mary Poppins and the Banks children and manufacture wooden objects signifying spring: cuckoos, lambs, branches laden with buds and snowdrops.

Lyndon was intrigued by these conversation lollies but more by the shopkeepers who sold them. Aunt Ellie's travel anecdotes included the tale of an English sweetshop kept by a decrepit old woman who had two lines of merchandise, one called Kiss Me Quick and the other Cuddle Me Close.[4] This old lady, combined with the Bowral sweetshop proprietor, were the basis for one of Mary Poppins's oddest friends, Mrs. Corry. She appears in several of the Mary Poppins books as a tiny, skinny old lady in a dingy store whose windows are decorated with old bits of colored paper. Mrs. Corry stocks gingerbread, sherbet, licorice sticks, apples on a stick (stale), and barley sugar. Her own fingers are made of self-renewing barley sugar and she tyrannizes her gargantuan daughters.

Mrs. Corry clearly comes from the world of legend and myth. She is a wise woman, a crone, a storyteller, a sibyl. Mrs. Corry knows William the Conqueror, Alfred the Great and Guy Fawkes, and, with her daughters and Mary Poppins, fixes stars on the roof of the sky with the help of a pot of glue and a very tall ladder.

The real Mrs. Corry in Bowral was just as fearsome. Lyndon was terrified of entering the dark recesses of the shop. With a quavering voice, she would ask for two fizzos—

glutinous sherbet lollies. Mrs. Corry cried "Fizzos!" in a booming echo, loud enough to wake the daughters, who came from upstairs to stare down at the girl.[5]

For all the rich lode of characters she found in Bowral, the focus of Lyndon's life remained her mother, Margaret, a woman who had never been mothered herself, except by Aunt Ellie, and who was now a widow in her thirties. At ten, Lyndon still did not believe her father was really dead. If things went badly wrong, she reassured her mother, "Don't worry, it will all be all right when father gets back from God." At this, Margaret's gray eyes turned black.[6]

Lyndon feared her mother would remarry, yet she might have suffered less if Margaret *had* found a man. She resented the burden of being the oldest child, the confidante. "I was the eldest and that is a very difficult place. So much is expected of you, an example to set."[7] Her mother even needed Lyndon's hand on her brow if she had a headache. Gradually the child came to feel inadequate to the task, resentful, as growing children do of a parent's needs. Her hair began falling out in little round patches; the family doctor, Dr. Throsby, said it was all too much strain on the girl.[8]

A continuing metaphor for her absent father was Halley's Comet, which she mistakenly knew as Harry's Comet. Waiting for Harry "is one of the things I've been doing all my life, imagining him out there on his appointed course, trailing his tail among the galaxies." When the comet came into view in 1910, the red-dressing-gowned Goff children were plucked from their beds to see the miracle and told, "You won't see him again...he won't come again for seventy-six years."[9]

In two accounts, one given in a letter in 1977, the other published in a magazine eleven years later, Lyndon told a story which was engraved on her mind. It concerned a magical white horse, but much more than that, the story signified the end of her childhood and explained, at least to her own satisfaction, this mystery: where did Mary Poppins come from? One night when Lyndon was about eleven, her mother turned in anguish from her children and rushed from the house threatening to drown herself in the creek. She had not recovered from her husband's death and knew no one well enough to share the pain. The rain was drumming onto the tin roof of the cottage, the trees outside were heavy with the day's downpour.

Lyndon was already mature enough not to panic. She stoked the fire, dragged an old feather quilt from the bedroom and wrapped it around herself, then Biddy and Moya. The three girls sat before the fire, watched over by the carved wooden fox on the mantelpiece, lit by their mother's china lamp. As they perched on the hearthrug, Lyndon told her anxious sisters a story of a magical white horse.

The horse might have been Pegasus, a symbol of poetry that would have appealed to the poet in Lyndon, but while it had no wings, it could still gallop over the sea like a shimmering comet, "its hooves flicking the foam." The colt was finely made with a neatly trimmed mane and tail. Was he going home, the girls wanted to know? No, the horse was coming *from* home to a place with no name. He could see that place in the distance as a great cloud of light. Can he do *anything*? Fizzle the world in a frying pan, fly into the air even without wings and dive to the bottom of the sea? Yes, yes, yes! Perhaps he will never even get to the light. What will he eat, what will he drink? Years later, Lyndon believed the magic horse ran underground, and came up eventually as Mary Poppins.[10]

The three girls cuddled tightly together as Lyndon thought of the creek. While her imagination flew to describe the horse's adventures, her logical mind considered the reality. How deep was the creek? Surely not deep enough for a woman to drown? And yet, if you lay down and let the water cover your face, like Ophelia...But the creek does become a wider pool downstream. Anyway, what would happen to us if she never came back? Would we go to a children's home and wear dressing gowns embroidered over to hide the worn holes in the fabric, or would Auntie Ellie take us back to Sydney? Maybe she would send Biddy to Aunt Jane and I would have to stay with Aunt Ellie and Moya would go to one of the cousins? No one would be the "little one" then. How long does it take to drown? Oh God, I will be good, if only Mummy comes back.

As the logs slipped sideways in the fireplace, the door opened. Margaret stood like Ophelia revived, her hair wet around her face, her clothes clinging to her body. Biddy and Moya rushed to embrace her, around the waist, the knees, tried to kiss her cheeks, crying and laughing, pulling at her clothes, pulling down the bedclothes for her, but Lyndon held back. She went to the primus stove, a place forbidden to the children, and boiled a kettle to fill the hot water bottle, which she silently took to her mother's bedroom. Moya and Biddy were already tucked into bed with her, one on each side, giggling and whispering the story of the magic white horse.

Margaret looked up at her eldest daughter. Lyndon threw the hot water bottle onto the bed with as much strength as she could muster, just as Margaret had once smashed the china doll on the iron bedstead. "Oh, you cold-hearted child. The others are so pleased to see me. What's the matter with you?" cried Margaret. Lyndon couldn't answer. She went to her own bed and lay cold, in her heart and body, and still as a stone. The pain, then relief, were impossible to bear. She could not even weep.

She had seen herself as a tight green bud, unable to bend to another's grief. Only as an adult, writing a letter to a friend, could Lyndon acknowledge the depth of Margaret's grief, that what "had been borne by two now had to be carried by one. Fullness had become emptiness." The empty bed symbolized the loss—the bed that once resonated with all the intimacies of marriage: "Yin breath and Yang breath flowing together, naked foot over naked foot, the day dissolved, absolved by night."[11] She realized that, far from being innocent, her mother knew a great deal. One day she saw Margaret looking down at her as she lay in the bath. Her mother was quietly weeping. "All the love had rushed to the gray eyes, they were black with concern and love and anguish and compassion, the desire to comfort. She said nothing. Neither of us could speak."

In May 1912, Margaret Goff advertised in the local *Wollondilly Press:* "Cottage furnished, to let. Mrs. Goff, Holly Street, Bowral." She intended to live for a while with Aunt Ellie while she enrolled Lyndon at a high school in Sydney. Ellie had insisted it was for the best; the child was bright and Ellie would pay the fees. Lyndon, who would turn thirteen in August of that year, was to be a boarder, returning to Bowral for holidays.[12]

Margaret fulfilled her duty by telling Lyndon (one day in Sydney's Botanical Gardens) that she would soon be a woman, and explained the reason for the monthly flow of blood.[13] Lyndon was quiet, full of unspoken resentment, which she was to unleash on her new teachers at Normanhurst Private Girls School in the inner west suburb of Ashfield. Normanhurst was considered "elegant" by Aunt Ellie. It maintained the pretense of being nondenominational but had links with St. John's Church of England and was a sister school to Abbotsleigh on the North Shore of Sydney.[14]

Lyndon began to be naughty, inventive about breaking the rules. The principal called her into her study but instead of berating her merely asked, "Do you know why you do these things?" Lyndon lied that she was bored. "Well," asked Miss Beatrice Tildsley, "what *does* interest you? Perhaps reading?" She ushered her into a corner of the study where she could read any book she liked. Lyndon began, she said later, with *The Decline and Fall of the Roman Empire* and went on from there.[15] She remembered Normanhurst as a place where she could read and learn, a preparation for the life of a writer and actress.[16]

Now she was apart from her mother, Lyndon understood that her father had definitely died. In fact, she thought he had turned into a star.

Lyndon dutifully studied music, passed a Trinity College theory exam in 1913 and fell passionately in love with the stage, thrilled by her first taste of watching a play when the hero was brought in wounded, his forehead covered in tomato sauce. (Her years at Normanhurst coincided with the Great War.[17]) Her first published article, under the byline Lyndon Goff, in the *Normanhurst School Magazine,* was a report of the "Grand Variety Entertainment" held in the third term of 1914. "As the different items were rendered, we were thrilled to find that these stars of the first magnitude had dwelt among us incognito, in some cases for years," she wrote. The proceeds from the concert went to war funds.

Lyndon progressed from acting to directing with her production of a fund-raising school concert in November 1914. It began with the "Marseillaise" followed by "Bravo!," a war recitation, and included "Gossip," a sketch for two old women (no doubt modeled on Aunt Jane and Aunt Ellie). The highlight of the evening was a melodrama, starring Lyndon and depicting kings, beautiful ladies in distress and dueling knights. The concert ended with the kaiser being toppled by the united efforts of England, France, Belgium and Australia, before the girls and teachers sang "God Save the King."

By 1915, the school magazine chronicled the loss of brothers at Gallipolli and earnestly reported that the girls' "hearts were full of reverence for those who have made, or are ready to make, this greatest offering of all." Lyndon's report of a

masked ball at the school later that year praised the flags of
the Allies suspended from the ceiling and, in each corner,
miniature flags intertwined with palms and ferns. At the Head
Dress Dance of winter 1915, "the bedrooms rang with cries
for pins, cotton, etc. as everyone rushed hither and thither in
a wild state of excitement...the cauliflower and turnip had to
be led in, the holes made in their paper head coverings not
large enough to see through."

Lyndon wrote well, in the direct clear style of a budding
journalist, but it was becoming clear that while writing came
naturally, acting would come first. Through her fascination with
acting, Lyndon was to meet the first of a long chain of men
who would, in her words, "pass her from one to the other."
These men were not just her mentors, but substitute fathers
and lovers, who would play Mr. Banks to her Mary Poppins.

He was Lawrence Campbell, a London-born actor in his
late forties who had taught drama and public speaking in
Sydney for twenty years. As a so-called elocutionist, Campbell
coached students at several schools, including Normanhurst.
In 1915 he cast Lyndon as Bottom in Normanhurst's production of *A Midsummer Night's Dream,* which opened in October
at the Ashfield Town Hall. Box office sales went to the Red
Cross and Belgian Funds. Lyndon wore a red wig, then an ass's
head, "quite transforming her," according to the school magazine review.

That year she also played the title role in *Le Voyage de Monsieur Perrichon,* and passed the Junior University Examination.
By 1916, now a school prefect, her thoughts skipped toward
escape from Normanhurst and a career as an actress. In May
1916 Lawrence Campbell took the fifth-form girls, including
Lyndon, to see *Richard III* at the New Adelphi Theatre. The
production was part of a six-play Shakespearean season presented by entrepreneur George Marlow. The star was an
English actor, Allan Wilkie, who played Malvolio, Shylock and

Romeo in the season but excelled as Richard III, whom he portrayed with both a limp and a horribly distorted mouth. Lyndon and her friends had a marvelous view of the tragedy from the stalls.[18]

Campbell was more than just a teacher who took his pupils on excursions. He was a professional actor, as well as a director of the Palace Theatre where he gave recitations of poems. He also played Jaques in *As You Like It,* in Allan Wilkie's 1916 Shakespearean season. He had an extraordinary suggestion to make to Lyndon. Why didn't she move into his home? His wife would be a sufficient chaperone, and he would train her as an actress.[19] When she later told interviewers about this suggestion, Lyndon gave no hint of a sexual motive but indicated that such a thing would have been impossible "in my kind of family," as Aunt Ellie and her mother were such snobs. For them, a life on the stage would have been a shocking thing for a girl to take up, tantamount to prostitution.[20] Instead, Lyndon said, "I had to earn my living and help my family...I had no choice."

Aunt Ellie took charge. There were no decent jobs for a young lady in Bowral. She must work in Sydney. There could be no choice; Margaret, Biddy and Moya would all move to the city, and Lyndon would live at home once again. Margaret Goff rented a modest cottage at 17 Pembroke Street, Ashfield, and the two younger girls were enrolled at Normanhurst. Aunt Ellie marched Lyndon along to the Australian Gas Light Company where she knew a board member, Thomas Forster Knox, a brother-in-law of her friend Edith Knox.[21] Ellie suggested Lyndon might become a shorthand typist. Thomas Knox only briefly protested, "My dear Miss Morehead, she might be too young . . ." before Ellie shouted him down with "Nonsense, she's perfectly competent and she needs to work."

Lyndon was sent to work as a secretary in the cashier's office. She dreaded having to make the money tally correctly at the end of each day. "Probably because of my early association with money, or rather the lack of it," she wrote later, she never once got the balance right. Somebody came to the rescue with an old adding machine and the management never knew of her incompetence. Lyndon was recommended for a raise. At the big black typewriter each day she heard Aunt Ellie's voice urging, nagging: Be a good girl. Help Mother. "That seemed to be my role and I wondered if there was anything else for me in life."[22]

At her bleakest moments, she said to herself that if stars were happiness, which would she rather have, the Milky Way or the two stars that point to the Southern Cross? Lyndon decided it must be the pointers. "It was so black, so dark, so terrible in between them—but I thought those two gold moments would be better than whole years of the Milky Way."[23]

4

The Creation of Pamela

By the time she was seventeen, Lyndon knew by heart all of Juliet's speeches and most of Lady Teazle's lines from *School for Scandal*. She was a typist in name but an actress by instinct. Under Minnie Everett's instruction, she continued her fancy dancing lessons, hummed little tunes which might accompany her own verses[1] and boasted that she saw every play that was staged in Sydney. Her obsession was more a matter of grief than pride for her mother and Aunt Ellie.[2]

Lyndon's grand ambition was to become a dramatic actress in the style of Kathlene MacDonell, whom she had seen in

1917 at the Criterion Theatre. She liked her in *Peter Pan* but loved her in Edmond Rostand's *L'Aiglon* and learned the play by heart. Two years later, Lyndon spent all her spare money at the New Olympia Theatre in Darlinghurst to see over and over again the visiting English actor, Sir Johnston Forbes-Robertson, in the play *Passing of the Third Floor Back*.

She watched with envy as the older pupils at Minnie's dance school were cast in the pantomimes staged at the city theatres owned by the flamboyant brothers Ben and John Fuller (motto: "Hilarity Without Vulgarity"), the Grand Opera House (formerly the New Adelphi) and Her Majesty's. The "pantos" were a regular fixture of the theatrical year, not just a Christmas attraction, and they all featured "beautiful ballets." They were based on European fairy tales, and there were few exceptions to the sweetly familiar stories of Cinderella, Aladdin, Dick Whittington, Robinson Crusoe, Red Riding Hood and Babes in the Wood. Now and again, the Grand Opera House audience might see a rare piece of Australiana, as it did in December 1916 with *The Bunyip,* a pantomime featuring the Wattle Blossom Fairy Princess.

After months of tantrums, when Margaret Goff and Aunt Ellie were alternately outraged by or contemptuous of the suggestion she should become an actress, they allowed Lyndon to perform in a pantomime.[3] Her debut took place in 1920 in J. C. Williamson's spectacular *Sleeping Beauty,* which opened in April for a six-week season at the Criterion. Of course she knew the fairy tale from childhood, and she had always identified with both the resolute princess and the thirteenth fairy, who took her revenge on being excluded from the christening party. Lyndon's involvement in the pantomime version helped reinforce its importance in her mind as a key to a woman's life.

Lyndon took part as a member of Minnie Everett's ballet troupe, some of whom spoke a few lines—to the scorn of the critic from *The Triad* magazine, who found their interpretation "intensely pathetic." But *Sleeping Beauty* had a successful season with the help of actors from England and New York playing the principal boy and girl.

During the run Lyndon made friends with Peggy Doran, billed in the cast list as "the noted Irish Character Comedienne." Lyndon asked Peggy if she would hear her practice the lines from *L'Aiglon*. She had rehearsed them already in the storeroom under the stage, amid the baskets of props and costumes. Peggy spread the word that there was a real actress among the dancing girls. Minnie was astonished, and she asked Lyndon where she had learned to act. Lyndon hung her head. "I never have." "Never mind, you'll now have a small part in the play," said Minnie. In true showbiz style, Lyndon stepped into the speaking role of a woman leaving the show.[4] Already stagestruck, she was now completely seduced. The stage fulfilled cravings in Lyndon for applause. Somebody, even if it was an audience of complete strangers, was now paying attention to little Lyndon. She longed to do this all the time.

The way ahead was through the Shakespearean actor Lyndon had idealized as a schoolgirl, Allan Wilkie. If Lawrence Campbell was her first Mr. Banks, Wilkie became the second. Liverpool born, Wilkie was a trouper and actor-manager in the Henry Irving manner who had learned his craft playing in melodrama and Shakespeare in companies run by Ben Greet, Frank Benson and Herbert Beerbohm Tree. He toured the English provinces, then traveled with an itinerant company of actors throughout the world. Caught in South Africa at the beginning of World War I, Wilkie and his actress wife, Frediswyde Hunter-Watts, sailed for Australia, where she had relatives.[5]

A traditionalist who shunned modern-dress versions of Shakespeare, Wilkie resembled Oscar Wilde and boasted that he could play Shylock any night with no preparation but needed twenty-four hours' notice to play Othello. For a generation of schoolchildren, he transformed Shakespeare from an incomprehensible jumble of words that the teacher made them speak aloud to poetry that came suddenly alive. It meant nothing that the Wilkie players' set might consist of a black backcloth, a wooden throne, a table, or a divan. What mattered was the passion, the loving, the embracing, the bloody sword fights and betrayals enunciated in the fruity tones of Frediswyde and friends.

In 1915 Wilkie found his first Australian financial backer—another showman from northern England, George Marlow, who had been the lessee of the New Adelphi Theatre and the Princess Theatre in Melbourne. Marlow suggested that Wilkie form a new company, and in January 1916 Marlow's Grand Shakespearean Company premiered in Melbourne with *The Merchant of Venice*. Marlow was the promoter and financier and Wilkie the star and artistic director. Lawrence Campbell had taken Lyndon's class at Normanhurst to see the Sydney season of this company.

In July 1918 Wilkie thrilled Sydney again in a long season at the Grand Opera House,[6] then finally formed his own permanent company in 1920. Defying theatrical tradition, he chose *Macbeth* to open the first season in Melbourne in September that year. In February 1921 his company came to Sydney for a six-week season at the Grand Opera House. It presented, in repertory, *Julius Caesar, Twelfth Night, Hamlet, The Merry Wives of Windsor, The Merchant of Venice, Macbeth* and *As You Like It*.

Lyndon met Wilkie just before this late summer season began. She told different versions of how she came into his orbit, but it is likely that she was introduced to him by Lawrence Campbell. As she walked through the city streets to meet Wilkie, whom she called the Great Man, or simply GM, Lyndon fantasized that his body would be as beautiful as Tarzan's and his face like a treasured picture of Sir Johnston

Forbes-Robertson which she kept at home. He would lead her, like a bride, down broad carpeted stairs to the stage where he would instruct her: "We shall rehearse *Anthony and Cleopatra,* and you will be Cleopatra."

Instead, Allan Wilkie resembled a weedy Lorenzo proclaiming his love to a stout and elderly Jessica. A felt hat was jammed down on his head, a cigarette butt clung to his lower lip, trembling as he spoke but retaining its perilous position. "Is this the girl?" Wilkie asked.

"This is she."

"Oh well, we'll try her anyway."

Wilkie looked down his chiseled Roman nose at Lyndon. He instructed her to run around a cluster of chairs masquerading as a fountain in a village marketplace. "You're a girl of the town being chased by a young man—go ahead!"

Lyndon obediently ran. One of the young actors caught her and kissed her full on the lips—violently, she later said. Young and innocent, she had never been kissed that way. Lyndon slapped him very hard, leaving a flaming hand mark on his face. He put his hand to his cheek. According to Lyndon he sulked to Wilkie, "Don't take her, she's dynamite," but Wilkie merely replied, "On the contrary, that's why I *shall* take her. We need a bit of dynamite around here. Good, now we'll do the scene again."

It is hard to know who felt the biggest thrill from the chase, the kiss, the smack, then the stinging cheek—Wilkie, Lyndon, or the actor. Wilkie asked her what else she could do. Lyndon boasted Juliet, Rosalind, Miranda, Portia, Beatrice, Mistress Ford, and even Lady Macbeth. Wilkie smiled at the last. Was she afraid of hard work? Hardly. Did she want to try? "Oh yes!"

She was engaged at two pounds a week.[7]

• • •

This time, Lyndon had less trouble with her mother and Aunt Ellie. After all—Shakespeare! She began her season with Wilkie as an understudy, sitting in the wings each night, in anguish for Ophelia, weeping out loud for Juliet. The leading lady, Frediswyde, was *never* ill. In the end, taking pity, Wilkie gave Lyndon a part as Anne Page in *The Merry Wives of Windsor*.

The debut was in March 1921. Trembling with fright, she could barely speak her first line, "The dinner is on the table; my father desires your worships' company." At the end of the engagement, Wilkie was satisfied with his Sydney reception despite the acerbic reviews in *The Triad,* which closely followed his company's fortunes. The critic, who hid behind anonymity, had found Wilkie's Mark Antony "eminently suburban...woefully deficient in light and fire" while the extras were "some of the queerest on this planet."[8]

Wilkie's plans included a new tour of Australia then New Zealand. Lyndon was desperate to travel, too. No, said Aunt Ellie, she was far too young to leave home with those *theatricals*. "Wait another year," said her mother. Lyndon sobbed as she waved the train good-bye.

In those few months on stage, Helen Lyndon Goff began her transformation from gauche little Lyndon to sophisticated Pamela. Her stage name, she decided, had to change. There was no romance in the name Lyndon and Goff was well, gruff, hardly mellifluous. There was, though, resonance in her father's Christian name, Travers. That sounded actressy. Lyndon knew of a Pamela from the Goff family tree. She thought it a pretty name whose rhythm flowed with Travers. In time, she grew to resemble her new name. Its translation from the Greek was "all sweet" or "all loving," and the name Pamela became increasingly fashionable in the 1920s and '30s. The new Pamela cultivated her hair into a frizzy halo and in publicity photographs learned to tilt her head beguilingly, so that she could gaze down at the camera through heavy lidded eyes. Pamela had full lips above a neat pointed chin, but her face was too long for true beauty.

In the spring of 1921 she was asked to tour New South Wales with a repertory company presenting a handful of plays, among them *Charlie's Aunt* and the melodrama *East Lynne*. They would also stage scenes from *Hamlet* and *The Merchant of Venice*, in which she was to play a boy's part, Lorenzo. "The family sat in council with me and the upshot, one very starry evening, I set out from Sydney with other actor people to get six months outback experience."[9] Pamela did not reveal the name of the touring company, but it was likely to be a group put together by the Fullers. *East Lynne* and potboilers such as *Her Road to Ruin* were favorites of Ben and John Fuller's Dramatic Players and had already been staged often in Sydney at the Grand Opera House.

The troupe included a leading lady, a leading man, a juvenile male lead whose sad face resembled a very thin horse, an old man who played character parts and, onstage, hid his lines in a dilapidated Shakespearean hat, and Pamela, the female "juve." They traveled in a lorry piled high with costumes, curtains and scenery. The six men rode Roman-chariot–style on top while the two women sat in the cab with the driver.

These were glorious days, seen in retrospect as if in a musical set in the 1920s, *Salad Days* or *The Boyfriend*, perhaps, or a chapter from *The Good Companions*. The tour was the making of Pamela, or, as she once put it primly, "this little company was excellent training for me, not only as an actress but as a person."[10] Waiting in the wings some nights, she saw the leading man look toward her with only slightly disguised lust. Pamela felt a surge of power. She knew she was at her peak of sexual magnetism.

"Wattle peered at us with little golden eyes" and the lorry sped through arches of eucalyptus. "The merriest group of barnstormers in the world" rehearsed new parts, sang, told stories and shopped at farmhouses for milk and oranges. Sometimes they journeyed by the light of the moon, so bright it turned the creeks silver. On the Dorrigo Mountains, inland from Coffs Harbour on the New South Wales north coast, the driver was so nervous he told Pamela and the leading lady to get out and take the next car to town. Of course they refused. Silly! With that, the wheels slid over the edge of a precipice. They all clambered out to push the lorry back to safety. Once they lost the juvenile boy over the back of the lorry, which rattled so loudly no one heard his shouts for help. He arrived at the theatre hours later, his feet and legs brown with dust, after a thirteen-mile trek.

The troupe often arrived at the village town hall just in time for the evening performance. The show might start at quarter to nine, the locals patiently waiting on benches with their lemonade, oranges and peanuts as the men pinned up curtains and hammered scenery into place. Pamela played Joyce, a servant to Lady Isabel in *East Lynne,* and Salarino in *The Merchant of Venice.* But "I longed to be in anything... I greeted each day with ardor," she wrote later.

Wilkie wrote to ask her to rejoin his company. Pamela traveled to Melbourne to find the company rehearsing *Julius Caesar.* "I loved the welcome the company—theatrical diehards—gave me, a novice. It gave me a kind of cachet of importance among the new ones but my smugness vanished under the sarcastic utterances of the GM at rehearsal."

Wilkie sometimes nodded approval, but the acknowledgment was rare and never came at just the right time, when she felt that she really was rather sweet as Titania. In this season, Pamela played a handmaiden to Olivia, a lady to Portia, a forest boy in *As You Like It,* a scarlet-garbed attendant to Lady Macbeth, then moved on to play Jessica, Olivia, Viola, Juliet and Lady Macduff. Now she was earning £4 a week and beginning to attract her first press notices, which she carefully clipped and posted to her family. "I told you so!" was the unwritten message.

She performed the opening dance in *Julius Caesar,* in "a very abbreviated green garment with flowers in my hair, cymbals in my hands. I stood trembling with a crowd of revelers and waited for the first note of my dance..." 2, 3, 4, there it was! "Clash of cymbals, clamor of the stage crowd, flowers tossed in the air and curtain up! How I kept in time with the music I don't know as my ears were dulled with the roaring of vigorous supers all determined to earn their night's wage of 6 shillings and eightpence," she wrote later. Pamela wanted her mentor's approval; Wilkie managed an approving nod one night.[11]

Back in Sydney's Grand Opera House in April 1922, Pamela was cast as Titania in Wilkie's production of *A Midsummer Night's Dream.* The *Triad* critic wrote "Miss Pamela Travers was human, all too human, as Titania. Whenever Titania is not all pure fire in ecstasy, the less Titania she. On the whole, this production was a workmanlike essay holding much mirth but little thrill."[12]

Pamela's acting career ended soon after a tour to New Zealand where, in sleepy Christchurch, she met a man who led her to a new life as a writer. It happened purely by chance when the troupe reached the southern city. Drunk with the freedom from any responsibility and tipsy with wine, the actors danced barefoot through the city square, playing leapfrog and giggling at the thought of the provincials tucked up in their beds.[13] The locals ogled the traveling players. One journalist from the afternoon paper, the Christchurch *Sun,* was so entranced by Pamela he started to follow her from town to town on his motorcycle.

From the evidence of her later writing, she fell for him with a sudden passion. In "Surrender," a poem written in 1923,

Pamela remembered how her heart had once been free from "all emotion's clamor"...until "the tree quivers before the storm...of searing love. Oh joyous overthrow...I feel your kisses warm upon my mouth."

"Surrender" appeared in an issue of *The Triad* on the same page as her poem "On a Circle of Trees in the Christchurch Gardens." Here in the gardens, she believed that

young Psyche, tremulous with love's pain,
first knew the wine of Eros's drooping mouth.

In the gardens, Diana might have paused,

mocking the lovers whom her deep eyes
led to woo her heart from chasteness to delight.[14]

Pamela had also written a prose version of the "Circle of Trees" poem, which she described as "a poetic imaginative piece," or "a fantasy about gardens." She showed it to the journalist, who in turn showed it to his editor, who published it. "The editor asked me to write for him regularly, articles and poems. I was so pleased at seeing my writing in print that I began to bombard the paper with material and the editor accepted it all."[15]

When the troupe returned to Sydney, she continued to write each week for the "Women's World" section of the Christchurch *Sun*. Her column was called "Pamela Passes: the *Sun*'s Sydney Letter." The acceptance of her work without effort, and the thrill of the byline, meant that "I knew I had found the love of my life, writing."[16]

Her output in Australia grew from an occasional comic essay or romantic verse to a more serious stream of freelance contributions. Among her outlets were the *Shakespearean Quarterly,* associated with Allan Wilkie, *Vision* and *The Green Room.*

Pamela considered a career as a journalist, although an editor once warned her against that addiction. "You're no journalist. Get away before you lose your soul." He had been caught in the trap of news making, but she must not be, he told her.[17]

Her father's voice continued to haunt her with his tales of Yeats and Russell. A real writer was not a journalist, she knew, but a poet. The prime place for an aspiring or established poet was page seven of *The Bulletin,* captioned "Various Verse" and featuring the work of David McKee Wright, Zora Cross, Roderic Quinn, Jack Lindsay and Mary Gilmore. On March 20, 1923, Pamela joined their ranks with an Irish fantasy called "Keening," in which she wrote of Iosagan, the Irish name for Jesus.

The poem began:

When I was young in green Athlone
The young Iosa played with me

Through the winter of 1923, *The Bulletin* published many of her poems, most referring to romance, stars, children sleeping, mouths and kissing. In one, she wrote of her own "wild, wild hair" and "tremulous breasts"; in another of her "pagan-scarlet mouth." The most erotic, called "The Lost Loves," began:

Now that he's gone and I am rapture-free
I shall return to my old loves again,
And seek from them some solace for this pain
That hangs me high upon a sorrowing tree.

The rope of kisses wound about my throat
Is tied with dreams upon a bough of grief,
Curving with my sad weight, and every leaf
A tear that I have wept for Love's lost note.

It spoke of her lover's "questing hands" and his "dream dark" head at her breast. Another poem, "Glimpse," described a man's "proud kiss-courting mouth" and his "dark head silk-pillowed on my arm."

In June 1923 Pamela wrote of the "Raggedy-taggedy Gipsy Man," which looked both backward to the gypsies of her youth and forward to two characters in her Mary Poppins stories, Bert, the itinerant matchman, and Robertson Ay, the servant-fool. But the most remarkable reference to the Mary Poppins of the future came in *The Bulletin* on July 5, 1923, in "The Nurse's Lullaby":

> *Hush, little love, for the feet of Dusk*
> *Stir softly through the air.*
> *And Mary the Mother comes to set*
> *A star within your hair*
>
> *Sleep, O heart, for the candle-light*
> *Out of darkness gleams,*
> *And Mary's mouth on your mouth shall fill*
> *The drowsy night with dreams*

Another poet published by *The Bulletin* was Frank Morton, who, Pamela knew, ran *The Triad,* which she thought "a rather good literary paper."

Although the focus of *The Triad,* edited by Charles Baeyertz, was literary, the magazine also boasted of its "outstanding coverage of Life, People, Places." Contributors included the poets Kenneth Slessor, Hugh McCrae and Mary Gilmore, and the writers Dulcie Deamer and Hector Bolitho.

But, as it was run on a shoestring, the editor and his business partner, Frank Morton, filed the bulk of the copy. Morton, who wrote under numerous pseudonyms, was to become the third Mr. Banks in Pamela's life. He sensed the energy and daring in Pamela, offering her regular work on the magazine. Aunt Ellie was again mortified. "Writing! Why can't you leave that to journalists!" Ellie thought Pamela had probably inherited the writing gene from her great uncle Edward, who wrote a book of religious sonnets, privately printed. Pamela sniffed that her talent had come from her own father.[18]

Unlike Lawrence Campbell and Allan Wilkie, both performers, Morton was an observer. While Campbell and Wilkie set out to impress Pamela, Morton was more interested in her mind. Or so he said. In fact, he was a total sensualist. Even his memorial notice in *The Triad* pulled no punches, admitting his detractors charged him with "lewd hedonism."[19]

Morton had been married for over thirty years but described himself in print as "the Great Lover, a disillusioned yet still dangerous roué."[20] As a journalist he worked in Singapore and in Calcutta, wrote as a special correspondent on the Indian tour of the theosophist Annie Besant, and contributed to *The Bulletin*'s literary pages, then edited by the grumpy A.G. Stephens, with whom he enjoyed a long-running feud over who was the better editor. Morton worked for the daily press in New Zealand and founded *The Triad* there. He joined the Australian edition of *The Triad* in 1915 and published volumes of poetry, including an erotic poem, "The Secret Spring." Morton was an odd and heady combination: a poet, a Don Juan, a gourmet, and a journalist so experienced he could write about summer fruit or French literature with equal speed and ease.

Pamela's first published work in *The Triad,* in March 1922, was a poem called "Mother Song." She wrote under the byline Pamela Young Travers. This was the first and only time she used the name "Young," which she undoubtedly felt. "Mother Song" was an unabashed piece of sentimentality, notable only for its mention of stars, the theme of so much of her later work, the phrase "time for bed," one of Mary Poppins's favorite orders, and the idea of a flying angel, in the form of the Dustman.

Little son,
You must soon be sleeping;
Baby stars are peeping,
One by one.

'Time for bed!' . . .
Hear the Dustman crying,
As he comes with flying
Wings outspread . . .

Morton and Baeyertz promised to publish her poetry, but what they really wanted was a sharp writer for the women's column. *The Triad*'s bylines included a few women's names, some of which may have been pseudonyms for Morton himself, especially the morose sounding Susan Gloomish. For three years, a Laline Seton Grey wrote every month under the umbrella headline "From a Woman's Standpoint."

In May 1923, when Pamela began to work at *The Triad*'s Castlereagh Street offices, the Sydney press had been busy hiring women editors and launching new women's sections. The new *Daily Guardian* ran a regular women's page of society gossip, fashion and shoppers' prizes, the *Daily Mail* gave women's news more and more space, while *Smith's Weekly* recruited the flamboyant actress Ethel Kelly as its society writer.

Morton and Baeyertz, who had seen the great success of the catty yet witty "Women's Letter" at *The Bulletin,* gave Pamela a luxurious free rein to fill four or more pages an issue under the new headline, "A Woman Hits Back." She could range from verse, to satire, to journalism, to fantasy. Pamela was both overjoyed and overawed. This seemed to be a dream job. She leapt in with unfocused, scattergun energy. (Morton and Baeyertz were the kind of editors who edited at long distance. Pamela once wrote that "the editors were not often to be found in the office, being too busy chasing Romance outside.")

She revealed more of herself than she knew in her pithy paragraphs, snippets, short stories, reportage, reviews, verses, snatches of overheard conversation, attempts to write in the style of the famous, observations of Sydney and its people, and thoughts on Australia. She wrote of love gone wrong and what men wanted, of desire, fantasy, feminism and memories of childhood.

The style varied wildly. Her strong suits were direct descriptive journalism and an ear for dialogue. Her weaknesses were occasional flights into purple prose or attempts at short stories set in places she could only imagine, such as Galway. Much of her work was tremulous poesy (a word she loved), in the style of Tennyson with references to Yeats.

But, perhaps to please Morton, erotic verse and coquetry ran powerfully through her pieces. Alongside them, *The Triad* published advertisements for Morton's soft porn books such as *Pan and the Young Spinster and Other Uncensored Stories*. Among her phrases of sexual longing, Pamela wrote of swooning "deep in an ecstasy of love," and in another poem yearned

Again to feel your fingers in my hair
Bending my half unwilling back...and back . . .
Until the fortress of my womanhood
Is shattered by your crushing, conquering arms.

In a short verse called "O-o-h, Shocking!" she wrote of "unutterable ardors...wake up, wake up! Hold me tight in your arms...tighter, tighter...crush me close, close against your heart...I am so afraid!"

She even told of the intimate pleasure of undressing: "The clip clip of fastenings giggling deliciously as they fly apart... and then the silky hush of intimate things, fragrant with my fragrance, steal softly down, so loth to rob me of my last dear concealment...but there is left this flower white, flower pink, radiant shy thing, tremulous. It's Me, Me, *Me*!...Ah, darling God, how dear of you to make me! My sobbing laughter is buried in the pillow's lavender. Life is so sweet...so sweet... God!" Pamela was a tease who sighed in one poem "You must take my No for Yes, my mouth will be a long caress . . ."

But despite all the heavy breathing, Pamela was more a flirt than a woman of the world. And she was well aware of the tricks of journalism, how one affects honesty to hide artifice. In the July 1923 issue of *The Triad* she wrote in a poem called "Friend (to HB)" that "the dress of passion that I sometimes wear has less of sorcery than this calm robe you fling about my life."

HB is likely to have been her *Triad* colleague, Hector Bolitho, who also edited the *Shakespearean Quarterly*. In the May 1923 issue, within a series of quips under the subheadline "So There Hector!" she declared, "Men are never interested in women. They are only interested in showing women how interesting they themselves are." In the style of Oscar Wilde, she told her readers that "A woman loves a man first, and then his face. A man loves her ankles, and then the woman." And, "There is only one thing more annoying to a woman than the man who doesn't understand her, and that is the man who does."

In another column, the two sides of Pamela were revealed in a piece called "The Moon and Sausages," in which she wondered how she could make money. Perhaps by sending a poem to the *Herald,* which might give her five pounds. "I think it had better be about love, all sonnets are about love...Here in the shade of this low whispering pine...What rhymes with moon, broom? No, swoon." Pamela's moon, June, swoon fantasies were interrupted by her mother asking her to "go and get a pound of sausages, and don't get chops by mistake...deep in an ecstasy of love I swoon...did mother say sausages or chops?"

As she went spinning around the city, Pamela watched with the intensity of a journalist or outsider. She saw "shabby" children in a toy shop, the partygoers at the Artists Ball, the crowds at the races with "orange sun-shades warring with red hats and shoes, shoes, shoes, shiny mirroring patent leather shoes very black and conscious of their blackness..." She watched the men at the fruit stalls, the statues in Hyde Park, the speakers in the Domain, the shoe sale in Pitt Street, and eavesdropped on gossip exchanged on the tram in William Street, in the auditorium at the Cat and the Canary, on the ferry to Manly (where Morton lived), at the State Orchestra and a private exhibition of etchings. She gazed at a green dress in a window and yearned to buy it. Next day it was sold, she thought to a fat lady who would wear it to the races.

Pamela showed more contempt than compassion for her countrymen. She thought Australians "took their fun very seriously...were incapable of undressing delight delicately, garment by mysterious joyous garment." She criticized the "stodgy, mutton fed" Australian sense of humor, complained that Australians were not a gay people, too self-conscious, too steeped in an overpowering sense of their own importance to let themselves go. "They are good fellows, hearty eaters, amusing companions but they lack the dancing, bird-like delight of the Gaelic races."

Australians had not found any "workable philosophy of life." Pamela, with the certainty of a woman in her early twenties, complained that "they sin, and then dear babes, regret, not knowing how to laugh at fortune. They brood, not knowing how to fling out their hands and say, well that's over, what's next!"

Australians were too intolerant of tradition to have any "legendary lore" of their own, she explained. She never mentioned Australia's Aboriginal people, then invisible to white city folk, but Pamela was hardly alone in her ignorance. Her myths all came from Ireland and England.

Pamela paraded her knowledge of literature with quotations from Rupert Brooke and John Keats, and with attempts to write in the style of Ethel Turner, Katherine Mansfield, Rudyard Kipling, Samuel Pepys, Henry Wadsworth Longfellow and even Shakespeare. Glimpses of her own storyteller, Mary Poppins, could be seen in some essays, one of which explained that the man in the moon was actually a woman. In another, "Nocturne," she wrote that at midnight, a crack of twelve seconds opens up throughout the world. Within the crack lie enchantment and magic.

And the stars kept creeping back, too. Some stars sang cadenzas above Pitt and George streets, but above Castlereagh Street they sighed and whispered lullabies and staves from old forgotten tunes. Then there was a little girl who asked of her mother in the tram "who put the stars in the sky?" and yes, she knew it was God, "but where did God get them?"

Beneath all the pieces was a sense of yearning, most notable in "Woman": "I want the moon...I want the world...I am a woman and the world sleeps on my breast." For all her idealization of women, though, Pamela was scornful of feminism. In one of her last columns written in Australia she explained that feminists wanted "all the rights of men and none of its [sic] drawbacks." Feminists were "drunk with the newness of their 'freedom'" and hated themselves for being women.[21]

For all the apparent certainty in her prose, Pamela confided to an interviewer that she "always felt rather reluctant to judge my bits of success. *They* praised my poems, and *they* liked my writing, but how can *they* be the judge? I'm afraid I felt that way about Australia, that there was nobody who could be quite sure, and consequently, I could never be sure. I decided quite secretly that I would save enough by my writing and acting to go to England."[22]

In fact there were some experienced literary editors, among them A. G. Stephens, who could have considered and reviewed her work, but it is more likely that she was afraid of their judgment. In any case, following the precepts and programming of

Travers Goff, she had almost no alternative but to sail away.

All these years, she never had a moment's doubt what she was saving for. It was "to slay the enemies of Ireland. The sorrows of that country got into me very early. How could it help doing so with father's nostalgia for it continually feeding the imagination."[23] Naturally, Aunt Ellie chimed in, "Don't be an idiot! Ireland! Nothing but rain and rebels and a gabble of Gaelic." And later, "What's this I hear about you going to England? Ridiculous nonsense. You were always a fool. Well, how much is the fare? I'll send you a cheque for it."[24]

At the end of September, *The Bulletin* published her poem "Song Before a Journey." It began:

> *Before I go to London-town*
> *Where streets are paved with gold,*
> *I'll buy me little flame-red shoes*
> *To keep my feet from cold,*
> *And skins of little rabbits grey*
> *Will wrap me tenderly*
> *When I go up to London-town*
> *That holds the heart of me*

The Triad was bulging with advertisements and free editorial for shipping lines and their luxurious fleets. Pamela studied the choices. Like Hector Bolitho who had sailed before her, she lingered at the windows of shipping offices decorated with posters of steamers floating on a background of Mediterranean blue.

Frank Morton suddenly died (of nephritis) in December 1923. His friend, the newspaper editor Adam McCay, wrote a full-page eulogy for *The Triad:* "Farewell Frank Morton, Lover of Beauty, Craftsman, Satirist" (and writer of "fantastic erotics"). The magazine was to continue until 1927, but Pamela was ready to search for another Mr. Banks.

In January 1924, with Ellie's money, she paid for her passage to England at the agents Dalgety and Co., giving her occupation for the passenger list of the *Medic* as actress. The White Star liner would take her to Southampton, calling at South Africa and the Canary Islands. A few days before she sailed, the feather of a bird flying above drifted down to her feet where she walked in Pitt Street. Pamela scooped it up. Black and white, soft, but finely shaped, the tail feather might have come from a magpie. She tucked it into her handbag. This omen was to travel with her, those fifty days to London.

She sailed at 11:30 on the morning of Saturday, February 9, 1924. "Not to cry, not to cry, so terribly difficult not to cry," she wrote when she remembered the moment when the streamers linking mother and daughter were about to break. For a column in the Christchurch *Sun,* Pamela described the scene that morning at Dalgety's Wharf on Millers Point. She saw herself as a wild-haired girl with a wild heart. Clasping flowers, a book or two and a few gifts, Pamela watched her slender gray-eyed mother and heard "Good-bye, good luck, laughter to you, sprite" as she clung as long as possible to the outstretched hands. "Rattling of many chains, and far away notes of old farewelling songs and tears dripping through a thousand voices." The flowers nodded against her face. She watched the waving hands grow indistinct as the rift of water widened. Suddenly there was "no land and no sea: only the blue of colored ribbons rainbowing my tears."[25]

Two days later, *The Triad*'s February issue announced: "When this issue of *The Triad* is in your hands, Miss Pamela Travers will be on her way to England, there to chase to its lair in London the will-o'-the-wisp of literary Fame and Fortune. Readers of *The Triad* will remember Miss Travers chiefly through her brilliant work in "A Woman Hits Back," that pageful of candid feminism which each month set so many of us blinking. By the time our impulsive young contributor reaches

London her book of verse (*Bitter Sweet*) will have passed through the Kirtley Press, thence to be scattered round the Earth in the bookshops of the Empire.[26] If youth and fiery enthusiasm and indubitable talents are a combination to ensure success, then Miss Travers has little to fear in her latest adventure. May the best of luck attend her!"[27]

5

Falling into Ireland

Pamela suffered dreadfully from seasickness. But as the
Medic plowed down to Melbourne then around to Cape
Town, she scribbled poems, features, fantasies and travel
articles to send back to her most faithful newspaper client,
the Christchurch *Sun*. She was too proud by far to rely simply
on Aunt Ellie's generosity. That might be needed eventually,
but first she was determined to pay her own rent.

When she allowed herself to dream, the pragmatic Pamela
faded behind her fantasy that she was now embarked on a
mythical journey. She believed she was sailing to her romantic motherland, to Ireland, a place of poets and druids still

living in the Celtic Twilight, the title of a book Yeats wrote in the 1890s. This Pamela she saw as a little brown hen, a plaything of her Irish ancestors, who had called her home with insistent voices.[1]

She had no way of knowing that Ireland now was far from romantic, deserted by many of its disillusioned writers and brutalized by the Easter 1916 Rising. By the mid 1920s, romantic Ireland had been buried under the realities of Sinn Fein and the Irish Free State.

In those seven weeks to Southampton, Pamela was often burdened by homesickness. She wrote poems for her mother, whom she remembered pottering about her garden, her feet slow and tender, "shadows of silver dappling her hair."[2] But she consoled herself with the knowledge that there could be no other course. Pamela thought she had not so much left Australia, as she had fallen from it, as an apple falls from the tree, and as if at the summons of a bell.[3]

On her journey around the world, each port offered a chance to make more contacts, essential to a freelance journalist. In Cape Town, she called on friends of Allan Wilkie, who promised her casual work as a publicist. Eventually this led to an assignment in London where she scribbled press releases for the International Variety and Theatrical Agency, which booked shows for South Africa. As Pamela once told a reporter, "I got into publicity writing for the theatres of South Africa. I had to see all the stars of the theatre who were going to South Africa."[4]

The Triad, though, remained her best outlet, even publishing travel features such as her article on Tenerife in the Canary Islands. Pamela first saw Tenerife at midnight, when "the moon had trodden a white path across the seas and was standing mature and arrogant upon the highest hill. Her silver train swung in and out of the shadowed valleys; she had dropped a feather from her hair on the sea's edge, and it bestowed upon the red glow of the little golden town a thousand shimmery and elusive witcheries."[5] Pamela was trying far too hard, burying the lighthearted style of her Sydney pieces under the dead weight of overwrought metaphors.

She had a standard story about arriving in London. It always went like this: "I had £10 in my pocket, £5 of which I promptly lost." Pamela only once disclosed that the pocket was not really empty. A financial safety net under her London adventure was thrown by rich relatives. "I was allowed to depart Australia on condition that I was met and stayed with specific members of the family. This happened as they had hoped. I was welcomed to a big house with three cars just outside London."[6]

These Morehead relatives, nieces and nephews of Aunt Ellie, were about to leave for their spring holiday in Cannes. Pamela must come too, they insisted, return in time for the season, and give up her dreams of art and literature. She begged off Cannes. By the time they returned, she had done the rounds of editors' offices and found a place to stay. Number 10 Mecklenburgh Square was not the poet's attic she had imagined, but it was a reasonable little place not far from the heart of Bloomsbury, near London's publishing heart, Fleet Street. "There, at last, I was where I wanted to be."[7]

Before long, she had a card printed with her London business address, care of Australian Cable Service, 19 to 22 Bouverie Street, EC4. She listed herself as a representative of the Sydney *Sun,* Melbourne *Sun,* Newcastle *Sun,* Sydney *Bulletin,* Sydney *Theatre Magazine, Green Room* magazine, Sydney *Triad,* Christchurch *Sun* and Hobart *Mercury.* Along with the card, Pamela gave editors a reference from *Theatre Magazine:* "Miss Pamela Travers, one of our most valued contributors, is going to London to report on theatres and matters theatrical and to interview prominent playwrights and producers."

At least that was the idea. Instead, she covered the rent by writing for the Christchurch *Sun.* She scurried around London for material, just as she had scoured Sydney for column fodder. By Christmas 1925 she had visited Paris—"absurd and adorable"—three times. Everything was a source of wonder, from the Sacré Coeur to the London tube.

All the romantic notions gleaned from her parents' books, then from Allan Wilkie, Lawrence Campbell and Frank Morton, hardly prepared her for England in 1924. The England she had imagined back home was as Edwardian as Disney's *Mary Poppins* movie, benevolently ruled by George V and documented by the author–heroes of her youth. This was the England of Kipling, H. G. Wells, Galsworthy and Joseph Conrad. Her father's old literary heroes, though, were now the ancients in the eyes of writers like Ezra Pound, who saw Yeats as "Uncle William, still dragging some of the reeds of the nineties in his hair." London was ruled by a new elite, the dandies, in the label given them by historian Martin Green. The dandies loved all things baroque, commedia dell'arte, and Byzantine painting. Among their leaders were Noël Coward, John Gielgud, Cecil Beaton and the Sitwells, all of whom, as D. H. Lawrence said, taught England to be young.

These were the sons who had survived the Great War, not bearded uncles or old literary figureheads but clean-shaven, their hair slicked into Pierrot-like skullcaps. It was all divine and modern and mad and sometimes, as Beaton said, "terribly unfunny, darling."[8]

The dandies identified with Serge Diaghilev's Ballets Russes, whose caravan of dancers and artists included such dandies' heroes as Cocteau, Picasso, Stravinsky, Anton Dolin and Leonide Massine. Diaghilev's troupe dominated London's cultural life in the 1920s but the whole stage scene was booming with the Blackbirds' review, George Bernard Shaw's *Saint Joan,* and the comedies of Noël Coward, "the spokesman of modernity," whose play *Vortex,* about drug taking and homosexuals, premiered in 1924.[9] Pamela, an outsider, knew little of the trailing comet of the Bloomsbury set, or of Pound, James Joyce and T. S. Eliot. While her ideas remained land-locked in the 1890s, London was moving on to *The Waste Land, To the Lighthouse,* and *Ulysses.*

The new Labour government, briefly in power when Pamela arrived, was led by Ramsay MacDonald; the mood was one of conciliation, progress and pacification, marred by the general strike in 1926.[10] "He wishes to do the right thing," sighed King George V in his diary the day MacDonald took power. The King stood for old power, MacDonald for progress and the new. (The dandies' royal hero was George's son, the Prince of Wales, the Pierrot figure who symbolized new England.)

In 1924, the British Empire Exhibition at Wembley summed up Britain's sense of pride in progress.[11] *The Times* thought that "many a young man of our cities will find it difficult to walk past the overseas pavilions—with their suggestion of adventure, and space, and a happy life under the open skies of the bush, the prairie and the veld—without feeling that almost irresistible tugging at the heart strings which drew the pioneers of old to cross the oceans and to blaze the trail for those who followed."

Pamela was not as enchanted by the pavilions as she was by the arrival at the exhibition of the King. As she reported for *The Triad,* "I was to see the King for the first time...and then he came...the crowd swept into a sobbing paean of welcome..."The King! The King!" went stepping from mouth to mouth as round the green the little happy horses pranced and bore him to the glaring dais...boom, boom, boom went the guns in Royal salute as the King led the Queen up the steps to a pair of gilt thrones...then the King spoke...The deep firm voice spoke to the Empire, and the Empire in the persons of those members of it who listened there, acclaimed him. I had seen the King!"[12]

In her first year in England she wrote for both *The Triad*

and the Christchurch *Sun,* admitting in print to feeling like a country bumpkin, overjoyed at the beauty of an English spring, rushing to New Zealand House to read back copies of the papers, buying Canterbury lamb, and all the time tempting her readers with glimpses of life in exotic London.

She wrote verse, too, including a sentimental sonnet to the memory of Frank Morton for *The Triad.* But her ambitions were greater. She had her eye on the *Irish Statesman,* a literary magazine published in Dublin and edited by George William Russell. In early 1925, Pamela sent him some poems, with no covering note, just a stamped addressed envelope for their expected return. On March 13, Russell wrote her a brief letter:

> *Dear Miss Travers,*
> *I like very much some of the verses which you sent me and hope to make use of one or two of them at an early date in the* Irish Statesman. *I do not remember seeing verse by you before. Have you published anything? I am sure a book of verse equal to the best of those you sent me would find readers.*
> *Yours sincerely,*
> *George Russell.*

The hook had been shaped, the bait taken. From now on, Pamela Travers would spend much of her life in an attempt to live out George Russell's ideas. She did not just love Russell. She felt as if he was her sun. He was Zeus, she once wrote, and Pamela just a page in his court.[13]

For all her years as a reporter, Pamela was a girl in love with the idea of being a poetess, so much in love that within one year, she became a pet and protégée not only of Russell but of a circle of men around him: Yeats, James Stephens, Padraic Colum, Oliver St. John Gogarty and Sean O'Faolain. These people "cheerfully licked me into shape like a set of mother cats with a kitten," which was "a blessing far beyond my deserving."[14]

Russell, almost fifty-seven when he met twenty-five-year-old Pamela, was flattered by her adoration. But by his own admission, he did not understand women and, despite a difficult marriage, kept them at emotional arm's length. He let many opportunities pass by. As Simone Tery, one of his young women friends, wrote to him, he was "a puritan without knowing it."[15] But for all the frustrations in their friendship, he turned out to be a force for good in Pamela's life. He was, by far, her supreme guru, her ultimate Mr. Banks, generous, big-hearted and selfless.

Until now, Pamela's world had revolved around poetry and the theatre, which ran through her life like parallel strands of hair. Russell introduced her to the meaning of fairy tales, to myths, the spirit world and Eastern religions. Now the two strands of hair became woven into this third, making a braid of esoteric, interlinked interests.

The joy she felt in reading his first letter was profound. She wrote back next day. It just so happened, she said, that she planned to come to Ireland to visit her relations. Could she meet him?

"Of course," he wrote, "I would be delighted if you would call to see me whenever you are in Dublin. I am found at the Plunkett House, 84 Merrion Square, any afternoon except Saturday and Sunday when I am at 17 Rathgar Avenue. I showed some of your verses to W. B. Yeats who thought they had poetic merit and that means a good deal from him."

This was his standard response, almost a form letter to aspiring writers. As Yeats's biographer, Roy Foster, has written, Russell was "well known for his undiscriminating adoption of young hopefuls."[16] But to Pamela, the invitation was miraculous.[17]

In the 1920s, Russell was seen as an intellectual colossus

in Dublin. His reputation had spread as far as Washington and New York as he transformed himself from artist to visionary, poet to playwright, economist to editor, then charismatic lecturer and later an adviser to the Franklin D. Roosevelt administration. Pamela thought his gifts "wheeled about him as a zodiac." They did not define Russell, who was, she thought, a spirit. "You might as well tie up a lion in a net of silk as try to fit him into a pigeon hole ticketed economist, journalist or artist."

A recital of his occupations never explained his impact on his contemporaries. Russell was described by the poet and doctor Oliver St John Gogarty as the anarchic angel, a teacher who taught nothing in particular, but who "communicated the best in himself, which consists of poetry, loving kindness and a passion for beauty more than anything else."[18] He was more like Plato, said Gogarty, than Tolstoy or Chekhov, whom he resembled.

Russell did not underestimate his own charisma. He made theatrical entrances, his bulky body draped in tweed, "his flowing tie half seen beneath the rich brown beard."[19] A memoir written by his friend John Eglinton described him as corpulent, moving heavily in his fifties. His brow was "hidden in a tangle of mouse colored hair never trimmed except by himself." He had a large full face, high cheekbones, round blue eyes behind small circular spectacles and a pugnacious mouth.[20] He smoked a pipe, which discolored his large teeth. The composer and novelist Lord Berners once described his kind of face as one that "looked like the pipe had been there first and the face had grown around it." Russell puffed constantly, packing his pipe with his favorite coltsfoot-and-tobacco mix. He affected the manner of a distracted artist, often slipping his lit pipe into his pants pocket, setting himself on fire. As well, he was careless about food, wasting no time over meals.[21]

Russell spoke with the mellow, musical accent of his native Ulster. He had worked in Dublin from 1890, as a clerk with the drapery store, Pim Bros., but his talent was for art. At the Metropolitan School of Art he met Yeats, two years older. They became involved in the occult, attending seances. Russell began to paint visionary paintings in the style of Blake and meditated so profoundly that he started to see spirits.

From Russell's trips into inner space came the idea for his pseudonym, AE. He had conjured up the most primeval thought he could, and the word *aon* passed into his head. "I was afterwards surprised at finding out that the gnostics of the Christian era called the first created beings aons and that the Indian word for the commencement of all things is aom."[22] His biographer, Henry Summerfield, thinks he embroidered this theory further into a kind of mathematical formula of the letters AEON:

A = Deity
AE = the first emanation from the Deity
O = static continuance for some time
N = change, that is the spirit returns to God

In the late nineteenth century, this was not as lunatic as it now sounds. The fashion of the time was for all things supernatural, for spiritualism, Eastern philosophy, gurus and spiritual experiments. In 1888, Russell attended meetings of the Dublin Theosophical Society and began to use AE, the first sound of AEON, as his pen name. The fashionable new religion of theosophy was based on Buddhistic and Brahmanic ideas, and revolved around the rather sinister figure of Madame Helena Blavatsky, a Russian who resembled an evil crone in a fairy tale. Blavatsky founded the Theosophical Society in 1875 and claimed that she was instructed in esoteric wisdom by a brotherhood of masters in the Himalayas. She maintained that "the universe was permeated by a kind of psychic ether called akasa through which clairvoyance and telepathy could operate and in which were preserved Akashic Records of the whole of man's history." One could gain access to these records through spiritual perception.[23]

Madame said the world was a conflict of opposites, that all souls identified with the Universal Oversoul and that every soul passed through the "Cycle of Incarnation in accordance with Cyclic and Karmic Law." The magic figure seven featured in all this. The soul had seven elements and it passed through seven planets. There were seven races, seven branch races and seven root races. Just to vary the formula, the soul had about eight hundred incarnations.[24]

Two years after he fell into this supernatural quagmire, Russell delved further into its depths to became a member of the so-called Esoteric Section of the Theosophical Society. He was now a full-scale, full-time mystic, even moving into the society's Dublin premises for seven years. AE was already fascinated by Eastern and Indian religions and had been studying the ancient sacred Hindu texts, the Upanishads and the Bhagavad Gita.

Russell studied with James Pryse, a Theosophist who ran Blavatsky's own press, and had lived with an Indian tribe. Even in old age, AE called Pryse his "guru" and believed him to be the only author to have written on mysticism from real knowledge since the death of Blavatsky.[25]

Russell already meditated on the chakras, the seven main centers of spiritual power which lie from the base of the spine, through the navel, solar plexus, heart, throat, forehead and crown of the head. Pryse explained that certain visions they both saw were chakras on the face of the earth; Indians, American Indians and Greeks also appeared in their visions.

Russell was also entranced by Irish folklore and believed he could see the little people. He was in the west of Ireland, lying on the sand, when he first heard "the silvery sound of bells." His vision sounds now like the sincere ravings of a spotter of UFOs. He saw "an intensity of light before my eyes...I saw the light was streaming from the heart of a glowing figure. Its body was pervaded with light as if sunfire rather than blood ran through its limbs. Light streams flowed from it. It moved over me along the winds, carrying a harp and there was a cir- cling of golden hair that swept across the strings. Birds flew about it and over the brows was a fiery plumage as of wings of outspread flame....there were others, a lordly folk, and they passed by on the wind as if they knew me not or the earth I lived in."[26]

His poetry at this time dwelt on spiritual journeys and the temptations that lay in store for the mystic. AE liked to linger around twilight and sunrise, explaining that the colors of the sky at these times of day were best for meditation. In this way, and with the emphasis of Yeats's twilight fantasies, the two poets reinforced in Pamela the significance of the magic of twilight that she had already experienced in Allora.

In 1898, AE married a member of the Theosophical Society, Violet North, who had succeeded Pryse as printer of the *Irish Theosophist* journal. Violet also saw visions. AE might have gone right over the edge if his common good sense and interest in literature had not acted as a counterbalance. He had joined the Irish Literary Society, which promoted a new Irish school of literature and he helped establish the Irish National Theatre (later the Abbey). Russell's middle years coincided with those two decades from 1890 to 1910 which saw a blossoming of the arts and literature in Ireland, inspired by the Celtic past. The leaders of the revival formed their versions of European salons, revolving around Lady Augusta Gregory, George Moore and Yeats, all Anglo-Irish and Protestant patriots.[27]

Before the First World War, his network grew from merely an Irish circle to an international group. Through his promotion by the former Irish politician and social reformer Sir Horace Plunkett he became a cult figure to many, including Henry Wallace, an American preacher and agriculturalist who advised the American president, Theodore Roosevelt. Wallace sent his grandson, Henry Agard Wallace, to Ireland to meet Horace Plunkett and AE. The grandson was most impressed. He shared with AE an interest in theosophy. It turned out to be a useful friendship for AE when Wallace became vice president in the administration of Franklin D. Roosevelt.

AE was not so much the seer that he grew into a downright bore. His friends loved his Sunday night salons, more casual than Yeats's salons on Monday nights. By the time he settled at 17 Rathgar Avenue in 1906, Sunday with AE was a feature of Dublin social life. He held center stage, explaining and interpreting anything, from dairy farming or the Bhagavad Gita to the Abbey Theatre. He clearly loved the sound of his own voice. Reading from books, or delivering his sonorous monologues, he emphasized the finer points with a flourish of his pipe.

Despite an uneasy tension between AE and Yeats, which lasted all of AE's life, the two men remained friendly. Yeats recommended to Horace Plunkett that AE become the organizer for a new agricultural banking network within the Irish Agricultural Organisation Society (IAOS), which Plunkett had founded. This was not merely a farming group but the basis for a new utopia, centered on cooperative creameries to be run by Ireland's poor farmers. Village communities would grow around each creamery. Communal marketing of eggs and butter might then lead to other, domestic and personal ways of sharing. Gymnasiums, libraries and galleries would all serve the people.[28] Such visions were shared by Henry Wallace Sr. and later John Collier, who was to become United States Commissioner for Indian Affairs. These men liked to talk of "cooperative life in precapitalist times," and praise noble savages such as the Eskimos.[29] All these connections were to prove important to Pamela.

AE took to the new job like a latter-day brother Grimm, not just talking soil and crops, but collecting folk tales as he went from farm to farm. In 1905, he also became the editor of the IAOS's magazine, the *Irish Homestead,* which promoted the cooperative movement's message, pushed Irish arts and crafts, and published James Joyce.

Two years before Pamela met AE, he had become the editor of the *Irish Statesman,* which Plunkett published from 1923, and which incorporated the *Irish Homestead.* Launched with the backing of a group of American Irish investors including the judge Richard Campbell, the group put in enough money for the magazine to last at least five years. The backers did not dictate its politics. It steered "a wide deep middle way, editorially."[30] But it supported the new Irish Free State and it was clear AE had Labour Party sympathies. His columns promoted the need for bigger schools and colleges and less expensive administrations.

AE wrote much of it himself, like Frank Morton inventing pseudonyms "to make the paper look as if it was written by many pens."[31] The magazine included his thoughts on local and international politics, art and literature, and ran contributions by George Bernard Shaw, Gogarty, Padraic Colum and James Stephens. But, always, there was financial stress. The *Irish Statesman* lost money every week[32] and the American guarantors, already edgy, were asked in 1925 to invest even more.

AE's editorial base was at IOAS headquarters in Plunkett House, at 84 Merrion Square, one door away from Yeats's home. The door, deep and wide, stood under an elegant semicircular window set in its Georgian facade. On the second floor, AE sat behind a pile of papers at a mammoth desk. Brown wallpaper was covered by his fantastic murals, among them heroic and supernatural figures, including a woman holding a flaming torch and, over a doorway, a wolf.[33]

Within this painted gallery of an office, AE offered Pamela some tea in his one unchipped cup. It was lavender. He introduced her to Susan Mitchell, his assistant, and to his deputy editor, Jimmy Good, who sensed the falseness in Pamela's name. Jimmy insisted she should be Lady Pamela. She liked the sound of that, Lady Pamela Travers. AE told her he would publish all the poems she had offered. He had a few suggestions on her work, of course,[34] and asked her to call again on her way back to England.[35]

In a daze of happiness, she went off to her Goff relatives in County Wexford, bursting to tell them she had met the great AE. They merely lifted their eyebrows. These Goffs had no use for poetry, preferring horses to the Celtic literary renaissance.[36] They dismissed *Cathleen ni Houlihan* as some kind of aberration, regarded twilight as simply a patch of time between night and day, and most definitely did not approve of Pamela's life in London as a writer. Fleet Street was home to "such frightful people."[37]

Pamela did return to Dublin. She walked once more to Merrion Square, AE and the painted room. But, once at the door, she found she could not touch the bell. AE had just been polite, she told herself. AE was a great and busy man. She turned away.[38]

Three weeks later, answering a knock at her own door in London, she found him there on her doorstep with a great parcel of books under one arm.

"You're a very faithless girl," AE told her. "You said you would come on your way back and then you never turned up. I had these books waiting for you." They were his collected works, each of the books inscribed.

From then on, AE wrote to her at least every month, often in response to her volley of contributions to his magazine. Always he told her his copy box was full or overflowing but that he could not resist one more poem. In May 1925, he had "enough sketches to last me for months but I like the verses so much I must keep them." In March next year, "the copy box was well brimmed up and running over but I couldn't resist the temptation of squeezing your last poem into it."

In 1925 he published three of her poems in the *Irish Statesman*. The first, called "Christopher," appeared in April, "The Coming" in July, and "Te Deum of a Lark" in November. Two poems he published in 1927, "The Dark Fortnight" and "Happy Sleeping," had strong references to the work of Yeats. In the last verse of "The Dark Fortnight" Pamela wrote:

> *I will go and find me a spear*
> *of wild goose feather wrought*
> *and fashion the ears of a hare*
> *to a parchment of silk*
> *and pray to the ewes of thought*
> *to let down their milk . . .*

An obvious inspiration was Yeats's "The Collarbone of a Hare," written in 1917, which ends:

> *I would find by the edge of that water*
> *The collar bone of a hare*
> *Worn thin by the lapping of water,*
> *And pierce it through with a gimlet and stare*
> *At the bitter old world where they marry in churches*
> *And laugh over the untroubled water*
> *At all who marry in churches,*
> *Through the white thin bone of a hare.*

In December 1925 AE gave her what he called the best Christmas gift, news that her verses had been "lifted out of the *Irish Statesman* to the *Literary Digest,* which has the largest circulation of any literary journal in the USA." Early the next year, AE was "sorry the box of poems is full but I cannot resist the temptation of keeping your delightful lyric, "Happy Sleeping," which I am sure will be in *The Best Poems of 1926* if such a thing comes out."

Many of Pamela's poems in the *Irish Statesman* are heavy with melancholy, including the rococo "Ghosts of Two Sad Lovers," published in October 1926, which begins "before we knew of grief we longed for grief" and concludes "no longer shall we pass imprinting warm foot-shapes upon crisp grass, and the sweet broken story of our loves is lost beneath a wind of living words." This poem had first appeared with a different ending in the Christchurch *Sun* in June 1926.

AE reassured Pamela he really did love "Ghosts of Two Sad Lovers" and, to emphasize the point, explained in detail how he gave unwanted contributors the cold shoulder. His letters were full of advice and wry hints about Ireland from one who had been through the Celtic twilight and survived. He warned her that her trips to Dublin would become addictive (they did) and that "we have all sorts here, from the most idealistic to a reality more absolute than any in Europe. I think 25 years ago, all the poets were trying to discover the heights in the Irish genius, now our writers are all trying to discover the depths."

Pamela's poems of the 1920s are, on the surface, lyrical and pastoral—never colloquial—yet they can be seen as dense with the need for experience in life. The author, the innocent nymph still, begged the muse to come. One poem, "Oh Break Her Heart," published in June 1926, was a cry to the gods to break her own heart—"from her grief distil loveliness for our need"—so that she might become a better writer. She revealed little of her inner self, and shunned simple words or references to everyday life.

AE not only allayed Pamela's insecurities about writing, he reassured her about life itself. His letters gradually reveal how concerned Pamela was for herself, not just her work, but her health. Almost all his letters comment on the illnesses Pamela began to suffer from the 1920s. He was sorry to hear about her influenza, bad colds, boils, and lung problems, which hinted at TB.

In early June 1926, Pamela moved to 14 Old Square, a corner of Lincoln's Inn, in the center of the legal district. It was, she told her Christchurch *Sun* readers, a cloistered life where porters touched their forelocks as she entered the gates, which closed at midnight. This column, headlined "Grey Towers: Pamela goes to Lincoln's Inn,"[39] ended with a description of her view by night of a carved boy angel. She talked to him, confiding to the stone figure that her new home was a sweet place. Could she want anything more? The angel replied, "Yes, much more."

In September that year, AE visited Pamela in London on the way to his first Parisian holiday, where he was to meet once again his friend James Stephens and the French writer Simone Tery. He wrote to Pamela, "Can you suggest anything I can do after my train gets in? I really don't want to do anything except talk to you. I think I would like to ride back and forwards in the top of a bus...and hear you talk about London. But you might get cold in the top of a bus, my precious child."

He walked with Pamela down the curve of Regent Street. Both felt a kind of nervy excitement, still shy of each other's gaze. Pamela said how odd it was they had met, "two people from the ends of the earth." AE stopped in mid stride. She glanced up at him then, to see his round blue eyes growing rounder. AE explained to her that this was not the first time they had met. They had known one another in a different incarnation. He told her of his law of spiritual gravitation which he explained as "your own will come to you."[40]

· · ·

For all her bravura, Pamela still felt isolated in London. It was all very well to hanker after the life of a poet but poets made no money and she desperately missed her mother. Pamela distracted herself with women's magazines while she continued to bombard AE with her verses. She paid the rent with the checks from her journalism and in 1926 worked out a way to earn enough to pay her mother's fare to England.

"And so," she confided to an interviewer, "having written only for the highbrow magazines, you know the literary magazines, I collected ordinary magazines, the flossies, and read them avidly. I got to see there were only two stories, fundamentally. There was "Get Your Man" and then there was "How to Keep Your Man." So I embarked on this, writing story after story, under another name, of course, and what do you think? I sent them to my agent and he said "Marvelous, these are certainly going to sell." And sure enough they did, and in a very short while, I had the necessary money for this big, this biggest expedition so far in my life. I saw my mother..."[41]

Margaret Goff and Pamela had written regularly. Pamela sent her mother her published stories and poems, and Margaret passed them on to Aunt Ellie, who liked the prose much more than the poems. Margaret wrote of her problems with money and the tension between her and Biddy, and Biddy's new husband, Boyd Moriarty. She was overjoyed, though, to tell Pamela in November 1926 that she had booked a berth on a ship due to sail in the (Australian) autumn of 1927.

All through 1926 Pamela wrote a different kind of story, not about women but about children and their dreams. These stories became the basis for the Mary Poppins adventures, which Pamela always claimed had suddenly come to her, unbidden, in 1934. Some of the adventures had their beginnings in stories she had written as long ago as December 1924, when *The Triad* had published her "Story for Children Big and Small." This told of a king, his chamberlain and a fool. The three characters, and the essence of the fable, were the basis for the chapter "Robertson Ay's Story" in *Mary Poppins Comes Back,* published more than a decade later.

For the Christchurch *Sun,* she wrote of a magical encounter in a Paris bookshop with a Pan-like creature who was reading in the *Just So Stories* about how the elephant got his trunk. An old man bought the book, to the dismay of the boy-creature. Pamela spoke to him; he ran away. She found him later, on a bronze pedestal in the public gardens. The story was published on March 8, 1926. Almost two decades later, the tale was the basis for a chapter in *Mary Poppins Opens the Door,* published in 1944. Called "The Marble Boy," it tells of a marble statue, Neleus, who reads the story about how the elephant got his trunk over the shoulder of an old man in the park.

On March 20, 1926, the Christchurch *Sun* published "The Strange Story of the Dancing Cow," accompanied by a panel boasting "Miss Pamela Travers, who writes this story for the *Sun,* is rapidly winning fame for herself in London. Few writers today can equal her in the realm of whimsical fantasy. Read here the quaint story of the Old Red Cow who awoke to find herself smitten with star fever." In the first Mary Poppins book, published in 1934, Mary told the same story of the cow and a king within a chapter called "The Dancing Cow."

In December 1926, again for the Christchurch *Sun,* Pamela wrote a fanciful piece called "Pamela Publishes—a Newspaper!" which purported to be a special news bulletin with gossip supplied by a cockney maid, "Mary Smithers." But it was on November 13, 1926, in a short story called "Mary Poppins and the Match Man," that Pamela really gave birth to her famous nanny. The story told of Mary Poppins's day out. For the first time, she had written of the Banks household and Mary Poppins, the "underneath nurse," aged seventeen. (There was no "top nurse" although Mr. and Mrs. Banks liked to pretend there was.) Her charges were Jane, Michael, Barbara and John

Banks. Mary Poppins, about to enjoy a day out, puts on white gloves and tucks a parrot-headed umbrella under her arm. Jane asks her where she is going, but Mary refuses to say. On the corner, she meets Bert, a match man and pavement artist. He loves her, and it is clear that she loves him, too. They admire Bert's pavement paintings and pop right into one showing a pretty scene of the countryside. Suddenly, Bert is wearing a striped coat, straw hat and white flannel trousers. Mary, in turn, is wearing a silken cloak and a hat with a long, curly feather. Mary and Bert take afternoon tea served by a man in a black coat. After the raspberry cakes are eaten, they climb onto the horses of a merry-go-round and ride all the way to Margate. When she returns home, Mary tells the Banks children she has been to fairyland.

As "The Day Out," this story, with many identical passages but some differences, appeared in Pamela's first Mary Poppins book published eight years later. It also formed the basis of the "It's a Jolly Holiday with Mary" song-and-dance sequence from Walt Disney's *Mary Poppins* movie. The fact that Disney had chosen this story as such an important scene for the film always irritated Pamela. She later called "The Day Out" chapter "false" and the weakest of all her Mary Poppins adventures, but never explained why. During her lifetime, no one ever discovered exactly when she had created Mary Poppins, and she certainly did not tell, although she did tell her favorite interviewer, Jonathan Cott: "When I was in my teens, I wrote a small story about someone named Mary Poppins putting children to bed. I can't remember what paper the story appeared in, but the name was a long time a-growing, a long time in existence, perhaps."[42]

Real writers, she always believed, did not write for children. And Pamela yearned to be a real writer, or rather a poet who could write of Ireland with the grace and confidence of Yeats. By December 1926, Pamela was confident enough of her relationship with AE to send him a photo of them together, which he found "not nice enough of you, my dear, as it makes you years older than you are. If I was the photographer I would have tossed your hair until it stood up like the mane of a lion in a rage."[43] He had just published her seventh poem in the *Irish Statesman,* "On Ben Bulben," another of Pamela's tributes to Yeats, referring to the mountain near Drumcliff in Yeats's home territory, near Sligo.

She told students years later that Yeats had a great influence on her,[44] but that she was in awe of the Bard, not the man. So much in awe that she adopted not only his writing style but also many of his characteristics. Like Yeats, she continually feared she had TB, studied eastern religions to help her create order from disorder, followed an Indian guru, used the lessons of fairy tales to support her philosophy of life, and embarked on a lecture circuit of the United States. Like Yeats, she adopted a variety of masks, freely admitting to the masks which did not just include pseudonyms, but a certain bluff and false self, in line with Oscar Wilde's maxim "the first duty in life is to assume a pose; what the second is no one yet has found out."

Yeats's biographer, Richard Ellmann, believed that Wilde's view was duplicated in *The Picture of Dorian Gray, Dr. Jekyll and Mr. Hyde,* in Mallarmé's poetry and in the pseudonyms and other selves of Yeats's contemporaries, W. K. Magee, Wilde, William Sharp and AE. Yeats was part of the nineteenth century's changing ideas on selfhood, and "came to maturity in this atmosphere of doubling and splitting of the self." AE wrote that by 1884 "Yeats had already developed a theory of the divided consciousness." Yeats came to see himself as the man who had created the other self—"The Poet." This was a significant discovery for Pamela, who had already adopted a pseudonym, Pamela Travers, and later obscured her true self further by writing as P. L. Travers, then claiming she would have preferred to be known as Anon, a variation of AEON.

In the late summer of 1926 Pamela again visited Ireland, mainly to enjoy days "full of poets, full of poems, full of talk and argument and legend-telling and delight."[45] She took the train to Athlone, in the Midlands, to met more elderly Goffs, then drove on to Galway, Clifden and Leenane. On the way back to Dublin, Pamela embarked on an adventure that she later remembered as a mythical journey that could have been called "When the Fool met the Sage, and learnt a Lesson."

Her destination was Lough Gill, made famous by Yeats's 1890 poem, "The Lake Isle of Innisfree." She asked a boatman to take her there. He said he knew of no such place, but Pamela, who knew by heart "I will arise and go now, and go to Innisfree," insisted there was. "It's known around these parts," sneered the boatman, "as Rat Island." The two of them set out under gray clouds with Pamela in the bow and a young priest with them, sitting in the stern. She found no hive for the honey bee on the island nor a log cabin, but the whole of the island was covered with red-berried rowan trees. She decided suddenly to take some branches back to Yeats. Pamela broke as many branches as she could, then staggered under their weight, in driving rain, to the boat. She could see the priest saying his rosary.

Back on shore, she ran with her burden of rowan to the station. In the stuffy carriage on the train to Dublin her clothes steamed as they slowly dried. Fellow travelers edged away. She arrived at Merrion Square, her hair dripping still, her arms full—still—with bedraggled branches. Pamela rang the bell at number 82. Yeats himself answered the door.

There stood Pamela, her face uplifted and full of yearning for approval, above the bundle of rowan. He called down the dark hallway to the maid, Annie. She took Pamela to the basement kitchen, dried her, gave her cocoa and took away the branches. The upstairs maid came bustling in: "The master will see you now." There he was in his blue-curtained room.

Yeats told her "my canary has laid an egg," and took her to the cage. From there, they went on a tour of the room, Yeats indicating which of his books he liked best. He explained that when he got an idea for a poem, he was inspired by reading again one of his own books. She saw on his desk a vase holding just one sprig of rowan. Was he trying to teach her a lesson? Why give armfuls when one sprig will do? But no, she decided, he would never do anything so banal. She knew that this one branch signified the art of simplicity.

The next day, Pamela lunched with AE who told her Yeats was touched by her rowan berry gift. He hoped, though, that when she visited him in Dunfanaghy, she would not cut down the willows. After all, as AE solemnly said, dryads lived in the trees.[46]

Pamela and AE had been talking for months of Dunfanaghy and Breaghy, in his favorite part of Ireland, County Donegal. By January 1927, she felt sure enough of him to suggest she might spend a summer holiday there, after her mother's visit.

For twenty years, AE had enjoyed his summer holidays in the northwest county of Donegal. He thought it the "wildest, loneliest and loveliest country I know, a country of hills, and hollows, of lakes and woods, of cliffs, mountains, rivers, inlets of sea, sands, ruined castles and memories from the beginning of the world. From the cottage I stay at, I can see seven seas between hills."[47] He loved the "unearthly beauty of the broken coast, its rocky inlets and silvery beaches" and came to think of this corner of Donegal as "his own peculiar, specialized kingdom." It was for him the spiritual center of Ireland, where he saw "the silver fires of faeries" and found "psychic population in both the water and the woods."[48]

Each summer, he set off by train from Dublin and spent part of the eleven-hour journey playing poker on a makeshift table of suitcases. He arrived at Dunfanaghy Road Station at nightfall, then traveled four miles to the village of Breaghy by jaunting car. Breaghy is close to Killahoey Strand beach which looks over Horn Head, the most beautiful of the Donegal headlands. Here AE stayed at a hillside cottage set behind one of the low stone fences that crisscross the landscape. Near the stone-fenced roadway, black-faced, black-legged sheep that looked like large shaggy calves stared at the horses as AE rounded the bend to the cottage. He rented a room from Janey Stewart, a spinster who filled the whitewashed cottage with her own handicrafts. Janey was a good cook, churning her own butter and baking cake as well as mutton in an iron cauldron slung on a chain over the peat fire. AE loved her dark brown, homemade bread and scoffed it down with pints of buttermilk. He slept in an attic bedroom that stretched the full width of the house. At night, AE could hear the cows moving about in their stalls below. If the weather was bad, he read a good part of the day. He had a weakness for Wild West novelettes and detective yarns. At twilight, he packed his crayons and sketchpad, pulled on his big boots, and strode over the hills.[49]

A mile away from Janey's was Marble Hill House, the graceful and perfectly proportioned gray stone home of the Nationalist MP for West Donegal, Hugh Law, who had been one of AE's closest friends since 1904. When AE tired of Janey's cottage, Hugh and his wife, Lota, let him stay in their children's old cubby house, adult sized, that they had built on the grounds.

The fairy house, as it was called, became AE's studio. He slept in a loft. Lota tried to make it comfy in an artsy-crafty way, embroidering a pattern of fishes and waves into a piece of cloth which she threw over the loft rail. Down in the big studio room below, above the hearth, AE hung one of his own paintings, featuring a sword of light.[50]

In the early days, AE took his wife to Breaghy. But by the

1920s, Violet preferred to stay home in Dublin. He invited others to share the peace, among them a few of his young women, including Simone Tery and Pamela. His friend John Eglinton knew AE always needed at least one friend to whom to whisper "solitude is sweet."[51] He liked to take the girls to dinner at the Laws or to walk and talk as he painted twilight sketches for canvases he might finish the next day. There were parts of the woodland or Strand which, he said, set up in him the strongest psychic vibrations. AE strode along the Strand in the same clothes he wore in Bloomsbury: a dark suit, broad hat, his trousers rolled up and boots hung around his neck. He talked without pause as he waded among droves of prawns and shrimp.[52]

The weather for Pamela's first visit, in June 1927, was atrocious, dark, rainy and threatening every day. She sat inside, at his side, absorbing his ramblings as voraciously as she devoured Janey's cakes and mutton. He teased her about how much she ate, "for a girl who is not hungry."[53] Once, when they were setting out for a walk, Pamela looked down through a break in the mist and saw a giant outline of a footprint bordered by flowers embedded in the grass. The shape was unmistakable, as though a monster from another planet had landed on earth, taken a step, then risen again. She told him "someone has been here." AE, of course, was hardly surprised. It often happened, he told his little protégée.[54]

When they visited the Laws, AE told her she could not walk the mile in her flimsy London shoes. He disappeared to his attic room and came down with the *Observer* and *The Times,* a bundle of string, a pile of socks and a pair of his old boots. "Sit down," he ordered. She was to wear six socks on each leg. Around one leg he wound the *Observer,* around the other *The Times,* tying the fatted calves with string before she wriggled into his boots.

Pamela said she bore this in "seething silence," but that

silence was more likely to have been full of intimate unspoken thoughts than hostility. It was possibly the most intimate
act AE could dare to perform: Pamela's bare legs, slipping on
the woolly socks, winding string around her calves.

They set off for the Laws, AE in front as usual, chanting
Eastern scriptures—again—his feet sure of every step. Pamela,
stuck in the bog, cried out to him. He turned and simply
laughed. He told her to take off the boots, to go barefoot,
he'd enjoy taking a dryad to lunch. She was silent. Just then,
AE seemed for a second to understand her. "I'm a fool," he
cried down to her. "You don't want a philosophy, you want a
life!" He knew and she knew that Pamela had heard enough
of the Eastern scriptures to last a lifetime. She wanted someone to clear the obscurity away, not add to it, not burden her
that day with another theory and another, but simply to live.
A young man might have kissed her then. AE let another
opportunity go by. He could see, but he could not react to
the little signs that say "come forward, don't retreat." Pamela
wanted AE to tell her who she was. "Acolyte, daughter,
apprentice?" she wrote later. "I never knew."

During these days on the yellow tongue of sand on the back
Strand, AE painted and sketched her, once in a tree looking
down on him. Once, he had started a landscape when he suddenly looked up at her. "Do you see them?" "No," she
answered, half regretful, half awed. Whatever his vision, she
knew he wanted her to see it, too. She had failed him.

AE had felt the old psychic vibrations again. He rapidly
sketched a host of fairies. Pamela watched smoke start to emerge
from his pocket. "AE, be careful, you're on fire!" He looked
down. The smoke was escaping from the pipe he had slipped
into the dark blue serge pocket of his pants. His wife, he told
Pamela, would have to reline another pocket. He showed her
his fairy canvas. AE had sketched her, too, on the branch, the
wild-eyed girl. He was soon to start calling her Pixie.[55]

AE wrote to her on July 1, "I was very sad that you went away after so many gray days in a beautiful country." He was sorry he could not amuse her. "My wretched old mind lost its spring. Even ten years ago I had a super-abundance of energy. I was young enough in my mind to make even you feel I was your contemporary. But you were very sweet to your elderly friend." At the bottom of the letter was his sketch of Pamela in her walking gear with the message, "Do you remember the paper leggings in the boots?"

AE praised her vitality, "so much vitality that I am sure when you are 80 you will be able to dominate your juniors or grandchildren and you may remember through the mists of time that you had an elderly friend who wrote poetry under the name AE who wanted to stroke her fluffy hair as you looked like a poor little duckling in a storm, but refrained lest you might think he did not treat you with sufficient dignity. Do you still have the dreams of the little house in the windy gap?"

He remembered how she dreamed of living up there, on a house on Horn Head, and how from Janey's he would call her to him by semaphore, for a chat. "You do feel better after your visit, don't you Pixie dear, I would be terrified if you had gone back from Donegal not feeling better than when you went. With Love, AE."

Late in 1927, Pamela told him she was tired of making plans and being responsible for herself. He reassured her that the "seer in me sees some very large man swooping down upon you and marrying you in the near future. I hope he will be very benevolent as well as a very large man. I think you deserve a gigantic husband with the powers like Aladdin to build you a tower in which you can write with ease and peace."

It could not be him, of course. "Dear Pamela," he wrote in December 1927, "pray for me...curse me for being an idiot going away." AE was about to leave Ireland for the first of his

American lecture tours, sailing from Liverpool on January 14, 1928. He left Jimmy Good in charge of the *Irish Statesman*. The magazine had continued to bleed and the American friends had suggested a lecture tour organized by Judge Campbell as the only way he could recoup the money quickly.

Pamela asked if he had time to go to London to see her before his three-month trip. No, "I have so many things to do here" before leaving Dublin on the boat to Liverpool. "It was delightful of you to suggest you should come down to see me off but do not go to the expense. Why should you empty your pockets for the sake of a handshake?" But, later, "do let me pay your hotel bill or your railway fare, which ever is largest, I can run to that."[56]

On January 13, the night before the *Albertic* sailed for New York, Pamela met AE in Liverpool. They went to the movies. Before the show, a man played the violin, badly. AE kept talking until he was hushed by the angry patrons. Pamela went to the dock the next day, in the rain. He held both her hands and stroked her wild and springy hair. "My angel," he said as they parted.[57]

6

Lovers, Gurus and the Glimmering Girl

AE's voyage to New York marked the beginning of
Pamela's own long journey from Ireland to America.
Where he led, she must follow. Just as she had caught
his coattails in Dublin, she eventually traveled in his wake to
Washington, to the universities of the East Coast, and to the
rose-amethyst mountains of New Mexico. But first, as usual,
came the practicalities.

Pamela was surviving on a tight budget in Lincoln Square
from her fees from *The Triad*. But this magazine, along with
so many others with literary pretensions, lived precariously.
She needed to woo new publishers. Before AE left for the

United States, she had asked him if she could work at the *Irish Statesman*. He replied, in October 1927, that he would love to have her for a colleague but it was impossible to employ any journalist full time other than Jimmy Good. "Much of it is written by professors, civil servants, and the like, in their spare time," he wrote. "All Irish weeklies are run this way, mainly to assist some cause, and in many, there is no payment at all. That is why I have never suggested to you to write articles for me because I know you get paid three times as well in London." And, he added, if the American friends, who now included a Senator Cullinan, did not help, "the paper will end at the middle of next year or autumn at the latest.'[1] AE ended on a flippant note, suggesting that if ever the magazine became rich, he would pay her an income so large that she could "afford to keep a husband."

Pamela was more in need of someone to share the rent. AE had suggested Madge Burnand, "an extremely nice girl" who was learning printing. "You want a companion," he wrote, "it is unpleasant to live alone." Madge was one of six daughters of the late Sir Francis Burnand, a prolific playwright as well as a barrister with chambers at Lincoln's Inn. For twenty years, Burnand had also edited *Punch,* which, under his reign, had expanded its coverage of art and literature.[2] His daughter Madge—tall, rangy, bony—was as well educated as her father. She liked Blake—another of Pamela's literary heroes.

When AE was in the United States, Madge moved into Pamela's flat in Lincoln Square. The two women remained together for more than a decade, the friendship growing more and more intense. In the beginning, Madge was mainly a financial prop—paying half the rent—but the relationship always had two other vital elements. The first was practical: Madge, born in Ireland and retaining strong literary connections there, represented an important link for Pamela to the Irish network she loved. The second was messy and emotional. Madge's practical-

ity was often overwhelmed by a sense of frustration and unpro-
voked anger, both of which developed as the two women became
closer.

In the late 1920s, the practical Pamela knew that as a freelance journalist she had to remain in London, close to Fleet
Street. But the romantic Pamela dreamed of working in Ireland, just like a real writer. AE had written to her in October
1927: "You talk of living in a little cottage in the Wicklow Hills.
It is very romantic and rather remote from Dublin. My experience of friends who went to live in the Wicklow Hills is, I
see them far less often than I did when they lived in London."
He thought Ireland might lose its glamour if she lived there
and pointed out she would have to do all her own cooking.
"Was my poem 'A Cottage on the Mountainside' responsible?"[3]

Whenever she was in Dublin, Pamela attended AE's salon
at Rathgar Avenue, where he had gathered "so many poets to
add to the number of your acquaintances and friends."[4] She had
loved that room where, AE told her, Maud Gonne used to sit
by his fire braiding her hair and "keening for the wrongs of Ireland."[5] One evening, AE took her to Yeats's sherry party in
Merrion Square.[6] Yeats insisted she accept copies of a couple
of his poems, including "The Song of Wandering Aengus," written in 1897, which tells of "a glimmering girl with apple
blossom in her hair, who called me by my name and ran and
faded through the brightening air."

Pamela said she set some of Yeats's poems to music. "He
asked me to sing them to him which I did. "Beautiful," he said,
"beautiful. I couldn't have imagined anything more like them."
Pamela was overjoyed. Next day she told AE. "You must sing
them to me as well," he said, but, breaking the spell, whispered "Yeats is tone deaf."[7]

Among the crowd at Yeats's and AE's salons, one man stood
out for his wit and his charm. He was Oliver St. John Gogarty,
whom Yeats called one of the great lyric poets of the age—

though he was better known as a surgeon. Gogarty drove a yellow Rolls-Royce and held his own soirées on Fridays, at home at 15 Ely Place. When Gogarty met Pamela he was almost fifty and married. She thought of him as "an old man... one of the old fathers."[8] But Gogarty had quite a different view of her. He dedicated his book *A Gathering of Swans* "To Pamela, with admiration" and wrote her dozens of poems, full of agitated excitement. "On First Meeting PT" gushed about her beauty for thirteen verses. It began:

> *She came and moved and shone*
> *and moving smiled*
> *a lovely woman grown*
> *yet dear as child.*

> *Trembling with speed her talk*
> *her form a quiver*
> *the way that saplings walk*
> *moored in a river*

It went on to praise her "clear blue eyes," her "sweet light," "silken vesture, her curving gesture." In May 1930, he wrote "To PT," in which he swooned over the "sheath of her flesh" and "her sweet presence, so lithe and intense." Pamela tucked the poem into her copy of another of Gogarty's books. She laughed off Gogarty, who eventually backed away.

To Gogarty's biographer, years later, Pamela explained how she felt about her rejected lover. He was only "a Lothario, a clown and writer of very good minor verse." It was "wonderful to talk with him... to be educated by him in the scandal of Dublin." But when poems arrived by the dozen, "I was not overwhelmed."[9]

If Gogarty was the noisiest guest at AE's literary gatherings, AE's wife Violet was the most shadowy presence. Pamela saw her moving among them "diffidently, almost invisibly replenishing cups, a fragile gray haired feminine figure," speaking little and to only a few before she disappeared into the kitchen. Here Pamela sought her out. Could she help? "No," said Violet. "People come to see George and not me." But Pamela insisted. At last, Violet let her slice the cake. Pamela wrote that AE might have drawn his strength from Violet. However, she also knew that by the 1930s, Violet did not have much strength to give. Her "nerves were bad and she was peevish...nothing he [AE] did or brought her was right."[10]

Violet might well have been sulking over AE's friendship with Simone Tery, and a student, Leah Rose Bernstein. The two young women were often on his mind. In 1928, on the way to New York on board the *Albertic,* he wrote to Pamela about Simone, such a "nice girl...You know I have much discrimination in girls, I have known many, and always made friends of the nice ones, like you."

During AE's months in the United States, when he spoke at five universities including Harvard, he wrote to Pamela often, with warmth and without self-censorship. He liked to boast of his adventures, including the day he met Simone in New York, how they hired a car and drove around and around a park for four hours, holding each other's hands. When he returned from the States in June 1928, after collecting an honorary degree from Yale University, he met a group of twenty young women from Wellesley College, on their way to Europe. AE succumbed to one of them, nineteen-year-old Leah Rose Bernstein. She was by far the prettiest. Leah Rose, who told him she was twenty-one, sat for him day after day while he painted her portrait in pastels. He did not hide Leah from Pamela, or Pamela from Simone, or Simone from Leah, but kept up a correspondence with them all, telling each about the others.

AE confided to Pamela that Leah Rose had "nothing to say,

but looked lovely. I was content not to talk as long as she sat there, you know the kind of girl." Leah Rose was one of those girls "you would like to have as an ornament about the house, but dread having to make up a conversation with them. I prefer girls I can talk to." But at the same time he wrote to Leah Rose, "I think if I would paint you every day for six months I would become quite a good painter, for good art is born out of the affections. You made the journey home delightful to me. There are all kinds of sweet things I would like to have whispered into your ears to awaken the Psyche, but I was slow and old and shy." The next month, he explained, "You see, dear Leah Rose, I am a poet and I fall in love with every pretty face and I am not fickle for I remember them all and never turn away from them. Dear Leah, you are young and I alas am sixty-two and it is a real friendship to give so much of your time to somebody forty years older than yourself when there must be so many handsome boys waiting to say adoring things in your ears. Sixty-two can never appreciate twenty-one as it ought to be appreciated. I send all my love to my pretty model."[11]

AE wrote to Leah for a year, upbraiding her for cutting in two a photo of herself with her boyfriend, Bernard. He wanted to see him too. AE now told her more about his enchanting friend Simone Tery who was "young, very pretty, very clever. We made friends quickly in spite of nearly forty years between our ages and she writes to me about her young man who is also very noble as yours is. They always are...There are some girls who are fixed stars and some who are erratic comets and my lovely friend Simone is an erratic comet."[12]

Pamela was always more of an erratic comet than a fixed star. In the late 1920s, she began to travel often, first to Europe and Russia, then to the United States and Japan. None of the journeys was purely for pleasure, but all took on the aspect of a search, a mission, or a cure; at the time she started her lifetime habit of restless travel, she began to feel almost continuously unwell.

In the summer of 1928, Pamela and Madge visited Spain and Italy. AE wrote to her: "I like to think of you splashing in water, your hair getting more and more like a lion's mane around your head. Beware, lest you fall in love with some gentle little man through the mere attraction of opposites, and have to look after him for the remainder of your life. Fall in love with some gigantic boss creature and run away from him if he is too bossy." AE wondered if she might have been stronger physically if he had insisted on "your walking in bare feet through the grass when you were in Donegal."[13]

On the Italian Riviera the two women stayed at the Grande Albergo Paradiso, at Diano Marina, where Pamela posed for a snapshot in a long-legged swimsuit, revealing hips and legs like a boy's. She peeled the top down to be photographed, showing off her young woman's lemon-shaped breasts.

The European cure did not do as much good as she hoped. AE wondered "how in heaven did you manage to get back so tired…you were so triumphant in Italy striding over the hills." Her side trip to see the Carrara marble quarries became an article for the *Irish Statesman*.[14]

By now Pamela wrote more prose than poetry, settling into a second-string role as a drama critic. Her reviews began to explore more complex ideas than the simple reporting and awkward jokes of her women's page for *The Triad*. Reviewing George Bernard Shaw's *The Apple Cart* for the *Irish Statesman*, she was intrigued by GBS's masks, just as she had been by the other selves of Yeats and AE. Who exactly was Shaw, she asked, "iconoclast, comedian, philosopher, poet? No sooner have we settled one mask upon him than Ariel darts away, thumb to nose, and puts on another…lest for a moment anyone should say 'at last we know him and have seen him plain.'"[15]

Pamela was learning from the masters the advantages of being evasive—of being many people in one, yet nothing specific. As a young woman she had a few masks herself, but then again, not a great deal to hide. In her twenties her writing showed an artlessness, the joie de vivre of a woman who was curious about life, a natural journalist. As she grew older, with many more secrets to conceal, she began to ridicule journalism and biography, expressing her deepest thoughts in more and more allusive ways.

Her poetry, though, never evolved from the romantic Yeatsian model she adopted as a teenager, although in the late 1920s the streak of eroticism in her verse grew stronger. By 1927 she was writing of "hiding your sword beneath a farthingale,"[16] how "Michael pulled me down into the speckled barley field and bent me backwards" and how she would milk a little cow and pour the milk into her lover's mouth.[17] There is no evidence that she actually had a lover in the 1920s, although her relationship with Madge is ambiguous—the bare-breasted photo is likely to have been shot by Madge, but that is hardly evidence that the two women were sexually intimate.[18]

Pamela's main income still came from journalism, mainly from a monthly column in the Sydney magazine now called *The New Triad,* in which she presented herself as the sparkly, blithe Pamela Travers, trying to work out how to be in five theatres at once, ridiculing Noël Coward's new plays, watching Charles Lindbergh's plane as she ate an ice in Hyde Park, finding this year's showing at the Royal Academy just a little dull, noting this year's red hats, shoes and bags, watching the Duke and Duchess of York at Hyde Park corner, and inventing a conversation with a policeman who talked of his fat little baby called Ellen Rubina, a variation of the name of Pamela's friend from Bowral.

In the way of almost every columnist desperate for material, her life was presented as a whirlwind of opening nights and intellectual stimulation. She found *Peter Pan* "a play so extraordinarily naive and engaging it would take a stonier heart than mine to let loose upon it the demons of criticism," she ogled at the circus at the Crystal Palace, saw *Macbeth* in modern dress, went to the opera at Covent Garden, read a new biography of Emily Brontë, danced the new craze, the Heebie Jeebie, far more fashionable than the Black Bottom and the Yale Blues, but "went to bed with Plato."[19]

After her mother's visit, Pamela continued to send money to her in Sydney. It was clear that Margaret needed help. When she moved, with Moya, to Devonshire Flats in East Esplanade, Manly, the two women were forced to take in boarders. Margaret's last letters to Pamela fussed over her health, her job, her happiness. In early October 1928, she was worried that Pamela's back was still giving her trouble. "God bless you and make you well and strong."

There were no more letters. Margaret Goff died at the Crescent Private Hospital, Manly, on November 6, 1928, of a heart attack. She was fifty-four. Her estate, like her life, was modest. She left £4,836. On her death certificate, the name of the first of her three daughters was given as Lyndon. For Margaret, her eldest girl never became Pamela Travers.

Pamela felt the loss of her mother "like a wound constantly bleeding." Friends spouted cliches but nobody offered genuine comfort except Gogarty, who wrote, "It is a sorrow that never ends...[but] the way-springs of life are not cut off. You have to be the way-spring." At last she felt someone understood the depth of her sorrow, its meaning and necessity. "I began at once to get over it," she claimed[20]—but her constant search for gurus suggests otherwise.

AE was too distracted to be of much help. He wrote from Dublin in November 1928 that "I wish I could be with you to say comforting things" but "this abominable case" had lasted ten days and "is not yet ended." (The *Irish Statesman* was fighting a defamation action in a Dublin court.) Pamela wanted to know if he could help her with the names of American editors, but AE replied, "I know none. Would it do if I wrote a statement about your talent as a writer that you could use?" He wrote her a testimonial: "In the hope that my sincere judgment of the literary talents of Miss Pamela Travers may incline editors who do not know her work to read with care any manuscript she may send, I would like to say that I believe her verse at its best is as beautiful as that written by any living poetess of whom I have knowledge, either in America or Great Britain, and my friend William Butler Yeats has also expressed to me his admiration of her poetry. She is also an admirable and picturesque journalist especially qualified to write on drama and literature as well as on current affairs and politics...I think if any American paper desired to have a readable London letter it could with confidence be entrusted to her."

By now, Pamela and Madge had moved to a cheaper flat at the Woburn Buildings, 38 Woburn Square, near Euston Station. Here Pamela completed a book of poems and told AE she would dedicate it to him. He urged her to begin some new enterprise. Had she thought any more about "the story of Keats? If you don't do it, someone else will." He told her how to start the biography—"swallow the whole, letters, poems, life, digest it for two to three months."[21]

AE's last years were marked by a physical restlessness as he acquired new friends, moved from place to place, rented a succession of homes and failed to dedicate himself to anything at all. He had become close to Kingsley Porter, an archaeologist, who had lectured in art history at Yale University but who spent much of his time in Ireland. Porter had rented the Laws' old home at Marble Hill, then moved to a lakeside mansion, Glenveagh Castle, fifteen miles inland. The castle was near Tory Island, a windy island separated from the mainland of Donegal by a rough stretch of sea. At his newly restored summer home, Porter, his wife Lucy and their guests became a new audience for AE. He talked all night, to whoever stayed awake, then finally retired to his room to read *The Arabian Nights* which he liked to analyze out loud over breakfast.

AE's son, Diarmuid, was about to leave his job at the *Irish Statesman* to marry and live in Chicago. The new editorial assistant was to be a twenty-one-year-old poet, Irene Haugh, another acolyte for AE to impress. He cooked for her, sketched her, and when she traveled abroad, wrote her letters wondering if she might come back "with a new continental way of arranging your hair. Why not let it stream behind you like a meteor on the wind?"[22]

Pamela's fragile health, meanwhile, had become steadily worse; she now suffered from bouts of pleurisy and was afraid of Gogarty's theory that "blonde hair and blue eyes are the favorite resting place for TB."[23] In the summer of 1929 Pamela, with Madge, tried a holiday cure in Ilnacullin, near Glengariff in County Cork, where Madge's sister Eileen lived. AE had told her of the island which had been turned into a neoclassical folly with Italianate gardens.

But by January 1930, AE was sorry to hear she had ptomaine poisoning and "had to survive on a diet of brandy and milk." She sent him a lucid review of an Italian art exhibition for the *Irish Statesman* but complained she was in a state of "muddledom" and might now need an operation for appendicitis. AE recommended coueism, a fashionable idea of the 1920s, based on the positive self-talk theories of a Monsieur Coue. "Imagine yourself the gayest and healthiest of women. It will do you a lot of good."[24]

AE had told the remaining American friends he wanted to close the *Irish Statesman,* retire, and perhaps return to the

United States. For its last issue, in April 1930, Pamela wrote an essay called "A Brand for the Critic," in which she dismissed most critics as superficial and slick. The true critic, she believed, must love and fully interpret her art form, and forgive the failures of artists. This ideal formula did not always tally with her own sharp asides as a critic. Pamela remained proud of her acting experience, firmly believing that it was a genuine schooling for her criticism. She would have blushed, though, if the actors she reviewed on the London stage knew the truth of that experience—small Shakespearean roles, on the road in rural New South Wales and New Zealand, and the pantomime chorus line.

In the final issue of the magazine, Horace Plunkett suggested that a decision to set the *Irish Statesman*'s cover price at threepence instead of sixpence meant it could never have covered costs. Irene Haugh helped AE clean up the detritus of twenty-five years. As they worked, the old editor brushed the dust of books long forgotten, stopped, read bits aloud to her, made piles of things to throw away, then changed his mind. That book could never go. And this one, save that, too! As AE retired to Donegal, Pamela and Madge cleaned out their own flat, moving around the corner to 13 Theobald's Road. But their new home was soon abandoned for Pound Cottage in Mayfield, near Tunbridge Wells. AE wrote that he hoped the move would be for her "what Donegal is to me, the fountain of youth."[25]

In the summer of 1930, AE was invited on another lecture tour of the United States by the philanthropist and patron of the arts Mrs. Mary Rumsey, the sister of Averell Harriman and a friend of the coming Roosevelt administration. "Rums," as she was known, financed the tour. He wrote to Pamela, "I leave Liverpool on 12 September and will be away for five or six months. This is to say good-bye." He did not really want to go, but, "I must make money somehow and it is the quickest way I know. I wouldn't go but that I have an invalid wife. Myself, I would live in a cottage in the country."

Despite his fears, AE soon became totally absorbed by the United States, remaining there for eight months, until May 1931. Once again he met his old guru James Pryse, his friend Henry Wallace, and stayed for a while with his son, Diarmuid. When his talks were broadcast, he was feted as a seer, an agricultural genius and a brilliant poet. People stopped him in the street to ask, "Are you AE?" They had recognized the face from the movie news.[26] The fame was splendid, but AE was more entranced by "magical Arizona with its rose-amethyst mountains" which he thought resembled "the mountains in a fairy book."[27] Pamela was excited by his description of Arizona and New Mexico, by his great enthusiasm for the cactus-covered desert. "If ever I was to leave Ireland," he had told her, "it would be to live in the desert under the rule of the rattlesnake and coyote."[28]

AE continued to respond to Pamela's expanding list of worries about her health and abilities. He boosted her flagging confidence with a description that she never forgot—who could?—that she had "a dangerous brilliance." He advised her to "indulge her fantasies." He meant literary fantasies, of course, which were "the record of spiritual experience." She should get a tan, as "doctors tell me when the skin is brown the blood changes and becomes electrified." But it was not just her body that worried Pamela, but a vague sense of anxiety that was to grow into feelings of dread. She told AE in 1930 that she was considering some form of psychology, which he told her was "rather dangerous in practice."

When he returned, they met for tea at the Euston Hotel near the station. Nothing had cured Pamela. She coughed and shivered and checked every little pain until her doctor suspected it really must be TB. In the summer of 1931, the doctor suggested a sanitarium—just in case—and urged her to live outside London permanently. Pamela decided to make May-field her home.

While she was in the sanitarium, she wrote to AE that her mind had become full of fantastic tales, of a witch whose broomstick would fly just as well by white magic as by black magic. AE was a willing, enthusiastic audience. After all, he said, Yeats "seemed to imply there *were* such witches." That summer, AE urged Pamela to "think over a tale which would use all your powers of fantasy." He thought she should call it "The Adventures of a Witch." It could be "the idea in letting you say all you want to say."[29] Pamela brooded on AE's suggestion. She had the time. *The Triad* was dead. The *Irish Statesman* was dead. She had the basis for a book in the stories she had written for children over the years. And she was about to go into the equivalent of a writer's retreat, the Sussex cottage.

Pound Cottage, just out of Mayfield, might have been the home of the wicked witch in "Hansel and Gretel," or Farmer Hoggett and his sweet pig, Babe. More like a stage set than a real house, the cottage looked as though a romantic heroine like Giselle might step through its rustic door to dance among the roses in the garden, except Giselle's home was in Germany and this cottage was deep in the heart of southern England.

Pamela heard from the locals it was mentioned in the Doomsday book but in any case, it could be dated as far back as 1632, the date carved on an oak beam over a cavernous fireplace. The cottage walls, between their skeleton of old beams, were so ancient they were made of wattle and daub. Pamela and Madge had to duck their heads when they walked in the front door, straight into the kitchen, then through to the living room. From there, a toy-sized door opened to a narrow stairway leading to three bedrooms above. The first floor was so cozily neat and compact, they thought it seemed just right for Goldilocks and the three bears. Pamela settled into the largest room, closest to the stairs; Madge took the middle room. The third room lay in wait, filled with junk, until house guests came down from London. Madge—who did all the cooking—wasn't too impressed with the kitchen. There was no fridge, of course, indeed no electricity. She cooked on oil heaters. Birds nested in the thatched roof, which drooped over the eaves like a wide-brimmed hat. Archaeologists came to gaze at Pound Cottage and ask if they might buy it. One wanted to export it, lock, stock and thatch, to Detroit.[30]

The Pound, once the stockman's cottage of the nearby Forge Farm, was one of many properties rented to farmers by the Glynne Estates, which owned four thousand acres in the south of England. When Pamela and Madge first took the cottage in 1930 it was surrounded by fields stretching far into the distance, all with a blanketing of white sheep. One could imagine Piglet and Pooh cavorting on their way to Eeyore's gloomy place, or Mole down by the riverbank. This was a perfect place for a writer, isolated, serene, except for the nightingales, which, Pamela complained, sang all night. Pound Cottage was at least a fifteen-minute drive from Mayfield, more if snow lined the narrow road where one car had to stop to let another pass, even one as compact as Pamela's black, canvas-topped, low-slung BSA sports car.

Pamela and Madge took day trips to Hastings, tended the vegetables, herbs and fruit trees, posed for the camera in the garden with flowers in their arms. Pamela thought they should keep a dog to scare away tramps, so along came the white bulldog Cu, whose name was Gaelic for "dog." He snuffled and snorted and farted as he slept in his wicker basket in the kitchen.[31]

Pamela loved it here, among the soft green fields. She watched them change color in the afternoon through the little windowpanes in a studio she added to the cottage. It was here, in the studio, that Pamela stored her scrapbooks. In one, she had pasted her tale of Mary Poppins and the Match Man.

AE was now approaching the end of his life. The death of his wife, Violet, and his friend, Kingsley Porter, signposted the way to his own passing. He was saddened and depressed by Violet's serious illness when a tumor "turned itself around too many organs to make recovery possible." He told Pamela, "The doctors tell me nothing can be done."[32]

Despite his depression, AE still wrote long, compassionate letters to Pamela. He hoped she was drinking milk by the gallon, eating eggs, and sleeping with windows "open to the infinite."[33] She was, but she was also far too wired up to simply relax into the country life. She had sent him two poems which AE thought "well phrased but a little artificial in comparison with others of yours. You say they are simple. Yes, simple in expression but I feel they are artificial beneath that. You seem to have a hankering for Biblical symbolism which I doubt is natural. Quality my dear is the thing, not quantity." He did think, however, that his judgment might be affected by the headaches from which he now suffered almost half the week. And no, he did not know anyone who was of "interviewing importance."[34]

Her move to the country made no difference to Pamela's health, and in January 1932 AE was very sorry to hear she had been so ill. He was only pleased she had Madge to look after her. "I think the best thing I ever did was bringing you and her together."[35]

Violet Russell died on February 3, 1932; after the funeral AE arranged to meet Pamela at the Euston Hotel in London where he was to stay a week. Once again, they simply talked, rode the buses, walked the London streets, held hands. At home in Dublin he wrote to Sean O'Faolain: "I would like to have seen you while I was in London... Pamela Travers is back in London but is ordered by her doctor to live out of it, and she will shortly leave. I don't know what she will do. I hope she will escape the tuberculosis which the doctors suspect. She has a touch of genius and should do good things and lead a rich life if her health keeps good."[36]

AE then began to slice away at his old attachments to Ireland. He wrote to Yeats that he was now completely disillusioned with his homeland, which seemed "like a lout I knew in boyhood, who had become a hero, and then subsided into a lout again."[37] He told O'Faolain that he had no further interest in Ireland, "indeed I have no further interest in nations at all." His friend, John Eglinton, thought the only thing that now kept AE in Ireland at all was Kingsley Porter. That summer he stayed once more with Porter at Glenveagh Castle.

By March 1932 Pamela was back in the sanitarium, where she heard from AE that "Lady Gregory died at midnight. All my generation are dropping fast." When Pamela returned to Pound Cottage in July, AE urged her to continue with the fresh air day and night, with sunlight and lots of milk and eggs. This time the cure worked, and by autumn she not only felt stronger, but brave enough to travel to Russia, a plan that amazed AE. He asked, "Why are you a moth seeking flames to dash itself against?"[38]

The idea of a woman traveling alone to Soviet Russia in 1932 astounded not only AE but all Pamela's friends, who saw it as either the chance of a lifetime or utter recklessness. The journey was in fact a carefully packaged experience with little risk. Pamela traveled with a party of English tourists herded about in boats, trains and museums by a guide following a strict schedule. Through AE's salon, she had spoken to other writers who had taken such a tour. One may have been the writer Hubert Butler, who had worked with AE and Sir Horace Plunkett. Butler sailed to Leningrad on the tourist ship the

Alexei Rykov in 1931. With his wife and a friend, he had traveled down the Volga then on to Moscow and Rostov. Butler wrote a book about the adventure, *Russian Roundabout*.[39]

Pamela's letters home from Russia later became a series of magazine articles and were then collected for her first book, *Moscow Excursion*. Published in 1934 by the Soho publisher Gerard Howe, *Moscow Excursion* hid the identity of almost everyone involved, including the author. The men and women she met in Russia were identified, in the style of a nineteenth century novel, as T— or M— or Z—. The author was simply known as P. T. Most mysterious of all was the dedication to HLG, which could well have been a joke of the author's, Pamela dedicating the book to her true self, Helen Lyndon Goff.

Her journey to Stalinist Russia—she called it "Red Russia" —was to include Leningrad, Moscow and Nizhny-Novgorod. Her companions were deadly serious academics, whom she referred to as the First Professor, the Second Professor, the School Teacher, and so on, and a couple of hangers-on—the Business Man and the Poultry Farmer. She portrayed herself, still, as a carefree young girl, a cigarette-smoking, modern young thing among a group of old fathers.

She realized, of course, that she was not going to see the truth about Russia, which she knew was "carefully concealed from the vulgar eye of the tourist," but rather a propaganda poster of Soviet Russia with its factories, crèches, museums and power stations. Across the Baltic Sea the party journeyed to Leningrad. The professors and teacher and businessman and Pamela were taken to the theatre, the Winter Palace, the Smolny Institute, the study of the last Czar, cathedrals, the cemetery in the grounds of the Alexander Nevsky monastery and the Rembrandts in the Hermitage, the whole an exhausting sightseeing marathon from breakfast until 4 P.M. each day. The increasingly grumpy group took the train to Moscow where they sat in a loge to see *Swan Lake* and caught a glimpse of Stalin. The party called at a crèche. Pamela was heartbroken to find babies propped up at a table, barely able to sit, expected to eat with a spoon when they were too little to even manipulate one.

She went to cuddle one of the babies, then scooped it onto her knee and fed it, but "somebody rushed in, snatched the child from my arms and dumped it down in the chair" and instructed her "look at the banner," which read "play is not just fun, it is a preparation for toil."[40] She did not reveal this instinctive need to nurture the baby in *Moscow Excursion,* only much later, when she was speaking at an American university, long after her childbearing days were over.

On her return to England, Pamela settled back into domesticity with Madge at Pound Cottage. They baked Christmas cakes, packed one for AE, and drank too many sherries by the hearth of the big old fireplace. The winter dragged on, Pamela more and more concerned with the state of her lungs. In March 1933 she decided to try a spring holiday with Madge in the south of France. This time, she told AE, she had hopes for a complete cure.

The next month she saw him in Dublin, asking for his help yet again. She wanted names and phone numbers of contacts for a series of articles on Irish politics which she planned to sell to Australian magazines. Pamela was unhappy with the result; AE comforted her: "Politics, as you will discover more and more as you live, are very complicated." But her journeys to and from AE in Ireland were about to end forever. As he told her in May 1933, "Ireland is dead to me, not the earth of course but the nation." He visited Kingsley Porter at Glenveagh Castle early in the summer. They yarned about his need to leave Ireland for a while. His biographer, Henry Summerfield, believed AE was preparing to act out the third phase of the classic four-stage Hindu life, following the stages of student and householder: that is, shedding his possessions in preparation for the final stage of life as a religious hermit. In the first week of July, he sold almost everything, including his house at Rathgar Avenue, keeping only some books and paintings. On July 8, he took the train to Donegal. That evening, the Porters' chauffeur picked him up from the station and took him to a spot on the coast where he was to meet Kingsley and Lucy, who had been visiting the little island of Inish Bofin, the nearest island to the coast in the Tory archipelago, where they had built a cottage. As the oarsman tied the boat up, AE saw there was only one passenger. Lucy told him her husband had drowned earlier that day. Summerfield makes no mention of any visit to the police, a request for help from a coastal patrol or anyone else, but merely states that AE and Lucy drove back to Glenveagh Castle where he spent a few days "comforting the widow." Lucy lay on the sofa while AE read to her from an advance copy of his new book, *The Avatars*. He dealt with the paperwork for the funeral and, after some days, left for London. There is no hint of an inquest or any further inquiry and the episode has the air of an allegory. This really was the end of Ireland for AE.

Early in August 1933, he moved to lodgings at 41 Sussex Gardens in London. It was a sweltering summer. Pamela asked again if he would please come to see her at Pound Cottage. He agreed on an overnight visit one Saturday late in September. AE boarded the train at Charing Cross in a three-piece suit, shirt and tie. At Mayfield, still in his Bloomsbury garb, he posed in the garden with Pamela. He placed one arm around her delicate shoulder and stared solemnly at the camera lens as Madge snapped the shutter. Pamela and Madge insisted he squeeze into their sports car to show him the Sussex countryside in its September colors.

That evening, Pamela told him she was worried about who she really was, that she had tried various guises but always felt

like an impostor. AE reassured her, "Why worry?" Back in
London, he told her by his next letter that he had seen "the
imp in her coming out from under the masks." But, what did
it matter? We all had "creatures within us, archangels, angels,
devas, fairy, imps and devils and why worry if one of the imps
in you [shows] through the mask?"[41]

Pamela now had another favor to ask of AE. She would love
to meet his important friend, Alfred Richard Orage, the editor
of the *New English Weekly*. AE had admired Orage for some
time, enthusiastically backing his theories on economics and
social credit. But now the two met regularly, as good friends,
at the Kardomah Café in Chancery Lane. Over the teacups,
they discussed Indian philosophy, Hindu scriptures and yogi
practices. Or rather, Orage listened while AE launched into
his monologues. Orage once asked AE what happened after
death. That had him stumped. He thought for a minute and
said, "I don't know."[42]

AE told Pamela, "If you wish to see Orage, I could bring
you to tea any Wednesday afternoon...we go out to a little
underground tea shop and talk for an hour or two, then go
our ways...if you time your London visit so as to have a
Wednesday 4 to 5:30, I will bring you to his office and out
to the tea shop."[43] She made the pilgrimage to London to
meet Orage—her next Mr. Banks—on the third Wednesday
in October 1933.

Orage and Pamela were to know one another only a year—
he died in November 1934—but in that year, Orage
profoundly influenced her life. More than just an editor and
another useful contact, he brought her into the orbit of the
most peculiar and most powerful of all her gurus, George
Ivanovitch Gurdjieff. If AE was her "literary father"—as Pamela
once said—Gurdjieff was her spiritual father.

She did not meet Gurdjieff until 1938. By then, her appetite was whetted by what she had heard of the master from Orage and another of Gurdjieff's disciples, Piotr Damien Ouspensky. These two men, the Englishman, Orage, and the Russian, Ouspensky, were to carry Gurdjieff's message to the world, acting as his interpreters for a gullible and willing audience of men and women who, like Pamela, had looked in vain for answers to their anxieties in religion and philosophy.

Gurdjieff, Orage and Ouspensky were all the spiritual off-spring of Madame Helena Blavatsky, whose Theosophical Society had so influenced Yeats and AE. Ever since she had heard AE talk of theosophy, Pamela had had a weakness for its blend of orientalism, Hindu philosophy and the occult. But from Orage onward, she was a total convert. Each of her Mr. Banks from now on would take her farther and farther down the path, one passing her to another, from AE to Orage, from Ouspensky to Gurdjieff, and finally to the New Age mystic, Krishnamurti. Orage was the critical link between her Irish theosophists of the nineteenth century and her Asian and Russian gurus of the twentieth century.

Just as Pamela had needed a mentor and found AE, Orage himself needed a guru. When they met he was sixty, a survivor of a turbulent life spent dabbling with the ideas of Nietzsche, Plato, Blavatsky, Fabianism, Hinduism, G. B. Shaw and H. G. Wells.[44] Orage had been a schoolteacher in Yorkshire, and studied the Bhagavad Gita and *Mahabharata* before moving to London in 1906. There, partly with the financial help of Shaw, he edited the *New Age* magazine from a tiny, chaotic office two flights up from a little courtyard off Chancery Lane. The *New Age,* promoted as "a weekly review of politics, literature and art," veered more toward culture than politics. It became a critical success, publishing Shaw, Galsworthy, Havelock Ellis and Anatole France, along with news of the theatre in Europe and of the Russian playwright,

Chekhov. There was little money for contributors and virtually none for Orage himself. He nicknamed the *New Age* "No Wage."

In 1921, Orage had fallen under the influence of Gurdjieff when he attended Ouspensky's lectures in London given at the Theosophical Hall in Warwick Gardens, off Kensington High Street. Ouspensky, also a journalist, had met Gurdjieff in Moscow in 1915. With his reporter's eye, he noticed "a man of oriental type, no longer young, with a black mustache and piercing eyes, who astonished me because he seemed to be completely disguised... with the face of an Indian raja or an Arab sheik."[45]

Although he caught a whiff of the fraud in Gurdjieff, Ouspensky believed in the truth of his philosophies. He became Gurdjieff's disciple, spreading his word to new audiences when he moved to London in 1921. Ouspensky's financial backing came from Lady Rothermere, the fey, estranged wife of the press baron, Lord Rothermere.

At Warwick Gardens, he lectured on his pet theory of eternal recurrence, telling his audience they had all lived their lives before, and would live them again and again, suffering endlessly, until they found a way out of the circle. O, as they called him, had written a novel based on the idea that a life could only have meaning when a person knew he was going nowhere. Ouspensky believed in déjà vu, hoping to understand the phenomenon by studying the fourth dimension. Along with Gurdjieff, he espoused the "fourth way," the first, second and third being the way of the fakir, the monk and the yogi. These paths involved giving something up at the start of a spiritual journey, but the fourth way involved inner work on oneself while remaining part of everyday society.

Early in 1922, Gurdjieff himself visited London, addressing newspaper editors, including Orage. Gurdjieff might have settled in London along with Ouspensky had it not been for the

British Home Office, which looked with suspicion on this caviar and carpet trader with a Nansen passport and refused him permanent entry, despite the intervention of Lady Rothermere.

At the Theosophical Hall at Warwick Gardens, both Gurdjieff and Ouspensky told their adoring followers that men and women were mentally asleep, with no real knowledge of themselves. These poor, unknowing fools lived in a mechanical state, as if in a dream, unable to reach their potential. They could wake only through a superhuman effort to "self remember." Part of the discipline of the Gurdjieffian way was for each person to unite and balance their three centers, intellectual, emotional and physical. Until they did so, they were simply machines or in Gurdjieff's word "idiots." How could they wake up? By following what he called The Work, which was in fact hard physical work done in groups. Gurdjieff also promoted various formulae, including "the law of Three" (in which "the higher blends with the lower to actualize the middle") and "the law of Seven," based on the musical scale. The theory was that every process had seven phases, including two semitonal intervals.

Like Madame Blavatsky, who claimed she had studied with secret Himalayan masters, Gurdjieff maintained his laws, special insights and sacred dances came from his travels to remote monasteries in the wilderness of Central Asia. Naturally there was no proof he had ever been to such monasteries or that they did, in fact, exist. Gurdjieff was above all a brilliant actor, playing the role of an Oriental mystic with a devastating blend of charm and rudeness.

Born in Russian Armenia about 1866, Gurdjieff had virtually trained for the life of a con man. He was a spy and a hypnotist as well as a dealer in caviar and carpets before settling in Moscow, where he began to attract a following as a guru in 1912. The following year Gurdjieff resurfaced in St. Petersburg under the persona of Prince Ozay, and began to

choreograph dances including *The Struggle of the Magicians.*
Gurdjieff was the contemporary of the wily Russian ballet
entrepreneur Serge Diaghilev, and in many ways his life ran in
a complementary path. Both were manipulators who won the
patronage of the rich in Paris and London. Not only was
Gurdjieff a messianic figure to his loyal troupe of dancers and
disciples, but again like Diaghilev, he cultivated an eccentric
manner and distinctive appearance. But while Diaghilev
commissioned brilliant artists to collaborate on classical ballets, Gurdjieff worked mainly alone, devising his own dance
vocabulary, which he taught only to his adherents. Unlike
Diaghilev, he seldom presented his work to the general public.
His ritualistic set pieces danced in white robes resembled a
mixture of Grecian dance, exemplified by the free and barefoot style of Isadora Duncan, and the movements of Emile
Jaques-Dalcroze, the Swiss music teacher who had set up an
Institute for Applied Rhythm.

Gurdjieff exuded a powerful sexual magnetism that he used
to maximum advantage. He liked to shock his audiences by
revealing their erotic fantasies and by graphically describing
their sexual organs. He never bothered with euphemisms for
lovemaking when he could say fuck instead. He seduced many
women and fathered many illegitimate children while at the
same time scoffing at his followers' obsession with sex. But
his greatest talent was the extraction of money. Whenever
Gurdjieff fell on hard times, he used his hypnotic powers to
convince newcomers, intelligent men and women, mostly
American, to hand over their dollars and follow him. This
process he called "shearing sheep."

By 1921, Gurdjieff had settled in Berlin. Later the next
year, with the backing of one of his "sheep," Lady Rothermere,
he established his Institute for the Harmonious Development
of Man at the Prieure des Basses Loges in a big park at Avon,
near Fontainebleau, about forty miles from Paris. Here, while

Lady Rothermere flitted through the garden and brought Gurdjieff black coffee, professional men who had given up their previous lives for Gurdjieff worked for him to near exhaustion. They had been lured to the Prieure by the promise of restorative therapies of all kind, from hydro to magneto, electro to psycho.

Far from the glories described in the seductive brochures, life at the Prieure was the equivalent of a lowly soldier's under a sergeant major who demanded absolute submission. Through pain, fasting and other deprivations, Gurdjieff promised his slaves self-discovery. The inmates, all voluntary, had to fulfill arduous tasks, involving hard physical work—The Work—as well as learning Gurdjieff's rhythmic movements and ritual dances. Like a child's game of Statues, the dances included his direction to "Stop!" When he did, the dancers had to remain stock still, as if statues, for up to ten minutes until he gave them the direction "Continue."

Gurdjieff, though, did not offer an unrelenting diet of privation. He reserved part of the Prieure for the really rich (these quarters were called the Ritz) while he indulged himself with good food and Armagnac, which he drank to excess. Personal hygiene was not his strong point. From veiled references to his habits in contemporary reports, it seems he did not care whether or not he quite made the distance to the toilet. Conditions at the Prieure were so bad that the kitchen was infested with flies.

Late in 1922, Orage decided to try the cure for himself. There at the Prieure, Gurdjieff allotted him a cell in the so-called Monk's Corridor, where he cried in the evening with fatigue. Orage was forced to stop smoking—another deprivation device of Gurdjieff's, who liked to take from his followers their most loved habit or possession. (Some were allowed to eat only soup while they watched others eating a three-course meal.)[46]

One of Orage's magazine contributors was Katherine Mansfield, herself in need of a guru. (Mansfield once wrote to Orage "you taught me to write, you taught me to think.") Despite his own treatment at the Prieure, Orage recommended to Mansfield that she move there herself, as a permanent resident. She willingly agreed, believing, as Orage said, "that it is not writing, as writing, that needs criticism, correction and perfection, so much as the mind, character and personality of the writer." Gurdjieff would be the master teacher. By the time she reached the Institute, Mansfield was fatally ill. Suffering from TB, her body had been tortured with mad medical experiments, strychnine tinctures, iodine injections and X-rays. Orage saw her almost every day at the Prieure and, as he wrote, "we had many long talks together."[47] She bled to death from a hemorrhage at the Prieure in January 1923. The night of her funeral, Gurdjieff hosted a huge feast at which he sat in his silken, shrouded, personal alcove.

Later that year, Orage was dispatched by Gurdjieff to America, mainly to scout for more money but also to spread the word of The Work. In New York, he held meetings at a bookshop called the Sunwise Turn, run by two women including Jessie Richards Dwight, half his age, whom he was to marry. Jessie was not impressed by Gurdjieff; the two men had a serious falling out. By late 1930, Gurdjieff demanded that Orage's American pupils forsake Orage. He forced them to sign a declaration stating they would have nothing further to do with Orage. Even Orage signed the document. In the words of one of Gurdjieff's biographers, "Orage without hesitation vowed to ostracize Orage."[48]

In 1932, Orage returned to London to his old life of journalism. His new magazine, the *New English Weekly,* was to publish the best writers of the day, as well as promising newcomers such as nineteen-year-old Dylan Thomas and AE's new friend, the writer Ruth Pitter. Orage, constantly on the alert for young talent, but with a tight budget, was impressed with the energy and output of AE's other friend, Pamela. Soon after the meeting arranged by AE he published her poetry, and before long she became the *New English Weekly*'s drama critic as well. In December 1933, Pamela sent Orage one of her letters from Moscow that pleased him, according to AE, and in the same month he published the first of the poems she wrote for the magazine. (Orage published four more of her poems early in 1934, but by then her poetry was becoming an occasional thing. Gradually she must have realized that she was not going to become a great poet.)

AE continued to respond to the vagaries of Pamela's health and work. In January 1934 he was sorry "your lung has been troubling you." By February he knew from Orage that she had been laid up and in April he was very sorry she had been laid up again, but he congratulated her on her first book, *Moscow Excursion*. "The preface is admirable. You add a delicious literary flavor to your journalism and I like your sly humor," he wrote.

All along, he kept soothing Pamela: "What a witch you are to get yourself laid up." But he looked forward to "your book of lyrics. Never forget you are a poetess."[49] The book of lyrics never came. Holding her first book in her hands, Pamela knew the addiction of every first-time author. If one collection of magazine stories on Russia could be made into a book so simply, then why not another.

She returned to the scrapbooks in the studio. The London letters were hopeless, she knew, so dated and striving for effect. But in among them were the short stories, about the under nurse, the match man and the dancing cow. AE had told her to think of a witch's adventures. Perhaps the witch could be the nurse?

Pamela tested the idea on AE. In a few weeks she had several stories to send him. He replied testily, "Why Mary Poppins and no word about yourself? I know Mary Poppins is an incarnation of some attributes of Pamela but I believe in wholeness, not in some partial incarnation, so please tell me how you are." He thought the adventures were "very good."[50] But AE, forever the editor, suggested an alternative ending. Mary Poppins "should not have gone up in the sky at the end without some transfiguration. Why picture her with that old umbrella and the carpetbag and the disastrous hat?" She might have left town in "less of a period garment" and more like the diaphanous slip worn in an illustration for the book by Maia, one of the seven stars who formed the constellation of Pleiades. AE and Pamela had fantasized about the origins of Mary Poppins, whose name could be a derivation of Maia. Had she come down from the heavens? Was she really a stray star, who had been placed in the constellation according to a tale from ancient mythology?

AE insisted all along that Mary Poppins had come from mythology. He thought if she lived in the days of old, where she belonged, Mary would have long golden tresses. In one hand she might carry a wreath of flowers, in the other, a spear. Her feet would be shod in winged sandals. But, as this was the Iron Age, she came in the clothes most suited to it.

AE had now known Pamela for a decade. The whole of that time, she needed a mentor and he wanted to fill that role. He could not stop now. In August 1934, AE wrote, "I hope you will think about my suggestion to write a [new] book with the inanimate things talking. Imagine a stone telling its story to the boy going back millions of years when it was flung out of a volcano, or a shell telling its history in...whatever age shells came into rocks. Or a chair gossiping about the people who sat on it, or a clock telling about the girl who came and looked at it every two or three minutes and who then sat down and cried. I only mention these possibilities, not that you need necessarily use them, but because they might start you thinking of things whose stories you could tell."[51]

Woven into many Poppins adventures to come, Pamela did write of inanimate objects coming to life to tell their tales— figures in a Royal Doulton bowl, a china lion, a marble statue who told the Banks children and Mary Poppins how he had come from Greece.

In October 1934, Pamela offered AE a small share of the money from her first Poppins book. He readily accepted "part of your treasure. Again, congratulations dear Mary Popkins." From now on, AE called both Pamela and Mary Poppins "Popkins." Pamela never knew if it was a deliberate mistake or not. "I hope the new Mary Popkins is adventuring in your mind or better still that poems are bubbling up," he wrote.[52]

The next month, Orage died suddenly of a heart attack. With the loss of yet another soulmate and listener, AE became even more melancholy. He was about to sail away for the last time, to the United States, returning home to London fatally ill.

Pamela would soon be thirty-five. Too old to be a nymph, still not a mother. She decided to dedicate *Mary Poppins* to her own dead mother, and began the search for the next Mr. Banks.

II

The Mother

1934–1965

'Out of the sky she had come,
back to the sky she had gone.'[1]

Tucked into her bed, Lyndon could hear Aunt Ellie complaining to her mother.

"The children are behaving abominably. Lyndon is the eldest and she must at least try to tidy up. The least she could do is put her toys away at night. My dear, I know money is hard to come by, but you really should think about advertising for a nanny.'

Lyndon wished Mummy wasn't so busy all the time, fussing over Moya. The baby was ten months old now, trying to walk but always falling over. Mummy never seemed to have a moment to just sit down and talk. Imagine if there was another mother in the house, someone as nice and sweet smelling as her, but funny too. Who might even make shopping fun, and take her for walks in the park. Instead, she had to act grown up and be a mother to Biddy and Moya when she was not even seven herself.

Lyndon knew she looked really grumpy and ugly. Mummy would say, "Better be careful or the wind will change and you will look crabby forever."

She pulled the blankets up toward her chin. Lyndon could hear the wind whipping up around the corner, rustling the grass out the back by the stable. She loved her mother, truly, but if only she could have a fairy godmother as well.

7

Poppins and Pamela in Wonderland

Who is Mary Poppins? In our mind's eye we see Julie Andrews in a pastel Edwardian dress, smiling as cheerily as the star of a toothpaste commercial, as saccharine as the spoonful of sugar that helped the medicine go down, as jolly as a jolly holiday with Bert, as cheery as "Chim Chim, Cheree." Such is the power of Walt Disney. The original Mary Poppins was not cheery at all. She was tart and sharp, rude, plain and vain. That was her charm; that—and her mystery.

Mary Poppins is snap frozen in the 1930s, a nanny of her day and age, not one of today's country girls dispatched by an

143

agency to mind the offspring of working parents—always half
wondering if they have a baby killer in the house. Mary
Poppins is a nanny from Wonderland or Neverland, who strolls
along the riverbank of *The Wind in the Willows* or through the
Hundred Acre Wood of *Winnie-the-Pooh*. She and her colleagues
could still be seen, mid-twentieth century, in Hyde Park or
Kensington Gardens, in a buttoned up, belted topcoat and no-
nonsense hat, pushing a high-wheeled Victorian pram.

That was the workaday Mary Poppins who blew in to the
Banks residence in 17 Cherry Tree Lane. But where did she
come from, and where did she go when she left at the end of
each book, lifted to the heavens by her parrot-headed umbrella
or a runaway merry-go-round? Why did she *have* to go? Children, academics, reporters, and readers from Sweden to
Trinidad, from the 1930s to the 1980s, all wanted to know.
Pamela Travers brushed them off, always. From the day the
first Mary Poppins book was published in 1934, she preferred
silence or allusion.

The many adventures of the magical nanny have their genesis in Pamela's childhood—her loneliness as a little girl,
daydreaming in Allora, her domineering great aunts, her precepts and rules for living—and in her love for AE and the
mysteries of creation she heard from him and read in the
poems of Yeats and Blake.

Each of the female characters in *Mary Poppins* contains a
little slice of Pamela. She appears in the guise of Jane, the
eldest child of the Banks family; as her mother, Mrs. Banks;
as Miss Lark, Miss Andrew, Mrs. Corry; a grab bag of weird
and magical hangers-on; and as Mary Poppins herself.

Mary Poppins represented one of Pamela's most treasured
beliefs: that a woman passes through three phases of life—first
maiden, then mother, then crone. By crone, she did not mean
a doddering old woman hobbling along with a stick. Her crone
was a woman who had "gathered up all the threads of life, and

all they've found and known, and had it there as wisdom."[1]

Mary Poppins has the superficial manner of a nymph or virgin waiting for the right admirer. But her next layer is one of a nurturing mother, not an absentminded one, like Mrs. Banks, but a mother sensitive to the needs of children, emotional and physical. That is why all children love her so much, why her disappearance is like a death, not like the death of a mother of young children but the death of a mother whose adult children have grown wise from her loving care. But peel back another layer and Poppins is revealed as a crone or grandmother, imparting the wisdom of the ages, a witch or wise woman. All these feminine qualities Pamela found, and loved, in fairy tales, the "marvellous heroines, the villainesses—all the women. I think the fairy tales have a very great deal to tell us about the life of a woman. I think they are all really one person rolled into one and tell us what we should be."[2]

She said every woman could find her prototype or a model for her role in life in the fairy tales collected by the brothers Grimm. They might be apparently passive heroines, such as Cinderella or the Goose Girl, a simple maiden like the Miller's Daughter, a heroine like the sister in "The Seven Ravens," who had to go to the end of the world—"to the sun and moon and stars and back"—to save her brothers, or the twelve dancing princesses who explored the mysteries of the world below our world. Or the grandmothers and witches in "Rapunzel" and "Hansel and Gretel," or the numerous queens, wise women, and priestesses.

Mary Poppins has been called the "mother Goddess," a witch, the good fairy, a wise woman, the "ecstatic Mother" as exemplified in Artemis and Sophia,[3] Mary Magdalene or the Virgin Mary. She is said to contain Zen secrets or to epitomize Zen. Professors have written books analyzing Mary Poppins. Earnest students and ordinary readers wrote to Pamela suggesting who Poppins might actually be. "*You* tell *me*," she liked to tell them, and shrugged in mock amazement: "The readers tell me things I never dreamed."

Although she shares qualities with Peter Pan and with Alice in Wonderland's surrealistic friends, the Queen, the White Rabbit and the Mad Hatter, Mary Poppins is unique: lovable because of her mixture of magic and sternness, her fantastic abilities hidden behind the facade of an extremely ordinary woman.

Walt Disney saw the fascination of Mary Poppins and, although his movie contained none of the mystique and symbolism of the original *Mary Poppins* books, it held enough magic to become a much-loved classic. Julie Andrews did not resemble the Mary Poppins created by Pamela and her illustrator, Mary Shepard. Andrews was sweet faced and exuded charm. The original Mary Poppins was never charming. Her appearance was based on a Dutch doll or peg doll that Pamela said she owned as a child. The doll had shiny, painted coal-black hair and a turned up nose, attributes she gave Mary Poppins, who also saw the world clearly through her rather small bright blue eyes. Mary had rosy cheeks, big hands and feet, and a bony frame. She wore shapeless coats and suits, cut to an unflattering low calf length, mufflers, gloves, sensible Mary Jane shoes and carried a businesslike handbag.

The Poppins adventures were written over a fifty-four-year period, but in the stories nobody ever gets any older and the adventures have the freshness of tonight's bedtime tale. The reader is led gently to the possibility that Number 17 Cherry Tree Lane might still exist. If Pamela was explaining it one more time she might tantalize the reader, "You will find it hard to find Cherry Tree Lane, exactly." She once wrote that it was one of those byways not important enough to show up on a map.[4]

Cherry Tree Lane appears to be in Kensington or Chelsea, but is definitely not in the most fashionable precinct of either suburb. A chemist's shop stands on one corner, a tobacconist at the other. On one side of the street is the entrance to a

P. L. Travers's mother,
Margaret Goff

P. L. Travers aged twenty months

P. L. Travers's father,
Travers Goff

The Goff family residence, Allora, Queensland

Left to right: Lyndon, Moya and Biddy Goff at the stream
opposite their home in Bowral, 1915

A youthful Travers in a checked shirt

A publicity shot taken for Travers in the 1920s

Travers photographed in 1923

Travers in a play
produced by
Allan Wilkie

Travers in costume for a
production of *Julius Caesar*

Travers and George William Russell (AE) at Pound Cottage, Mayfield, 1934

Madge Burnand at
Pound Cottage, 1930s

Pound Cottage, Mayfield

Mary Poppins arrives at the Banks
home in Cherry Tree Lane

Jane and Michael Banks with
Mary Poppins

Michael and Jane watch Mary go

The balloons illustration
from *Mary Poppins
Comes Back*

Detail of the balloons illustration: Travers and Mary Shepard
holding their named balloons

George Ivanovitch Gurdjieff   Travers in 1941

Travers with Camillus in 1941

park as big as the imagination of a child. Inside the grounds are a merry-go-round, a lake and classical statues. A row of cherry trees goes dancing down the middle of the street. On the other side is a handful of houses. The most eccentric, at one end, is the home of that cheery soul Admiral Boom. The house, built like a ship, is crowned with a gilt weathercock resembling a telescope. The garden is dominated by a flagstaff.

An elderly spinster, Miss Lucinda Emily Lark, and her pampered hound, Andrew, live next to the Bankses. Miss Lark has the grandest home in the street, with two entrances, one for friends and relations, the other for tradesmen (not tradespeople—this is the 1930s). Number 17 is rather dilapidated and the smallest house in Cherry Tree Lane but somehow big enough to accommodate five children—Jane and Michael Banks, the twins John and Barbara, the new baby Annabel— Mr. George Banks and Mrs. Banks (whose first name is a mystery), a nanny who never stays long, a cook, Mrs. Clara Brill, a maid, Ellen, and an odd, odd job man, Robertson Ay.

Mr. Banks can afford either a smarter house, or all those children, but not both. As a banker, he is keenly aware of budgets and often complains, as Pamela's father complained in Allora, that there is no extra money to bring home today as "the bank is broken." George Banks, balding, is neither handsome nor plain. He wears proper banker's attire, bowler, suit, overcoat. George is short tempered and expects the worst. Once he threatened to leave home for good. He is finicky, even obsessive. Everything has a place and everything *must* stay in that place. Yet there is also something rather wistful and boyish about George. One day of the year—only one—he sings in his bath. He likes to smell the tulips in the garden and has a secret longing to be an astronomer. Just last summer, he told his children about the constellation called Pleiades, the seven sisters. He is forever hopeful that a new star might light up in the sky.

Mrs. Banks seems vain and proud but is really terribly insecure and succumbs easily when Mary Poppins tells her she has no references, because producing references these days is *frightfully* unfashionable. Nor do smart people give their servants every third Thursday off each month. To be really chic, Mary tells Mrs. Banks, they should allow her every second Thursday off. Mrs. Banks is a bit silly, anxious and soft.

Jane Banks is a proper little girl, quiet and thoughtful, occasionally naughty, and wishes so much that she was not the oldest. She broods sometimes and pretends she is a hen about to lay seven nice white eggs. Pamela told a university student in 1964 that the tale of Jane in the chapter "Bad Wednesday" laying imaginary eggs was "a definite element" in her own childhood.[5] Michael, Jane's younger brother, is like all younger brothers in children's stories: naughty, quick to speak his mind and then to regret it.

None of the servants is quite up to his or her duties. Oh, they cope, just, but when the unsuccessful nannies leave, the other servants fall apart. Not that Robertson Ay even needs to cope. A sleepyhead, not much more than a boy, Ay is supposed to shine the shoes and keep the lawns in order. Instead he snoozes all day in the broom cupboard or garden. Robertson Ay, we learn later, is not like the other servants but really one of Mary Poppins's mystery gang, one of the Ancient Ones, the supernatural creatures from myth and fairy tale. He is the Fool or the Dirty Rascal to the Wise Woman of Mary Poppins.

Not that we know, in the beginning, that Mary is anything but a servant with an unconventional way of arriving at the door. The Banks household is in a state of disorder if not chaos, as the previous nanny, Katie Nanna, has just disappeared. As Mrs. Banks writes advertisements to send to the newspapers for a new nanny, the East Wind suddenly flings Mary Poppins against the front door, complete with carpetbag, umbrella, shallow-brimmed straw hat, long scarf and a bad attitude.

She gives the strong impression that she is doing the Bankses a favor by accepting their offer to become the new nanny. The children are astonished to see that she slides up the banisters and that from her ordinary-looking carpetbag she takes out a starched white apron, a large cake of Sunlight Soap, a toothbrush, a packet of hairpins, a bottle of scent, a small folding armchair, a package of throat lozenges, and a large bottle of dark red medicine that is as magic as *Alice in Wonderland*'s "Drink Me" bottle. Mary's luggage and its contents seem rather like Aunt Ellie and Aunt Jane Morehead's travel requirements, especially when it comes to the next layer of contents: seven flannel nightgowns, four cotton nightgowns, one pair of boots, a set of dominoes, two bathing caps, one postcard album, one folding camp bedstead, blankets and an eiderdown.

Mary settles into the nursery for the night. When Michael asks her if she will stay forever, Mary displays her disagreeable habit of responding with a studied insult or threat. If he persists in this line of questioning, she will call a "Policeman" with a capital P.

Mary Poppins seems the epitome of the punishing governess, the bullying woman who has an apt saying for every occasion, and who subdues children as they were subdued in the Victorian age, when they were seen and not heard. "Spit spot into bed" is her most famous order, but Poppins is an absolute compendium of instructions, cliches, declamations and proverbs, among them: Strike me pink; Early to bed, early to rise; Curiosity killed the cat; Trouble trouble and it will trouble you; Don't care was made to care. She carefully hides her compassion. Almost sadistic at times, Mary is never really nasty but often very sharp. She is a controlling force, making order from disorder, making magic, then never admitting magic took place.

Mary has one great weakness: her vanity. She is endlessly fixing her hat and checking her clothes, always pleased with her reflection, and clearly believes in retail therapy. She is especially chirpy about her new clothes. Mary loves her blue coat with silver buttons, white blouse with pink spots, the hat with the pink roses, the hat with the daisies, the brown kid shoes with two buttons, white gloves, fur-trimmed gloves, and of course the parrot-headed umbrella, which is also her means of transport to the stars.

Mary Poppins threatens to leave at a point of time which only she controls. She tells her charges she will be with them until the wind changes or until her necklace breaks. She never tells where she has comes from, where she intends to go or who she really is. But she leaves many clues. Like Francis of Assisi, she is close to animals and birds, with whom she can talk. Like Jesus, she helps the poor and weak. She understands the universe and seems to take part in its creation and renewal. She is known as the Great Exception, the Oddity, the Misfit.

The shopkeepers and neighbors treat her with respect and bluster and bumble when she is around. Mary takes the Banks children on many adventures to visit her most peculiar friends and relations. It is the contrast between these adventures in Fairyland, or Wonderland, or Neverland, and the reality of life in Cherry Tree Lane and its environs that gives the Mary Poppins stories their special charm. The real world is one of teatime, and sensible shoes, and being tucked into bed, of the ice cream man, the butcher, fishmonger, the grocer and above all the nursery food, the gingerbread, raspberry jam, buttered toast, thin bread-and-butter slices, crumpets, plum cakes with pink icing, warm milk, baked custard, apples on sticks, lamb cutlets, wholemeal scones, arrowroot biscuits, porridge, coconut and walnut cakes, rice pudding with honey in it, macaroons, tapioca, conversation lollies, chocolate drops, sherbet and licorice.

In the real world live forlorn and rather lonely figures: Mr. and Mrs. Banks; Miss Lark, bedecked with brooches, bracelets and earrings, cared for by two maids, and mothering silly, silky, fluffy Andrew, who wears leather boots and is awfully spoilt; and the power-crazed Park Keeper, Frederick Smith, whose badge of authority barely disguises that he is a boy at heart. He is the voice of authority—no litter here, obey the rules, this won't do at all, it's against the regulations!

In the unreal world live happier folk, fantastic creatures who float upside down, laugh so much they fly to the ceiling, or construct the universe by painting springtime or gluing stars to the sky. The fantastic people are often relations of Mary Poppins. The bald Mr. Alfred Wigg, who is her uncle, is round and fat. On his birthday (if it falls on a Friday) he floats in the air. Mr. Arthur Turvy, her cousin, mends broken things, even hearts, but every second Monday he is compelled by supernatural forces to do the opposite of everything he wants to do.

Her first cousin, once removed, is a scary snake, the Hamadryad, also known as "the lord of the jungle." Mary Poppins is also intimate with the ancient Mrs. Corry who runs the sweet shop and who knows Guy Fawkes, Christopher Columbus and William the Conqueror. Mrs. Corry likes to paste stars on the sky, breaks off her fingers (made of barley sugar), and has a soft and terrible voice. She is the Queen of the crones; Mary Poppins treats her with the utmost respect. The Bird Woman is another Ancient One, as is the old woman in a chapter called "Balloons and Balloons." All the old people in the Mary Poppins books appear to be happy—crones who have found the meaning of life.

The animals and birds in the stories are also members of Mary's fantastic world. Mary Poppins speaks to Andrew the dog and to the starling who knows how to talk to babies. Animals at the zoo behave like humans, locking the humans in the cages and laughing at the baby children.

Most of the adventures in the first Mary Poppins books, *Mary Poppins* (published in 1934), and *Mary Poppins Comes Back* (1935), are concerned with flight, flying, or simply the air. The first book begins with Mary being blown in on the East

Wind and ends with her floating away on the West Wind. Men, women, children, and animals all float or soar in space—on laughing gas, over the moon, around the world with the whirl of a compass, over St. Paul's, up to the heavens. A naughty starling flies in the window to talk to the babies and Maia, a star, flies down from the sky to do her shopping.

In the second book, Mary arrives on the tail of a kite, a baby tells how she flew through the world, everyone flies on balloons and Mary disappears on an airborne merry-go-round. The Banks children understand simply this: out of the sky she came, and back to the sky she must go.

The theme of stars constantly recurs in the Mary Poppins books, with the first imprints decorated with printed stars. Mrs. Corry glues stars, the Cow jumps about the stars, Maia is a visiting star, and shooting stars guide the way to the zodiac circus.

Pamela constantly returned also to the idea of the unity or duality of things. She really did believe, along with the god-like snake, the Hamadryad, in the "Full Moon" chapter of *Mary Poppins,* that birds and beasts and stones and stars are all one.[6]

The books can be read as an ode not just to "oneness" but to the dual nature of every creature, and of the world itself. Not only are there two distinct sides to Mary, goodness and sharpness, reality and unreality, and to George Banks—softness and crankiness—but there are twin babies, day and night, the sun and the moon, the East Wind and West Wind, the seasons and opposing points of the compass.

Pamela's fourth Mary Poppins book, *Mary Poppins in the Park,* published in 1952, was the most mystical, made up of discrete chapters or incidents which could have happened at any time. The first three books, culminating in *Mary Poppins Opens the Door,* published in 1944, have a different kind of symmetry: in each, eight to twelve adventures are sandwiched between chapters heralding Poppins's arrival and departure. The adventures range from visits to Mary's bizarre relations, whom she is often able to save from outlandish trouble, encounters with the neighbors in which Mary puts things to right, misadventures of the Banks children in disagreeable moods, and sometimes, a story within a story. The emotional climax of the books is a fantastic or surreal journey ending with an apotheosis. At the end of the adventures, which involve another dimension, someone leaves a sign or souvenir of the visit with Mary or the children. If the children point this out to Mary, she angrily denies anything has happened.

The first two books mirror one another, even to chapter titles—"Bad Tuesday" and "Bad Wednesday," "Miss Lark's Andrew" and "Miss Andrew's Lark," "The Day Out" and "The Evening Out." Mrs. Corry and the Bird Woman of the first book relate to the Balloon Woman of the second, and the Dancing Cow in the first book and Robertson Ay's story of the second both tell nursery rhyme tales mixed with parable.

In *Mary Poppins,* the most eerie and fantastic story concerns Mrs. Corry and her two big daughters Annie and Fannie. In *Mary Poppins Comes Back,* an equally frightening adventure, "Bad Wednesday," is a cautionary tale; Jane in one of her rare naughty moods gets trapped in time, inside the lives of boys who live on a Royal Doulton bowl. She might have been there forever if Mary had not dragged her back home. The most charming adventure in *Mary Poppins* is "John and Barbara's Story," the tale of the baby Banks twins who know the language of the universe but only for a year or so, until they become fully human. The most wistful adventure concerns the visit of Maia, the second-eldest of the Pleiades, who has come to earth to do some Christmas shopping for her six sisters.

Both *Mary Poppins* and *Mary Poppins Comes Back* include chapters in which Mary guides the children to the secrets of the universe. In "The Evening Out" (*Mary Poppins Comes Back*), Mary is the honored guest at a huge circus in the sky. The Sun is the ringmaster while Pegasus, Orion, Pollux and Castor, Saturn and Venus are among the entertainers whose finale is the Dance of the Wheeling Sky.

This great cosmic dance, with its literary and mythological connections, touches on Yeats's theory, explained in his book *A Vision*, of wheels and gyres, and on the dance of the spheres in Dante's *Paradiso*.[7] "The Evening Out" reveals how much faith Pamela put in astrology and has its precursor in the Grand Chain dance of the animals in "Full Moon," in *Mary Poppins*. One night—the night of Mary Poppins's birthday—there is a full moon. The Banks children and Mary visit the zoo where the animals strut around outside, laughing and pointing at the antics of the humans inside the cages.

In both "Full Moon" and "The Evening Out," the children appear to encounter God in the shape of the Hamadryad and the Sun. In "The Evening Out," Mary Poppins dances with the Sun who plants a kiss on her cheek. Next day, back at Cherry Tree Lane, the Sun's lip marks can be clearly seen by the children, burnt into the flesh of her cheek.

Mary Poppins Comes Back contains one chapter that takes the reader beyond the fantastic, to the realm of myth, religious symbolism and poetry. Called "The New One," it is inspired by Wordsworth, and by AE's favorite poet, William Blake, whom Pamela also revered. The "new one" is Annabel, the Banks's new baby, who has traveled on a long journey through the universe to arrive in the Banks household. She is not just a time traveler, but part of the universe itself, every part, from the sea, to the sky, to the stars, to the sun. Eventually, she forgets her origins, just as her older siblings, John and Barbara, have forgotten their journey and how they could talk to the sun and wind. Pamela wrote "The New One" with no experience of staring in awe at a newborn baby of her own, with that instinctive feeling that a child has come from God.

But she did have the example of Blake's view of children,

Songs of Innocence, and especially one poem in that series, "A Cradle Song," which expresses each parent's wonder at their baby and the feeling that this child must have come with the blessing of "all creation." In his "Immortality Ode," Wordsworth puts forward the same idea that "our birth is but a sleep and a forgetting...trailing clouds of glory do we come from God who is our home..." Staffan Bergsten, the Swedish academic who wrote *Mary Poppins and Myth* in 1978, pointed out that one of the poems of Blake's *Songs of Innocence* was one Pamela applied to herself, "The Little Black Boy."

An adult looking for deeper meaning in the books will understand that Mary Poppins lives in a land where religion, fairy tale and myth combine. Despite her knowledge, she does not moralize, but simply allows the Banks children to experience mysterious other worlds. She tells parables and allegories. Lessons can be learned. The grass is always greener, but don't always want what you haven't got. Things are not what they seem; don't judge a book by its cover. Have faith.

Mary Poppins was a direct descendant of the heroines Pamela had loved since she was four. Her closest literary relative was Alice in Wonderland. Back in 1928, Pamela wrote in *New Triad*'s "London Letter" that everyone loved Alice who "delighted our mothers...The world began to change with the advent of Alice. How could Alice help changing a world that was preoccupied with stories of little children dying prettily and with their last breath bidding their parents not to grieve... Before Alice came...literature for the young was sentimental and unreal. It needed the cold philosophical thought of Alice to put things right."[8]

Mary Poppins has much in common with the girl who fell asleep one summer afternoon. Mary travels to Fairyland. Alice goes to Wonderland. Mary meets weird floating creatures and flies through the sky or sinks to the ocean floor. Alice sinks down a hole in the ground. Mary talks to animals who talk right back to her. So does Alice. Mary Poppins might be only a fantasy, just an ordinary nanny whose adventures happen in the dreams of the Banks children. After all, Alice dreamed her entire adventure.

Mary springs from the same family tree as Peter Pan, another night flyer who comes to a London household as middle class and respectable as the Banks's. The head of the family, Mr. Darling, loves his children but is always worried about money. The children, Wendy, John and Michael, are minded by a nanny who is in fact a sheepdog called Nana. (John and Michael are also the names of the two boys in Mary Poppins's care.) Peter Pan, the boy who never grows up, arrives one night and teaches them how to fly to Neverland, his magic island. Mary Poppins, who seems to be twenty-seven but is in fact ageless, is also a children's escort for night flying adventures.

Both *Alice* and *Peter Pan* were part of Pamela's childhood, but then again they were part of the childhood of every middle-class child in Australia and Britain. *Alice in Wonderland* was written by Lewis Carroll in 1866. *Peter Pan* by James Barrie was published as a play in 1904 and a story in 1911. Both helped create a new fashion for children's fantasy, acknowledging the child as a reader with his or her own interests, yet, at the same time, appealing to adults.

The Victorians had romanticized childhood and invented the idea of children's books, but it took the Edwardians to make a cult of it. They were "fixated on children's pursuits," wrote Jackie Wullschlager, who studied Carroll, Barrie, A. A. Milne, Kenneth Grahame and Edward Lear for her analysis of Edwardian children's literature, *Inventing Wonderland*.[9] From the 1860s to the 1920s, England was awash with children's fantasy books, among them the riverbank tales of *The Wind in the Willows* by Kenneth Grahame, published in 1908, and the Bastable books, by E. (Edith) Nesbit, begun in 1898. Both Nesbit and Frances Hodgson Burnett, with *The Secret Garden* in 1911, brought the idea of magic to the lives of children, while A. A. Milne's Winnie-the-Pooh books in the 1920s were a reminder of a prewar idyll where Piglet, Eeyore, Pooh, Owl, Kanga, Roo and Tigger were as cozy in their Hundred Acre Wood as Mary Poppins, Jane, Michael and the twins were in their park next to Cherry Tree Lane.

Mary Poppins drew on the traditions of nonsense and anarchy in Victorian children's books and the romance, whimsicality and middle class settings of the Edwardian books. Like A. A. Milne's characters, the Banks family and Mary herself would be perfectly happy in Harrods, frolicking about a Sussex garden or cozily tucked into a Chelsea or Kensington nursery. Wullschlager wrote of the Winnie-the-Pooh books "what draws both adults and children to the books is the ironic, biting tone mixed in with the safe setting." *Mary Poppins* adopts the same tone, sharp, unsentimental, but with the certainty of the most comforting moments of childhood.

Part of Mary Poppins's appeal lies in her streak of rebelliousness, a quality she shares with the naughty Peter Pan, with Peter Rabbit created by Beatrix Potter, with Toad of *The Wind in the Willows,* and the peculiar fantasy animals of Wonderland. All these creatures influenced Pamela, who acknowledged her debt to the authors. But it annoyed, even "pained" Pamela when Mary Poppins was called a direct descendant of Peter Pan. "Must you say that?" she grumbled to one analyst of her work.[10] Pamela's literary heroine was Beatrix Potter. "To me she was one of the archangels." She loved "her understatement, her bareness, her surrealism, her non explaining."[11]

Potter had said "I painted most of the little pictures [of Peter Rabbit, the Flopsy bunnies, Mr. McGregor and the rest] mainly to please myself." Pamela loved that phrase, repeating it ad nauseam and adjusting it to apply to herself: "I write to please myself." Potter's sweet little animal tales, published from 1902, were on the Goff family's bookshelves in Allora. Pamela devoured them all. She adopted some of the characteristics of Potter. Pamela liked to say she was educated by a governess (Potter was), she took up gardening with passion (Potter loved gardening), moved to a country house that looked like Potter's animal farmhouses, and began her serious analysis of fairy tales. Potter illustrated traditional fairy tales and was so interested in "Cinderella" that she once wrote her own long and detailed version.[12]

Pamela saw that each of Potter's tales was built on a simple everyday happening, without sentimentality, but suggesting magic. Each had an element of irony, toughness, danger, suspense and even terror. She was impressed with the sudden, wild inconsequence which from time to time took Potter into a "mad and beautiful, almost surrealist dream where everything is a non sequitur." And she loved the sweet femininity of Mrs. Tiggy-Winkle, Jemima Puddle-Duck, Mrs. Tabitha Twitchit and Mrs. Tittlemouse, four creatures who seemed to sum up women's ability to nurture and put things to right.[13]

But the essence of Beatrix Potter that appealed most to Pamela was the "non explaining." Mary Poppins never explained and neither did Pamela. The reader had to discover where Mary went between sojourns with the Banks family. In one interview Pamela added, in an arch and infuriating way, that if she knew where Poppins went, she would have said. "She never explains, that is her chief characteristic, and I think it must be mine." Then, Pamela threw in an extra piece of *Alice in Wonderland*–like nonsense: "I don't not explain because I'm too proud to explain, but because if I did explain, where would we be?[14]

"Mary Poppins is never explicit. Perhaps she has Oriental blood. Did you know there is a Chinese symbol called pai? It has two meanings: one is explain, the other in vain. If the book were to be publicly translated [into Chinese—it had been privately], I think it would have to be called *Pai*."[15] The kind of writing she liked was done between the lines. "I like understatement, hints."[16] The Poppins stories all revolved around questions.

Pamela maintained there was never anyone remotely like Mary Poppins in her life. "Perhaps as a child I may have wished there were. I did not even visualize her. She just appeared fully armed with umbrella and carpetbag rather in the way that Pallas Athene sprang from the brow of Zeus."[17] But while Mary Poppins did not really refer to her, "there must be some element in me to which she hooked herself I suppose."[18]

One element was Pamela's apparent strictness. In Mary Poppins, the strictness was, she said, only skin deep, the wise woman's strictness. She denied that Poppins's authoritarianism was a masculine characteristic, and pointed out "how the men all turn to her," just as the Irish literary set all turned to Pamela. Mr. Banks, the Lord Mayor, the Butcher, the Baker, Bert and even the Park Keeper all had a special feeling for her.[19] "Men do fall in love with her."[20]

Mary Poppins's impact on men and appreciation by Mr. Banks is an expression of Pamela's own desires. The vanishing act of Poppins into the sky at the end of the first two books recalls the death of Travers Goff, a disappearance that Lyndon knew mysteriously as "Daddy going to God." Years later she felt the true impact when she gazed up at the night sky. Pamela visualized her father transforming into a star, just as Mr. Banks believed Mary Poppins's ascent into the sky on a merry-go-round was a new star. As an adult she could make another connection—in many Greek myths heroes turned into stars and constellations.

From the very first Mary Poppins book, it is clear that Mr. Banks has adopted many of the traits of Travers Goff. He harbors the same mixture of melancholy and gaiety. Like Goff, his abruptness is softened at odd times as he searches the sky for his favorite stars. Pamela knew Mr. Banks had "a strong inner urge to be an astronomer."

Pamela said Mr. Banks was the complement of Mary

Poppins because he "almost knows."[21] Without understanding anything consciously, he was involved in the adventures. Somewhere in his masculine nature, he understood Poppins's feminine being.[22] It was Mr. Banks, not Bert, who was Mary Poppins's opposite number, who sometimes subconsciously understood who she was.

Other characters from Pamela's childhood appear in the books, Nellie Rubina and Uncle Dodger from Bowral feature in *Mary Poppins Comes Back* as the couple who live in an ark and prepare the world for spring. The Goffs' maid, Kate, appears as Banks's former nanny. Miss Quigley, the sad woman with a music box in Bowral, was written into *Mary Poppins Comes Back* as a piano-playing governess who arrives and departs quickly after Mary Poppins's first disappearance.

Pamela also borrowed from her adult life—the Pegasus she won at a fairground at Tunbridge Wells and the woman she called the "Duchess of Mayfield," apparently a snob from the local village. In the "Balloons" chapter in *Mary Poppins Comes Back,* the illustrator Mary Shepard sketched herself, Pamela and her pet dog, Cu, all holding balloons with their real names on the side.

The Poppins adventures are crammed with other, incidental, autobiographical detail. Pamela wrote that "every Mary Poppins story has something out of my own experience... several record my dreary childhood penance of going for a walk. But against that is set the blissful forgiving moment at bedtime when I suddenly felt so very good. Of the glimpse when the fire was lit and the lamp glowed, of the nursery reflected upon the garden."[23]

Pamela always insisted that both she and Mary Poppins were servants who served a purpose. Pamela became a servant of a succession of gurus while Mary Poppins was both guru and handmaiden. She claimed that Mary had lived for centuries, that she was "the nurse of Beauty, Truth and Love" (an idea developed in the fourth Mary Poppins book, published in 1952) and that "she knows an awful lot about the stars,"[24] implying she might be part of the Pleiades or another constellation.

Like Mary Poppins, though, Pamela never became too pompous about it all. She continually stressed that her nanny represented the business of ordinary, everyday life. As Pamela said, "We cannot have the extraordinary without the ordinary. Just as the supernatural is hidden in the natural. In order to fly, you need something solid to take off from. It's not the sky that interests me but the ground...When I was in Hollywood the [script] writers said, surely Mary Poppins symbolizes the magic that lies behind everyday life. I said no, of course not, she is everyday life, which is composed of the concrete and the magic."[25]

Pamela claimed she scribbled the Mary Poppins stories on any bits of paper that came to hand at Pound Cottage, old bills and envelopes, even income tax demands.[26] But it's more likely that one evening, she showed Madge Burnand her old stories, pasted into scrapbooks.

Madge, who had many contacts in London publishing houses, might have encouraged Pamela to expand her articles into a book of short stories that Madge herself could try to sell. Pamela did say that the stories were taken by "a friend" to show publishers. And it was Madge who eventually found a buyer in Gerald Howe, head of a small publishing house in Soho. Howe asked to see the author.

Pamela insisted that her rules applied from the start. She told Howe she wanted a major role in the publication, suggested she would find an illustrator and would even choose the type—in consultation with him.[27] It was not a happy beginning. Pamela later remembered Howe as an enemy. He was, she said, only a very small publisher and she an "innocent," without an agent. She complained that the contract was "bad," but in any case it hardly mattered because the manuscript was sent to the United States, where more than ten publishers wanted to publish.[28] She settled with Eugene Reynal of Reynal & Hitchcock (later taken over by Harcourt Brace and her agent, Diarmuid Russell, AE's son in Chicago).

Pamela claimed she wanted the author of the book to be called "Anon," but "the publisher threw a fit and put my name on it.[29] I signed my name P. L. Travers originally because it seemed to me at the time that all children's books were written by women and I didn't want to feel that there was a woman or a man behind it, but a human being."

She definitely did not want to be "one more silly woman writing silly books. That's the idea, among publishers: "Oh yes, these curly headed women, they do it very nicely." It's never respected as literature, it's never given a high place in that sense."[30]

Mary Poppins was dedicated to her mother, who had died six years before. About a year later, the sequel was published by Lovat Dickson & Thompson.

The period charm of the books lies not just in the text but in the delicate drawings of Mary Shepard, the daughter of *Winnie-the-Pooh* illustrator Ernest Shepard and his artist wife, Florence. Pamela had wanted Ernest Shepard himself to illustrate the Mary Poppins books. She knew his cartoons and drawings from *Punch,* essential reading at Pound Cottage, partly because Madge's father had once been the editor. Ernest Shepard illustrated A. A. Milne's *When We Were Very Young* verses, which had appeared in *Punch* in 1923. Pamela never admitted she had asked Ernest Shepard, but in unpublished autobiographical notes Mary Shepard wrote: "In 1933 Pamela Travers approached my father with her first *Mary Poppins* book of the series, but he had to turn down the offer, very regretfully, because by this time he already had too much work in hand."

Pamela found his daughter's work by accident, through a Christmas card sent to Madge. Florence Shepard, who had died in 1927, was an old friend of Madge's. At Christmas 1932, her daughter, Mary Shepard, sent Madge a card which she had drawn herself. It showed a gloomy horse, resembling a rocking horse, ridden by a little knight holding a banner. He soared through the sky, just like Mary Poppins. In the snow underneath was a hoofprint.

There it stood among the many other Christmas cards on the old mantelpiece at Pound Cottage. "Of course it wasn't Leonardo, but I didn't need Leonardo," said Pamela in a later interview. "I was after a happy imperfection, innocence without naivete and, as well, a sense of wonder. The flying horse did indeed look dejected, as though it had just received bad news. But the rider was joyfully waving his banner, sunlight behind him, snow light before, a paradigm for the human condition, and, best of all, down in the castle courtyard the horse, as he took off into the air, had left in the snow a footprint!"[31]

She thought there was something happy about the drawing, imperfect though it was, and asked Madge to introduce her to Mary Shepard.[32] Shepard, then twenty-four, had just left the Slade School of Art. From the day she agreed to illustrate the books, the relationship of teacher and pupil was established. Shepard felt she had to do whatever Pamela asked her to do. Privately, she called herself Eeyore, after the downcast donkey in *Winnie-the-Pooh*.[33]

Pamela explained to interviewers that Mary Shepard "struggled nobly with the text."[34] She found her first drawings impossible. Pamela showed them to AE and Orage, who both suggested she should try another illustrator. But she persisted, taking Shepard for walks in Hyde Park, pointing out children as suitable models.

"We walked, like explorers... 'There,' I would say, and again 'Look, there!' And still Mary Poppins was not in the sketch book. Other young ladies. But not she."[35] At last they discovered the right look when Pamela found a Dutch doll—

like the one she had as a child—and gave it to Mary, "and suddenly it seemed as though she...came to life, tentatively, very imperfect, but some of the atmosphere of the book came through." At various times Pamela said she came across the doll in "an antique shop," while at other times she claimed the doll had been found in an attic. Shepard maintained that it was she who bought the Dutch doll, and that it was only then that she managed to get a suitable-looking Mary Poppins.

"Eeyore" was overruled on many suggestions. She wanted to show Mary Poppins standing in the fifth ballet position, feet turned out, the heel of one foot lined up with the toes of the other. As a compromise, Mary usually did appear with turned-out feet, but in first or fourth position, or up on half pointe. This was appropriate as the books are full of dancing. Mary dances, of course, but so do inanimate objects, from the trees to the stars. In her normal nanny mode, however, there was nothing balletic or theatrical about Poppins. Pamela even insisted to Mary Shepard that she "must have no figure."[36]

Later, Shepard's Mary Poppins drawings tended toward the comic, becoming too pert, and rather like the cartoons in *Punch*. Pamela believed Shepard was greatly influenced by *Punch* and the *Strand* magazine. Gerald Howe was very skeptical about Shepard, asking Pamela, "But has she any experience?" "Well, no, not really," she answered, "but then neither have I." "Mmm," Mr. Howe said and, when he was shown the scrapbooks with Shepard's first attempts, muttered, "Mmm" again.

Mary Shepard illustrated all the Mary Poppins books, completing the first two at her father's Surrey home. In 1937 she married the editor of *Punch*, E. V. (Edmund Valpy) Knox, whom she met through her father. After the war, when the Knoxes lived at Hampstead, "Evoe" Knox, as he was known, sat as a model for Mr. Banks in the fourth book, *Mary Poppins in the Park*.

Despite the obvious appeal of the Mary Poppins books for

children, Pamela always denied that she wrote with an audience in mind. "I wouldn't say *Mary Poppins* is a children's book
for one moment. It's certainly not written for children."[37] "I
never know why *Mary Poppins* is thought of as a children's
book," she grumbled to an audience of students at Radcliffe
College at Harvard in the mid-60s.[38] "Indeed I don't think
there are such things. There are simply books and some of
them children read. I don't think there is any such thing as a
children's book...I dislike the distinction very much. People
say "tell us the secret, how do you write for children?" I have
to say that I don't know because I don't write for children."

She knew she would be more readily accepted as a serious
writer if she was not labeled a children's writer, but there was
another, private reason for her insistence. She was writing to
please a man she was beginning to love—Francis Macnamara,
whom she described over the years as "an Irish poet," "the great
Irish critic," "a great friend," "very beautiful, fair, highly intellectual, loved by women and much liked and envied by men."
He had warned Pamela not to expect him to read *Mary Poppins*.
He hated children's books. She sent it to him anyway and he
read it, reluctantly. His reaction had a profound effect on her.
He wrote, "Why didn't you tell me? Mary Poppins, with her
cool green core of sex, has me enthralled forever."[39] Pamela
believed Francis Macnamara understood more of Mary Poppins
than anybody ever had, even more than she did herself.

The trouble was, Pamela did not understand Francis at all,
though he understood women perfectly. He knew what they
wanted to hear. Francis told them how he loved their minds,
so funny and bright and witty, and watched as their pupils
dilated as they grew more and more sure of their own charm
and wit, until suddenly they were laughing all the way to bed.
Other women he reserved for vestal virgin status, fantasizing
that they *were* actually virgins, his untouchable ones.

In her never-ending search for Mr. Banks, Pamela could not

have chosen a worse candidate than Francis Macnamara, but it was easy to see why she fell. Tall, golden-haired and blue-eyed, Francis was a wit, dandy, thinker, poet, sometimes riotous and great fun but more often slipping into a maudlin state. Francis Macnamara was expected to make a fortune or write a masterpiece. He did neither. Like most of his contemporaries, he was a boozer, happy in any pub from Chelsea to Galway Bay. There he flirted, said his daughter Nicolette Devas, in the manner of Fielding's Tom Jones.[40] He told anyone who would listen that he believed in "free love," that "women were a blank slate for a man to scribble on."

Francis did not have to struggle. He was the son of the high sheriff of County Clare, Henry Macnamara, who owned a great deal of land in the county including the market town, Ennistymon. His Australian mother was Edith Elizabeth Cooper, the daughter of Sir Daniel Cooper of Woollahra who made his fortune from gin distilling. She delivered all her children in a suite she booked specially for the purpose at Dublin's Shelbourne Hotel.

Francis was sent to Harrow and Oxford, but the temptations of a bohemian life were too great. He gave up his legal studies to mix with the Bloomsbury and Slade School of Art sets who congregated around Augustus John. He wrote a book of poems, *Marionettes*, in 1909, and became close friends with Augustus John, who wrote that Francis was "much given to solitary and gloomy cogitation" until, "warmed with what he called the hard stuff, became genial, popular and, the police were apt to think, dangerous."[41]

In 1907, Francis married a pretty Frenchwoman, Yvonne Majolier, whose sister was even prettier, according to Oliver St John Gogarty, who spread the word that "he slept with his sister-in-law and wife in the same room to save hotel expenses."[42] But in 1914, Francis abandoned Yvonne and their four children, including Caitlin (who was to marry Dylan

Thomas), for another woman. In the 1920s he married Edie McNeil, the sister of Augustus John's wife Dorelia. He liked to call Edie the "Virgin Goddess."

Francis was equally at home in Dublin, on his yacht, the *Mary Anne,* or at the family seat, Ennistymon House, a Georgian mansion overlooking a valley across to the town of Ennistymon, or at his flat in Regent's Square, London. Like many of his homes, the London flat was arranged with the compact look and efficiency of a ship. At Ennistymon and the nearby fishing village, Doolin, he was treated as the hereditary squire. His daughter Nicolette heard it rumored that Francis had fathered many illegitimate children "trying to produce a child worthy of himself."[43]

He met Pamela through the Irish literary network. Francis had idolized Yeats, and was the guest of Yeats and Lady Gregory at Coole Park during his honeymoon. Yeats offered to help him with his writing, but Macnamara did not take him up on the offer. Many years later, Yeats said, "Francis Macnamara had some poetic talent once but he lost it by not attending to the technique of verse."[44]

When Pamela sent Francis her Mary Poppins adventures in 1933, Francis was preoccupied with his next big affair, this time with a sensual young woman, Iris O'Callaghan. She lived on his yacht, then moored in Dover Harbor. Iris had pursued Francis like a stalker. Her great weapon was her youth. At twenty-two—less than half his age—she had him thoroughly flummoxed. She might have been almost illiterate, with a chaotic mind and a tendency toward screaming matches in which clocks and crockery were thrown and clothes cut up. But Iris, full-lipped and absolutely ripe, was a lethal weapon herself. While Pamela dreamed of life with Francis at Regent's Square, Iris had already moved in.

8

A Beautiful Night for a Death

There is an intersection in a woman's life where she feels like the many-armed Shiva, juggling the roles of mother and lover, daughter and wife, child and grandparent, the all-purpose female, all in one. She is the night nurse, gliding through the wards at midnight soothing anxious patients, wondering who is going to soften the blows when they fall on her. Between 1934 and 1939, Pamela became that woman. It began with AE's death.

Late in 1934, AE was suffering from bowel cancer. He did not suspect it, nor did his doctors. He was tired but not tired enough to reject an offer, which came though a bombardment of cables from Mary Rumsey, to visit the United States in December. Rumsey wanted him back in Washington, D.C., to lecture and advise on American rural communities. He might also give advice, she said, on the repatriation of the Mexican Indians.

AE was fascinated by the spiritual lives of American Indians. He always told his Irish acolytes that the Native Americans had religions of "a rather profound pantheistic character. Nature, its works, trees, earth, lakes, clouds, are Being to them." But he did want to warn his friends in America that he was four years older than the last time he saw them, not yet senile, but "out of harness." After one of the cables arrived, AE had asked Pamela's advice. She told him "Go at once." And he sailed on the *Aurania* on December 13, 1934.[1]

When he arrived in New York City two weeks later, he found Mrs. Rumsey had died. AE felt old, tired, finished himself. But once again, the Americans greeted him as a seer. He lunched with the president, Franklin D. Roosevelt, and his secretary of agriculture, Henry Wallace, who was, he told Pamela, "my special friend, a great man." John Collier, who had been commissioner of Indian affairs for two years, was overjoyed to see him back in the States. Early in January, Collier invited him to "go south to see the Indians on the reservations."[2]

Collier had seen Taos as a Red Atlantis that held secrets needed by the white world.[3] This impressed AE, who regarded Collier as a mystic who "loved the Indians and thinks I, as a pantheist and visionary, could get into the minds of the chiefs of the tribes and expound to them the cooperative policy which Collier thinks will strengthen the Indian organization." He thought it amusing that Collier, who had read his poems and his book *Candle of Vision*, "should have picked me as a kind of possible ambassador to the tribes." Collier wanted him to beguile the Indians "into safeguarding their ancient culture and industries by cooperative methods. I would love to see them...

but I feel too aged for such adventure, going so many thousand miles." In the end, he rejected the New Mexico adventure.[4]

For Pamela, AE had a great piece of news. During a trip to Chicago to see his son, Diarmuid, and meet his daughter-in-law, Rose, he had had lunch with the head buyer in the book department at the giant store Marshall Field's. As AE told Pamela, "She was the person whose enthusiasm for *Mary Poppins* gave your book a send off. The [commercial] traveler gave her a copy. She read it and ordered 500, to the traveler's astonishment. She actually sold over 1,100! I heard the book talked of with delight, to my great delight. I said with pride I knew you, and they wanted to know all about you." A special advertisement had been placed in the Chicago papers to promote the book which was "a best seller, Pamela dear. Hunger and cold fade from your horizon."

The Marshall Field's buyer assured him that if Pamela ever came to Chicago she must visit. The buyer would "show you around and get you to give talks which means dollars," he wrote to Pamela. Overall, Pamela thought AE's letters from the United States were tired and dispirited but she had no idea just how exhausted AE felt by February, when he sensed the full extent of his illness. The main problem was his frequent, urgent need to empty his bowels. He sailed home, again on the *Aurania,* arriving in mid-March 1935, and found new lodgings at 14 Tavistock Place, near Euston Station.

Pamela heard nothing more until late March, when AE wrote that he had "some inflammation in my insides and they are investigating me bacteriologically." His doctor and friend, Hector Munro, diagnosed dysentery and ordered a diet of milk, barley water and junket. Pamela did not trust Munro. She sent AE barley sugar and homemade treats, and worried even more, although his letters to her in April reassured her that he was "getting better rapidly."

Pamela's instincts took her to him in London. It was obviously very serious. AE was going to the lavatory every few minutes. At last, in despair, she brought him all the medicines she already had stashed away in the medicine cupboard for enteritis. They didn't work, but AE was cheered when she told him how long she had suffered enteritis without it getting worse. Pamela thought he looked gray, and she begged him to see a specialist.[5]

Her own doctor recommended one. AE promised that if he didn't get better in a week, he would see the man. In the meantime, Munro decided to call in a specialist himself. AE saw a surgeon in Cavendish Square who X-rayed him seven times and pronounced diarrhea in the lower bowel and constipation in the upper bowel. He amused the doctor by telling him then of the chakras, the seven spiritual centers of the body, to which the doctor replied, "Oh surely not, Mr. Russell."[6]

Pamela asked AE to stay at Pound Cottage, where she could nurse him in peace, among the early greenery and bluebells, but he felt "I must postpone all thoughts of shifting to the country until the doctor gives his decision."[7]

Although Pamela was living mainly in Pound Cottage with Madge, she traveled to London often to visit the office of the *New English Weekly,* then edited by Philip Mairet and directed by a board that included Jessie Orage, the American widow of its founding editor, A. R. Orage. During 1935 Pamela became close friends with Jessie, a tall, fair woman who was descended from generations of Connecticut clergymen and scholars.[8]

That year, Pamela sometimes stayed at Jessie's apartment when she visited London. For many years, Jessie kept a diary whose pages reveal much of Pamela's life for the next decade, sometimes in detail, but at other times in mysteriously allusive phrases. The diary shows that by April 26, 1935, Pamela and Jessie "talked all night," as they did again the next evening. When Pamela stayed at a hotel, the two women had breakfast together and Pamela often invited Jessie and her two young children, Dick and Anne, to stay at Pound Cottage. By the end of May, Jessie was writing in her diary "I like her so much."

The two women had been calling on AE in London who was, by then, very ill. On June 14, he signed a new will. A week later he traveled to Bournemouth by train with Dr. Munro and Charles Weekes, a friend from London who had been his publisher and agent. AE had decided to stay at Haven-hurst, the convalescent home of a Miss Phoebe Myers. He gave up his flat at Tavistock Place—the specialist thought he would be better out of London. At Havenhurst, overlooking the sea, he lay in a deck chair under the trees.

On July 4 he wrote Pamela a card, which she found an odd way of writing, for him,[9] saying, "I don't know how long I will be here. This is a lovely place but I wonder if I will ever get better. I am no further in spite of sun, sea air, kindness, that I often feel my holiday in this place is nearly over. Thanks, dear P, for the invitation [to Mayfield] but I can hardly rise out of a chair."[10]

AE began to write farewell letters to friends, asking every day if there was news for him from Yeats. There never was. He asked Munro to write to Pamela to tell her he needed "a serious operation for stoppage." By then the doctors had discovered secondary growths. Pamela rang Dr. Munro to learn that AE had only a month or so to live. Munro told her that the doctors had never examined AE's rectum until he got to Bournemouth. A new doctor had been called in, and after the examination said he must have a surgeon. It was the surgeon who broke the news, and he was so moved by the way AE received it that he broke down himself and had to leave the room.[11]

The news had come on July 9. The following day, AE underwent a colostomy operation at the Stagden Nursing Home. Pamela could bear it no longer. On Saturday she drove down from London to Bournemouth, where she booked a room at

Havenhurst. She was greeted by William Magee, AE's friend, another writer (who wrote under the name John Eglinton). "I'm glad you've come," Magee told her. "He keeps asking, and I can't make up to him for you."[12]

In the morning, she visited AE. Pamela sat on the chair by his bed and put her head on his pillow. He lifted his hand and put it on her hair and said, "You're a kind, sweet girl." She found him terribly changed. Pamela thought he looked like a prince, the gray of his beard changed to gold, "the face so slender and dear and the eyes so deep and blue. Oh...I could not restrain my tears." She managed to say she had come to be near him, that she would not leave him. AE asked for news of *Mary Poppins Comes Back*. She said she had brought it with her and would work at it there. She kissed his hand again, then left, asking if he would like her to look after his letters and he said, "Yes."

The next day she went to him, stood by his bed, and took down in pencil many farewell letters, including this letter to Henry Wallace:

My dear Henry,
This is to say good-bye to you. My illness can't be cured either by medical or surgical means. I do not know how long I have to remain here, possibly less than six months, death does not make much matter, we understand each other.[13]

She did not weep. The doctor asked if there was anything he could do. AE said, "Perhaps a little Chinese tea."

On Tuesday, back at Stagden, he asked if she had been swimming. They talked of tides. AE was in a much worse condition. He could not sign the letters, asking Pamela to sign on his behalf. They said their farewells. He said he wished he could have lived long enough to see her poems published. She said they would be dedicated to him. Pamela spoke to AE's doctor; death was imminent. AE asked, again, if there was any message from Yeats. Nothing. Pamela sent the poet a cable: "AE dying and daily looking for a word from you."

She was relieved when Con Curran, one of AE's Irish friends, arrived with news that the Irish Academy intended to recommend AE for the Nobel Prize. Until then, her only other support in Bournemouth had been Magee. She was on the phone each day to Charles Weekes, back in London.

On Monday and Tuesday nights she hardly slept, waiting for a telephone call from the nursing home. As he lingered, she felt herself thinking, "Oh be gone my darling, do not wait. Be gone!" A nurse from Stagden called on Tuesday night, but it was only a false alarm. Oliver St John Gogarty sent her a telegram on Tuesday: "Kindly say if I shall be in time to see my friend Russell if I leave this evening Dublin." She wired back, "Come quickly."

On Wednesday AE was given morphia and was mostly unconscious. Jessie heard that Pamela might need help and drove down from London in her black BSA sports car. Madge had also arrived. A telegram finally arrived that morning from Yeats: "Give my old friend my love." AE was asleep when Gogarty came. He woke at four.

Before he entered the room, Gogarty kissed Pamela's hands and said, "Be ever blessed with this!" Then he straightened himself, "already weeping," and went in. Before the door closed she saw Gogarty on his knees beside the bed, with his cheek on AE's hand.[14]

Outside in the sunny garden, his friends sat talking, waiting. Pamela looked up at a porch to see a bird wildly fluttering.[15] AE fell into a deep sleep. They all knew he would die that night. The nurses suggested they wait in a downstairs sitting room, and they assembled there: Pamela, Madge, Jessie, Con Curran, Charles Weekes, who had returned to Bournemouth, Gogarty, Magee and Hector Munro. Pamela begged to see him one more time, but they said it was better if she did not go into his room.

At about ten o'clock, Munro said AE's breathing was now "only automatic, he himself has flown." An hour later, Munro told them AE was "in the death rattle." Pamela felt sure that could not be right and asked Munro to return upstairs. The doctor came down once more to tell Pamela that AE had passed into a peaceful sleep. He died at twenty-five past eleven.

As if in church, Con Curran stood and said, "Let us now praise famous men." Each one stood, the circle of friends. The moon was very full. Pamela thought everything was bright and rich and lovely at its zenith. Jupiter and Venus were high in the heavens and the moon was streaming out to sea.

His body lay in the bed next morning. Pamela went up to the room. She had never before seen a dead man. He seemed noble, almost majestic. In his hands he held two sprigs of rosemary Pamela had taken to him from Pound Cottage. She asked the nurse if they could be buried with him. Simone Tery arrived from France and wanted his coffin opened to photograph him but Pamela was glad the funeral home would not allow it. Sean O'Sullivan made three sketches of AE's head, which, pressed into a pillow, resembled an ethereal halo. That night, Pamela followed the hearse to the mortuary. Charles Weekes's oversized wreath sat propped up in the back seat of her car. She saw that the moon was gold and full over the sea. She noticed the smell of death in the mortuary.

On Friday, Pamela and Con Curran traveled on the train with the coffin to Euston Station. Pamela remembered thinking, "I shall never travel again with my genius." In London, they were met by the Irish high commissioner and Helen Waddell, an academic and London friend of AE's. They went for a drink at Euston Station hotel where she had met him often. Brian Russell, AE's elder son who remained at loggerheads with his father until the end, joined them later on the ferry to Ireland. AE had said he wanted to be buried there.

His body was taken to Plunkett House, the old office of

the *Irish Statesman,* where he had worked for so long. The coffin lay in the hall; his friends came with flowers. On July 20, AE was buried at St. Jerome Cemetery. Yeats and de Valera walked in the long funeral procession. Frank O'Connor gave the oration, quoting from an Arabic poet: "He saw the lightning in the east and he longed for the east, he saw the lightning in the west and he longed for the west, but I, seeing only the lightning and its glory, care nothing for the quarters of the earth." Pamela had asked that words be spoken from Ecclesiasticus, the book of the Apocrypha: "Let us now praise famous men and our fathers that begat us...the people will tell of their wisdom, and the congregation will show forth their praise." The night he was buried was, she thought, as beautiful as the night he died. "Everything about him was lifted to its fullness and that is a triumph for a man."[16]

In the days and years that followed his death, Pamela sifted through her memories of AE, raking them as a Zen garden is raked, making patterns and sense. She wanted to make clear she "wasn't a fan of AE's. I did nothing for him. What does a flower do for the sun? Nothing, it just lives and grows by it."[17]

She wrote to her friends that as Orage gave rise to intellect in men, so AE gave rise to the spirit in them. Although she had grown closer to him in recent years, he had not spoken much of his feelings to her. Pamela thought he accepted her constant need of money and her bad health as "part of my karma" but found out from others that both made him anxious. She had taken "everything" to him and from him all her good had come, material and immaterial. He knew she loved him. She had tried to tell him but it was too difficult.

Pamela leant on Diarmuid Russell who arrived a week too late to see his father alive, and in August went to stay with Lota Law in Donegal for six weeks. She felt AE's presence everywhere in Breaghy and Dunfanaghy, that sense of a soul hovering above, not yet willing to fly away. Lota Law looked after her like a mother.

As C. S. Lewis said of grief, the emotion which so shocks the survivors is the sense of nervousness. She hadn't been well since he died, and feared her sense of loneliness. The worst moments, as every grieving child, husband or wife knows, come when drawers and wardrobes must be cleared, when everyday reminders are spread before you, the hairbrush with hair still entwined, little poems on yellowing paper, safety pins carefully saved in a tin, a scarf that still smells of a neck you once loved to kiss.

When Pamela sorted out his clothes and personal possessions she found a little reel of black cotton and a needle and realized how often he must have mended his own things. "It was simply heart breaking. He never let people do things for him. He was very contained and aloof...I find myself so often thinking, "I must tell AE" or "I must ask AE" and then—I realize!"[18]

She no longer felt afraid of her own death, unless it might be a sudden disastrous one, with no time to compose her heart or mind. After AE died, she had terrible nightmares about him, as she did about her mother after her death. In the nightmares he was always ill and sad. But one night she dreamed he made her a little tucked apron. Then, when he found out she was cold, he produced a warm cloak, green, embroidered with rough lines of blue. This, she thought, was exactly what he did in life. AE wrapped up his friends warmly, but also had the gift of giving cold, stark comfort, the kind which said, "It's your battle, you must fight it without weapons, you may lose but I can't help you."

She bundled up copies of his collected poems for the nurses at Stagden—women whom she found full of tenderness. Pamela had hoped she could make a selection of his essays for magazines, but AE's friend, the writer Monk Gibbon, had started something similar while AE was alive. Although AE didn't like it, his son Diarmuid felt that Gibbon should have the first chance to compile the memoir.

Yeats had suggested to Pamela that she should prepare a special selection of his Irish writings but she believed that this would step on Gibbon's rights. Diarmuid asked her to write AE's biography, but again, she felt unsure if she could do it well enough. How could you tell the "story of a soul," as she saw his life?

On her first visit back to Dublin after his death, she took lavender from the garden at Pound Cottage and planned to sprinkle it on his grave, but couldn't tell which it was. There was still no headstone.[19] Eventually a stone was erected, engraved with the lines: "I moved among men and places and in living I learned the truth. At last I know I am a spirit and that I went forth in old time from the self ancestral to labours yet unaccomplished."

By late October 1935, after long days and nights spent at the typewriter, Pamela finished *Mary Poppins Comes Back* in an exhilarating burst of three weeks. It was published in both the United States and England in November, in time for the Christmas trade. Madge thought it was a better book than the first.

Eugene Reynal, the American publisher, had been in England in October and was "kind and generous and touchingly gentle to me." He asked her how much she needed to live on and assured her he would try to boost *Mary Poppins*'s sales in America. "And it wasn't just bluff and hard headed business but something real and quick and human and generous."

Now, at thirty-six, Pamela felt fatherless, for there was "nobody to whom one may go for the deeps of life and being." She wrote to friends that "AE would expect us to do now for ourselves what he did for us. And I will try to do that."[20]

9

The Crossing of Camillus

Only a woman as tough and brave as Ellie Morehead would embark on a sea voyage from Australia to England at the age of ninety. Aunt Ellie was determined, though, to attend the wedding in London of a great niece. She looked like a little old crone, shrunk to the height of Pamela's shoulder, when the two women greeted one another in London in 1936.

Pamela showed her great aunt the first of her Mary Poppins books, typed on the typewriter that Ellie herself had given her. The old lady stroked the cover, opened the crisp pages, then read the dedication to "My Mother." She turned away so

Pamela could not see her face. Ellie's eyes reddened and her
voice was unusually low when she looked again at Pamela.
Meg would have been pleased, the old woman said. Ellie liked
the cover. Then in her old grumpy way she asked, was the
inside as good?

Ellie Morehead returned to Australia the next day. From
her home in Darling Point, Sydney, she wrote one last letter
to her sister Jane, then living in England. The date was September 24, 1937. The letter ended: "I love you all. I have had
a long and happy life. God bless you. Goodnight." The last
wavering strokes of her pen seemed to drift away like a plume
of smoke. Ellie had died as her hand left the paper.[1]

In her will, the old lady had been generous to Pamela. As
well as her equity in the Colonial Sugar Refining Company
and the Commercial Banking Company, Ellie left Pamela a
share in all her real estate and personal estate. Now Pamela
had three secure sources of income: the money from Aunt
Ellie, royalties from her Mary Poppins books, and regular pay-
ments from the articles she wrote as a freelance journalist for
the *New English Weekly*.

She had been an occasional contributor to the journal since
1934, but in 1936 Pamela increased her output to three or four
articles a month. Under the bylines "P. T." and "Milo Reeve,"
she reviewed many plays and films, from *A Midsummer Night's
Dream* to *Peter Pan,* from *Snow White* to *King Lear*. It was the age
of the great stars of the London stage. She saw Ralph Richard-
son as Othello, Leslie Howard as Romeo and Alec Guinness as
Hamlet. Dismissive of Chekhov, Eugene O'Neill, Noël
Coward, the films of Walt Disney and many children's writers,
including A. A. Milne, Pamela praised most of Ibsen's plays
except *Peer Gynt,* which she dismissed as "a jumble." Her sharp
rebukes reveal an immature critic's voice—the need to sound
certain and authoritative at the expense of genuinely helpful
or insightful comments. The only writers she consistently

praised were G. B. Shaw and T. S. Eliot. By then, Eliot was a consultant and contributor to the *New English Weekly*.[2] Glimpses of a more personal, everyday world peeped into her infrequent essays. She wrote of motor shows and dog shows (did she display her hound, Cu?), a picnic in winter, or her clapped out BSA sports car with its hole in the carpet and bent nail in the door.

With her new streams of income, Pamela had enough to buy the freehold of Pound Cottage from the Glynne Estates. Not only did she now own her own house, but she decided, like Mrs. Banks, to hire help. Pamela knew that little Doris Vockins, who lived with her big family a ten-minute walk away, was about to leave school. She went to see her mother. Doris, who was fourteen in 1935, left school on a Friday and started work with Pamela as a daily maid the next Monday morning.

Doris was impressed by Miss Travers and Miss Burnand, as she called them. Ever so happy, they seemed, and Miss Travers so pretty with her curly hair and lipstick and smart-looking slacks. Doris had a long list of duties. She started at 9 A.M. First there was the general housework, the cleaning, the fires to be lit in winter. The oil lamps and oil heaters had to be cleaned every day. There was no electricity. She pumped up the geyser in the bathroom for the hot water. Doris swept around the two big armchairs near the fireplace, then cleaned the long oak-paneled table. Cu kept her company, trotting around on his squat little legs.

The mail and newspapers came each day; the wind-up phone rang often with news from London. The kitchen was Madge's domain. Doris was fascinated by how much pasta Miss Travers and Miss Burnand got through. The milk came from Mr. Firrell's Forge Farm nearby. Miss Travers always made an early start with her writing. Doris lit the fire in Pamela's new study, added to the house in 1936. "Bring me coffee at eleven," she instructed

Doris. At lunchtime, she liked a whiskey. Every morning she sent Doris outdoors to tickle the carburetor of her car.

Often Pamela talked of America. Doris never really knew where her boss was going next, or why she was going, only that she seemed to be forever traveling. When Madge and Pamela were both away, Doris would check on the cottage, making sure the locks were secure, running a duster around the furniture.[3]

In January 1936, Pamela joined Jessie and her children on a skiing trip in Switzerland. Jessie's diaries at the time reveal a new intensity in her relationship with Pamela. The diaries are not proof of intimacy, but there are many allusions to a lesbian relationship. From 1936, these are not specific and could refer just to a close friendship. Later, in the 1940s, the references are specific but still not conclusive proof.

In the spring and summer of 1936, Pamela and Jessie together attended meetings in London conducted by Jane Heap, a lesbian disciple of Gurdjieff who confided in friends "I'm not really a woman." Heap, who wore scarlet lipstick and masculine suits, and looked a little like Oscar Wilde, was an American who had edited the radical arts magazine *Little Review* in Chicago with her lover Margaret Anderson. Both women had then studied with Gurdjieff in Paris, but Heap had recently moved to London, on his instructions.

Heap and Anderson, along with their lesbian entourage, had been fascinated with Gurdjieff since they met him in New York in the 1920s. He in turn was fascinated by them, and in January 1936 formed a special lesbian group in Paris called the Rope, whose members and associates included Margaret Anderson, Georgette Leblanc and Elizabeth Gordon. (After Gurdjieff said he had metaphorically roped them together, Kathryn Hulme, one member of the group, said "We knew... even from the first day what that invisible bond portended. It was a rope up which, with the aid of a master's hand, we might be able to inch ourselves from the cave of illusory being which we inhabited. Or it was a Rope from which, with sloth and lip service, we could very well hang ourselves.")[4]

Unlike the members of the Rope, both Pamela and Jessie loved men, but their relationships with men were often frustrating in different ways. When they became close friends, both were feeling the loss of important men in their lives: Jessie with Orage's death and Pamela with the death of AE a year later.

Jessie Orage's diaries show that she spent many days with Pamela in 1936, going to the theatre and movies, having dinner, taking holidays together, or just talking, often all through the night. In May, Jessie went shopping for Pamela, who wanted some coral. Jessie wrote in a diary entry: "She wants to wear it for her melancholia." A few days later, after Jessie found just the right piece, a coral hand token she bought from a man in Chancery Lane, she went down to Pound Cottage for a "delightfully mad afternoon and evening with Pamela." Next day, they walked in the woods in the rain. And the day after, "Pamela and I did not get up 'til late."

In the middle of the year, Pamela's American publisher, Eugene Reynal, suggested she visit New York, Detroit and Chicago to promote *Mary Poppins*.[5] Jessie accompanied Pamela to Southampton, where she boarded the *Queen Mary*. Jessie wrote in her diary, "I shall miss P. terribly." Pamela rang Jessie from the ship and then the United States quite often, with Jessie feeling "great excitement" at each call. Pamela returned in December, ill with pleurisy, almost too sick to walk from the boat. In her luggage, she had an extravagant present for Jessie: a luxurious evening cloak. That New Year's Eve, Jessie and Pamela went to King's Hotel in Brighton. Jessie's diary records: "P. and I have a room overlooking the sea. At 12, P. rang Madge and sang 'Auld Lang Syne' into the phone."

Madge was hardly a disinterested party in this relationship. In 1937, tensions grew among the three women. The entries

in Jessie's diaries for this year reveal a complex web of emotions and references to other tumultuous relationships in
Pamela's life. In May, Jessie drove down to Pound Cottage to
find "P. not very well having had an emotional week. Damn
Madge. I've always been suspicious of her temper and the cru-
elty of her nostrils."

Jessie recorded that Pamela had suffered several "dizzy
spells" in June. On June 29, "P. and I drove back to London.
P. seemed happy but became more and more silent, not completely, "til after she rang Madge." After a summer holiday at
a beach in Ireland, during which Jessie squabbled with Pamela,
the two women met Madge in Dublin where Jessie also fought
with Madge. The next month, Jessie wrote, "P. told me many
things about herself she'd never told me. It pleased me very
much...we talked in front of the fire. I understand many
things now."

Those many things remain frustratingly hidden, but it may
have been that Pamela told of her love for Francis Macnamara
who, in 1937, succumbed to marriage for the third time. His
new bride was the woman who had been his sexy young house
guest in London, Iris O'Callaghan. The couple went to live in
Ireland. Francis was a serial lover who compartmentalized his
affairs, ignoring the trail of broken hearts and adopting the
position that each affair was just a game, and that his women
should take them as lightly as he did himself. Each game ended
more messily than he hoped. Pamela cared for him a great
deal more than he ever knew. She carried a torch for Francis
Macnamara for the rest of her life, forgiving him, preserving
him in her mind as the perfect man, though she knew all along
he was a Don Juan.[6]

Despite her intimate relationship with Jessie, the loss of Macnamara represented a serious passing of hope for Pamela, and

left a great emptiness in her spirit. His place was filled to some extent by Gurdjieff, whom Pamela first met with Jessie in March 1936 when the women took the boat train to France, visited the vacant Prieure at Fontainebleau, then drove to Paris to meet Gurdjieff in Paris at his favorite Café de la Paix.

As Jessie wrote in her diary, "Gurdjieff didn't know me at first. We went to his flat...Margaret, Georgette and Elizabeth Gordon there. Same old ritual, drinks to idiots etc., very good food cooked by G....Pam and I did all the talking. I found I felt quite indifferent to him."

Pamela, though, was entranced. Here, in the Gurdjieff work she had already studied with Heap, was a philosophy that appealed to both her intellect and senses for different reasons. It satisfied many parts of her, from her need to set herself apart from others to her need to find relief from dreadful anxiety. The Gurdjieff way was clearly not for the strugglers of the world. Firstly, he demanded money and secondly, he insisted on more self-absorption and more time than strugglers could afford. Gurdjieff attracted the emotionally needy and most of all, he was a magnet for artists of all kinds, among them Georgia O'Keeffe, T. S. Eliot, Frank Lloyd Wright and Lincoln Kirstein, the rich associate and backer of the choreographer George Balanchine.

Pamela was a snob. The exclusivity of the Gurdjieff work for the fortunate few appealed to her. There were other attractions: the emphasis Gurdjieff placed on studying oneself, and his promise of peace partly through dance. The first rule of his work was to know thyself, to practice deep inner observation. The student was to ask, "Do I actually know myself in the here and now, know myself with objectivity?" The Gurdjieffians constantly practiced turning in on themselves. Negative emotions had to be banished as they worked daily on their inner health in order to become "conscious" and transformed. Students took mental pictures of themselves, watched their sensations, moods, emotions, thoughts. The idea was to experience non-desire over desire. Such introspection suited Pamela perfectly.

All this self-study ran in tandem with Gurdjieff's ritualistic dances and movements. He had about a hundred of these, derived from sources in Turkey, Turkestan, Tibet and Afghanistan. The dances represented a kind of meditation in action or body semaphore. Among them were six obligatory exercises as well as dervish dances for men and prayers in motion. Throughout his life, Gurdjieff affected the humble persona of "an old dancing teacher," but that affectation was close to the mark.

In her soul, Pamela was a dancer, too, not trained but instinctive. She found the calmness she needed as she executed Gurdjieff's sacred dances in various halls of London. Through dance, she met and became close friends with Gurdjieff-trained student teachers, among them Rosemary Nott, who was also a pianist, and Jessmin Howarth. Pamela eventually called Nott her mentor; she loved to hear her play for the movements, particularly the obligatory exercises.

The Gurdjieff work undoubtedly helped calm her mind to some extent, but Jessie's diaries show that Pamela remained in a state of high tension through many of the next few years. She appeared to be in a double bind with Madge Burnand. Both women needed one another, yet hurt one another over and over again. At the end of 1937, Madge sailed on the *Queen Mary* for a long break in the USA, but by mid-May of 1938 Jessie's diary notes, "Pam very depressed. She dreads M.'s return." A week later, "M. is putting her through it all right." In October, Pamela visited Jessie in London and after dinner, "cried and cried." Jessie thought she was crying because Madge had taken a job that meant leaving Pound Cottage, although she was not specific about the place Madge was to move to.

At the cottage, Doris knew nothing of all this anguish. But

one day, she was astonished to find Miss Burnand had packed up and left. She hadn't told Doris she was going, and Pamela never mentioned Madge's name to Doris again.[7]

Now, even Doris was to be drawn into Pamela's unhappiness and uncertainty. For several years, Pamela had observed how easy Jessie was with her children, how a mother and her child can be even closer than lovers, snuggling into one another, giggling, hugging, sharing nothing specific yet everything.

Pamela quietly, without saying why, arranged for a new bedroom to be built at the cottage, next to her study. She called on Mrs. Vockins up the road. Pamela summoned up all her acting talent. In her most persuasive and charming way, she suggested that as Mr. and Mrs. Vockins had *seven* children, and because Doris was already working at Pound Cottage every *day,* would it not be an excellent idea if she took one of the children off her hands, and formally adopted Doris?

The plan failed dismally. The Vockinses just wouldn't have it. And Doris herself told her she definitely did not want to live at Pound Cottage, despite Pamela's offer that she would show her the world. To that, Doris replied: "I don't want to see the world!"

On January 13, 1939, Jessie's diary noted: "Tempestuous day. P. sacked Doris. P. and I rowed again, she is so snide, rude to my children, and flares at them."[8]

Pamela now felt in desperate need of someone to love and control. Her sisters in Australia meant little to her. She had no parents, no permanent lover, no children, and even Madge had gone. The adoption fantasy remained firmly in her mind. She told Jessie, who wrote in her diary in February 1939: "P. is disappointed because I didn't support her idea of adoption wholeheartedly."

All through spring the women talked of the plan, Jessie trying not to tell Pamela she thought the scheme quite harebrained. Her growing obsession that she must have a baby coincided with exterior stresses—the certainty that there was going to be a war involving all of Europe. Jessie's diary entries began to alternate between the fateful dates of Hitler's advance, and the minutiae of life in Pound Cottage and Jessie's own home in London. The escalating tensions before the declaration of war were also recorded in a poetic and dreamy way by Pamela, in a series of articles she wrote for the *New English Weekly*. From as early as 1937, when she reported on how Edward VII's coronation was celebrated in her village, Pamela had chronicled the doings of Mayfield for the *New English Weekly*. She referred to Mayfield as either as "a Sussex Village" or "M—." In the series, subtitled "Our Village," she made the personal universal, gently mocking the fusspots of Mayfield while painting a picture of an English country town as romantic as a Constable landscape. Only an outsider, an Australian who had dreamed of the "Mother" country, could capture the essence of a Sussex village as well.

On the day war was declared, Pamela clambered into her BSA and drove to Mayfield "to see how the village was taking it." The place was in turmoil, "worse than market day." The butcher's boy ran past her shouting that an air raid was in progress. She watched in alarm as the tobacconist—a warden—hurried along the street in a waterproof cape, clanging a dinner bell. It turned out to be only a fire at the Frogling Farm. A local boy, John Eldridge, stood at his front gate to be greeted by two passersby: "You'd better get indoors, war has been declared!"

The frenzy of those days had a parallel in the messy breakdown of the friendship between Pamela, Jessie and Madge, who was to make a reappearance in Jessie's diary that autumn. By the end of September, Jessie and Pamela were squabbling at Pound Cottage whenever Jessie came to stay. Jessie wrote: "I must be independent even if it means getting a house of my own." The next month, when the three women met for a drink at a hotel, Madge was very reserved and silent. Then, in an explosion of awful anger, Pamela yelled "Madge, you're a goddamned bitch!" The outburst was followed by ghastly scenes, with Jessie recording that Madge actually hit Pamela and Jessie.

Pamela by now was determined to adopt a baby, despite Jessie repeatedly telling her it was "a crazy idea." On October 23, Pamela received a letter from Dublin telling her a certain infant was ready for collection. She wrote of the journey in the *New English Weekly,* not revealing the reason for traveling from London, with its "sandbags, blackened windows and carefully staged humiliating atmosphere of Safety First," to the quiet, diurnal and "comfortably realistic Dublin" with its "soft radiant light." In such a place it was "impossible not to melt into whatever is one's true self."[9]

Pamela had first gone to Ireland in 1924 believing it was her own spiritual homeland, so it was hardly surprising that she would return there fifteen years later to pick up a piece of Ireland for herself. Her adopted baby was not to be just any old Irish child, but the grandson of a great friend of Yeats, the publisher of AE's works and a cousin of Francis Macnamara.

The baby's surname was Hone. His grandfather, Joseph Maunsell Hone, was a central figure in the Anglo-Irish literary network, Ireland's most distinguished literary biographer. He had founded Maunsell and Company in 1905, which published works by Yeats, Synge and AE, and knew all the writers worth knowing, among them Gogarty, AE and Hubert Butler. In 1939, when he was in his late fifties, Hone had written *The Life of George Moore,* and he was soon to write the first biography of Yeats.

Francis Macnamara often came to stay with Hone at his big

old house at South Hill, Killiney, on the coast south of Dublin. The home, inherited from his wealthy father, was open to all the literary clan. With its five bedrooms and three living rooms, there was more than enough room for Hone, his American wife Vera, their three children and all their friends. Madge Burnand, who knew Hone through her father, stayed at South Hill in the 1920s and Joseph and Vera Hone's daughter, Sally, remembered that Pamela was a houseguest from the late 1920s. Joseph liked her very much, Vera less so.

The baby Pamela was to adopt was more like Vera in personality than Joseph, who was as cautious and canny with money as Vera was extravagant. For many years the Hones spent their winters at the Grand Hotel in Gardone, near Genoa. Vera had accounts at all the best shops in Dublin. When the parcels and boxes arrived home Joseph complained, "You're spending far too much money!" Although he was sociable, and amusing, Hone harbored a pessimistic, conservative streak. He gave his two sons names that had been in the Hone family for centuries. The elder son was called Nathaniel, after the best known of all the Hones, an eighteenth-century painter.

Nathaniel, shortened to Nat, lived life recklessly but with a certain style and great charm. He went to New College, Oxford, then in 1933, when he was twenty-one, inherited about £10,000. From then on, Nat lived the life of a rich young man about town.[10] He joined the Royal Air Force Volunteer Reserve, planning to take a group of Irish Republicans to fight for Franco in the Spanish Civil War. Or so he said. The plane he was piloting did not fly beyond Biarritz. His son wrote of the adventure: "He and the rest of the bibulous Irish brigade spent a week at the Imperial Palace instead, ambushing the champagne before flying back to Dublin."

Nat was a publican's nightmare, with a habit developed in the 1930s of moving around Dublin's cocktail bars with a loaded .45 under his coat, blasting the tops off the brandy and Benedictine bottles.[11] One day in the King's Head and Eight Bells in the Kings Road, Chelsea, Nat met a nurse—Bridget Anthony, one of twelve siblings from a poor County Kilkenny family. Like her own father, the pretty Bridget (nicknamed Biddy) was very fond of a drink. She married Nat in August 1936. Biddy, a Catholic girl, was already pregnant.

When little Joe was born six months later, Nat and Biddy lived in comfort in Surrey. It seemed as though the inheritance would last forever. The next year, Nat and Biddy had another baby, Geraldine. Soon after, Biddy became pregnant yet again, this time with twins. She decided to go home to Ireland, to give birth in Dublin. Anthony Marlow Hone and John Camillus Hone were born on August 15, 1939. By now, the strain of raising four children on an ever-diminishing pile of money was beginning to tell. In the summer of 1939, with the war between Germany and Britain so close, the Hones decided the family must scatter. Little Joe Hone, only two and a half, was sent to his grandparents at Killiney. Grandmother Vera Hone wanted to bring him up herself, but old Joseph, still fussing about money, said he would not allow it.[12] Instead, he was unofficially adopted by Joseph's friend Hubert Butler and his wife, Peggy, at their family home in Kilkenny in the southeast of Ireland.[13]

Biddy had taken the twin boys straight from the Dublin hospital to the home of Joseph and Vera Hone. By now, and not surprisingly, Joseph was beginning to get rather fed up with all these children.[14] But, they muttered, "Biddy, poor Biddy" could not cope, emotionally or financially. And Nat had told everyone, straight out, that he could no longer afford to keep all the children.[15] Little Geraldine was sent to Biddy's parents. But who would take twins? Joseph Hone knew someone who might take them off his hands—Pamela Travers, AE's close friend and Macnamara's castoff.

Nat's sister Sally Hone, then twenty-five, remembers the scene when Pamela called. The baby boys, Camillus and Anthony, lay in two separate adult-sized beds in a guest room. Camillus was much better looking. Pamela gazed down on each one. Joseph said to Pamela: "Take two, they are only small." Biddy also tried to orchestrate the choice. "You want to have Anthony, he is a gorgeous boy." Camillus was crying. Anthony was not.[16]

On October 28, Jessie wrote in her diary "P. rang up from Dublin at 12. She is coming back Tuesday without the baby. She didn't like him enough." A fortnight later, Pamela confided in Jessie. She liked Camillus much more than his twin, the baby she was supposed to take. Just to be sure, Pamela had both babies" horoscopes prepared by an astrologer, an Edward Johndro of Fresno, California. The astrological chart for Camillus concluded: "All in all, it would be a rare thing to find better cross rays between a child and its <u>OWN</u> mother. So I would say, by all means, ADOPT HIM."

Little Anthony was now dispatched to Biddy's mother and Camillus made the crossing to England, with Pamela, in mid-December 1939. From then on, Pamela wore a wedding ring, a simple gold band signifying respectability. Five days before Christmas, "P. had bad night as Camillus screamed all the time." The doctor came, but "she now talks of sending him to a babies' home in Tunbridge Wells." Jessie told Pamela it would be a mistake to send Camillus away as he'd settle down soon. On Boxing Day, though, he yelled constantly. Jessie recorded in her diary: "Poor Pam. P. asked my advice about sending him to TW to get his feeding right and have the rash on his face looked after. P packing for Camillus."

A few months before Camillus moved to Pound Cottage, young evacuees from London had begun to arrive in Mayfield, complete with their little food kits of corned-beef tins and condensed milk. Pamela heard them complain of the " 'orrible quiet down there. The condensed milk stood unopened on larder shelves, for, at the end of the year, it seemed the war was not going to arrive. On Christmas Day, Mayfield tucked into the usual Norfolk chickens and Stiltons.

The weeks of the phony war passed. While the locals blew the froth off their pints in the public bar, declaring there would be no real war, the main street was blacked out at night. That was fine. The locals always went home in the dark anyway. New rabbit guns could be seen in the saddler's window. The petrol boy from the garage was in uniform and everyone tried on his steel helmet. They all had gas masks, too.

By early 1940 Mayfield's comfy retired major, a gentle soul who had canvassed the village in search of the conservative vote, was appointed chief warden. Sporting new trousers, he ordered the villagers to black out those damned windows, immediately. Each day, the young men disappeared from the streets and shops and houses. Pamela saw that the ironmonger's boy and the lad who drove the milk lorry had gone, "as leaves drop from a tree."

Khaki filled the public bar and the saloon and leant with "a rattle of brass against the counter, elbowing out the regulars." Pamela's old gardener had returned from France after a series of adventures and limped the three miles to Pound Cottage to see her. They toured the garden, Pamela apologizing for the daisies and clover on the lawn. "Dainty, that's what they are," he said, "let them bide." And, still, Mayfield stood serenely under "the great marquee of heaven."[17] The romantic image was washed away, eventually, by the sheer number of evacuees and the troop buildup in the area. Without a special pass, it was hard to get anywhere closer to the coastline of England than Mayfield.[18]

All through winter and early spring, Camillus remained

fretful, in and out of hospital at Tunbridge Wells. On April 18, when he was eight months old, he was returned to Pound Cottage, still tiny for his age, still not able to sit up or turn over. Two days later he was back in the hospital again.

Jessie and her children spent most of their time at Pound Cottage, but in March Jessie told Pamela it was impossible to continue the arrangement. They fought more often than not. Jessie longed for her homeland.

By May, troops were billeted around Mayfield, patrolling the streets. German planes flew overhead; then bombs were dropped on nearby Ticehurst. A few days after the Germans marched into Paris in June, Jessie told Pamela she planned to leave England. She and her children would sail soon for New York. Pamela was "very sad," Jessie wrote in her diary. A couple of days later she hoped to take Pamela too, but when the S.S. *Washington* sailed on July 7 with Jessie, her children Ann and Dick, and 150 other mothers and children, Pamela was not on board. Jessie wrote once more in her diary: "Darling Pam, so broken up and sad." Pamela thought she should stay, although she yearned to follow Jessie.

At the dock in New York Jessie was greeted by a Gurdji-effian group, including Rosemary Nott and Jessmin Howarth. By the end of July, she opened her first letter from Pamela— "very distressing, if only I could get her over." On August 3, another letter followed. This time, Pamela was on her way, via Canada. By now Mayfield was part of the front line, with planes streaming in from Europe and battles raging overhead. Some aircraft came down in and around Mayfield. Pamela asked the local real estate agent to rent out Pound Cottage, indefinitely.

10

Through the Door to Mabeltown

The ship carrying Pamela and Camillus to Canada sailed with three hundred children on board, almost all evacuees from London's East End. They were to cross the Atlantic in convoy with seven other passenger ships, three destroyers and a battleship. At the Liverpool wharf, before they boarded the big ship, Pamela stroked the ground. "I must feel it once more," she said, "just once more."[1] For two days, they stood at anchor at Liverpool; U-boats had been spotted nearby. Several women, distraught at the sight of land, begged to be taken ashore. The children had wept as they squeezed their parents good-bye. But on the second day, the novelty of their new surroundings dried their tears. The boys and girls swarmed all over the railings, scampered across the deck. Some even tried to climb the rigging. They had no idea how dangerous the journey might be.

By August 1940, thirty-five hundred British children had been evacuated to Australia, New Zealand and Canada. Escape from southeast England seemed the sensible thing to do, but many might have been safer at home. In early July 1940 one of the first evacuee ships, the *Arandora Star,* was attacked by U-boats in the Atlantic. There were no casualties among the children on board, but from then on, the British Admiralty decided all ships carrying evacuees should sail in slow convoy. In late July, a ship taking children to Canada was attacked by submarines. At the end of August, after Pamela's ship had sailed, another evacuee ship, the *Volendam,* left Clyde. It was torpedoed 215 miles out to sea. Over three hundred children were on board that vessel, but none died. On September 17, the ship *City of Benares* sailed from Liverpool to Canada. It was torpedoed in the Atlantic with the loss of 260 lives, among them one hundred children.[2]

In a series of articles called "Letters from Another World," Pamela wrote of her journey for the *New English Weekly*. In the first, she compared the convoys with their fragile cargo to the voyages of many *Mayflowers*, each traveling from the known world to a new life of which they knew nothing except "a promise of hope."

She felt overwhelmed by her responsibility to Camillus and to the other children from Mayfield and Tunbridge Wells she was escorting to Canada. The adult passengers, she thought, had little to say, little to offer. Among them, though, she found someone she could talk to, a woman with a gentle voice. Often she was bent over a sketch pad. Gertrude Hermes was an artist, quite a good one. "Call me Gert," she told Pamela. The women sometimes teamed up with two of the ship's officers.[3]

The first officer liked the poetry of T. S. Eliot, whose "Burnt Norton" seemed to speak of wartime. One day, when he mentioned "the still point of the turning world," Gert picked up her pencil and began to draw. She told an inquisitive child she was only sketching "the still center." What did she mean, the still center? Gert just smiled.[4]

Each night the little band of travelers tried to decipher the crackly shortwave BBC radio broadcasts reporting the bombing raids over England. By day, they listened for warning blasts that meant lifeboat drill—six blasts for mustering and seven if U-boats were sighted. Pamela felt dreadfully guilty that she was not facing up to the war in England. By saving the children, she felt she was missing her own life. She told Gert she felt as if her body was made of the woods and rivers of England. The worse the news of the war, the worse her body felt.[5]

The ship docked at Halifax, which smelled of pine—a sweet relief after all the salty air. Pamela and Camillus took the train to Montreal, spent a week at the Windsor Hotel, then on August 30 flew to LaGuardia Airport, New York, Pamela arguing all the way with a finance journalist about the concept of social credit, which at least distracted her from the awful storm that meant the journey lasted five hours instead of the usual two.[6]

LaGuardia had been a rubbish dump when she last saw it in 1936. Now, all around the airport were the wild shapes of the World's Fair and there before her, across the Triborough Bridge, as familiar as a returning dream, lay the "delicate airy towers and those tongues of flame turned stone that are Manhattan." Pamela wrote in the *New English Weekly* that she loved the roar and hum of Manhattan, loved to feel part of a band of poets and artists in New York "on a mission, who have it in their power effectively to join the hands across the sea."[7]

That was the propaganda, but in truth, Pamela was miserable, despite her new but increasingly intimate friendship with

Gert. The big reunion with Jessie Orage went badly. Both women were agitated, unsettled and missing England. Pamela rented an old fashioned apartment at 142 East 52nd Street and hired a Finnish maid, Pauline.

Pamela, Gert and Jessie met, talked, then recognized that the ground rules had changed utterly. The three women made an uncomfortable triangle. In October 1940, Jessie felt she had told her diary too much. Later, she ripped out the pages she had written over ten days, but left intact the words "I'm free somehow, thank God." Gert, she confided, was the cause of her freedom. A few weeks later, the three women met for a drink—"a very funny situation," wrote Jessie.

Jessie never planned to stay on the East Coast, but to drive with her children to New Mexico to join a community of Orage and Gurdjieff followers, among them Jessmin Howarth. She was also in search of the architect Frank Lloyd Wright, a Gurdjieff disciple who had invited Rosemary Nott and her husband to his house, first in Wisconsin then in Phoenix, Arizona. At both homes, he welcomed those who worked in the Gurdjieff way. Pamela told Jessie she would visit her one day in New Mexico.

All through her first year in the United States, Pamela felt like a lost child, forlorn and lonely, a prisoner of the war raging across the Atlantic.[8] At times, life was "so bad I thought I couldn't endure it."[9] Pamela even consulted a Jungian analyst who told her, "You don't really need my help. What you should do is read your own books."[10] In her little apartment, Pauline helped her feed and change Camillus. She brushed his soft, light brown hair and washed his baby smocks and later his matching shirt-and-short sets. There was only one true solace, as there had always been. Writing.

In 1940, she wrote a short story, "Happy Ever After," in

which Mary Poppins reads the Banks children *Mother Goose's Nursery Rhymes*. Eugene Reynal told her he would publish a special edition, just for fun, and a thousand came off the presses of Reynal and Hitchcock, their covers dotted with silver stars. She mailed a few as Christmas presents to her friends.

Reynal suggested she write an account of her journey to New York. The result, *I Go By Sea, I Go By Land,* was published in 1941 by W. W. Norton. Written in diary form by a fictional eleven-year-old, Sabrina Lind, it tells the story of "Pel" of "Thornfield," Sussex, who escorted the children of friends to America and made friends with "Mrs. Mercury" (Gertrude Hermes). Among Pel's eight charges were Sabrina, her eight-year-old brother James Lind, and Pel's baby, Romulus. "Pel" is Pamela and Romulus is, of course, Camillus, who by now had recovered his health to become a more placid and almost chubby baby boy.

The Lind family's decision to evacuate their children to the United States followed the shocking arrival over Thornfield of a German plane. At 1 A.M., it dropped five bombs. One exploded in Farmer Gadd's cornfield, killing two horses—who could be seen, bloody and lifeless, at the bottom of a crater. The cowman, who had been up all night nursing a pregnant cow, was taken to Tunbridge Wells hospital with bomb splinters in his leg.

Just as Mayfield is called Thornfield, many local characters make a barely disguised appearance in the book, including "Mr. Oliphant, the Vicar of Thornfield" (the real vicar was the Reverend Theodore Oliver). Mrs. Lind is "Meg," named for Pamela's mother, and the Lind children are greeted in London on the way to the boat by their rude Great Aunt Christina (yet another incarnation of Aunt Ellie).

Pamela dismissed *I Go By Sea, I Go By Land* as "a mere bibelot...written at the request of my publisher...all of us took assignments which weren't properly in our line."[11] The book was all founded on fact, and, as she once said, "the feel-ings much resembled my own." She described herself in the book as a solicitous but playful minder of the evacuee chil-dren, especially caring of the little girl Sabrina Lind. The writer and guardian of the children, Pel, tells Sabrina, "you have a full cup, and the thing to do is to learn to carry it without spilling over. Nobody can help you, you have to do it by yourself. And it takes time, I am only learning it now." As Pamela later said, "Sabrina Lind is an aspect of me…my cup was always full."[12]

Pamela wrote another, much shorter, book in 1941. Her mind had drifted back to Aunt Ellie in Woollahra, to the death of her father in Allora, the great aunt coming to rescue Meg and her little girls, to the fairy stories that had sustained her. The book was *Aunt Sass,* the story of Aunt Ellie. Pamela called Ellie "Christina Saraset" or Sass for short. *Aunt Sass* became her second personal gift book. It was dedicated to Reynal, who printed five hundred copies. Their yellow covers were decorated by a locket, surrounded by stars. (*Aunt Sass* was fol-lowed two years later by another gift Christmas book, *Ah Wong,* about her family's general dogsbody, a Chinese man who was largely a figment of Pamela's imagination. She dedicated this book to Camillus and the children of her friends, including the children of Jessie Orage, Diarmuid Russell and Eugene Reynal. Pamela sent a copy of *Ah Wong* back to Madge, inscrib-ing it "To Madge Burnand, with faithful love, Pamela.")

Words clattered out of her typewriter, as they always had, worthy but dull pieces written for the *New English Weekly*. In these, she claimed with phony authority to understand the mood of America. Some were laced with the journalist's old standby, the views of barmen and cab drivers. One such piece was written from Washington, D.C., which she was visiting when the Japanese bombed Pearl Harbor. With the entry of the United States into World War II, the Roosevelt administration launched a national and international propaganda campaign, coordinated by the Office of War Information (OWI). Pamela became drawn into the effort.

She knew two ministers in the Roosevelt government, Henry Wallace and John Collier. Both were old friends of AE, and she maintained the contacts. The OWI and Britain's Ministry of Information developed strong networks of staff and contributors among the literary and journalism communities. The poet Archibald MacLeish and the playwright Robert Sherwood played major roles in the formation of OWI. MacLeish, a dedicated antifascist, worked mainly on the domestic side of the operation, claiming that the principal battleground of the war was American opinion. He became the OWI's first director.

Sherwood, who had been writing Roosevelt's speeches before the war, headed the overseas branch. He gathered around him hundreds of journalists, writers and broadcasters who shared his views. Before the war he had spent summers in Surrey and knew many English writers as well, although there is no evidence he knew Pamela then. A major part of Sherwood's overseas branch was the radio news and features division, which asked Pamela "to do some broadcasts to all the occupied countries." Pamela thought, "Good gracious, why ask me? You can all tell the news of the day or something interesting." But they said "No, we want you to do something." But what kind of thing? "We don't know, but we think you will come up with something."[13]

She couldn't sing or act or play an instrument. But she did have one idea. "How could I speak to anyone except speaking to their child? And so to every country I did broadcasts on their fairy tales, their legends, their folklore. If I didn't know it, I learned it and discovered it and it was very useful to me afterwards." Then there were the nursery rhymes. "I would tell them...have them sung, say where they came from, and reminded [the listeners] that there would be a time they could be told again." In broadcasts to France, she played recordings of "Frere Jacques" and "Sur le Pont d'Avignon," told the history of the songs, and reassured her listeners. "All they had made of France was still there, and one day would be free again. And then we came to Greece. I could only talk to them of their great heroes."[14]

After the broadcasts, the division received messages from all sorts of places saying "let her go on, let her go on telling us the stories." "Mind you," said Pamela later, "it was partly my voice and partly somebody translating into every language, but something in them was welcome. One was able to speak to their childhood, and even now I meet people who discover that it was I who had done those broadcasts. They remembered it was an important moment for them. So you see how much I owe to myths and fairy tales, they opened so many doors for me."[15]

In her apartment on 52nd Street, she opened her old books on myths, pored over them into the night, felt the satisfaction of studying a jigsaw of names and connections that helped her make order of her own life. At night, when Camillus was tucked into bed, she read him the fairy tales that had comforted her in Maryborough, Allora and Bowral, tales of vindictive queens, of princes and frogs, and of pumpkins that turn into coaches.

She claimed that fairy tales had "great things to teach us." They were "carriers of a very old teaching, a religion, a way of life, a chart for man's journey."[16] For *The New York Times Book Review* she wrote of her love of the Grimms, describing the brothers Jakob and Wilhelm with lavish affection. She told the readers of the universality of fairy tales, how she had heard them in Ireland and told by an Aboriginal woman on a sugar plantation in Australia. Fairy tales, she thought, "live in us, endlessly growing, repeating their themes, ringing like great bells. If we forget them, still they are not lost. They go underground, like secret rivers, and emerge the brighter for their dark journey."[17]

At three, Camillus, the infant twin separated from his other self, was already showing a fairy-tale-like ability to be two people in one. He declared: "I am two boys, Goodly and Badly." Pamela wanted to know which he was right now. With an angelic smile, Camillus replied "Goodly," then closed the door behind him. Immediately, it swung open again. He looked now like a demon. "This is Badly!" he declared and then, with a dubious, anxious look, asked her which she liked best. Pamela quickly replied that she liked them both the same. Camillus threw himself on her with joy.[18]

He was not a calm child, nor was he easy to read. Camillus was frightened of cracks in the ceiling, and he took a sudden loathing to the hot water radiator in the apartment because it clanked and fizzled each night when he went to bed. Pamela stood by the radiator, whispering privately to it each time it hissed and laughing out loud when it honked. Camillus begged to be let in to the private conversation, then became the heater's confidant himself each night until he fell asleep. Pamela remembered her own fear of the captain tap-tapping behind her bedroom wall at home in Queensland.[19]

The boy showed a stubborn determination to know the grisly truth and scolded Pamela when she skirted around the details of Ginger's death at the knackers in *Black Beauty*. But she was proud of her little boy's vivid imagination. He told her: "Once upponer time, I were walking along and I came to a house with three wise old woman ladies. I knocked on the door and they said who's there and I said Camillus John. So they bited me and I spanked them." Pamela felt this contained all the elements of a profound legend.[20]

She spent much of the summer of 1941 on holiday in Maine, but by autumn her mood was no better than before. One day she called Jessie in Santa Fe, sounding, Jessie wrote, "very low." Jessie's diary contains the only remaining evidence of the cause of Pamela's mood, hinting at a worsening relationship between Pamela and Gert. During 1941, Gert had been staying with relatives in Canada but wrote to Pamela to say she planned to move back to New York. Pamela asked her to stay with her, at the apartment. While Pamela was at work, Gert decided to create a bronze bust of Camillus, then a wood engraving showing a wild sea after the sinking of a submarine.

At the end of the year, the two women rented a house in upstate New York, at Mt. Kisco, where early in January 1942 Jessie called on them during a visit to the East Coast. After she saw Pamela and Gert at home in their "nice house," Jessie told her diary she was relieved to find herself "at peace about Pamela at last."

In July, Pamela wrote to Jessie that she had been "ill in body and mind." Jessie does not record why, but it is likely that Gert was the reason. Jessie's diary and Pamela's travel notes indicate that Gert and Pamela separated some time in 1942.

Eventually it was Camillus who led Pamela out of depression. When he turned four in 1943, her boy needed more than the routine of the New York apartment. Playschool, outings, the corner store, his new round made her part of the city, where she discovered that "I had, in fact, a very large family." She planned to write about the release, scribbling notes for an article under the headline "The Big Family."[21] From then on, she wrote, "I really felt I belonged here as much as I do in England."[22]

Pamela saw New York "in the light of its history. I called

by its two rivers, letting their currents flow over my grieving mind so that it became peaceful and limber enough to write a book again. Perhaps I found my third Mary Poppins book in those very waters." Summer, with its expansive heat, invited friendships. She felt the links between herself and all the nameless people she saw on the street, in groceries, in drugstores. Windows and doors, inner and outer, seemed suddenly to open. The odd-job man in the apartment block, Sam Gloriano, became her friend. Sam was the ice-and-rice man. He carried ice up to her apartment and one day tossed out the rice that was burning on her stove and started over with a new pot of water.[23]

She took Camillus to watch the organ grinder at the playgrounds by the East River. The monkey, Rosine, dipped into her begging mug and handed Camillus a nickel. That meant lots of return visits. Others in the big new family were the staff at the grocery store. One reached under the counter and slipped her five Hershey bars on a day when she hesitantly asked for candy. At that time, chocolate was worth its weight in diamonds. The store messenger, a black man called Charlie, took Camillus to playschool one morning when Pamela was ill in bed.

Once, Camillus brought a stranger to the apartment after school. "This is my friend Solomon—I found him in the drugstore." She discovered he was Charlie's grandson. His mother had died. Solomon was three years older than Camillus but centuries older in wisdom. At nightfall he would linger, chortling over Camillus's bedtime story. "That Peter Rabbit! He certainly was some fella. I guess ma Mammy'd have laughed." Pamela took his photograph with Camillus outside the drugstore, in front of the scarlet signs advertising Coca-Cola and Chesterfields. They wound their arms around each other. Camillus smiled up, Solomon smiled gravely down. Pamela said she learned from Solomon "how to surmount grief.

I think only a child could have taught me this, Solomon all unwittingly and wordlessly said to me: Be Happy, all things pass."[24]

Pamela set her mind to what Eugene Reynal most wanted: a third collection of Mary Poppins adventures. She planned to call it *Good-bye Mary Poppins,* "because I thought it would probably be the last one...it seemed I had said all I wanted to say about her." But Reynal said, "Oh, you must not. I beg you not to! You never know what will happen. How does she go away this time?" Pamela told him that she just opened the door and disappeared. Reynal said, "Let's call it *Mary Poppins Opens the Door*."[25]

The book came together in the summer of 1943, when Pamela felt haunted by the terrible bombings of Coventry and the Ruhr.[26] The picture she paints of England in this book is more nostalgic and sweetly sentimental than the previous two Poppins collections. It opens with a foggy winter day in London and imagines nightingales singing in the city, recalling the poignancy of the wartime ballad "A Nightingale Sang in Berkeley Square."

Mary Poppins Opens the Door tells eight separate stories, which start with Mary arriving by umbrella on Guy Fawkes Day. Mr. Banks is enraged because there's been no nanny to bring order to the house. He is so furious he kicks the furniture. Somewhere in the heavens, Mary knows it is time to return to Cherry Tree Lane. She flies in as a dying ember of the fireworks display in the park and in the Banks's nursery unpacks her carpetbag, complete with tape measure which sizes up the children and finds them "Worse and Worse" or "Willful, Lazy and Selfish." The tape measure shows Mary as "Better than Ever" and "Practically Perfect."

Mary tells Jane and Michael she will stay until the door opens. The children settle into bed and watch, astounded, as the parrot's head on the end of her umbrella dips its head and plucks colored stars from the silky folds below, then shakes the stars onto the floor where they gleam silver and gold before they fade.

In the style of the two earlier books, Mary visits an odd relative, Fred Twigley. Fred, like Miss Quigley of Bowral, keeps large and intricate music boxes. In a story within a story, Mary Poppins tells the tale of a china cat who comes alive to give wisdom to Old King Cole. Her fascination with fairy stories is evident in both this chapter, "The Cat That Looked at a King," and in "Happy Ever After" (already published as her gift book of 1940), in which all the fairy-tale characters come out and play in the crack which emerges between New Year's Eve and New Year's Day. "Inside the crack," she wrote, "all things are one. The eternal opposites meet and kiss." The fairy tale people dance and, unlike Pamela, "everyone had a partner and no one was lonely or left out."

Mary also takes the children under the sea in a tale which reads like an inspiration for the "Under the Sea" segment of Walt Disney's *Little Mermaid,* when the lobster, Sebastian, and his fellow crustaceans jam to a West Indies beat. In Mary Poppins's sea adventure, also called "Under the Sea," the cornet fish play silver cornets, the flounder blows a conch shell and the bass beats on a bass drum. The great god of the underwater world, the Terrapin, greets Mary as another of the ancient ones. But not that ancient. The Terrapin calls her his "young relative."

"The Marble Boy," the fourth adventure in the book, borrows from her 1920s fantasy for the Christchurch *Sun.* The boy, a statue of the Greek god Neleus, comes to life and talks to the Banks children about his brother Pelias and father Poseidon, who are still back in Greece. Mary Poppins, it turns out, is a very old friend of Poseidon's. The book closes with Mary disappearing on a cool spring day through a mirage door. The children see their entire nursery reflected in the window. Mary escapes into that reflection and makes her way out to the sky through the reflected door. As Mary leaves, Mr. Banks falls in love once more with his wife. He calls her "my dear love" and waltzes in ecstasy to "The Blue Danube." The melody had wafted to 17 Cherry Tree Lane from a hurdy gurdy in the park. Miss Quigley in Bowral had once waltzed with Pamela to the same sweet waltz. Peace and happiness cloak Number 17. Mary has made everything right. Now she can go once more—for a while.

This book, dedicated to Camillus, was published in America by Reynal and Hitchcock in November 1943, and in England by Peter Davies in 1944. Both editions included Mary Shepard's illustrations. Pamela had scribbled many letters from New York to Shepard in London, all with detailed instructions on how each character should look. She told Shepard that Mrs. Clump should be huge and hideous, with a knob of hair at the back of her head. Mary Poppins, she said, must have a new hat, with a big bow perkily and primly placed in front. Mary obediently did as asked and used her husband, "Evoe," to pose in his office overcoat as a model for Mr. Banks.

Pamela told Shepard she was so glad to have the book written. She hoped they would do another, sometime, "but not a Mary Poppins. She is away for good now and I am filled with other ideas."[27] Pamela was homesick for Pound Cottage and the soft fields of Mayfield, soon to be scarred by flying bombs launched from the coast of France and dispatched at 180 miles an hour toward London. On June 12, 1944, Mayfield looked up to see the first of Hitler's doodlebugs. Pound Cottage was saved, but in the next four months at least seventeen doodlebugs crashed around the village, carving huge craters in the ground.[28]

But Pamela's need for home was washed away when John Collier, the Minister for Indian Affairs, suggested that, as a cure for her homesickness, she spend a summer or two in the southwest, on an Indian reservation. As she wrote of the offer, "it seemed an unlikely antidote," but, in the end, she found it a healing process.[29]

She later felt Collier's offer came as a kind of magic. The next two summers were to be among the greatest experiences of her life. Pamela moved from the gray reality of New York to the brilliantly colored fantasy of the southwest, just as Poppins moves through a mirage door from her earthly Cherry Tree Lane to her heavenly friends in the sky. Here, Pamela discovered what so many artists and writers had found before and after her: spiritual peace and meaning within a beautiful landscape, brittle, red, gray-green. Even the air was different here, rarefied, dry, and mixed with juniper, sage and piñon.

Like AE before her, Pamela loved the landscape of New Mexico, the mesas—tabletop mountains—painted rose, white or yellow, standing in brilliant relief against the blueness of the horizon. The mountains fell to the ground in folds, like Grecian robes. In the red sandstone of the mesas, dinosaur remains had been found. But now the only danger came from snakes. Pamela loved the feminine architecture, the houses as round and plump as newly baked bread.

She wrote that with "its dryness, its sage brush and its desert, the southwest reminded me of the extreme beauty of parts of Australia." Pamela found it "a wonderful place for an artist...nature is at its purest, and you cannot draw a breath without finding a new truth. My writing has deepened and matured in America, but especially during the few months I spent in Arizona and New Mexico."[30]

Her first visit to the southwest was in September 1943, when she took the train from Chicago to Santa Fe. September was the best time of the year to see the town, the month when Santa Fe celebrated the Spanish conquistadors' resettlement of New Mexico in the late seventeenth century. Jessie, who was living in Santa Fe, found Pamela "looked well but very self-assertive." She drove her to the fiesta and listened patiently as Pamela read her a chapter from her new Mary Poppins book. Later they talked, once again through the night. On September 29, Jessie wrote in her diary: "She told me about Gert and her unhappiness. Quite a revelation to me and very distressing." In Pamela's many personal papers, some left for posterity, others at her London home, there is no evidence of her relationship with Gertrude Hermes or its outcome, and virtually no word, either, of her friendship with Jessie Orage, another relationship to end badly.

A year passed before she saw Jessie once more, in summer 1944. This time, Pamela stayed in the southwest for five months. She had accepted John Collier's suggestion that she live for some weeks in Window Rock, a tiny Navajo settlement in Arizona, near the New Mexico border. It looked like a train stop at the end of the world. Named for a big rock studded with a circular hole which might have been molded by a giant melon ball scoop, Window Rock was the home of the Navajo Tribal Council. The council had been formed by the U.S. government after minerals and oil were discovered on the Navajo reservations in the 1920s. Dirt roads wound between a dozen flat-roofed, squat buildings, all resembling the basic building blocks of a Lego set. The buildings were set among eruptions of rocks and mountains that seemed to grow from the flat ground like camel humps.

John Collier spent little time here himself, leaving the supervision of the Navajos to the Superintendent of Indians, James M. Stewart, who worked for the United States Department of the Interior. Stewart lived in the government-owned hillside settlement built of native stone, south of the town, along with the few hundred Anglos who worked on federal programs. The Navajos lived on their reservation at the base of mountains on fertile land in the Fort Defiance area west of the town.[31]

Pamela liked to say she spent the summer on a reservation,

but photographs in her albums show that she and Camillus lived in a western-style building that Pamela indicated in one interview was a boarding house. On the grounds in front, grinning for the camera, Camillus sat perched on the back of Silver, a white horse.

Pamela was driven from place to place in an old jeep or a truck. She waited each day at a given spot to be told who would be the guide. On the reservations, she tried to "speak little but hear much," folding herself away so she did not seem to be listening to the Navajos' stories. She wanted to share the dances and songs, share the silence.[32]

In the mother phase of her life, Pamela understood and appreciated the matriarchal society of the Navajos, the way girls were specially honored at puberty, with a public ceremony. Friends and relatives all gathered to celebrate kanaalda: the girl who had just had her first period ran toward the sun at dawn, a little farther every day. Pamela took notes of the Navajo ways, religion, hierarchy, spiritual leaders: first the Holy Ones who can travel on a sunbeam or the wind, the Changing Woman, the earth mother who teaches people to live in harmony with nature, and her children, the Hero Twins, who keep enemies away.

Pamela felt as though she was learning the Indian myths "direct, not put on for an audience. Gradually I was able to hear some of their stories, elements of their myths and religions, and so to see that these were related, distant cousins but still related to the stories from the rest of the world. I loved…the sparse hot land, the quiet people."[33]

She ate with the Indians in their octagonal homes, called hogans, sat around fires burning sagebrush, "listened among the mountains to the strong high-pitched voice of the rock." Camillus was "taken by the hand by grave red men, gravely played with, and, ultimate honor, gravely given an Indian name. Its strange beautiful syllables mean "Son of the Aspen." I would not ask a better thing for him to go through life protected by that strong, sensitive tree that springs so hardily from its native rock, putting on its round green coinlike leaves in summer and dropping them in autumn as golden money."[34] Pamela was given a secret Indian name and told "I must never reveal it and I have never told a soul." Her secret name, she said, "bound her to the mothering land," that is the land of the Earth Mother—her own motherland was far away.[35]

The most mystical experience of her summer came one night in the middle of the desert, when she rode out "a long, long way and it was full moon and there was some ceremony of dancing. Some two thousand Navajos were gathered, and there wasn't a sound amongst these men, not a sound, except a bridle clinking." They had made a fire to heat water. All she could hear was the crackle of the sagebrush on the fire or a baby crying. Nothing else, not a sound. "There they were, just sitting, meditating, and one man got up and started to sing and the others began to take it up, and then they were quiet again for a long time and then they got up and danced and then again were quiet." This marvelous capacity for being quiet enchanted her.[36]

The day after she received her secret name, Pamela rode at twilight through the Canyon de Chelly, believing her name had been borne on the wind before her.[37] The canyon, sometimes called "the baby Grand," was to Pamela "marvelous, so subtle and lonely. You know there wasn't a tourist for a hundred miles." (Pamela might have felt the same sense of mystery in Uluru in Central Australia, had she not been such a stranger to her own native land.) Even the most skeptical traveler falls under the immense spell of the Canyon de Chelly, pronounced "chey" but named for the Navajo word *tsegi,* meaning rock canyon. Here, the Anasazi tribes lived for four thousand years, then the Hopi and Navajo people. Pamela had already traveled through it on horseback. At first she wore what all the Anglo women wore: blue jeans, high boots, cowboy shirts. "Then suddenly I saw the Navajo women wearing those full skirts, seven yards around...with velvet jackets."[38] She had to have one, too. From these days she adopted two fashions she wore until old age: tiered floral skirts and Indian jewelry, turquoise and silver, with bracelets stacked up each forearm like gauntlets.

At twilight, she found the canyon "most mysterious, because...you go up and it looks as if it is a blank wall and the two sides close in and you don't really know but your sense tells you that there is a turning. And it is like going up door after door, rising through this opening and the next one. And it was very dark and then the opposite happened, you see and the doors were closing behind me." There, she was stopped by a group of Navajos who asked her to share their meal and told her how, the night before, they had danced away a nightmare of a woman who had been called by the wrong name. They danced the nightmare to the lip of the canyon, so it was finished with, danced away.[39] Pamela thought if only she could dance her nightmares away she would have no pain, no need of any psychiatrist.

Pamela wrote to Jessie to say she was returning to Santa Fe. "Well," Jessie huffed to her diary, "I'm not very pleased about it. Why can't she go somewhere else?" But the old friendship survived—just. On July 19, Jessie found Pamela ill in bed at her Santa Fe hotel. When Pamela recovered Jessie did her social duty, playing hostess, taking Pamela on the rounds of Santa Fe. She drove her seventy miles north to Taos, the cultural colony dominated by Jessie's friends Mabel Luhan, her Indian husband Tony Luhan, the painter Dorothy Brett and the widow of D. H. Lawrence, Frieda Lawrence.

Mabel Ganon Evans Dodge Sterne Luhan was the presiding spirit of Taos. A writer, arts patron and indefatigable hostess, she was a figure of fun to many. Mabel saw Taos as a garden of Eden where the innocents lived in the Taos Pueblo. Home for centuries to the Tiwa Indians, the pueblo resembled an organic sculpture made up of adobe apartments, each reached by a ladder. The pueblo was a magnet for artists as well as social scientists and Jungians, including Carl Jung himself, who after a visit in 1925 saw the Indians of the Taos Pueblo as "the manifestation of prehistoric archetypes."[40]

Mabel had lived in New Mexico since 1917, when she followed her third husband, Maurice Sterne, to the capital Santa Fe, where he set up an artists' studio. They moved to Taos, where she presided over a famous salon of artists and writers who half-loved her, half-loathed her. They sat at her feet or mocked her, just as they had at her equally famous salons in Florence and Greenwich Village. In Taos she found her Shangrila, a place where "the whole world [was] singing in a new key."[41] Mabel and Maurice bought twelve acres of orchard and meadow next to the pueblo and began to invite groups of Indians to their home, Los Gallos, named for the decorative ceramic roosters on the roof. At Los Gallos, the Tiwa Indians played their drums, sang and danced. Mabel, who had led a Dionysian life up until now, regarded them as Apollonian. She cut her hair into a bob, wore a serape, shed Maurice and married Antonio (Tony) Luhan, a full-blooded Pueblo.[42]

Mabel, they said, had "talons for talent"[43] and, once smitten by Taos, was desperate to have it documented by writers, poets and musicians. She said she willed them to come. Around Mabel, one did as one was told. As a friend once said, Mabel was like "an aeroplane laden with explosives." Her first important recruit to the Taos way of life was John Collier, whom she met in New York when he was a social worker. Next, Mabel lured D. H. Lawrence. She had read his *Sea and Sardinia* and decided he should write about Taos. Mabel summoned him from Australia, willed him into submission in 1922. At first he was drawn to "the secret essence and mystery of the American continent." Deeply stirred by the pueblos, desert, the mountains and the Indians, Lawrence found that "the moment I saw the brilliant proud morning sun shine high up over the deserts of Santa Fe something stood still in my soul and I started to attend." He described New Mexico as "the greatest experience from the outside world that I have ever had." But Mabel herself overwhelmed him. With Frieda, he moved to a ranch outside Taos and later wrote with venom about his patroness, whom he described as a "culture carrier who hates the white world and is in love with the Indian out of hate." Taos, he sneered, was "Mabeltown."[44]

Mabel also tried to hook George Gurdjieff. She had heard Gurdjieff and Orage speak at public lectures in New York in 1924, and offered Gurdjieff $15,000 and the use of her ranch as a branch of his French institute. It came to nothing. Gurdjieff wasn't interested and Orage recommended against it. But, in 1934, Gurdjieff decided to take up the offer. This time Mabel rejected him.[45] By the 1930s, Mabel had called to Taos the artist Georgia O'Keeffe, the photographer Ansel Adams, and writers Edna Ferber and Thornton Wilder.

Jessie Orage had been mixing with the Mabel circle since her first year in New Mexico, and in July 1944 she took Pamela to see them all, chronicling in her diary a round of social engagements with Mabel, Tony and Dorothy Brett. But by now, Jessie was near the end of her patience with the self-absorbed Pamela. She asked her friends, was it just her? No, of course not. One said Pamela was too "grasping," or "too tiresome to bother with," another found her "too egotistical for words." By the end of October 1944, Jessie decided: "I think it's best not to see Pamela again."

A month before, she had helped Pamela find a house to rent in Santa Fe. It was, perhaps, the oddest house in town. Known locally as the round house, it was the only circular residence in a city of square ones. El Torreon was at 808 El Caminito, near Canyon Road, the long and winding street which later became a street of artists' studios. The house had been designed to resemble a Spanish colonial torreon, or defensive tower. It might have reminded Pamela of the martello towers along the coast near Killiney in Ireland, where she had picked up Camillus as a baby.

Inside her tower, Pamela longed for home. By November 1944 she was obsessed by the war in Europe, studying the bad news in the *Santa Fe New Mexican,* which reported that summer: "German flying bombs have killed 2,752 persons and wounded 8,000 others since blind robot attacks centered on London started three weeks ago." Storm clouds often thundered over Santa Fe. She told Camillus not to cry, it was only the angels moving the furniture in heaven. Sometimes, after the storms, she sensed that the mountains were prowling around the house, in two opposing lines, like a grand chain. After a giant storm one day she walked, as usual, up the back road from El Torreon. Back at the house, she wrote that the mountains had stalked her, like hunters. But when she turned to face them, they all stood still, seeming to say "Well, here we are." She imagined the piñons were undergoing a secret experience. Maybe the rain was trickling down their roots, as they stood still "as we stand still sometimes, to feel love trickling down to our hearts' fibers. The world was still and washed and I was, within myself, on my knees with the adoration of it all, the mountains and the sun and the pale blue thread of the road running out to Tesuque [north of Santa Fe] and I feel a passion of praise for whatever brought me here, even though to suffer."[46]

Camillus loved to go with his mother on "jewel walks." She told him the pieces of mica they picked from the road were diamonds, rubies, sapphires.[47] What was under all the sparkles? he asked, and opened his eyes very wide when she answered: "a great ball of burning fire." One night, he stared through the high windows of El Torreon, then came running to her. "The moon is broken, the moon is broken!" Tears rolled down his

cheeks. She went outside and, sure enough, there was only a
sliver of moon in the sky. All she could do was to watch with
him, night after night, as the moon mended itself, growing
and growing.[48]

That autumn, Pamela prepared her fourth Christmas gift
book for her friends. *Johnny Delaney,* she called it, in honor of
another romantic figure from her mythical past. Delaney was
supposed to have been the groom on her father's sugar plantation. The book was dedicated to "Frieda Heidecke Stern, for
showing me the way through the canyon." The canyon is both
the Canyon de Chelly and a metaphorical canyon, the kind a
woman of forty-five has to cross, from nymph to middle age,
from hope to acceptance.

But who was Frieda Heidecke Stern? An extensive search
in New Mexico proved fruitless. Perhaps she was an amalgam
of Frieda Lawrence and Mabel Dodge Sterne (with the Sterne
misspelt.) "Frieda Heidecke Stern" was obviously German, as
was Frieda Lawrence, whose maiden name was Frieda von
Richthofen. Under the name "Frieda Heidecke Stern" in
Johnny Delaney are the words "Wenn ein Tuer zue geht an
anders Tuerle geht uff." This is misspelt German for "If one
door closes, another opens." The fragments Pamela left of her
life are sometimes barely adequate to piece together what she
hoped to conceal, and this is one such gap in her life. The pain
she felt, whether for Francis, Jessie or Gertrude, or all three,
remains her secret.

In February 1945, when Pamela had been back in New York
for a few months, Jessie wrote to say she planned to return
to Britain. The Atlantic was now relatively safe. Pamela said
she would follow, soon. On their last day in New York, the
iceman Sam Gloriano came to say good-bye. He dropped a
medal of St. Christopher into Pamela's palm.[49] "That Atlantic's

a pretty big sea," he remarked, "but the kid will be safe with this." Camillus's friend, Solomon, stood in the apartment block doorway, watching them climb into the cab. He didn't wave. He simply held his hand above his head and kept it there until the car turned the corner. At the last moment, Pamela thought he bent and trembled, but perhaps "I saw him through tears."[50]

They sailed in March. On the ship, as the last of the bombs were flying over Mayfield, she wrote for the *New English Weekly* that a lone remaining wolf pack was harrying the convoys bound for home. Once she had visualized the Atlantic as a "sea space separating two countries dear to me." Now it was the link that joined them—the place where the waters of the Thames and the East River ultimately met.[51] The door to both countries now remained always open.

On the ship, Pamela contracted mumps. She was met at Liverpool by officious representatives from the Board of Health and taken by ambulance to an isolation hospital, cut off from friends, forbidden even to use the telephone. Pamela began to feel she had gone mad and "been tidily put away."

Camillus had been collected by Madge and taken to her new home in Devon. To everyone's surprise, Madge had married during the war. Her husband was a diplomat, Don Gregory. Camillus wandered, lost, sad and sniffly, among the big trees and huge spaces of the Gregorys' garden. When her fever had gone, Pamela was free. She traveled by train to Sussex, overcome by the greenness of the grass. The other passengers pointed to the sweet spring lambs, but Pamela could only stare at "the spread and solidity" of the many little fields.[52]

VJ Day, August 15, 1945, was Camillus's sixth birthday. The radio crackled out the news of peace from the kitchen into the garden of Pound Cottage, where Pamela sat with Camillus. That night, all Mayfield marched in a torchlight procession to the High Street. The Mayfield Silver Band led the way. At the war memorial, a war widow laid flowers. The villagers marched down Fletching Street to Dunstan's Croft where they lit a bonfire. After the fireworks, they sang their favorite songs. Over and over came their most favorite, "Bring back, bring back, oh bring back my Bonnie to me, to me..." Someone read a poem, "A Saga of a Village's War Effort," written by Major Morris of Little Twitts, Five Ashes. Pamela felt a twinge of guilt. She had not been part of it all.[53] But, she later wrote in the *New English Weekly,* peace—that "cold moment"—was full of possibilities and for Pamela, "the door is hardly opened."[54]

11

Monsieur Bon Bon Says Au Revoir

She posed for a snapshot at the door of Pound Cottage in her gingham skirt, layered and frilled in the Navajo style. Pamela seemed the epitome of happy motherhood, a young matron from the pages of a summer fashion catalogue. In her arms was Camillus, his arms entwined behind her neck. She called him "my treasure," made him drink up all his milk at lunchtime, read him *Squirrel Nutkin* and *Peter Rabbit,* worried about his education and decided it must be good, it must be proper. She had gone to the Allora Public School and a college for young ladies in Sydney. He would attend the French school in South Kensington, then Dane Court prep school in Surrey.

At times, Pamela still felt the westward pull of America. It was bracing there. In a piece for the *New English Weekly,* "Notes on a Homecoming," she contrasted the United States, vibrant, electric, with sleepy England. America took measurements, asked everything, waited for nobody. England, after the war, made no demands, asked no questions, was without curiosity. England was "heavy and intimate, soft, but firm at the core; sluggish, forever waiting, half asleep on her feet at the crossroads." Pamela felt a stranger in this stoic, mustn't grumble land.[1]

She beat Jessie back to the offices of the *New English Weekly* by one day. From the quarantine hospital in Liverpool, Pamela had written to the *Weekly*'s editor, Philip Mairet, asking whether she should resign. She explained something of the tension between Jessie and herself. In any dispute, she had the weaker hand; after all, Jessie owned the *New English Weekly*. Its masthead listed the editorial committee as "Jessie R. Orage (sole proprietor), Maurice B. Reckitt, Pamela Travers, T. S. Eliot, W. T. Symons and T. M. Heron."

"Getting in first is typical of Pam," Jessie wrote in her diary. "When she saw him she said she had thought it over and would let it rest for a time. Philip wanted to know if I minded seeing her. Of course I said no, nor did I see any reason why she should resign or stop writing." In October, an editorial board meeting was "a bit grim for me because of Pamela, and I was the first to leave although Philip and Symons expected me to dine after. But the thought of a whole evening of Pamela's presence was too much. I preferred not to waste my emotions. When she came in she swarmed all over 'Dear Philip.' 'Dear Travers.' I nearly laughed."

Pamela never relinquished her place on the board nor her role as a major contributor. From 1945 until 1949, when the *Weekly* collapsed, she wrote for almost every issue under the bylines P. L. Travers, PLT, or Milo Reeve. In all these pieces, Pamela's tone was confident, superior, as she reviewed films and

books, but mainly theatre. Jessie occasionally objected to remarks
in her reviews, with Mairet forever playing the diplomat.

Just before Christmas 1945, Jessie and her children moved
into the bottom half of a house in Oakley Street, Chelsea.
Above them lived Stanley and Rosemary Nott. Jessie's diaries
end in February 1946, her relationship with Pamela still unre-
solved, but Pamela's own sketchy diary notes show the two
remained on reasonably friendly terms until Jessie moved out
of her life, leaving London for Kent in the 1950s. Pamela may
have kept a diary for years, but at the time of her death the
only notebook remaining covered 1948 and 1949. Because of
the gap in dates, there is no record by either woman of a trau-
matic event in Pamela's life.

In early 1946, the man she had loved was dying. Francis
Macnamara's illness was a mystery to both his doctors and his
friends. He seemed shrunken, his skull shape clearly visible
through papery skin. He had decided to move to Dalkey, outside Dublin. His last home stood on a cliff, its garden plunging
down to the coastline. Macnamara ordered renovations but
never saw them completed. At the age of sixty, he died in his
upstairs bedroom. The builders had left most of the house
unfinished, in total disorder. Macnamara seemed to have vanished at midpoint in an unsatisfactory journey. One of his
German friends, an old professor, compared his death to Tolstoy's death in a railway station. Just before his death, on
March 8, 1946, Macnamara had said to his manservant:
"Weighed and found wanting."

On Macnamara's own instructions all his papers, including
a cupboard full of old letters, had been burned. Joseph Hone
thought the best of his writing could be found in his "tempestuous and intensely personal letters," all written in an
ornate hand. Hone wrote Macnamara's obituary in the *Irish
Times:* "He broke a good deal of crockery on his way through
life, that of others as well as his own, but I have never heard

that he made an enemy. Perhaps only Ireland could have produced a Francis Macnamara and only Ireland could have so failed to give direction to his remarkable gifts."

In Pamela's copy of *Two Flamboyant Fathers,* a book of memoirs about Macnamara written by his daughter Nicolette Devas, she slashed the margins with a bold pencil line on two pages. The first marked the place where Devas wrote "not long before he died, Macnamara said 'I have just found out that affection and tenderness are important.'" Devas went on to write: "These words, this confession, seem to me to sum up the failure of all his intimate relationships." Pamela's second mark highlighted the words "the papers beside his bed were never sorted, they were all burnt one day on his orders. And burnt too, a cupboard full of old letters and other papers."

Decades later, when she thought she was going to die herself, Pamela began to dream vividly of Francis Macnamara. One night, she imagined that she was alone with him. She told him how much she loved him. They could never speak of their love when he was alive. In her dream, she was free to do so. Macnamara listened, nodded, and murmured that he understood completely.[2]

In April 1946 Joseph Hone wrote to Pamela to ask whether she had heard of Macnamara's death. He didn't miss him, Hone wrote, but felt as if the world was different since he had gone.[3] Hone was now in Enniskerry in the Wicklow Mountains, while his son, Nat, lived in a seedy mansion flat in Battersea, having worked his way through his inheritance. Pamela had moved into a house not far from Nat, in the more salubrious suburb of Chelsea, where she bought a three-story Georgian terrace at 50 Smith Street, on the corner of the Kings Road.

This was reasonably close to Camillus's first school, the French school in South Kensington. When he was nine, Pamela decided it was time to start his serious education, at Dane Court in West Byford, Surrey. Early in September 1948, after a summer holiday in Switzerland, she drove him down to the prep school. He confided in her: "Oh, you are going to miss me!" never realizing how much he was going to miss her.[4] The house was "so empty without C," she wrote in her diary. That month, she decided to sell Pound Cottage. She drove to Mayfield, cleaned the cottage and told Nightingales, the local real estate agent, to list it.

Now, as before, Pamela was dogged by illnesses, not of a desperate kind but the same array of colds, flu and stomach upsets that had nagged at her from the late 1920s, when her letters to AE disclosed a similar trail of problems. Late in September she felt unwell, overtired, missing Camillus and very upset in the stomach. She dragged herself to an evening meeting of *New English Weekly* contributors on September 28. The magazine was in its death throes but the directors resolved to start afresh, hoping they could pay the creditors.[5]

The magazine was to close within a year, but Pamela hoped she might earn enough from her Mary Poppins royalties for the upkeep of her new house and to pay the wages of the first of a long line of housekeepers. The books had been moderately successful and were always in print. The first daily was Mrs. Ritchie, with whom relations were stormy, at least much more difficult than the tensions between Mrs. Banks and Mary Poppins. By year's end, Mrs. Ritchie said she was ill and threatened to leave. (She didn't.) Pamela was uncertain about Camillus, partly guilty that she had sent him away, partly worried that he was not growing up quite the way she planned. In autumn, he wrote that he was "in-joying" school thoroughly. Still, she felt low and lonely.

When she drove down to see him at Dane Court, Pamela found Camillus tense and homesick. He had some grounds for complaint. At first he found Dane Court ramshackle, with everything rather worn. For tea, the boys were offered only bread and butter. Camillus was very cold in bed, his mattress was frightful and far too small. The boys all slept in dressing gowns and socks. When it was time to go, he hugged her tightly, but wouldn't cry. Pamela felt proud at this show of a stiff upper lip.

At Christmas 1948 she found comfort in Dane Court's end-of-year concert. Camillus stood in the front row as the boys all sang "Away in a manger, no crib for a bed." Pamela felt her own hot, prickly tears at the innocent words. He looked so sweet in his gray suit.

Camillus came home to Smith Street for Christmas on December 21. Pamela recorded in her diary that this was one of the happiest days, if not the happiest, of her life. They shopped, they drove with Mrs. Ritchie to see the Christmas tree in Trafalgar Square. She read him two chapters of *Dr. Dolittle* at bedtime and, as she left his room, thought to herself: "Oh, God bless him always."

But in January, when she took him back to Dane Court, he did not adjust to the new term and promptly got the flu. The principal decided it would be better if she did not see him so often. Mrs. Ritchie quit in February, which was even harder on what she called her "digestive upset." With the help of a new daily maid she just managed, though she did not feel well.

In the spring Camillus came back to Smith Street to cry "Home at last!" They played Ping Pong, bought treats for lunch—mushrooms and frozen strawberries—and went to Harrods to have his hair cut and to Selfridges to buy a bow and arrow. At night she read, again, *Squirrel Nutkin*. All along she felt waves of anxiety, the same sense of uneasiness that had dogged her for years.

Pamela's one comfort came from being part of the Gurdjieff family, dysfunctional though it was in the late 1940s, when each group of his followers maintained a haughty distance from the others. After the war, Gurdjieff tried to reconcile all the warring factions that had formed around him in France, England and the United States. It was tough work as, often, the leader of one group didn't talk to another, except perhaps through their lawyers. The most influential group was in France, led by Jeanne de Salzmann, one of the founders of Gurdjieff's Institute at the Prieure, which had collapsed when the Wall Street crash led to a shortfall of American funds. But now, needing funds to pay his wartime bills, Gurdjieff called in his flock, telling them "you are sheep without shepherd, come to me."

Pamela had retained her connection to Jane Heap's group, but had links to another group outside London led by one of Ouspensky's protégés, John Gondolphin Bennett. An obsessive who had recited the Lord's Prayer a thousand times a day for nine years, Bennett fasted, put himself through ordeals and vigils, and offered Gurdjieff the gift of many influential people, among them Dr. Bernard Courtenay Mayers, a French Canadian who played an heroic part in the French resistance movement. Courtenay Mayers was to become Pamela's lifelong adviser and doctor.

Pamela was one of the many postwar visitors to Gurdjieff's apartment, which, from 1948, was packed with the spiritually needy—including Bennett's sixty disciples from England.[6] Pamela's need for her guru was so urgent she was on one of the first trains to Paris after the war. It wasn't far from the heart of London, on the Golden Arrow boat train, to Gurdjieff's first-floor apartment at 6 Rue des Colonels Rénard.

Gurdjieff had survived the war in an Aladdin's cave of begged and borrowed goods. A magpie by nature, his mirrored apartment was stashed with knickknacks and figurines, from mountain hussars to ballerinas, galloping Arab sheiks to Nubians on camels. He had stacked his floor-to-ceiling pantry shelves with sugar, salt, flour, dried fruit, lentils and spices. From Hediard, the emporium behind the Madeleine, he bought Beluga caviar, halvah and dried figs, chocolate, peppermint balls, sugared almonds, crystallized fruit, cartons of Gauloises (Bleu), bottles of vodka, calvados, and Larresingle Armagnac. Gurdjieff bought on credit, promising to settle after the war when his profits would roll in from a Texas oil well. The "oil well" turned out to be his American friends, who eventually paid his bills. From the country he brought hams, bacon and sacks of goat cheese. Apartment 6 smelled like a rakish Middle Eastern bazaar. Across the ceiling, festooned in loops and garlands, hung sprays of mint and rosemary, onions, scarlet peppers, dried eels, smoked sturgeon, and sausages that might have been made from camel's meat. Gurdjieff was addicted to thick black coffee, constantly ready in an old thermos flask. On his shelves and in his pockets was a neverending booty of candies and lumps of sugar. Children called him Monsieur Bon Bon.

Behind the artifice lay the tackiness. The apartment was dingy, the furniture shabby, the dining room carpet holey and patched. After the war, Gurdjieff himself looked older, tireder. His belly stuck out—he called it his "valise"—yet his eyes remained as hypnotic as ever, tending to stare in different directions. His silences were as eloquent, too, and his rages as effective. He spoke with a muffled Asian accent, in pidgin English, affecting odd habits of speech. The letter *h* in the middle of a word came out as *g,* so that he pronounced "behind" as "begind."

Yet in 1946 Pamela saw only a hero, a patriarchal host, massive of presence, radiating a kind of power that was both formidable and reassuring, like a multibranched old oak tree. But he was always unpredictable as he often spoke in parables. Gurdjieff had an alarming tendency to strip off his pupils' masks. Underneath his gaze, everyone was naked.

During that visit, he engaged Pamela in one of his typical plays for attention and domination. "You English," he accused her, "even when there is butter, you prefer margarine." No, she said, yes, he said, no, yes, no, yes, like a child's game, until she felt close to tears. Next day, at dinner again, she tried to hide but he singled her out, demanding: "If I should say Yes would you still say No?" She nodded her head. "Good," he said, with a beam. This was a classic Gurdjieff exchange. First the student was reduced to a childlike state, then when they least expected it, he relaxed his apparent rage, smiled "bravo" and offered the victim a sweet.[7]

Pamela and all the pilgrims in Paris took their medicine with joy. "Now," they thought, "is the harvest of our lives." Gurdjieff saw the need in each. He read Pamela in a way that AE, too wrapped up in himself, could not. Gurdjieff perceived her loneliness, her hunger for esoteric wisdom, and the potential for funds from her powerful American friends. She went to see him in his own private rooms at his apartment. He never sent her away, answering all her questions.[8]

At number 6, all his followers waited for his words of praise and wisdom. First they watched him eat, one foot folded under him as he sat on his divan. Gurdjieff fingered his food as he fingered women. He liked to assemble his own salad, fiddling with sauces, pouring out a whole bottle of chutney, slicing up cucumber with his bent fingers, adding a spoonful of cream, picking up cubes of lamb, chunks of goat's cheese and fresh tarragon leaves. Only then would he sit back, replete, and grunt "Who fresh come from England?"[9]

Before dinner his students often read from the manuscript of his book *Beelzebub's Tales to his Grandson*. After, he gave them the benefit of his insights. "Mathematic is useless," he might say one evening, "you cannot learn laws of world creation and world existence by mathematic." Or, another night, "Useless study Freud or Jung. This only masturbation." He recommended that his students read Mesmer on hypnotism and told them they must have an enema every day.[10]

In the late afternoon, he liked to adjourn to a café in the Avenue des Acacias. There he exchanged his fez for a Panama hat. At dinner he changed to a bright but pale turquoise pajama jacket or, more formally, into a loose gray cashmere suit, open-necked white shirt and soft kid slippers. Halfway through dinner he liked to slip on his tasseled magenta fez in the style of the Ottoman Turks. After dinner, he laid his accordion piano on his knee and played music in a sad, minor key. "This is temple music," he said, "very ancient." Pamela told him how she loved the music. He sat back, smoked, told the assembled company, "See now how my life is roses, roses, and I only a poor old dancing teacher!"

At this late hour, most of the guests were relaxed if not almost comatose after numerous toasts to "the Idiots." (Pamela's interpretation was that he used the word "idiot" in its original Greek meaning of private person.) Gurdjieff had invented a ladder of twenty-one Idiots, up to God who was "the Unique Idiot," but toasts were usually drunk only to the first layer of twelve idiots, who were ordinary, super, arch, hopeless, compassionate, squirming, square, round, zigzag, enlightened, doubting, or swaggering. Only Jeanne de Salzmann was considered bright enough to be "going out of idiocy." Sometimes dinner didn't finish until 3 A.M. The guests would keep talking at a café, reconstructing what the master had said.

In October 1948, having emptied many English bank accounts, Gurdjieff embarked on one last shearing visit to the United States. He returned to Paris in spring 1949, bringing a brace of young women known as "the calves," not rich followers but girls who would be the next generation of his dancers, including Jessmin Howarth's daughter, Dushka. He then dispatched Jeanne de Salzmann to England to check on the students of one of the London groups. There she ran movement classes which Pamela attended, afterward feeling both tired and strengthened.[11]

Pamela saw Gurdjieff for the last time in September 1949. With Camillus, she took the Golden Arrow to Paris, then drove straight to the Rue des Colonels Rénard. Monsieur Bon Bon was charming, of course. He offered Camillus sweeties. The boy was unself-conscious, just as disarming as the guru. Camillus told Gurdjieff he didn't have a father. Mummy had told him Daddy had had some kind of an accident and died in the tropics. Gurdjieff assured Camillus he would be his father. Camillus told Pamela he loved him. Gurdjieff took them both in his arms and kissed them.

Within a week they were home, Camillus back at school, Pamela agitated and again unwell. It was the old problem again: churned up bowels, constant diarrhea. A specialist found nothing but recommended an X ray. She thought of the last weeks of AE and the dreaded Dr. Munro.[12]

In October, Jeanne de Salzmann made another flying visit to London to give movement lessons to almost two hundred students in a west London studio. There, wrapped in the peace a dancer feels as her body and the music become one, Pamela was intensely happy and convinced she should return to Paris to see Gurdjieff. She wanted him to give her a "task," a special exercise for her soul. It was her body that needed help. But she was too ill to leave her bed.

By October 24 Jeanne de Salzmann knew Gurdjieff was so ill himself that he might die. She hoped the Gurdjieff disciple Bill Welch could administer a radical liver treatment and asked the doctor to come at once from New York. It took Welch nineteen hours to fly to Paris. Exhausted, he went straight to the Rue des Colonels Rénard to find what he saw as the mark of death on Gurdjieff's face. The doctor sent Gurdjieff to the American Hospital at Neuilly. Dressed in bright pajamas, smoking a Gauloise Bleu, he was carried into the ambulance announcing *"au revoir, tout le monde!"* In his private hospital room on the first floor, he kept up his insouciant patter as

Welch administered the treatment, puncturing the old man's abdomen. Gurdjieff no longer ate, but he continued to drink black coffee and to smoke through a black cigarette holder.

On the afternoon of October 29, Rosemary Nott rang Pamela to tell her the worst had happened. Gurdjieff had died at ten thirty that morning. Pamela went to Victoria Station to book a seat, then rang Camillus to say she couldn't visit him the next day as planned. Many Gurdjieff followers, among them Jane Heap, traveled with her on the Golden Arrow the next day.

Gurdjieff's embalmed body was to remain in the chapel at the American Hospital for a week, but Pamela saw him that first day in his room, trembling before entering, then, to her surprise, not shocked. She sat for a long time, gazing at him. Other friends came too, watching and praying.[13]

In the chapel Pamela felt a sense of intense calm and containment. For a week it became her refuge. Chairs were arrayed around the bier. People sat quite still for a long stretch at a time. When one left another filled his place. Each afternoon, a black-bearded Russian priest said prayers while a lay singer intoned responses in a large bass voice slightly hampered by a heavy cold.[14] After the service, Pamela knelt at Gurdjieff's feet and made her promises. Each day he seemed a little farther away. She thought of AE again.[15]

On November 2, she went alone to the hospital to see him for the last time. He seemed very far away now. The undertakers arrived to collect his body, and in a macabre twist which suited his macabre life, they found Gurdjieff's body too big for the coffin. A fresh one was ordered. At the Alexandre Nevski Cathedral in Rue Daru the congregation was puzzled by the delay. The mourners stood waiting, each holding an unlit candle, from 4 until 6 P.M. Gurdjieff was finally borne in.

At that moment, Pamela heard the massed voices of a hidden choir in what sounded like a musical cry of both anguish and welcome. The noise was so sudden, tears rushed up to her eyes then subsided. She told herself the funeral was too great for that. The service was sung, flowers piled up, and suddenly every light in the cathedral switched off. The mourners were left in the darkness lit by their candles. Somebody asked a sacristan if they could stay and watch through the night but he said no, the priests would watch now.

Many of the mourners went on to Jeanne de Salzmann's, where they read from Gurdjieff's books. She offered tea, soothed them, advised them to go on with the exercises he had given them and to work at the movements. Pamela lingered.

The day of the funeral was cold and bright. Pamela returned to the cathedral for High Mass. This time, the priests wore grand ceremonial dress, gold and white and pale blue, with towering headdresses, which Pamela noted with the eye of a drama critic. At the end, when the priests had gone, one after another they filed up to the coffin, knelt down and kissed the shaft of a little cross that was there. Pamela felt that everybody was making the best promise they could.[16]

Four huge buses followed the hearse to the burial place. They edged past the flat at the Rue des Colonels Rénard, bowled past L'Etoile with the sun frostily shining through it, through the brown leaves of the avenues. Pamela thought the flowery hearse bounded almost gaily in front. Through the window she saw a fairground with a merry-go-round in full swing. Coconut men collected centimes for the shy. The mourners sped past slums, shops, people carrying on their everyday trade. It must have seemed like a Brueghel canvas, these old black-shawled women hobnobbing in the sun, a mother holding out her baby.

The procession rolled past fields with their new winter wheat, big white bullocks coming home from plowing. Pamela hoped she, too, would have a happy funeral. They arrived at Avon near Fontainebleau. The brightness of the day had faded, the sky was graying, it was very cold. Each mourner threw a little earth into the grave. Pamela saw Katherine Mansfield's grave nearby, and inscribed on it: "Out of this nettle, danger, we pluck this flower, safety." She picked a little leaf from another grave and laid it on Mansfield's stone. Somebody handed each mourner a spoonful of wheat cooked with honey and raisins. Pamela watched the faces, saw how they had changed in grief.

Everyone stood so still by the grave, unwilling to go away, but night was coming. They drove back through the dusk to Gurdjieff's apartment, so crowded they could hardly move their arms to pass the plates. She looked one last time at the room where they had sat to read, "seeing many things," then said good-bye. She left Paris that night from the Gare du Nord, a cake and banana from the last supper tucked in her bag for Camillus.[17]

Camillus came home from school the next day, home to Smith Street. Pamela held him close. In grief and pain, she thought, a child offers the warmest comfort. From her bag, she pulled a picture of Gurdjieff on his bier. Camillus said little. They spent Guy Fawkes Day pottering about, playing Happy Families, making a face for the guy that they decided to call Sir Stafford Cripps. That night, with his friends, Camillus watched the guy's head blow off with a bang. He'd put crackers inside him. Camillus told his mother he loved her. Solemnly he said there was no other house so sweet or a mother so kind.

The next day, Pamela decided he must return to school by train. He cried and said if only the other boys liked him more he wouldn't mind going back so much. Pamela invented a word game to distract him on the way to Waterloo station. He waved good-bye cheerfully enough. On the way home she thought how similar they really were, the adopted baby and the last-minute mother who was once a little girl whose parents were so kind, reasonable, so distant. He took things hard, as she did. His pride pushed people away. Still, he seemed so much happier this term than ever before at school. Yes, she was sure he was all right.[18]

But she wasn't sure at all. Camillus's parting made an uneasy end to the year. What was left now? Both her guru and the *New English Weekly* had gone. There was comfort, though, in her Gurdjieff network of friends and, most of all, in the movement hall, the calming music of Rosemary Nott.

In grief, sometimes, women clean up, sweep, dust, put away. Mrs. Ritchie helped Pamela attack a kind of chaos at Smith Street. They stored clothes, bits and pieces of mismatched furniture, Camillus's baby things, books. Up they went, into the loft. Pamela had decided to rent out some rooms. England had not been the soft landing she had hoped. If only she had been Mrs. Banks, she could have hoped for the return of a comforting nanny. Mary Poppins would have helped her find peace in everyday things: cups and saucers, stars and rocking horses. She would have been someone to lean on, to pick up, tidy up.

That pain in her gut and bowels came back again, worse than before.

12

Shadowplay

After three books, Pamela planned to let her magic nanny fly into the sky and never return. She felt bound by her own creation, as if she would never produce another character as fascinating. Almost as soon as the first book was published in the 1930s, film and TV executives, including Walt Disney, had jostled for the rights to the stories. She refused to sell them; the offer was never exactly right. Pamela wanted to move on from children's fiction, but she knew that Poppins was all that anyone wanted.

In the early 1950s T. S. Eliot, then at Faber and Faber, asked Pamela if she would be interested in his publishing the books.

She declined, remaining faithful to Eugene Reynal. Eliot's approach followed another tempting offer; Reynal told Pamela that the American network CBS TV was interested in buying the rights for a TV production, possibly with a musical score. Reynal was keen to see the proposal succeed. At the same time, he reminded Pamela that their original contract stipulated up to four Mary Poppins books, all to be published in the United States. And although his old firm Reynal & Hitchcock had been taken over by Harcourt, Brace & World, he remained with the merged firm. Reynal wanted a fourth book, which he personally would carry through to publication.

Pamela agreed, although she warned him the nanny would eventually have to stay away for good. In a preface to the new book, *Mary Poppins in the Park,* she wrote that the nanny could not keep arriving and departing forever. The author wanted to make it clear that the six adventures in this book, published in 1952, could have taken place during any of the three visits of Mary to the Banks family.

The new stories came quickly and effortlessly, appearing on her typewriter as if by magic. Mary Poppins was now much more than a servant with a secret life. Pamela invested her with all manner of insights and powers, telling Reynal she "saw further" into Mary Poppins. She realized that George Banks had an instinctive understanding of the nanny and that Poppins had a reason for coming to the Bankses—to find something for herself. Once she found it, she was free to leave. Mary Poppins was happy in her role as a conduit. Through her, people found balance and a sense of their true worth.[1]

Pamela, now fifty-one, had absorbed all the theories of the pundits on what Mary Poppins actually meant. She began to mix Gurdjieffian ideas into Poppins's adventures and personality; the nanny was more than ever a guru, or seer, and seeker of spiritual truths. Pamela thought *Mary Poppins in the Park* gave "certain clues" that the other books did not. It was her favorite in the Poppins series as the book carried certain ideas she loved. Among them is the nature of identity, our real selves, and other selves. Pamela was fixated on shadows, doppelgangers and duality, partly because of her own complex identity but also because the truth about her son and his twin was locked stubbornly in her mind. *Mary Poppins in the Park* is peppered with references to twins, triplets and shadows, and other selves of every kind.

Pamela herself appears throughout the stories. Like little Lyndon Goff, Jane Banks in this book wishes on a star and makes miniature parks for poor people who never quarrel. Mrs. Lark, the Banks's neighbor, is now more dreamily nostalgic than before, recalling her girlish days when she wore a pinafore and button boots, when her curls were blond, when she played imaginary games with fairy-tale creatures and never dared step on an ant. That was the little girl who "meant to marry a king." Mrs. Lark is Pamela in her fifties.

The book begins with the story "Every Goose a Swan," in which Jane Banks says she is only Jane on the outside, but somebody quite different on the inside. "Every Goose a Swan" is threaded with people yearning to be someone else, among them a goose girl who says she is really a princess in disguise. Jane herself pretends to be the daughter of an Indian chief. A wise man disguised as a tramp warns that every alternative life that looks so tempting is disappointing and difficult in reality. The moral is so simple it's a cliché: be yourself. Pamela told an interviewer later that everyone's inner self is not so much hidden as lost. Adults lost their inner self when they were children. Each person longs for his inner self for the rest of his life.[2]

In the second story, "The Faithful Friends," a policeman tells the Banks children he is a triplet. His brothers left him to go to a distant land. One brother came back but met with an accident. The other wrote a note, reassuring his brothers they were not to worry about him. They never heard from him again. Pamela struggled with this story, explaining how she first thought the policeman should be a twin, but after taking a walk in her favorite thinking place, Battersea Park, across the river from Chelsea, said out loud to herself, "Of course, the policeman is not twins but triplets!"[3]

In another adventure, "The Children in the Story," Pamela again asked who is real, who is fictional: three princes in a fairy book or the Banks children themselves. Both the princes and the Bankses have read of each other in books, and each group of siblings is excited to meet the others in the flesh. They have in common their flighty nanny, Mary Poppins, who is likely to leave the princes—Florimund (Beauty), Veritain (truth) and Amor (Love)—at any time, just as she flies away from Jane and Michael Banks.

In the fifth adventure, "The Park in the Park," Jane wants to know if everything in the world is not quite what it seems. She visualizes an endless chain of worlds within worlds, where one park, for example, is inside another, inside another. Jane realizes she herself can be in two places at once. In this story, an illustration by Mary Shepard shows Mrs. Hickory, the mother of twins, holding her two baby boys, Dickory and Dock. Mrs. Hickory's face is Pamela's.

The last and most lyrical story in the book concerns Halloween, when the Banks children are invited to a party in the park. Only their shadows attend, to mingle with the shadows of the other guests—fairy-tale shadows, nursery-tale shadows, and shadows of Mary Poppins's friends, among them two crones, Mrs. Corry and the Bird Woman. All the lonely people in the park are searching for their own shadow. The Bird Woman remarks that our shadows are the other part of us, the outside of our inside. The Park Keeper is astonished that a star, and the light in the Banks nursery, are so alike, he can hardly tell the difference. At this, the Bird Woman explains that one is a shadow of the other. At midnight, the shadows reclaim their owners. The story anticipated what Pamela must have known: that one day her own son would find his other half.

Camillus spent his high school years as a boarder at Bryanstan, a public school in Dorset. During the school terms, Pamela moved between her home in Smith Street and New York, where she rented an apartment and spent much of her time with Dr. Bill Welch and his wife Louise, who ran a Gurdjieff group in Manhattan. In September 1956 she took Camillus for a spring holiday to Trinidad. It was to be their last few weeks together before he discovered the truth about his adoption. Back at boarding school for his final few months, he wrote home to his "dearest Mama" that he had failed French but was optimistic about his English exams to come. After graduation, he planned to spend a few months studying in France, at the University d'Aix in Marseilles.

Camillus waited for the academic year to begin at home in Smith Street. Pamela gave him an allowance of £2 10s a week, some of which was spent at the bars of the Kings Road pubs nearby. One day in one of the pubs Camillus, now seventeen, began drinking with a young Irishman. His name was Anthony Marlowe Hone. The two young men looked similar, but were not identical. Anthony was shorter, darker. Like the shadows in Halloween, Anthony had been looking for somebody else. He knew he was one of at least three siblings, but there had been talk of more, perhaps even a twin. Anthony wanted to know why his parents, Nat and Bridget, had abandoned their babies all those years ago. One drink led to another, and another, and eventually to the truth. The two young men discovered the sequence of events.

When Pamela took Camillus from his bed at grandfather Hone's Irish home in 1939, his twin was sent by their natural mother, Bridget, to her own mother in Piltown, County

Kilkenny. This grandmother, called, confusingly, Mrs. Anthony, raised him as an Irishman and Catholic. He always knew who his parents were, and his sense of family and identity was enhanced by the generosity of rich relatives. His grandfather's sister, Olive Symes, paid for his secondary schooling at Blackrock College in Dublin.[4]

Seventeen was the very worst time to find out the truth. Pamela was even more devastated than Camillus when he told her he knew. For months after, she could hardly work in the face of Camillus's anger—which was unbound. In the spring of 1958, Pamela wrote to Mary Shepard that she could work only when she felt well and when "domestic tribulations" smoothed themselves over. Camillus went up to Oxford early in October and then, at last, she would be able to concentrate. When he was at home, the house rattled. Camillus was a great time waster, but so were all teenagers.[5]

After two terms, Camillus and New College, Oxford, parted company. The temptations of driving down to London in fast cars had been too great. By March 1959 he was back at Smith Street, and Pamela asked her solicitor if he could find him a job. If anyone could find a job for Camillus it would be Arnold Abraham Goodman, one of the best-connected men in the City. Known as "the universal fixer," the unmarried Goodman was at the center of an extensive network of contacts in politics, publishing and the arts, and was to become Lord Goodman in the early 1960s. Tall, bulky, with black hooded eyes under untamed eyebrows, Goodman had worked with Rubinstein Nash, a law firm known for its defamation practice, before he set up his own firm, Goodman Derrick, in the 1930s. A *Times* profile once described him as "the most influential man in England who...probably knows more secrets of the great than anyone else in the country." The Goodman contact came good, but not immediately. While he waited, Camillus took a job in a furniture workshop. Pamela had hoped for much more.

Women, she thought, absorbed tension into their colon and stomach, and this time her own pain was so persistent she booked herself into the Salvadore Mundi Hospital in Rome for a cure. The Salvadore Mundi was one of the best and most expensive hospitals in Europe, staffed by American and other international doctors. Pamela probably heard of its treatments from her American doctor friend, Bill Welch. The hospital offered a solution to her problems in the form of an all-potato diet developed by a Dr. Simeon in India as a cure for spastic colon and dysentery. While Pamela was in Rome absorbing potatoes, Madge Burnand, now a widow, wrote her sweet, resigned letters from another hospital, in Chichester, where she was dying. The hospital fees and her doctors' bills had been paid by Pamela.

Madge had asked the doctor whether she was about to die. He replied: "That is in God's hands." She smiled and said she knew what that meant and could they send for her lawyer so that she could write her will? Camillus attended the funeral, posting Pamela a handful of tiny flowers from the graveyard of the church. He told his mother the furniture place didn't pay a fortune but it kept him out of trouble and out of debt. Goodman still had no news of any job, but she was not to worry about that or about her accumulating bills, which he was sending on to Rome.

Goodman found Camillus a position in the city with a stockbroker, but it was not enough to distract him. Pamela thought someone his own age and gender might help calm him down. She asked Peggy Butler if Joe Hone, then twenty-two, might travel from Ireland and introduce himself to Camillus. Perhaps he could even stay at Smith Street? In the late summer of 1959, Joe moved into her Chelsea house, sleeping in Pamela's little studio in the garden. It was all so awkward, extremely awkward. Camillus worked in the city in the afternoon, gambled at private parties in the evening and slept all morning.

In the late afternoon, Joe and Pamela sat in the drawing

room overlooking Smith Street. On the landing nearby, she took from the drinks cabinet one red and one white Martini bottle, and mixed her favorite cocktail. They sipped a single cocktail each, talked politely, waited. Camillus remained stead-fastly not at home.[6]

Late that year Camillus's father, Nat Hone, died in Dublin, his poor diseased lungs unable to carry him one more day. He had made his peace with a Catholic God. In a last gasp con-version, Hone had embraced the Catholic Church, becoming close to Dr. John MacQuaid, the Archbishop of Ireland.

The deaths of Nat and Madge, and the nagging problem of Camillus, might have meant that 1959 was the blackest year of Pamela's life but for one quite marvelous piece of news. It came in a long letter from the offices of Goodman Derrick in Bou-verie Street in the City, on July 3. For months, Pamela's New York lawyers had been negotiating the possible sale of Mary Poppins to the Walt Disney organization. Arnold Goodman had seen William B. Dover, their executive story editor, and his side-kick, a Mr. Swan, who had made what he believed was a firm offer to turn Mary Poppins into a movie. This was the moment that would transform Pamela's life. The offer propelled her into a decade of fame and wrapped her in financial security which even in her old age amounted to millions of pounds. Disney did not just buy the Mary Poppins story but swallowed it whole, as a shark takes a minnow. It became, officially, "Walt Disney's Mary Poppins." P. L. Travers became merely a consultant, with most of her requests to Disney charmingly but firmly turned away. She fell into Walt's embrace like a lovesick fool, but the fortune he gave her almost made up for the betrayal.

The July letter to Pamela from Goodman was a well-drafted, concise document from a tidy legal mind. He covered three parts of the Disney offer. First, Pamela was to prepare

Travers with Camillus in Gstaad, 1947

Camillus aged 19

Julie Andrews with Tony Walton

"She shelters the posies on her hat in a *Mary Poppins* rain scene"

Julie Andrews and Walt Disney

Julie Andrews, Walt Disney and Travers at the premiere of *Mary Poppins*, 1964

"Andrews gets her face dirty in a chimney-sweep scene"

Choreographer Marc Breaux had a lot of fun rehearsing dance routines with the film's stars.

POLICE PASS

Walt Disney's

MARY POPPINS

GRAUMAN'S CHINESE THEATRE

6925 Hollywood Blvd.

THURSDAY EVENING, AUGUST 27, 1964 AT 8:30

Police pass for *Mary Poppins* premiere, August 27, 1964

PRACTICALLY PERFECT IN EVERY WAY

September 4, 1964

Mrs. P. L. Travers
c/o Mrs. M. W. Coward
R. F. D. 2
Box 271
Mount Kisco, New York

Dear Pamela:

I received your very nice letter and note with care its contents, and understand it very clearly. I am enclosing three copies of the program bearing Walt's autograph, which you requested.

I am also enclosing another comment by George Todt of the Los Angeles Herald-Examiner. He is not a motion picture critic, and very rarely, if ever, refers to anything pertaining to the entertainment industry. He confines his writing to politics, international affairs, etc., etc., and it is quite unusual for him to give his whole space to our film.

Rather than compile a scrap book, I thought it best to continue to send on the reviews as I receive them here. I am going to ask Charlie Levy in New York to forward to you directly the reviews that are published in the New York press following the picture's opening. Likewise, Arthur Allighan will be happy to give you a collection of the reviews from the British press as he receives them. It would be quite difficult for me to attempt to get a complete collection from this point.

You will also be happy to know that MARY POPPINS, as of the conclusion of business Thursday night, smashed the house record, grossing the largest amount of money and the largest paid attendance since the Grauman's Chinese Theatre first opened its doors. The previous house record was $53,000 for a week's business. MARY POPPINS grossed slightly more than $60,000. If this is any indication of what can be expected, I feel that this picture will make history.

Best regards.

Sincerely,

William B. Dover

Walt Disney's **Mary Poppins**

PRACTICALLY PERFECT IN EVERY WAY

September 28, 1964

Mrs. P. L. Travers
c/o Harcourt Brace Inc.
757 Third Avenue
New York, New York

Dear Pamela:

Thanks very much for your note bringing me up to date as
to your contemplated plans. I have been away for a week
on holiday, and just returned, I saw a collection of the
New York reviews, and they are extremely gratifying. The
New York reviewers are by and large pretty sophisticated
people, and it was difficult to anticipate how they would
react to a picture of the nature of MARY POPPINS.

I know by now that you have seen most of them, but inasmuch
as some may be missing, I am sending you this collection,
and will forward others that come in directly to your London
address.

I have every conviction that the London premiere will be a
source of great satisfaction to you, and that as time goes
on you will be more and more pleased with what emerged out
of that first meeting we had in Cyril James' office when it
appeared that there was a chance for MARY POPPINS to reach
the cinema screens of the world.

I certainly appreciate your attitude, and trust, and will
certainly keep in touch and post you on all that comes my
way.

                              Warm regards,

                              Bill

                              William B. Dover

WBD:ks
Enclosures

SAMUEL GOLDWYN

September 11, 1964

Dear Walt:

Once in a lifetime -- and only once -- a picture comes along which cannot be compared to any other and to which no other can be compared. A picture which writes a new page in motion picture history. A picture which has such universal appeal that it is a pure delight to father, mother, children, grandparents and grandchildren -- it makes no difference who.

You have made it -- MARY POPPINS.

You have made a great many pictures, Walt, that have touched the hearts of the world, that have spread your name and your fame to every corner of the globe, and you have deserved every bit of acclaim that has come to you. But you have never made one so wonderful, so magical, so joyous, so completely the fulfillment of everything a great motion picture should be as MARY POPPINS.

I hope everyone in the world will see it -- that is the nicest thing I can possibly wish them.

Sincerely,

Sam

Mr. Walt Disney
Walt Disney Productions
500 South Buena Vista Avenue
Burbank, California

Travers in her residency at
Smith College, 1966

"The books wrote themselves,"
P. L Travers said of *Mary Poppins*

The character of
Mary Poppins:
from literary
heroine to film star
to advertising icon

Travers's collection of mementos presented to the New York Public Library, including the original Dutch doll that was the model for the Poppins illustrations

Travers in 1966

Travers at home in Shawfield Street, Chelsea, 1995

a story outline or "treatment" for submission to Disney as soon as possible. The Disney lieutenants had told Goodman this did not prevent the boss from enlisting the services of other writers to put a fresh slant on the work. Disney would then give Pamela the completed treatment for her approval. She would be asked to give her blessing to this. It had to be understood that such a treatment was not a shooting script. There would be reasonable latitude to depart from it as the film went on.

Secondly, she would be *consulted* (Goodman's emphasis) on casting and other artistic questions as far as possible. Finally came the matter of money. There would be a $100,000 down payment against the percentage she would receive from the receipts of the film—that was, 5 percent of the producer's gross (the distribution receipts after the cost of prints, distributors' costs and advertising). They would not pay for the treatment, since the whole deal was conditional on it being used, but would pay for the time it took—say, £1000. Goodman thought this a fair fee for very little work. He told her this was not to be any form of script but merely a succinct statement of her conception of how different Mary Poppins stories could be used.

Goodman advised Pamela she should think not only about the $100,000 but about the 5 percent. As she knew, Disney films were timeless, with little "contemporary aspect," which meant they were released over and over again. This meant, for her, a form of income for life. On the other hand, of course, she might only be left with the $100,000.

If she agreed, the transaction would mean she had to grant full rights to the stories, other than the written word, which in turn meant that control of any possible theatrical, musical, TV or radio production would pass to the Disney organization on terms to be settled.

Arnold Goodman, the ultimate fixer, suggested they meet to discuss the deal urgently.

13

The Americanization of Mary

She called it "uneasy wedlock." Walt Disney and Pamela Travers danced around each other—he the great convincer, she the reluctant bride—then, after the slow courtship, came the quick consummation and a lingering cool down. The result of their five years locked in this awkward embrace was Disney's greatest film of the 1960s, a movie about American values and family reconciliation. Made in America in 1963, Walt Disney's Mary Poppins was released the following year, when Lyndon Baines Johnson promised to heal a fractured nation with his concept of the "Great Society."

Created by Disney, a fervent anticommunist and family man who stood four square for the American way, the movie *Mary Poppins* was only loosely based on Pamela's original books of Mary Poppins adventures. Disney seized upon the fantasy world of the books but eliminated their mystery. He made a film of no ambivalence, no depth, and very little sadness. But then his aim was not to mystify and challenge, but to show how peace was restored to a family in strife. His happy family and jolly songs helped cheer middle America.

Few in the movie audiences knew the name P. L. Travers, which appeared in small type in the opening credits. And certainly no one knew or cared how Mary Poppins arose. Later, many interviewers quizzed this unknown P. L. Travers to try to discover what inspired the nanny. Only a few suspected that she was born from a need in Pamela, whose own childhood had been out of joint and whose own little family of two was now in disarray. While the film was in production, with Julie Andrews and Dick Van Dyke prancing with penguins to "It's a Jolly Holiday with Mary" at Disney's Burbank studios, Pamela herself sat on a tatami mat in Kyoto and tried to meditate away her anxiety.

The film's great success, critical and financial, helped soothe the pain for the rest of her life. Walt Disney's *Mary Poppins* cost $5 million to make, grossed more than $75 million, launched Julie Andrews on a movie career, earned her an Academy Award, and produced a handful of hit songs which remain lodged in the subconscious of three generations. Thirty-five years after the movie was first released at Grauman's Chinese Theatre in Los Angeles, grandmothers and mothers sit with their children in front of the *Mary Poppins* video or DVD knowing, as if learned by rote in a dusty schoolroom, "Chim Chim Cheree," "A Spoonful of Sugar" and "Supercalifragilisticexpialidocious." To those generations, Julie Andrews is Mary Poppins and Mary Poppins is Julie Andrews, an amalgam and culmination of all her successful roles from Eliza Dolittle to the singing nun, Maria, in *The Sound of Music*. Julie's Mary Poppins was not the sharp, plain nanny created by Pamela and Mary Shepard but a sparkling, reed slim, sugar-sweet soubrette, with rounded vowels and a voice *Time* magazine described as "polished crystal."

Disney had lusted after the Poppins stories for almost twenty years, ever since the evening just before Christmas 1944 when he walked by the room of his daughter, Diane. He heard his eleven-year-old laughing out loud. What was so funny? She held up a book—*Mary Poppins*. The book had sat on her bedside table for most of her childhood. Her mother, Lilian, liked it too, often reading a chapter to her daughter before she fell asleep. For years, Lilian and Diane had both asked Walt if he would make the book into a movie. In 1945, when he heard that Miss P. L. Travers was in New York, Walt Disney sent his brother Roy to see her. Roy—dull, diligent, without the charismatic manner of his younger brother—could not convince her to sign over the rights.[1]

Disney, a master of persistence, did not give up. He had survived the Depression years brilliantly with sweet Mickey Mouse and grouchy Donald Duck. In the decade to 1941, Disney had won thirteen Oscars, and, as America was getting ready to go to the war, could boast of three hugely popular movies: *The Three Little Pigs, Snow White and the Seven Dwarfs,* and *Pinocchio*. He was soon to release *Dumbo,* about a baby elephant who could fly, and was planning *Bambi,* the feel-good film about childhood. Disney had taken a gamble with *Fantasia,* a success with movie critics if not with the music world's intelligentsia. By now, his manipulation of the American consumer market was unsurpassed. But although the turnover of Disney-branded goods had reached about $100 million a year, Disney wanted more. Throughout the 1940s, Disney searched for new properties and continued to make what Pamela called "forays into the jungle" for the rights to *Mary Poppins*. She consistently refused.[2]

But Disney was about to move from the pure slapstick of his earlier short cartoons into a new, more ambitious phase. In the 1950s, he began to adapt the best-loved fairy tales and classics of children's literature into full-length animated features. The shift in emphasis from Donald Duck and Mickey Mouse probably changed Pamela's mind about Disney and her distaste for what she called "the vulgar art" of moviemaking. In 1950, Disney released the charming and top-grossing feature *Cinderella,* with its catchy song "Bibbidi Bobbidi Boo." This was followed by *Alice in Wonderland* in 1951, *Peter Pan* in 1953, *The Lady and the Tramp* in 1955, and *The Sleeping Beauty,* with music adapted from Tchaikovsky's ballet score, in 1959.

Early in 1959, Disney had made the fresh offer for *Mary Poppins* through Pamela's New York law firm, then sent his emissaries, Dover and Swan, with a precise offer to Goodman Derrick in London. This time she succumbed, telling her friends it was such a generous contract that it would not be right to refuse any longer, despite her view that Disney was without subtlety and emasculated any character he touched, replacing truth with false sentimentality.[3] But Goodman was right. It would have been foolish to refuse $100,000 and a possible income for life at a time when sales of her four Mary Poppins books were languishing and she had no steady income except from her lodgers' weekly rent.

Disney was so determined now that he had already asked Bill Walsh, one of his most trusted writers, to prepare a story outline. Walsh had been an all-around organization man for Disney for a couple of decades but in the last few years had teamed up with the screenwriter Don Da Gradi, director Robert Stevenson and songwriters Robert B. Sherman and Richard R. Sherman to produce many hit Disney films. Walsh knew what an audience wanted and he knew how to gut a book.

For his outline, he went to Pamela's first book of 1934, visualizing the nanny's arrival out of and departure into the clouds.[4]

In the face of the seductive insistence of Disney's two outriders in London, Pamela stood her ground. Yes, she would agree, but she made sure the movie would not be an animated cartoon and insisted that she should have final script approval. Walt Disney Productions and Pamela's company, John Lyndon Ltd., signed a preliminary agreement in April 1960. Then, on June 3, they signed a "service agreement" that was to last six years. Under its terms, Pamela remained entitled to the copyright in any material she wrote before the agreement and was also entitled to the copyright in material she would write while she was employed by John Lyndon Ltd. The agreement was vague about any subsequent live stage rights for *Mary Poppins*, but Disney did insist on his right to impose a freeze on any radio and television productions.

Despite Goodman's reassurance that a treatment would be simple to prepare, Pamela recruited the TV scriptwriter Donald Bull to help. Disney had given Pamela just sixty days to come up with a treatment. She made the deadline, though the words came slowly.

All through the negotiations, Pamela had something far more pressing on her mind. Early in 1960, she had asked for help from one of her Gurdjieff friends, the Harley Street surgeon Kenneth Walker. The problem was urgent: how to deal with Camillus's drinking problem and increasingly odd behavior. During 1960, he had lost his driver's license but continued to drive and one night, on a Middlesex road, was stopped by the police for driving drunk and without a license. He was sentenced to six months in Stafford Prison, a maximum security jail, where he spent his twenty-first birthday in August 1960.

Pamela longed for a piece of good news. Disney had not

responded to her script. Maybe he had dumped the whole project? On December 20, a Western Union telegram broke the drought with the news from Disney that enthusiasm was still high for *Mary Poppins*. He would set a date for presentation early in the new year. But no further word arrived until February 13, when Disney reassured her that the completed treatment was close. The more he thought about it though, the more he thought she should come to Los Angeles to spend at least a week at the studio, meeting everyone who would carry the picture through to completion. They would show her storyboards to indicate the nature of the visual presentation... "particularly with regard to the trick photography we want to incorporate to make the story properly come across on the screen."

Disney suggested she travel to the West Coast early in April. Naturally he would pay for the airfare and hotel. His letter ended with a slight warning. While Disney was "very respectful" of Pamela's wishes, there were certain things that would be best discussed at first hand. Late in March, she checked into the luxurious hacienda-style Beverly Hills Hotel. At the studios in South Buena Vista Street she met Walt Disney, then sixty, surrounded in his office by more than twenty-five Oscars, and riding high on the success of his recent *Pollyanna* and *The Absent-Minded Professor*. By the late 1950s, Disney knew what the American public most wanted to see—a happy family. Now, once again, he had got just the right property to do so with *Mary Poppins*. He saw Mary, as he called her, as assertive but still sexy, cool yet hot, as pretty as the shapely dreamgirls Cinderella and Tinker Bell that his animators had drawn. This new angel would rid the Banks home of chaos, just as his *Parent Trap* of 1961 transformed a dysfunctional, divorced family into a happy home.[5]

Pamela, middle-aged, a touch frumpish yet sharp, and Walt Disney, dapper, pencil-thin-mustached, were alike in some surprising ways. Both were driven to the point of physical exhaustion, both were burdened by the same work ethic, the same conservative values. Pamela, two years older than Disney, was a small-town girl at heart, though she liked to hide it, while he boasted of his small-town childhood in the midwest, wearing his Main Street origins like a cartoon costume. They both avoided talk of sex, claiming to be shocked by any obvious salaciousness in print or in art, and, oddly enough, both spent a lot of time worrying about defecation. Pamela was obsessed with her problem bowels while Disney joked often and loudly of turds.[6]

Disney had been married for decades. He and Lilian lived comfortably and reclusively in Holmby Hills in Los Angeles, spending their weekends at their thousand-acre Smoke Tree Ranch near Palm Springs. He loved trains and built a model railway around his Holmby Hills property. But apart from his comfortable marriage, there was one big difference between Disney and Pamela. Disney's purpose in life was entertaining people...bringing pleasure, particularly laughter, to others rather than being concerned with expressing himself or "obscure creative impressions." Pamela specialized in obscure creative impressions.[7]

Walt Disney was "the great convincer" in the words of his marketing director, Card Walker. He liked to exercise his famous eye-lock technique in which he caught his victim's gaze and held it tight. If he or she turned away, Disney would say "What's the matter, aren't you interested?"[8] Still, Pamela was his match. She called him "Mr. Disney" (almost everyone called him "Walt") and did not turn away during their long talks in Burbank that April. She often talked later of one particular exchange: Disney had said to her "I think you're very vain!" She replied "Oh, am I?" "Yes," he went on, "you think you know more about Mary Poppins than I do." "Well, vain or not," she smiled, "I think that I do know more than you." Disney trumped, "No you don't!"

Pamela had scribbled all over the script written by Bill Walsh and Don Da Gradi. It certainly wasn't the one she and Bull had prepared so painstakingly in London. For a start, she had planned to use at least seventeen episodes from three of her books: "East Wind," "Mrs Corry," "Laughing Gas," "John and Barbara's Story" and "West Wind" from the first book; "Miss Andrew's Lark," "The New One," "The Kite," "Balloons and Balloons" and "Bad Wednesday," "The Evening Out" and "Merry Go Round" from the second book; and "The Marble Boy," "Mr. Twigley's Wishes," "The Cat That Looked at a King," "High Tide" and "Happy Ever After" from the third book.

Walsh and Da Gradi, though, had created completely new adventures for Mary Poppins, and had adapted just three stories of Pamela's—"East Wind," "The Day Out" and "Laughing Gas," while incorporating a few details from "The Bird Woman," "John and Barbara's Story," "The Kite" and "West Wind."

Each day for ten days, Pamela went into the production studios. Line by line, she scoured the treatment prepared by Da Gradi and the Shermans. The Sherman brothers, Richard and Robert, were more than musicians. As staff writers for Disney, they had written the songs for *The Parent Trap* and *Summer Magic,* and were to play a major part in developing the script of *Mary Poppins.*

On day one, the Sherman boys began at the beginning, reading from the script: "Autumn in 1910, London. 17 Cherry Tree Lane, the Banks household is in an uproar."

Pamela immediately cut in: "Hold it!"

In the first of her objections, interruptions and interjections, she took alarm at the possible look of Number 17 Cherry Tree Lane. Pamela promised to give them a photograph of 50 Smith Street so they could see the Banks house was quite like hers, except with more to the garden.

"The father comes home to find the children misbehaving. Mr. Banks talks of his wife's job."

"Just a minute. That's, that's, not job, ah, ah..."

"Domain?"

"Er, yes."

"Responsibility?"

"Well, we can't have job. Let's leave it for the moment."

"Sphere of influence?"

"Oh no no no no no. She just lived. That's far too, you know..."

In the archives of Disney and in the records Pamela kept of her encounter with Disney are transcripts of six audio tapes made during the ten days of conferences. The tone of the writers is deferential, the tone of Pamela is both anxious and dictatorial. She wanted to make one thing *very clear* to them. It was integral to the book and to the story in whatever form that Mary Poppins should never be impolite to anybody, and particularly not to Mr. or Mrs. Banks. The comedy came from this grave, quiet person through which magic happened.

As the days dragged on, it became clear that Pamela wanted signposts to her own family story scattered throughout the film. For a scene in which Poppins measures Jane and Michael Banks she urged the writers to use the kind of long, roll-up tape measure her mother had when she was a little girl. Later, she issued instructions that Mr. Banks must be in pajamas. She remembered *her* father in pajamas. And again, the children must tell Mary Poppins not to put tapioca on the shopping list. Pamela said she hated tapioca when she was a child, so she wanted this put on record. One of the writers remarked that Mr. Banks was not always tender with his wife. This reminded Pamela of her own parents. Mr. Banks was "only untender" in the way that "any husband was in the daily misses of life." In the manner of her own father in Allora, he was not even indifferent, but merely unable to express his love.

Pamela's efforts to explain that Poppins was on a private search of her own fell on uncomprehending ears. They wanted, she thought, "magic for magic's sake."[9] But the biggest gap between Pamela's ideas and those of the writers revolved around the critical relationship between Mary Poppins and Mr. Banks, one which reflected her own idealized relationship with her father. In the movie, Mr. Banks is a disturbed and unhappy man until he is propelled into almost hysterical glee after being fired by his employer, the ancient chairman of the bank. In the books, George Banks is more grumpy than disturbed, more out of sorts and vague than he is a depressed curmudgeon.

The writers were frank with Pamela. Before they could establish a comprehensive and cohesive story, they wanted to interpret her Poppins books in one sentence: what did Mary do and why. They decided that Mary Poppins saw an unhappy family, arrived, then, through her presence, showed the family how to understand one another. When she succeeded, she left. Pamela smelled the odor of psychoanalysis. Yes, that was right in a way, but it was not so much an unhappy family as a worried one. Pamela thought any family would be upset when a nanny had left and they couldn't find another. After all, she had been in this predicament herself. She remembered when one maid was leaving and she had not been able to find another. The Banks family was only at odds with life, not with each other. She wouldn't like anything to creep into the script of "a psychological quirk" or any hint of "Freudian unhappiness." The Banks family was just—at odds.

But just at odds did not make for a dramatic script. Nor did her gentle short stories, with their Victorian ambience, amount to a cohesive story with a beginning, climax and denouement. The writers needed a storyline of black-and-white sentiments within a brilliantly colored setting, which is one reason why Mr. Banks in the movie was, outwardly, tough and chilly. She fought them on that, Pamela told interviewers later. In fact, she said, "I could hardly bear it...I've always

loved Mr Banks. I did ask in Hollywood why Mr. Banks had
to be such a monster."[10]

Why, she demanded, must they have Mr. Banks tear up an
advertisement his children had written, setting out their needs
for a new nanny? Not only that, he threw it in the fireplace.
She asked the writers if they had children. Yes, they had. And
did they write letters and make pictures? Yes, of course. And
would they tear up their pictures? Certainly not. Then why,
she asked, do you do it in a film for the children of the world
to see, why be untruthful?[11]

They smiled and asked her simple questions, apparently
pandering to her superior knowledge. She chiseled away at
them, tried to eliminate the worst of their Americanisms ("go
fly a kite") and succeeded in cutting a scene in which Mary
Poppins took the children to Timbuctoo where animals played
in an orchestra. That scene was defended by one of the writers as a sort of stylized Disney touch.

The Shermans talked constantly of fantasy—a word, Pamela
noted, much used around the studio. But to her, fantasy was
unreality. They told her earnestly they understood the meaning of Mary Poppins. It was the miracle that lay behind everyday
life. No, she replied crossly, she didn't agree. There was no
miracle behind everyday life. Everyday life *was* the miracle. The
boys did not quite cotton on to the Gurdjieffian theory.

By now, the Disney machine was too far down the track
for any retreat. Pamela signed further agreements, including
her approval of a long list of merchandising.[12] She did try to
influence casting and boasted that it was one of her conditions
on signing the contract that the whole film be played by
English actors. (In the end, Bert and Uncle Albert were played
by Americans.) The two conditions on which she would not
budge were that the film be set in the Edwardian period, and
that there be no love affair between Mary and Bert, the pavement artist. But, as she said afterward, while Disney agreed

in principle, ultimately Mary Poppins and Bert were too close for her liking, mainly because Disney was not sure Julie Andrews could carry the whole movie herself.[13]

One night at the Beverly Hills Hotel, Pamela wrote a nine-page letter to the writers, warning them against showing Mary Poppins as "a hoyden." If she was nothing but a hoyden or a tomboy servant girl, then what would happen to the magic? It was Mary Poppins's plainness of person, her absolute rightness without being pert, her calm and serene behavior in the middle of the most unlikely adventures, that made the fun in the story. She wanted them to understand that if Mary Poppins's gravity was not maintained, the whole point would be lost. In their script, the nanny had become an impertinent person. Their luck would hold if they stayed close to the books. It would not do otherwise.

On April 14, with Pamela safely back in New York, the Shermans wrote her a formal, old-fashioned thank-you letter. Its contents show that she feared she had gone too far with the Shermans. They thanked her for traveling so far and for giving them so much. She was an invaluable inspiration and guide to them all. She had referred to her "temperament" but they would like to interpret her behavior as "an ardent desire" for them to fully comprehend Mary Poppins. In that way, they might be faithful to her.[14] And Disney himself sent Pamela a telegram. The Mary Poppins project was so important, he said, that he would go along with her two suggestions if that would make her happy.[15] She had reiterated: no love affair and an Edwardian setting.

Pamela fell back easily and happily into the rhythm of New York, into the arms of the Welches' group. She thought she had squared up to Disney and won. With the glow of victory about her, Pamela impressed one newcomer to the group as a woman at the height of her confidence and power, over sixty yet with elan, vibrant blue eyes, and bubbling with energy and enthusiasm. At last, Pamela felt she was back among intellectual equals. Away she went again, leading the group into circuitous spiritual journeys as she analyzed out loud fairy tales and obscure Persian tales.[16]

Pamela was now brimming with ideas for three books to follow the publication of *Mary Poppins from A to Z*, a money-spinner for the gift market. They were *Mary Poppins in Cherry Tree Lane* (a title not published for over twenty years) and an allegory about giving called *The Fox at the Manger*, plus a novel whose main character, Mallow, would share much with little Lyndon Goff of Queensland.

Pamela needed Mary Shepard once more, first to illustrate *Mary Poppins from A to Z*, an alliterative picture-to-a-page book. This time, Shepard was not as amenable as before, especially when she heard of the Disney deal. Shepard wrote to Harcourt Brace & World: "I understand from Miss Travers that a film is to be made by the Walt Disney Co. of the Mary Poppins books. If this is so, I should like to know whether my drawings are to be used in any way and if so, I think I ought to be informed."[17] Furthermore, Shepard wrote to Pamela, she was not at all sure if she would agree to the new *A to Z* as she had so much to do.[18]

Over the next few months, the two women corresponded in a tetchy, formal kind of way, Pamela from Mt. Kisco, where she was staying with an American friend, Vanessa Coward, and Shepard from her home at Hampstead. Both women complained of their illnesses. Pamela told Mary it was not an easy time for either of them. She had suffered four years of great anxiety with no end in sight.[19] In fact, she was in such a bad state of health that she must do nothing but rest. It was not so much a serious illness as bad digestion and a queer kind of overtiredness. Pamela planned to take another cure, this time in France, then

work in the autumn. There were so many new ideas for Mary
Poppins, but she had no energy to write. She was, she told Shepard, in a state she defined as "between the acts."

In August 1961, Pamela wrote again to Shepard to tell her
she had made a start on *Mary Poppins in Cherry Tree Lane,* although
every good day was followed by a bad day. On the bad, she
could not even think let alone write.[20] At the end of September, she flew home to London. Shepard, who really was ill and
needed an operation, was not mollified by Pamela's advice to
take things calmly. Pamela advised Shepard to go peacefully to
her operation. She had tried to do this herself but had not always
succeeded. But, in the process, Pamela had seen glimpses of the
meaning of life. "Such rare glimpses meant I would not *not* have
had my burden for anything," she wrote to Shepard.

In February 1962, Shepard told Pamela she had hired an
agent, a Mr. Knight, who wanted everything in writing. The
whole relationship must be set out in a formal arrangement.
This sent Pamela into a frenzy of letter writing. She hoped no
agent would come between them, spoiling what had been a
loving and appreciative friendship. Why, she had always maintained a "punctilious duty" toward her "dear illustrator."

Next month, she wrote Shepard the letter of a woman
betrayed. Pamela had the feeling that she was being pressed
into the role of a wicked giant whereas she saw herself as a
goose who had laid five valuable eggs for them both. Did Shepard not realize that a spoken word was binding to her? She
could not understand Mr. Knight's distinction between formal
and informal agreements. After all, an IOU was the same,
whether it was written on embossed notepaper or an old envelope. She assured Shepard that she would always be able to
market her own original drawings (to which Shepard held
copyright). Furthermore, she was paying her a fair fee for
translations, and in any case, there would be no translation of
A to Z. (This turned out to be a lie.)

As to the film, she had spoken to her lawyer who said there was no question of any arrangement with the artist. Disney was using the books in live action, not animation. Pamela told Shepard not to bother to reply unless there were points she had not taken up.[21] But Shepard persisted and responded within the week that she needed more money for *A to Z* than the previous books because it required more work and effort from her than from Pamela herself.[22] In autobiographical notes she wrote for her family, Shepard later said that "for the film, my drawings were not needed and my agent won me something for compensation."

Now that Disney funds had started to flow to Pamela, she decided to sell her Smith Street house. The rental money was superfluous and the three-story Georgian house seemed far too empty without Camillus, now out of prison and living in a flat. She put her books in storage and in the summer of 1962 rented a place nearby, in Cheyne Row, while she waited for her new house at 29 Shawfield Street to be renovated. Again, it was in a street running off the Kings Road, but the Regency house was smaller and narrower than Smith Street, only two stories, with room on top for a study.

It was true, Pamela knew, that nobody wanted anything from her but Mary Poppins,[23] but W. W. Norton in the United States had agreed to publish (in November 1962) the new Christmas book, *The Fox at the Manger*. All her Christmas stories had been autobiographical and here was another: her memory of Camillus as an innocent child in 1945 when she had taken him with two of his friends to the carol service at St. Pauls, home of the Bird Woman. Each of the children in the congregation was to donate a toy to the poor. But her three little boys were unable to part with theirs: a lion whose beady eye hung by a thread, a toy bus whose paint had chipped, and a rubber mouse. "X, Y and Z," she called the three friends, as anonymous as the initials PLT.

She wished the manger held one of her favorite black sheep. She told X, Y and Z a legend about Christmas night, when a donkey, a cow, a sheep and a dove came to the Christ child in the crib with presents. The animals are given the power of speech. The child, X, asked if there were any wild animals at the crib and Pamela says yes, a fox who gives his gift of cunning to Christ. Pamela later explained to an interviewer: "I've always loved the fox, because he had a bad time at the hands of Aesop and la Fontaine and mankind generally. He's the untameable creature, that's why man dislikes him."[24]

Years later, that Christmas of 1962, she couldn't help but think of the fate of X—Camillus—whom she once described as Romulus, the twin reared by a wild wolf. The dedication in *The Fox at the Manger* read: "For C. to remind him of X."

Walt Disney was besotted with his grand new movie. He slept at the studio, filled rooms with drawings of how Mary Poppins would look, stayed in the office after the animators had left, emptied their trash cans and next morning waved discarded roughs in their faces, urging them to "go back to this." *Mary Poppins,* the musical, was to be nothing less than revolutionary stuff. In one scene, he planned to mix live action with animation when Mary, Bert, Jane and Michael would pop into one of Bert's pavement pictures. There, within a painting of one bucolic scene, they would dance with cartoon penguins, turtles, a pig, horses, and a farmyard of Disney pets, all trilling "It's a Jolly Holiday with Mary."

Disney knew the casting of Mary Poppins herself was the real key to the success of the film. In the spring of 1962, he saw Julie Andrews as Queen Guinevere in a Broadway production of *Camelot.* When she sang "What Do the Simple Folk

Do?" Disney knew he had his Mary. She could even whistle!
He raced back to her dressing room after the show, lavished
praise on her performance, and next day offered her the part.
There was something so perfectly natural about Andrews, a
beguiling candor, which belied a toughness bred into her from
years on the road as a child prodigy. From the age of five, she
had sung and danced in an English vaudeville team with her
mother and stepfather, astounding audiences with her strong
adult voice. In the 1950s, Andrews made her New York debut
in the musical *The Boyfriend,* in which she played a sweet young
thing—without affectation and with great success. But the
greatest of all her roles was the cockney flowergirl Eliza
Dolittle in Lerner and Loewe's *My Fair Lady*. Although Andrews
was a faultless Eliza, she was rejected for the film version of
My Fair Lady by the director Jack Warner in favor of Audrey
Hepburn, who looked gorgeous but could not sing at all.

Andrews had been hurt, but the rebuff must have put doubt
in her mind. She did not say yes to Disney's offer right away.
There were reasons to reject a movie career right now. She
was still young—just twenty-six—and expecting her first child
with her husband, the set designer Tony Walton, who had
recently enjoyed his own more modest Broadway success with
A Funny Thing Happened on the Way to the Forum. But Disney, the
great convincer, offered him a job, too, as *Mary Poppins*'s design
consultant. He suggested they both visit his West Coast masterpiece, Disneyland. Disney planned to escort them around
Disneyland in person. Once there, Andrews and Walton felt
as if they were in the presence of a god. "See that tree?" he
asked Andrews. "There are three million leaves on it and four
million flowers." Then he paused and added, "They said only
God could make a tree."[25]

He played her the Shermans' songs. That was it, the decid-
ing factor. She heard in them a slight flavor of vaudeville, and
knew she could sing those songs. Andrews signed a contract

for $150,000.[26] There was just one potential problem: Pamela. Disney knew that a middle-aged Poppins would be a disaster. He thought perhaps that Pamela envisaged the nanny as her own age, maybe a bit younger, and nervously asked her, just how old is Poppins? When Pamela said, precisely, "twenty-four to twenty-seven," Disney knew he was home free.[27]

Still, Pamela was desperate to see this Julie Andrews. On November 27, 1962, Andrews gave birth to Emma Kate. The next day, Pamela rang Andrews in hospital. "P. L. Travers here," she said. "Speak to me, I want to hear your voice." Andrews, still weak, told her she wanted to recover first.[28] Pamela invited Andrews and Walton to lunch. When they met, the first thing she said to Andrews was, "Well, you've got the nose for it." In any case, Andrews adored her: "She was so honest and direct."[29]

Pamela, too, was charmed at first sight. She told many interviewers she was completely won over. "I hadn't spoken to her for five minutes before I realized she had the inner integrity for the part." Andrews had confided, "I haven't read these books, I don't know anything about them and I've never been brought up on them. Tell me how to play Mary Poppins? Should I have an accent?" Pamela replied, "I won't tell you anything, you just play her as you truthfully think. Don't play it any way but yourself."[30]

At Christmas, Pamela's publishers sent her author's copies of her latest books; in a mood of exuberance, Pamela asked her publishers to send a gift set, the Mary Poppins Library, to President Kennedy's wife, Jacqueline. Her social secretary, Letitia Baldridge, replied that the president's daughter, Caroline, was charmed with the Mary Poppins Library. She knew that within a few years John Jr. would also love the books.[31]

Next, Pamela bundled up a copy of *Mary Poppins A to Z* for Walt Disney and mailed it in December with a letter, explaining that the book was for his grandchildren. She wanted him to know she had talked to Julie Andrews and found her, even in the first flush of motherhood, "very alert and intelligent." Although she had not seen Andrews act, Pamela thought she had the inner honesty and dependability necessary for Mary Poppins. Nor had she seen the actor Dick Van Dyke, who she heard was to play Bert. She hoped, in vain as it turned out, that he was English and could speak cockney. Pamela told Disney that Mary Poppins definitely did not speak cockney but had a most demure unaccented voice.

Then there was the matter of casting. She suggested Margaret Rutherford as the Bird Woman and Karen Dotrice as Jane. The children should be dressed in clothes similar to those she had marked in pages torn from *Punch* and the *Illustrated London News*. She was sure the Edwardian atmosphere would give an air of magic and fairy tale to the film. No taxis and cars, but hansom cabs, street cries and penny farthing bicycles. Disney would disappoint his audience if he did not include the Banks twins in the film, and she cautioned him that Mary Poppins was not referred to as Mary in the books except by her odd relatives. The Banks should refer to her by her full name, as if it was a title.

By now Pamela knew that Disney's writers had built up the role of Bert far beyond anything in the books. Disney's Bert was to be a one-man band, a chimney sweep and an artist who knows all about the magic of Mary Poppins and is clearly her equal in magic. Pamela wanted Disney to know that Bert must never appear as Mary's lover, but could only appreciate her from a distance. Shy, humble and loving, he would never hope that his love was reciprocated. She reminded Walt that she had never agreed to a planned love song for the two characters in the "Day Out" animated sequence and hoped he, too, had come to this conclusion. However, she did see Bert singing a song with no emotional overtones . . . something "jingling yet sincere," perhaps a melody like "Lily of Laguna."

Disney appears to have accepted her next idea that Bert should sing and dance soft shoe, while Mary looks on smiling, tapping her foot, looking prim and ladylike. Pamela also suggested Bert should seize the parrot umbrella and dance with that, telling the umbrella about Mary Poppins, then, at the end, shyly putting out a hand to Mary. The two would dance at arm's length, no words of love spoken. She reminded Walt Disney, the great sentimentalist, that if you keep things light, deep feelings can seep through.

Although Pamela was unmusical, she advised Disney on the score, suggesting that all the musical numbers should have the rhythms of Edwardian songs. In this way, old melodies would filter through the new ones, like ghosts, hints and reminders. "Lily of Laguna" could counterpoint Bert's song. "Ta ra ra boom de ay" could peep through a song sung by Admiral Boom, and "Brahms' Lullaby" could be heard through "Feed the Birds." The old songs, she reminded Walt, were not only wonderful, but back in fashion.

At this time, the film was still not cast and Disney was considering Stanley Holloway, a hit in *My Fair Lady* as Eliza Dolittle's father, for Admiral Boom. In the end, the Admiral was played by Reginald Owen and the role enlarged and broadened. (His habit of firing a gun at 8 A.M. and 6 P.M. became a running gag so simple and broad, it appealed only to children.)

Disney honored his promise to use mainly English actors with his best piece of casting: the partnership of Glynis Johns and David Tomlinson as Mrs. and Mr. Banks. He chose Karen Dotrice and Matthew Garber as Jane and Michael Banks (they were both in his previous film, *The Three Lives of Thomasina*). Three talented English character actors appeared as the maid Ellen (Hermione Baddeley), the Banks's former nanny, Katie Nanna (Elsa Lanchester), and Constable Jones (Arthur Treacher). One of John Ford's character actors, Jane Darwell (who had played Ma Joad in *Grapes of Wrath*) was the Bird Woman, and Ed Wynn played himself in the guise of Uncle Albert, who couldn't stop laughing and floated up to the ceiling on a steady diet of "boom boom" music hall jokes.

To direct the array of English talent, Disney recruited another Englishman, Robert Stevenson, who had directed *The Absent-Minded Professor* in 1961. The Shermans, Bill Walsh and Don Da Gradi had also worked on that successful Disney film, which had starred Fred MacMurray with a flying Model T.

In February 1963, Disney sent Pamela the latest script and told her his casting plans. She sent back a fourteen-page letter, her longest and most detailed yet. She was very happy with progress, she said, and felt that his film would be a great success, for it was, she thought, "a tremendous box of tricks and adventure and merriment." Yes, it was a long way from the books, but she did see that the inspiration came from them. Most of all, she was happy that Mary Poppins retained her own unknowable integrity, no matter what happened. Bert, too, was now in the right relationship to her, and so was Mr. Banks. There was no love affair, and nothing too cruel. (In handwriting she wrote on a carbon copy of this letter that it turned out not to be right in the finished film.)

But after the praise came the warnings. Pamela was horrified that her gentle Mrs. Banks had been transformed into a suffragette. However, she could see that by his choice of Glynis Johns, who was a great favorite of hers, Disney intended that Mrs. Banks was the most flustered, feminine and inadequate suffragette ever. Just why Mrs. Banks had to be a suffragette is not clear, but she was clearly a feminist in name only, and one who deferred on all matters to her husband—as did Lilian Disney. The portrayal of Mrs. Banks as a dippy dame carrying a Votes for Women banner could be seen as a sly adult joke against the new American feminists stirred by Betty Friedan's early 1960s book, *The Feminine Mystique*. This, however, did

not concern Pamela, a woman born in the late nineteenth century who got her own way with men by flirting or bullying.
Her understanding of feminism was so narrow that she told
Disney in this letter that a silly suffragette such as the movie
version of Mrs. Banks would always vote for the most handsome candidate. Indeed, Pamela added, so would she. Her main
concern was that the feminism joke would be lost on children
who would not even know what Votes For Women meant.

Then there was the problem of a new adventure written
into the script, when the Banks children visit their father's
bank which we take to be the Bank of England. Michael Banks
inadvertently starts a run on the bank by demanding his
twopence back from the chairman, Mr. Dawes. The customers
overhear his demand and rush the tellers. (If Pamela saw the
irony in this scene, invented by Walsh and Da Gradi, she did
not tell Disney. It was the Bank of England that, in 1891, had
precipitated a crisis with the Queensland National Bank, whose
directors included Pamela's Uncle Boyd.) This banking scene
remains one of the funniest in the movie, with the final credits revealing that Dick Van Dyke also plays the chairman who
eventually dies laughing at one of Uncle Albert's gags. Pamela
had told Walt the death was too gross a joke and suggested
that he merely retired, then spent the rest of his days laughing.

She was worried, too, about the opulence of the Banks
family home, which she had described in her books as "rather
dilapidated." Nor did she think the scriptwriters understood
where the Banks family stood in the social scale. Servants in
England were not rough cockneys. In this script, she said, Mrs.
Brill the housekeeper and Ellen were too common and vulgar
for English servants for that or any period. An *h* dropped occasionally, a lively phrase, were fine, but these were people who
thought of themselves as respectable and would never use
phrases such as "old sow." Even Bert was far too much of a

cockney. She remembered that the cockneys in Disney's 1961 film, *A Hundred and One Dalmations,* were very difficult for her to understand. The whole essence of cockney speech was its clarity and directness.

Page after close-typed page, she objected to each detail. Mary Poppins had been described in the script as an attractive young woman. This was more cause for concern. Poppins should not be pretty but must keep her Dutch doll appearance: black hair, turned-up nose. She begged Disney to give Mrs. Banks a more sympathetic and Edwardian name than Cynthia, which she hated. Somehow she felt the name was unlucky, cold and sexless. Why not Arabella, Victoria, Caroline, Julia, Gwendolyn, Araminta, Lavinia, Lydia, Alexandra, Olivia or Winifred? In the end, Disney chose Winifred.

Once again Pamela scoured the script for American figures of speech, objecting to "on schedule," "six-oh-one," and "outing." The last, she said, meant "a general gathering, like a Sunday school picnic, or the Elks going to Atlantic City." The British would say "going out." Nor would Mary say "larking about." She never used slang. "Freshen up" was a contemporary phrase, and would have been repugnant to an Edwardian. The writers must remember it should be "let's go <u>and</u> fly a kite." Still, she realized this was only a first draft. (It proved not to be, to her consternation.)

In the middle of 1963, Julie Andrews, Tony Walton and their baby settled into a rented house in Studio City in the San Fernando Valley of Los Angeles. When shooting began, it became clear to Andrews that she was Pamela's only contact with the progress of the movie. She received long letters from Pamela in England with innumerable suggestions about how things should be done.[32] Andrews tried to reassure the nice old lady in Chelsea.

After filming the "Jolly Holiday" and "Uncle Albert" scenes, Andrews wrote to Pamela that they were all working like fiends. She assured her that Ed Wynn was "delightful" as Uncle Albert and that Dick Van Dyke was "good" as Bert. His cockney was really not too bad. He would be an "individual" cockney instead of a "regular type" cockney. The children looked adorable, although the little boy who played Michael hated heights and there had been tears once or twice. The planned "Chimpanzoo" scene had been eliminated but her lullaby scene was back in. Pamela's letter had done the trick. Andrews urged her, "Please don't worry about anything."

Andrews was a little more forthcoming about the problems of filming the movie in an interview with the *Christian Science Monitor;* she explained that Matthew Garber did not like to fly on wires and for a long time could not be persuaded. Then someone offered him a dime if he would. After that, "he made a fortune." He was "an intelligent monster of a boy, a born charmer, a businessman in the making." For Andrews, flying was not much fun either. With wires attached at her hip level, she could rise up into the air easily enough but had a tendency to remain upright, whereas Mary Poppins had to fly on an angle. "This meant that the pull was all on my back."[33]

With the filming over, and Disney working toward a 1964 release, Pamela felt a sense of relief. She decided to spend some of her advance money. Through her Gurdjieff friends, she had learned more, and wanted to know more, of Zen. Perhaps meditation would help her gut, and those waves of vague anxiety that came so often in the night. These were before the days of irritable bowel syndrome, and her doctor must have thought that the constant churning and feeling of urgency in her bowels was psychosomatic. She had been told already that her Poppins adventures were "full of Zen,"[34] an idea that intrigued her more than any other theory.

Pamela had been haunted for years by a picture of a ninth century statue of Buddha in the Koryu-ji Temple in Kyoto and now, with a financial safety net beneath her, was the time for a spiritual journey to Japan. She decided on a quick side trip first, to see her sisters. Pamela flew to Bangkok late in July, then down to Sydney, to find Biddy and Moya living like a couple of maiden aunts in the comfortable middle-class Sydney suburb of Mosman. It was Pamela's first visit back to the city she had abandoned at the age of twenty-four. And her last. She stayed just two weeks. Ever since Boyd Moriarty had died in World War II his widow Biddy had lived with Moya, who had never married. Pamela refused to give their names to a reporter from the *Australian Women's Weekly,* as "they wouldn't care for publicity."

Her Australian publishers, Collins, had organized a modest publicity campaign for the famed children's author and in the course of one day she did her interview duty, wearing a plain tweed suit and white embroidered blouse, and, incongruously, eight Navajo silver-and-turquoise bracelets on each wrist. The press photos showed she had been to the hairdresser, her copper hair sprayed tight into a curly bubble, but the glossy coating could not hide the signs of deep fatigue around her eyes.

For the Sydney reporters, Pamela trotted out the usual tales of how she liked to be known as Anon yet cautioned the *Sun-Herald* reporter that she had recently passed a note to an American TV journalist, ending an interview on the spot because he had not even *heard* of Mary Poppins. The reporters did not ask, "And how do you like Australia, Mrs. Travers?" but if they had, she might have answered, as she did a couple of years later, with a pat answer: "I found I loved Australia—not that I want to go back there, because I don't think that's my place."[35]

In the long summer months in Kyoto, Pamela studied Zen with Ruth Sasaki, an American married to a Japanese, whom she met through her friends the Gardiners, fellow Gurdjieffians. Pamela said Sasaki was the only American woman ever to become a Zen abbess. In Kyoto, Sasaki had her own zendo, a place for meditation.[36]

Pamela studied the statues in the lecture hall and treasure house of the 622 A.D. Koryu-ji Temple, one of the oldest temples in Kyoto,[37] and read R. H. Bly's *Zen in English Literature,* "the most marvelous book." She meditated in a stone garden, was handed a rake by a monk and tentatively combed wavy lines around the pebbles. She read haiku. Pamela liked the "gnomic quality" of all haiku. As she sat on a tatami mat, her life seemed to make more sense than before. She knew of a Zen koan (a problem or riddle with no solution, used in meditation) which said "not created but summoned." This, she thought, must refer to Mary Poppins. The nanny must have been summoned by some need in Pamela.

Yet for all her new insights, Pamela never relinquished a need to control. In February, when she returned to London, she began again to manipulate Mary Shepard, telling her that a Japanese publisher was to produce a big colored edition of the first two Mary Poppins books. The publishers had suggested an illustrator's fee of £10 but, luckily for Mary, she had managed to get this doubled. With the London release of the Disney movie planned for late 1964, Collins wanted new jackets for the first books, and had asked her to approach Shepard. On the other hand, a German firm soon to publish *Mary Poppins from A to Z* did not want Shepard, planning to use their own illustrator. At long last, she said, France had decided to translate the books but the publisher, Hachette, also planned to use its own illustrator. This was a great disappointment but, alas, Pamela had "no power of veto."[38]

Pamela's thoughts now were fixed on the Hollywood premiere of the Disney movie. She was pitifully eager to attend, while Disney himself seemed just as keen that the irascible P. L. Travers did not. The big night was set for August 27, 1964, at Grauman's Chinese Theatre on Hollywood Boulevard. In a precursor to the Disney merchandising frenzy of *The Lion King, The Little Mermaid* and *Beauty and the Beast,* the Disney marketing department had signed agreements for forty-six Mary Poppins products, including girls' dresses, dolls, jewelry, and books labeled "Walt Disney's *Mary Poppins.*" In these, the story was "adapted" by various writers and artists. (One version was written with so little care that the nanny blew in on a west wind.) Pamela's American publisher, Harcourt Brace & World, produced a new combined edition of *Mary Poppins* and *Mary Poppins Comes Back,* but Disney versions outsold hers by five to one. The biggest of the Poppins promotions was the "A Spoonful of Sugar" campaign by the National Sugar Company.

Like a forgotten lover whose heart jumps at every ring of the phone, Pamela waited for an invitation from Walt Disney to attend the premiere. When none came, her lawyer, agent Diarmuid Russell, and her American publisher all asked and protested, to no avail.[39] One morning she woke knowing what had to be done. She sent a telegram to Disney. He might like to know she was in the United States (staying again in Mt. Kisco), and that she was coming to Hollywood for the premiere anyway. She was sure somebody would find a seat for her. Would he let her know details, time and place? The whole embarrassing episode was essential, she told her English publisher, for the dignity of the books and for her relationship with Disney.[40]

Disney's story editor, Bill Dover, responded quickly to tell her that Walt was sending an invitation. He offered to escort her to the premiere. Disney wrote too, wriggling out of a tight spot by telling Pamela he was counting on her presence at the London premiere of Mary Poppins but was happy to know she was able to attend the Los Angeles world premiere. They would, of course, hold a seat for her.[41] Harcourt Brace & World paid for her to fly to Los Angeles on August 26 and stay for three days at the Beverly Wilshire Hotel. Harcourt executives told her they were shocked by the Disney books of the film, agreeing with Pamela's assessment—"ghastly."[42]

Walt Disney was too busy to spend much time with Pamela at the premiere. Oh, he posed with her for a couple of pictures, but there was Julie Andrews to attend to, not to mention the photo opportunities when the miniature train rolled down the boulevard accompanied by the Three Little Pigs, the Big Bad Wolf, Pluto, Mickey Mouse, Snow White and the Seven Dwarfs, Peter Pan, Peter Rabbit, a skunk and four dancing penguins. The actors in costumes danced around Disney, ten thousand balloons were released from the train. A band in pearl-buttoned costumes played songs from the movie. From 1 P.M., more than three thousand fans had gathered to see the stars arrive for the eight thirty start. Disneyland girl guides walked guests to the doors; Disneyland staff were dressed as English bobbies. Ushers in Edwardian costumes escorted Disney executives (the men resplendent in white dinner jackets) to their seats.

The opening titles appeared as the camera panned over a luscious view of London at dawn: Big Ben, St. Paul's, the Thames, the sleepy houses of Chelsea and Kensington. Mary Poppins could be seen sitting on a cloud, powdering her nose, waiting to fly down to the Banks with her umbrella aloft. From the heavens and the city, the scene narrowed to Cherry Tree Lane with Bert, the one-man band, talking to the camera. Bert says he will take the audience on a tour of the lane (where Admiral Boom's fanlight doorway is identical to the one at Pamela's old home at 50 Smith Street).

Through the next two hours, the first-night audience enjoyed a blend of Pamela's magic with Disney's magic. His overrode hers. Yet for all its loud, vaudevillian, "aw shucks," pseudo-cockney humor, for all its whizzbang special effects, the film retained some part of the irony and subtlety in Pamela's characterization of Mary Poppins and George Banks. The Sherman brothers had produced fourteen original songs, some derivative but many unique, from "Spoonful of Sugar" and "Supercalifragilisticexpialidocious" to the anthemlike "Fidelity Fiduciary Bank." The audience loved the complex "Jolly Holiday" animation sequence with its merry-go-round horses galloping free, its dancing, kissing penguins and a barnyard of animals. The Disney studios had pulled out all its most expensive special effects (children flying up the chimney, toys putting themselves away), then mixed in delicate costumes, rich settings, and strong choreography in the style of *Seven Brides for Seven Brothers.*

Yet while the movie looked like a fin de siècle bonbon, the tone was small-town, God-fearing, in support of nuclear family values. The lasting qualities in the film proved to be brilliant performances by Andrews and Tomlinson, good dancing in the loose-limbed Ray Bolger manner from Van Dyke, very catchy songs, many spoken like those of Professor Higgins in *My Fair Lady,* and the surrealistic, stylized bank scene, which retained its impact through the film's reissues. The film story is resolved when Mr. Banks is fired from the bank, then reconnects with his family. Mary Poppins is no longer needed. The final scene, when Mary talks to her parrot-headed umbrella and flies off into the clouds, remains true to the tone of the books, bittersweet rather than cloyingly sentimental.

During the premiere, Pamela cried, to the embarrassment of Disney and his staff. It was such a shock, that name on the screen, Mary Poppins. So sudden.[43] It hardly mattered, then, that *her* name was in such small type, listed as a "consultant" at first, then in the line "Based on the stories by P. L. Travers." (Her name was even smaller in the press ads.) Afterward, Technicolor Corporation hosted a champagne party held in an English garden setting. Chimney-sweep dancers swirled guests to the music of the pearly band. Pamela, in a long white gown, felt regal, and tried to make it clear to whoever would stop for a minute that her books were still alive and would remain so, along with the film version. One woman rushed up to her and began commiserating in front of Disney. Pamela swept through the faux pas by announcing it was "a splendid film and very well cast."[44]

On the morning after, she wired "Dear Walt" her congratulations. His confection was beautifully cast and acted, lovely to look at, and true to the spirit of Mary Poppins. She carefully kept a copy of the telegram, noting on the bottom that Disney "needed praising," that there was much she couldn't say at the time. He replied formally. Disney was happy to have her reactions and appreciated her taking the time before she left town. Such a pity that "the hectic activities before, during and after the premiere" meant they saw little of each other. Bill Dover had told him she enjoyed the festivities.[45]

From Mt. Kisco the next day she wrote "THANK YOU" again and explained to Disney that she had gone to the premiere to prove to all that author and filmmaker were in harmony. His picture was "splendid, gay, generous and wonderfully pretty." The premiere was also wonderful. But, she felt she must say the real Mary Poppins remained within the covers of the books. Naturally, she hoped the movie would turn a new public toward them. And another thing. She wanted to let him know the picture fell into two halves. The scenes in the Banks home retained some contact with the books while the musical numbers were pure Disney. David Tomlinson, as Mr. Banks, held both halves together. He was absolutely right. Julie Andrews's performance was also beautifully understated.

Again, for posterity, she kept a copy of the letter and wrote on the end that it was a letter with much between the lines.[46] Pamela told her London publisher that although the film received a rave reaction, it contained little of the essence of her books. The film was "Disney through and through, spectacular, colourful, gorgeous but all wrapped around mediocrity of thought, poor glimmerings of understanding," and over-simplification. In short, it was truly a Hollywood movie that would make a fortune. Although it was the best thing Disney had ever done, for her, the finished product was simply sad. Still, she had made peace with Disney by going to Hollywood, remained friends with the writers, and was glad to have a fat-tened bank balance. Underneath all her bluster, she told her publisher the truth: that in a certain sense she enjoyed the fame and attention but she knew that her life had turned a sharp corner.[47]

After the film's release, it took about a decade for Pamela to return to the state of "Anon" from which she had sprung. She stayed on in New York for the premiere at Radio City Music Hall in September, gave interviews to build up book sales and, by night, read Yeats's "Reveries" on his childhood, recognizing something of her own family reflected in it.

Disney was aware that his competitor for awards and box office, *My Fair Lady,* was to open one month later than *Mary Poppins.* His publicity campaign took advantage of the head start. One of his press ads featured an open letter from Samuel Goldwyn. Dated September 11, 1964 and written to "Dear Walt," the letter gushed:

Once in a lifetime and only once, a picture comes along which cannot be compared to any other and to which no other can be compared. A picture which writes a new page in motion picture history. A picture which has such universal appeal that it is a pure delight to father, mother, children...you have made it MARY POPPINS. You have made a great many pictures, Walt, that have touched the hearts of the world...but you have never made one so wonderful, so magical, so joyous, so completely the fulfilment of everything a great motion picture should be as MARY POPPINS. I hope everyone in the world will see it—that is the nicest thing I can possibly wish them.

Sincerely, Sam (Samuel Goldwyn)

On September 25, the first important review appeared in *The New York Times*. The critic, Bosley Crowther, who put Pamela's name in the first paragraph, called the movie "sparkling...a beautiful production" with some "deliciously animated sequences...a spinning musical score, the nicest entertainment that has opened at the Music Hall this year. This is the genuine Mary Poppins that comes sailing in on the East Wind...a most wonderful, cheering movie." Crowther pointed out similarities in the score and look of the film with *My Fair Lady,* and Judith Crist in the *Herald Tribune* described Andrews in *Mary Poppins* as "the fairest lady of them all. She is superb, only the grouches and nit pickers should stay at home."

The ads ran the rave lines from the reviews: "It glows and it gladdens," Archer Winsten in the *New York Post;* "Walt Disney has bestowed an eye popping family package," *Cue* magazine; "A delight, wonderfully imaginative, entrancing," William Peper, *World Telegram and Sun*. A critic bylined "JWL" at *The New Yorker,* though, grumbled "Why Mr. Disney has chosen to mingle two utterly dissimilar mediums [*sic*] is his secret. Miss Andrews and Mr. Van Dyke wisely make no effort to out act the talking pigs, laughing horses, and urbane turtles...Miss Andrews as Miss Poppins is less acerbic than the original and the wistful air with which she finally packs her magical bot-

tomless carpetbag and abandons her little charges would seem
to hint at a not too distant reunion."

The sharpest slap came from Francis Clarke Sayers, once
the director of children's services for the New York Public
Library, whose letter to the *Los Angeles Times* sparked follow-up
interviews. Sayers said in her letter that "the acerbity of Mary
Poppins, unpredictable, full of wonder and mystery, becomes,
with Mr. Disney's treatment, one great marshmallow-covered
cream puff."

Pamela yearned to speak out about her own, real, Mary
Poppins but she was too frightened of Disney and too cautious
about a possible sequel to do so. She told an interviewer that
"there is provision for a sequel but on terms to be agreed." A
Mary Poppins Comes Back was unlikely, however, as Disney was
"against sequels on principle" and Julie Andrews didn't appear
interested. She read that Andrews, who had gone on to make
the movie *The Americanization of Emily,* and would soon star in
The Sound of Music, now demanded $1 million or more for a
picture. Pamela was so keen for a sequel that she was going
to speak to Julie and "if he [Disney] wants her, she must be
generous... He gave her her first chance. If he wants to do a
sequel I'm on his side."[48]

In 1965 two magazines asked her for articles about the
making of the film, and she hoped, when the publicity died
down, she might do this honestly. The only problem was a
potential sequel. Pamela knew she must remain silent, not
wanting to work with "a prickly porcupine." Disney, she knew,
could be ferocious. Once, when she made a disparaging
remark, he turned on her with anger. Why had she spoken
against the film? He gave her bread and she had paid him back
with a stone. Pamela wrote to a friend that she had tried to
maintain a harmonious relationship with Disney but it always
amounted to "uneasy wedlock." She thought Disney wished her
dead; after all, until now, all his authors were dead and out of

copyright.[49] He was cross, she said, that she hadn't obliged him.[50]

By 1966, all thoughts of a sequel were abandoned. In a message to stockholders in his company's annual report, Walt Disney said he was not going to make a sequel to *Mary Poppins*. By then he was near to death from lung cancer, and died a few months later, on December 15, 1966.[51]

Gradually, timidly at first, Pamela spoke against the movie, in both letters and articles that she kept, copied and labeled for her files. The first was a letter to a student at Illinois State University. In this, she explained how much she minded seeing the words "Walt Disney's *Mary Poppins*" on billboards everywhere. Filmmakers should be humble enough to say "P. L. Travers's *Mary Poppins,* screened by Walt Disney."[52]

Next, she told a contributor to *The New York Times* that the movie went against the grain of the books, that it was merely a colorful extravaganza, as far from true magic as it was possible to be. The introduction of Bert as a "co-magician" with Mary Poppins ruined the film and made nonsense of the character of Mary. But no, she told the journalist, she could not quote her in the *Times*.[53]

Even before Disney died, Pamela confided in Janet Graham, writing for the *Ladies' Home Journal,* that she hated some parts of the movie, including the animated horse and pig. What's more, it was all quite shocking when Mary kicked up her Edwardian gown and showed her underwear. (Nevertheless she had to admit that children loved the film, which led them in great numbers to the books. Since the movie, sales had tripled.[54]) By the time Roy Newquist quoted her in his book, *Conversations,* in 1967, Pamela inflated the impact of the movie to an emotional shock that left her deeply disturbed. It was all so externalized, so oversimplified, so generalized. Not vulgarized really: "The movie hasn't simplicity, it has simplification." By 1968, she "couldn't bear" the movie. "All that smiling, just like Iago. And it was so untrue—all fantasy and no magic."[55] Definitely, she did not want to be remembered for the movie.[56]

In October 1964, when Pamela returned from New York to London, the press was full of "this unknown Englishwoman" who had inspired the hit movie. Collins brought out its new edition of the first *Mary Poppins,* wrapped in a pink-and-white candy-striped jacket with a picture of Julie Andrews on the back.

"Now," said *Trade News* reporter Ruth Martin, "people are asking, "who is P. L. Travers?" She is, in fact, a bright eyed, slim and lively woman of middle years with a bubble cut hairdo and a determination to remain as anonymous as possible in the present circumstances." Martin interviewed Pamela at 29 Shawfield Street, her "charming, newly done over Regency house in Chelsea with its white painted exterior and dove gray, elegantly fanlighted door, spanking new decor, gleaming modern kitchen, little patio garden where she grows spinach and has barbecue suppers, white-walled top floor studio, with its picture windows and tiny balcony." Pamela told Ruth she wasn't too happy about the line "Walt Disney's *Mary Poppins*": "It is *Mary Poppins* arranged for the screen by Walt Disney, just as it is J. M. Barrie's *Peter Pan,* cartooned by Walt Disney— that would seem to me the proper way of describing it."[57]

The "Royal European" premiere of *Mary Poppins* was held at the Leicester Square Theatre on December 17, 1964. Inside the Walnut Lounge, above the foyer, Pamela curtsied deeply as she was presented to Princess Margaret and Lord Snowdon. She stood with Julie Andrews, David Tomlinson and Hermione Baddeley. Walt Disney didn't make it. He sent along a couple of directors of the company instead. (The next week, Collins's public relations department dutifully sent the Mary Poppins books to Princess Margaret, for her children.)

The reviews confirmed Pamela's fears. London was not as addicted to sugar as middle America. This was swinging

London, the city of Pete and Dud, Carnaby Street in full psychedelic flower, and the Kinks in pink jackets and black silk stockings singing "You Really Got Me." Dilys Powell, London's senior critic, was disappointed by the flat, cartoonish tone of Disney's *Mary Poppins*. Powell had done her homework by rereading the original book—"created by an Englishwoman" —and found "I haven't liked a children's story as much since I was introduced to *The Borrowers*. The success of the book seems to me to lie in its fusion of magic and the everyday. But in the movie, the talented Dick Van Dyke has been persuaded to portray Miss Travers's pavement artist as the American cinema's idea of a cockney card, all smirk and bounce." And as for the magic adventures, "instead of being an imaginative extension of the everyday—instead of coming from within—the characters are nearly always piled on from the outside." Another critic, David Robinson of the *Financial Times,* sniffed at *Mary Poppins*'s "lurching unevenness," and "rather dated and common flashiness."

The four months from Hollywood to Leicester Square amounted to both more, and less, than Pamela hoped. Who would really understand what she had been trying to say with her magical nanny? Her heroine had been hijacked. Who was left to tell? Not Frances, not Monsieur Bon Bon, not Madge, not AE. All dead. The media, hungry for a new celebrity to boost for a minute, had clattered around her, distracting her for a while, but by midwinter it was all over. Pamela took refuge in a bad bout of pneumonia. She planned to recuperate at Todtmoos-Rutte, in the Black Forest. Almost missing a deadline, she mailed a commissioned piece for the spring book review on children's books to Belle Rosenbaum, an editor of the *New York Herald Tribune,* who sympathized, "Pneumonia is a nasty business and I hope it has disappeared for keeps. The clear piney Schwarzwald [Black Forest] air should be a cure."[58]

Pamela told Rosenbaum to return her original manuscript

as "my papers have been asked for by a university." They hadn't, but she hoped she might sell them. After all, her name remained newsworthy in the United States. She had left for Germany with the news that *Mary Poppins* had won five Oscars: best actress, best editing, best song ("Chim Chim Cheree"), best original musical score and best sound. But in the end, it was to be *My Fair Lady*'s night out. That musical won nine Oscars, including Best Picture, in competition with *Becket, Dr. Strangelove, Zorba the Greek* and *Mary Poppins*.

The more the awards, the higher the gross, but for Pamela, the better news came in a letter from Dr. Dennison Morey, a Californian rose grower. He had read in the magazine *Saturday Review* that her favorite flower was the rose, that the heroine in "Sleeping Beauty" was sometimes called Rose, and that she was working on a new book, *About the Sleeping Beauty*. He eventually bred three new roses: Pamela Travers, Mary Poppins and Sleeping Beauty. Pamela told Morey she "could hardly believe such an honor." To her, the rose was "the flower of all flowers." Furled, curled, it never gave anything away. A rose was to be envied, obviously, for its secretive nature.[59]

Like Mary Poppins, and her favorite Buddha, Pamela was now an expert at not explaining. No one but her closest Gurdjieffian friends knew what she was really doing in Todtmoos. The piney air was not the reason she went to the Black Forest. The real attraction was the latest Mr. Banks in her life: the psychoanalyst Professor Karlfried von Dürckheim, a former German professor of psychiatry whose so-called initiation therapy combined Christianity with Zen Buddhism. Von Dürckheim had lived in Japan for eight years, until after the war, when he returned to Germany and, in 1948, established his Existential Psychological Training and Encounter Institute in Todtmoos. He wrote as much as he practiced psychiatry, and from 1950 began to publish books: *Japan and the Culture of Silence,* then *Hara: the Vital Center of Man* and *Everyday Therapy*. Von Dürckheim promised Pamela peace of mind if she practiced meditation and breathing exercises. He did not offer a complete physical cure to his patients suffering from acute physical problems, but told them his therapy would lead them to insights into themselves.

For Pamela, insight came slowly, despite the daily breathing exercises and long discussions with von Dürckheim about her life.

In her mid-sixties she was still a fractured woman, frazzled but still flirtatious, jittery, yet reveling in the limelight, as fascinated by herself as a lonely woman can be. Eventually these pieces coalesced into an eccentric whole as she adopted the role of a grand and wise old lady. The flirt in Pamela, all her playful instincts, were never to resurface. They had gone out for one great public farewell late in 1964.

That winter, when she was trying to sell more books in New York, she had given an interview to Haskel Frankel of the *Saturday Review*. He confided he had no interest in meeting P. L. Travers but found himself, the night before the interview, reading *Mary Poppins* in bed and scrunching up, with that sensation of digging deeper under the covers. Every time he straightened, he caught himself digging down again into a deeper scrunch. By dawn he was "hopelessly in love" with Pamela. Frankel found her the next day "in a darkish corner of a restaurant sipping something mild." At one stage in the interview he took out a sketchpad, noting her blue eyes, curly hair. Reddish brown, was it? She answered, "If you can imagine a blond mouse or perhaps a mousy blonde, I think you will have it." What was he doing? Nothing much. Just a sketch. Suddenly she said, "I wish you could see my feet. I'm very vain about my feet, but I don't suppose I can put those on the table for you?"

His soup arrived—Italian spinach. She looked suspicious. He made her take a spoonful and she asked whether he liked women. He did. She smiled. "I knew it! Many men say they like women but what they really mean is that they like one woman. You can always tell men who really like women: they always want to share things from their plate." He looked at her. She asked, "Please don't make me an éminence grise. I'm really quite a lunatic, that's what saves me from being carted off."

She tried, then, to get him back on the narrow path of questioning she expected from interviewers. Why hadn't he asked her why she wrote for children? But Frankel wouldn't play, telling her he had hardly needed to ask her anything. She did so nicely by herself. Undeterred, Pamela sniffed, "Well I don't write for children." Then he came up with the standard line, why did she call herself P. L.? Because she did not want to have this label of sentimentality put on her, so "I signed by my initials, hoping people wouldn't bother to wonder if the books were written by a man, woman or kangaroo." She looked up at him: "Won't you ask me something different?" He thought. She looked hopeful. "You do," she drawled, "come from that nice, intelligent magazine. Do ask me something that others don't." "Okay," he said, "what are you doing on Saturday night?"

Pamela shrieked, clapped hands, hit the table. "Oh, put that in, that's different, do put that in." Then she turned coy again, confiding that her greatest joy would be to have a rose named after her. The daisy was a child's favorite flower. It was open. But the rose was never open, not until the last moment. Frankel saw her arms come up about her and somehow turn into petals as she whispered, "It's the folded rose, the secret rose...aahhhh."

This "secret rose," which, he suspected, "was more P. L. Travers than even Mary Poppins, folded herself into a sensible tan raincoat." She departed, gurulike and enigmatic. "Intimate life is the only life I can bear. I'm not interested in the passing scene because it passes." Then, "a smile, a wave, and P. L. Travers, world famous and happily unknown, slipped away into a gray New York day. On very pretty feet, may I add."[60]

Pamela later told an interviewer that Frankel's piece was "charming." She just wanted to correct one point. She had written to Frankel to say "I never, ever wore a tan raincoat. It would be *beyond* me to wear a sensible tan raincoat. It was pale blue and *French silk*."

With that, the flirt seemed to fold herself back into a bud. That month, she complained in a press report that she had recently been rather dismayed by the American attitude toward grandmothers: "The object of many women's lives is to be a grandmother and looked to as the storyteller, the wise woman, the funny woman."[61]

The French silk flirt was going to subsume now, into the wise woman and storyteller. In the summer of 1965, at Shaw-field Street, she submitted to a long interview with a writer, Janet Graham, in which she said, "I think the whole purpose of a woman's life is to become a grandmother. I've said this again and again and again, nymph, mother, we have to become wise old crones, carrying the traditions we've learned. You see that should be our aim, to gather it all up at the end of our life." This was the role of women, of the "triple Goddess"— which reminded her that AE had called Mary Poppins a goddess.[62]

But behind the new persona of crone, Pamela seemed to be trying to stamp out all traces of the sad child within her. The transcript of the interview, which she kept, is a summation of her life at the age of sixty-five. She spoke of her mother and sisters, and how she spoke comfortingly at times to her dead father. When the article eventually appeared in *Ladies' Home Journal,* it carried the headline "The Cup of Sorrow in Every Woman's Life." Much of the interview had revolved around the way women return to an almost basic state of sorrow. To Pamela, sorrow was the opposite side of the joy she found in Blake and Mozart. It was how she felt, still, at sunset. That was always "terrible sorrow." She told Graham that the "cup of sorrow" was always full. This was a big theme of hers. That afternoon, Graham talked of the sorrow of unrequited love which could be "a kind of secret joy." At that, Pamela took fright: "Ah well, *that* I'm not going to put my opinion upon." She did make veiled references to Camillus, but never once said the words "my son."

III

The Crone

1965–1996

"An old woman in a rocking chair . . .

Lyndon crept out to the bedroom window and looked up. The sky was so clear she could see the setting of the great constellation of Orion. It was the end of April now, not long before the cold winter months forced her inside to the fire grate.

They told her at school she had to go to Bible study and learn about Jesus, but she had discovered a book in the library about Buddha and one night took it under the covers and read about the giant statues they made in his honor.

"Ginty, turn out the light!" She could hear her mother's voice, then silence. Five minutes passed. Lyndon thought her head might burst with all it held. Shakespeare's words were mixed up in there along with a poem she wanted to write for her teacher.

She tried to sleep but the west wind was whipping up over the sleepy town of Bowral, the elm tree branches arching and dancing. Daddy had never talked about death. He just wasn't there anymore. Perhaps he had gone to play in the sky with Orion and Hesperus.

Pamela climbed out of bed and stood at the window. At the end of the paddock, she could see the creek quite swollen now, the driftwood rushing downstream fast. She felt an emptiness in her tummy, a black kind of feeling as if it no longer belonged to her. What was that lullaby mother used to sing to her: "So la *is like the earth's clock ticking."*[1]

la la la bye bye, do you want the moon to play with, and the stars to run away with?"

Lyndon could see mother rocking to and fro in her creaky rocking chair. Do you want the moon to play with? Mummy seemed to know everything, Mummy and the great aunts. When shall we three meet again? She loved that line. And the wise fairy in "The Sleeping Beauty." It wasn't her fault she didn't get an invitation to the party. Lyndon wanted to be brave and strong and wise like them. She was going to have to do it by herself, though. What were the last words of the hymn at assembly this morning?

> *We know we at the end*
> *Shall life inherit.*
> *Then fancies flee away*
> *I'll fear not what men say,*
> *I'll labor night and day*
> *To be a pilgrim.*

Lyndon's eyes closed.

14

A Crone among the Sleeping Beauties

In 1966, Pamela told a journalist from *The New York Times* that crone was "such a beautiful word, like dove—quiet and full of overtones. I would like to live so that I could become one of those old crones in the fairy tales, the last stage in the business of living as a woman." Still an actress at heart, Pamela was ready to play the role of the wise woman for the last third of her life. In theory, she knew that a crone was not a pitiful old dear, but an admirable woman combining all the qualities of Mother Goose, a prophetess and a nurse, who could transmit her old wives' tales to the young, in the manner of Juliet's nurse. This archetypal crone went back to the Queen

289

of Sheba. She was both fairy godmother and fool, enchantress and houri.[1] Perhaps, in becoming such a crone, Pamela could abandon her lifelong search for a male guru and become her own guide.

In reality, though, Pamela fought cronedom, as every woman does. After all, who would want to listen to the seer she planned to become? With no little boy of her own to hover by her rocking chair she had to turn elsewhere, and in the 1960s found a willing audience in the undergraduates who literally sat at her feet in a university dormitory. Pamela spent the autumn semesters of 1965 and 1966 as a writer in residence at two women's colleges in Massachusetts, first at Radcliffe College, part of the Harvard University campus at Cambridge, then at Smith College in Northampton.

The invitation to Radcliffe came early in 1965 from Barbara Solomon, the dean of Radcliffe's East House. In February, Pamela wrote back to say she had a warm feeling for the college because she had once met a special Radcliffe graduate, Helen Keller. Pamela thought no fairy tale heroine was ever more heroic than the deaf, blind and dumb Keller. As for the details, Pamela told Solomon not to worry about paying her, that she needed no facilities and that just breathing American air was "a delight" to her.

Defensive about her simple education at Allora Public School and Normanhurst, she also felt bound to tell Solomon that she could not come to Radcliffe "trailing any noble letters" after her name. She had been educated "by governesses" and at private schools. They never gave her enough of what she wanted—myth, legend, fairy tale, poetry.[2]

In late summer, she flew to New York. From the Cosmopolitan women's club on East 66th Street she wrote apprehensively to Mrs. Deane Lord, the director of Radcliffe's news office, that nobody had told her what they wanted her to do. "Never mind, I am a bit Poppinsish myself and will just let that work itself out." As for the press, she warned, she had two strict requirements. Reporters must have read her books, and they could not ask personal questions. She told Lord that ideas were much more important than "gossip." In any case, if these requirements were set, the papers would send their more intelligent reporters. Lord must not have journalists waiting for her arrival at the college, as they would ask foolish questions, such as "What do you think of Cambridge?"[3]

At Radcliffe, the staff and students were expecting a cross between the spirit of the East Wind and Julie Andrews. This was their first encounter with the strange new breed, a writer in residence, and preparations went by in a flurry of nervous anticipation. Miss Travers was to stay at East House, the grand name for a ragtag collection of old-fashioned women's dorms on the eastern side of the Radcliffe quadrangle. She would live in the East House dorm Whitman Hall. But where could such a celebrity sleep? Barbara Solomon hijacked two rooms occupied by the secretary to the master of East House, Tony Oettinger, who moved his files to Harvard. The newly named "guest suite" was plain and simple. They tried to make it look snug, installed a kitchenette without a stove, pushed in the most basic furniture.

Whitman was ruled by a house mother, senior resident Ethel Desborough. She was the last of her breed, a remnant of the mistresses who guarded the ten Radcliffe dorms from 1901. Five years after Pamela's time at the college, the administration allowed men from Harvard to take up residence in the Radcliffe dorms. But for now Harvard and Radcliffe were far from fully integrated.

Before the campus revolutions of the late 1960s, both Harvard and Radcliffe were still trying to emulate the British models of Oxford and Cambridge. There were indications of ferment, some beginnings of liberated thought that led on to the politicization of students within a few years. Oettinger was

friendly with Daniel Ellsberg, who later leaked to the press
Pentagon papers outlining the secret history of the Vietnam
War. Oettinger asked Ellsberg to speak to the Radcliffe women
and invited intellectual friends from Boston to call at the college.[4] Some Radcliffe students even marched against the
Vietnam war, which was to become such a focus for student
revolt—the "stain" on LBJ's Great Society. But Radcliffe was,
on the whole, dominated by a masculine ethos. The acting
president, Helen Gilbert, signed herself by her husband's
name, Mrs. Carl Gilbert, while the dean of East House des-
ignated herself Mrs. Peter Solomon.

When Linda McVeigh broke a ninety-three-year masculine
tradition and became the first female managing editor of the
university daily, the *Harvard Crimson,* in1966, the *Harvard Lampoon* printed a special commemorative edition in bubble-gum
pink and saturated with cheap scent. The *Lampoon* claimed the
male staff on the *Crimson* had staged a walkout, and that
McVeigh planned to paint the *Crimson* newspaper walls pastel
pink and issue "princess phones."

This Radcliffe world of "slender pretty girls who laughed
as they ate big slices of cake, who filled lecture halls with
bright balloons and looked at the world through magical colored glasses" was one which Mary Poppins would "thoroughly
approve," wrote Boston's *Sunday Globe* in an article celebrat-
ing Pamela's move to the campus.[5]

All the local media knew the author of *Mary Poppins* was
coming to Radcliffe, of course. The news office had made sure
of that, despite Pamela's instructions. She arrived at Whitman
Hall on October 5. Linda McVeigh was waiting with another
reporter from *The Harvard Crimson* to interview her in front
of an audience of students. Oettinger was surprised by this
"gray nondescript lady—our first impression—like a World
War II British movie character. Ordinary, very nice but ordinary." McVeigh didn't see the niceness in Pamela. "Now what

did you put down?" she asked the reporter. "You must quote me precisely, you know, you must put it down exactly as I say, otherwise it won't be me, it will be you. Reporting must have the same precision as poetry. I ask this not for myself, but out of a respect for writing." She discussed rocking chairs—"I like rocking because you can go anywhere, they are like merry-go-rounds"—said she had never been to university as she was privately tutored and, to a question on the Disney movie, instructed, "Don't ask about something you already know."

Pamela was happy here, though, in her hastily converted suite. She unpacked her Japanese paintings, scattered jars of candy on the shelves, just as she remembered from the apartment of Monsieur Bon Bon, and lined up her books, among them *African Genesis*, and six volumes of Stith Thompson's *Motif Index of Folk Literature*.[6]

Outside, she found the golds and auburns of the Massachusetts fall too bright, sometimes wishing for the lavender and pearly gray of England. To Oettinger, she made it clear she wanted seclusion. They all left her alone. In the Widener Library, she reveled in that heady mixture of tranquility and the excitement of discovery. She felt free there, looking up mythological references, filling in all the associations. It didn't smell of old men and socks, like the library at the British Museum, where she felt drowned by the sheer volume of books and guilty she had added to their number. Sometimes she thought she was lazy, remembering a poem by Randall Jarrell called "The Girl in the Library": "the soul has no assignments, it wastes time, it wastes time." (She said later unless you know how to waste time you don't know anything about time at all.)

Because her own fairy tale of Mary Poppins had been cheapened by Walt Disney, Pamela was more intent than ever on recapturing fairy tales for herself, on affirming the power of allusive storytelling, not spelling everything out as Disney thought necessary. For her next book she was tracing "The Sleeping Beauty" back to "unsuspected beginnings." The heroine's sleep might represent our sleeping souls, in need of awakening, like the lines from a Scottish poet, "wings folded within a heart." She also lay in bed thinking of the great Indian epics she discovered through AE, the *Mahabharata* and *Ramayana,* and especially the monkey in the *Ramayana,* Hanuman. She could not talk of this with the staff or students because "once you speak the words they are lost and will never come again."[7]

Through the autumn months, she sat with her head bowed over reference books in the library, drawing out the many versions of the sleeping princess, from Giambattista Basile's *Sole, Luna e Talia,* with its twin babies, to the interpretation of the Brothers Grimm, *Dornroschen.* In the erotic tale about femininity, she could see the elements of her own sixty-five years. "The Sleeping Beauty" was, she thought, a fairy tale fundamental to herself, one she had always loved above all others.[8]

As autumn grew into winter, Pamela saw the symbolism of the nature myth in "The Sleeping Beauty," how the earth in spring, personified by a nymph, woke from the long sleep of winter. She left the library bleary-eyed, surprised by the lateness of the hour. She walked through the dusk to her dormitory. Tucked into their rooms, their own heads bent over Eng Lit texts, the women of Radcliffe were yet to unravel into anger or subside into resentment as housewives. Before the revolution of the late 1960s, when they woke to the words of Betty Friedan, Gloria Steinem and Germaine Greer, these women expected to graduate onto the marriage market. Docile, long-haired, self-consciously academic, they seldom asked questions.

It was one of the last ironies of Pamela's life that, while she was acting out her role as a crone, one who respected and made sense of the lives of women, she was agitated by her isolation within women's colleges. "I am always happier," she told the *Radcliffe Quarterly,* "when there are men as well as girls who come to my evenings...the questions are better then, when men are around." She wondered whether "Radcliffe girls haven't got too big a feast spread before them, how can they choose between all these splendors, because after college, what do they have before them but babies and the washtub? Still, how good to have plenty to think about when one is busy at the kitchen sink."[9]

She confided in Barbara Solomon that she was quite unsure what a writer in residence should do. Solomon said "Nothing, my dear, just be here, that's what we want." Yet somehow it didn't feel right. Perhaps, Solomon added shyly, she could receive students? Slowly, the Radcliffe women and some Harvard men made appointments to talk of their poetry. One Harvard undergraduate asked how to make sense of an interview he had done with Auden. She advised "write the whole piece about his face." Pamela agreed to a regular open house at the suite. Each Thursday evening the students filed in at about eight o'clock, taking their place at her feet. She reclined on the sofa, in a kimono, her bangles glinting, her glasses on and off like a stage prop.

Like Gurdjieff before her, she did, at first, try to draw them out, told them her role was not to talk and teach, but to hear, elicit questions. She ended her own sentences with a question mark, her voice lilting upwards in the Irish way. Now you tell me? Or, what do you think, Robert? It was the men she loved, and patted, a hand on the shoulder, a reassuring "go on." Some of the Harvard boys brought her a frisbee painted "P. L. Travers." The talk was good, she remembered, the students open to ideas, and "so ready to fight me for them. I liked that."[10]

In fact, only one person fought for her ideas, one person dominated the conversation, which might stretch to midnight, sustained by cups of instant coffee. Recordings of the open house evenings feature the voice of Pamela overriding all others, driving out the questions which got too close to the personal for her comfort.

"Where were you born?"

"Oh, we're on that kind of question are we?"

"You wouldn't believe in writing an autobiography?"

"No, being born, going to school, having measles, being married or not wouldn't really be an autobiography for me. An autobiography would be an inner statement, how one grew within, the hopes, the difficulties, the aims. But as I never do want to write anything about myself, no autobiography." Robert obligingly chipped in, "You wouldn't read a biography of a writer, you would read the work?" "Yes," she sighed, "that's a beautiful question Robert, because the work is the biography."

Though Pamela insisted she could not talk about her writing as it was a very secret process, a few personal details escaped. No one had educated her, she became a journalist because it was "close at hand," she wrote very little, very slowly, had to grapple with the text, wanted to "bring much to little. I whittle and whittle…until there is only a spindle, a sliver." The first draft was torture, the second not so easy but the third "a wonderful experience." Her kind of writing was "done between the lines."

They could ask all they liked about other writers, about Yeats, and Wordsworth, Tolkien and Auden. She told them she loved *The Hobbit* and the Narnia chronicles, but felt C. S. Lewis was "looking over E. Nesbit's shoulder…Nesbit is purer." You could not help but love Alice, although she harbored "a lurking, sneaking lack of liking for Lewis Carroll himself…*Wind in the Willows,* certainly, *Charlotte's Web,* and *Pooh.*"

And again, she insisted *Mary Poppins* is not for children. When one timid student said every child in America read the Mary Poppins books she slapped him down. They were very often read by "grown men," attorneys, doctors, all sorts of people. They might be going to university, "and they write 'ah, now we see what you mean.'" But her great interest, she told them, was the small perfection of the fairy tales which had been ground down by the centuries until only the essential remained. These were not entertainments for children, but the last remnants of myths. Until a hundred years ago they were told orally to adults. The material in them was for grown-ups, "a way of facing up to life."

Once in a while, the lecture would become a free exchange of ideas. When she offered her favorite phrase that "thinking is linking," one student saw the point immediately: "Yes, only connect!" and began searching for pencil and paper but Pamela begged her not to write it down. E. M. Forster had already made the connection. But in any case, "once you write things down you've lost them."[11]

From time to time the press came to see her, often to be sent away empty-handed. *The Boston Globe* found out almost nothing from the famed author but a false date of birth, 1906. When they asked what she thought of the state of American letters, she shot back, "That would be far too pompous, too bombastic for me to answer...too broad...what I care about is the intimate, local."[12] Paula Cronin from the *Radcliffe Quarterly* was apprehensive about her interview before she opened the door to the suite. "I was about thirty, she jumped on me. I felt quite unable to carry on as I would have liked. She was legendary for being that kind of person."[13]

Pamela asked Nora E. Taylor from *The Christian Science Monitor,* "Did you prepare questions?" She insisted on "exact quotation, no paraphrasing." Asked about the origins of Mary Poppins, she strode about her room and said, "You're trying to find out my secrets. A secret is something that must not be told. Nevertheless I will tell you a secret, and that is, that I don't really know." With that she sat down, ankles crossed, wrists bangled and jangling in silver and turquoise. She waited serenely. Nora asked, "What type of adult is it that retains the childlike quality of regarding fantasy and actuality as equally real?" But "up comes the doubled fist and she disappears behind it. 'No type of adult.' 'Okay,' said Nora, 'how long was Mary Poppins aborning?'" Oh, she liked that, "what a beautiful phrase," just as she liked Nora's "big and beautiful" question: "Since Mary Poppins arrived, has she altered your life?" The film had, she admitted, "rather pulled me out of my socket." Her main aim at Radcliffe? "To arouse questions."[14]

At Christmas, not long before Pamela's time at Radcliffe came to an end, the Oettingers suggested she hold a children's party. She agreed, reluctantly, and sent handwritten notes to about twenty children. Not many wanted to go. They had heard of the cranky lady in Whitman Hall. Some children were bribed to attend and one even had to discuss it with his psychiatrist. It turned out to be not so bad. A flautist recruited from Harvard played carols. Pamela turned off the lights, and in the semidarkness the children each held a candle, stood in a circle and obediently sang the Christmas songs. They drank ginger ale with maraschino cherries, scoffed Vienna sausages on colored toothpicks and Mary Poppins cake, stuffed with dimes.

Pamela's manner with children was clearly revealed in a question-and-answer session on Boston Forum, a radio program hosted by Palmer Paine on Boston's WNAC—"your companion station." Alternately bullying and charming, threatening and motherly, she alarmed the children who had phoned to ask questions. She instructed young John to make a fuss when he could not find her books, demanding he tell the bookstore owner that "the author is very cross, really. Go and tell them that."

A little girl wanted to know if there would be another Poppins book, to which Pamela replied, "I can't bring another book out of my hat! It takes quite a long time to write a book, you know. Have you read all the Mary Poppins books? No?

Then you jolly well read those before you ask me for more!"
The little girl whispered "Oh. Bye."

The program reveals more clearly than any other interview
or college recording the public personality of P. L. Travers at
sixty-five, and, coincidentally, the acquiescent nature of the
media at the time. Palmer Paine appeared to be on automatic
pilot, smoothly reading ads for Prudence in the Pantry Roast
Beef Hash for "all you modern young women, when your husband brings home unexpected guests." In between promos, he
asked Pamela questions and interjected at regular intervals,
"This is Palmer Paine. Our subject—*what* [pause] do our children read. Our lines are open now. Good evening, you're on
the air, may I have your question or comment please?" Nothing appeared to surprise him, no quirkiness was allowed to
upset the even, fruity patter.

In contrast, Pamela was vividly alive, stressing her words
in an actressy manner, at times lowering her voice to a breathy
sigh, at others enunciating crisply, "That pleases me verrrry
much!" She responded to Paine's questions like the Allan
Wilkie Shakespearean actress of her past. When he asked, without much interest, "Where does Mary Poppins go?" she replied
"You're asking *me,* as if I *knew*." She did offer, though, that
when Mary had flown away, her typewriter was "*drenched* with
tears!"

When the conversation moved around to "young people
today" she advised listeners to follow the recent advice of the
head of the women's college Girton and "stick to your own
values no matter how much young people attack. You must
stand like a rock amid the tide, amid the storm." She confided
that one young person she knew told her, "You live in a fug
of values." Nevertheless, she told this young person, not
naming Camillus of course, "'They are my values, they may
seem very fuggy to you.' And he said to me rather shame-
facedly, 'Oh, but they're my values too.' And I said, 'No, no,

they had to be worked for very hard and suffered for, these values. And they're mine. They might be yours one day.'"[15]

In early February, Pamela said good-bye to Radcliffe with all the right polite words. She told the staff and girls she had never received a prize or gold medal for writing but this semester past was her prize, to be the first writer in residence at Radcliffe. She was sorry that she couldn't stay longer but "I have a home, you know."

Shawfield Street welcomed her home, the narrow house embracing her with its odd blend of Kyoto and Chelsea decor. She thought of number 29 as a person, disconsolate and lonely when she first found it, now a warm haven behind the front door painted lolly pink. (The other doors in Shawfield Street were sensible brown or green or blue.) The architect had tut tutted at the narrowness of the front hall. Where was she going to put her books? She had suggested taking off the roof, and suddenly his eyes had gleamed as he began to design in his mind a top-floor studio with big sliding glass doors. This became her sanctuary. Up the three flights of stairs, up there in the studio, she could dream on the sofa by the window, sit at the desk with its modern paper-shaded lights that swung to and fro. She loved the straw scent of the tatamis and the Buddha on the big terrace, loved to see the sun set over the chimney pots of the Georgian roofs. A bookcase ran the length of the room, the volumes of Blake in the best spot, by the window.[16]

In her bedroom overlooking the street, Pamela drew the curtains she had specially chosen for their whirly night sky pattern, and lay down in bed. But nothing was as she hoped. The meditation she had practiced in Kyoto would not push away the fear which often felt impenetrable, solid, separating the upper and lower parts of her body. She felt as if she was becoming this black fear, which at its worst, extended dark rays into the other parts of her. Even when she wrote of the fear, to herself, her breath came up too quickly to her chest. Pamela began to type out little notes, which she stashed in her desk, expressing her fear—a fear like the devil, she thought.

It helped if she faced the sun, as if the heat might flood the blackness away. She wanted all her rooms to face west. As she had told the Radcliffe students, all she wanted now were two comforters, "a rocking chair and a west window." They went back "to my early anxiety and love for the sun, and the anxiety of seeing it go down...I've always gone westward, this westward pull...In any house I have, all rooms should be turned to the west, I don't want to lose any part of the sun." The rocking chair "means so much to me. Sitting on a rocking chair is like sitting on a merry-go-round horse, even as a child I used to feel I was going somewhere and when the music stopped and I had to get off, I felt the same sorrow I felt when the sun went down. Rocking, I can go almost anywhere. It goes tick tock tick tock."[17]

Again, she returned to von Dürckheim in Todtmoos and tried to focus her thoughts on another autumn in America. Pamela wrote to Smith College, a couple of hours' drive from Boston, would they like a writer in residence?[18] They would. Like Mary Poppins who went to the Banks home with a mission, she had two reasons to go to Smith, or rather two people to find. One would translate her Mary Poppins into Latin, the other would translate it into Russian. Or so she hoped. Pamela had had an obsession with a Russian version since the early 1960s. In 1962, she told *The New Yorker,* "My great hope is having her [Mary Poppins] translated into Russian. I know we don't have any copyright agreement with Russia, but I say to my agent, never mind, leave her around where the Russians can steal her."[19] (Her agent, Diarmuid Russell, had in fact told her to be careful. He thought "a Russian nibble might turn out to be a shark's bite.")

Three years later, at Radcliffe, she was still complaining to students and journalists that although *Mary Poppins* was now in seventeen languages, there was no Russian translation. In an interview with *The Harvard Crimson,* she grizzled, "I've told my agents not to worry if the Russians steal them. I've told them I'd like them to hide the books in lavatories and in parks—anywhere people might pick them up and steal them."[20]

A Latin translation became more pressing when she heard of the plans to publish *Winnie-the-Pooh, Alice in Wonderland* and *Pinocchio* in Latin. Pamela wrote to the news director of Smith College, Peggy Lewis, asking for the names of all suitable academics at Amherst College, a brother college of Smith's. Lewis suggested she get in touch with Professor Peter Marshall, chairman of Amherst's classics department, and thought someone at Smith College's Russian department might be just right for the task.[21]

Pamela had already given Lewis a list of instructions of how she was to be treated at Smith and had filled out a questionnaire for the Smith College news office. In the questionnaire, she gave her date of birth as 1907, and under "place of birth," coyly wrote "British Commonwealth"—less shameful, obviously, than Australia. Her initials, she explained to Lewis, were sacrosanct and she was to be known only as P. L. Travers. She pointed out that Smith College was also host to another English author, commonly known as V. S. Pritchett, not Victor Pritchett.[22]

Fall was the prettiest time of year at Northampton, a small-town hub of four colleges, two of which were for women only. Northampton maintained the look of Main Street, USA, as nostalgic as a Norman Rockwell cover with its tall and tidy brick buildings and churches columned and porticoed in the Greco-Roman mold. Smith College was a microcosm of the town, a delicate collection of red-brick buildings, aloof and stately, each a hubbub of girls intent on a liberal, though ladylike, education.

The college had been founded in 1871 by Sophia Smith to "furnish for my own sex means and facilities for education equal to those which are now afforded in our colleges to young men." The poet Sylvia Plath had been there in the 1950s when the girls played bridge and had a rigid code of what was right for casual and dressy occasions. (Plath felt she never had the proper clothes.) Now, in 1966, the education for the twenty-three hundred students was still going to lead most of them to the altar. They hoped. In the English faculty—Pamela's hosts—only seven of the eighteen professors were women and it was to be nine years before Jill Ker Conway became the first woman president.

Late in September, Pamela was taken to her guest suite downstairs in Lamont House, a dormitory built eleven years before on money bequeathed by another benefactor, Florence Corliss Lamont. Immediately, she felt confined in a beautiful prison. As she wrote to Deane Lord at Radcliffe, after three days in her suite she felt like a dog turning around in its basket. Making sense of being a woman was all very well, but Pamela still hankered for men. She kept her distance from Pritchett, busy in another suite with his biography of Balzac and giving lectures on "Certainty and Uncertainty." The charming Victor Pritchett, now sixty-six and a practiced writer in residence, told interviewers he found it "rather engaging to live in a small town in such a beautiful part of the country. Smith is a very civilized place and incredibly hospitable."23

Pamela found it much less so. Unlike Radcliffe, neither students nor faculty had much interest or respect for the supposedly famous author. And it was, after all, a year later. The mood of the nation's universities was creeping toward revolt, to the ferment of the shootings at Kent State and the love-in at Woodstock. Smith students, like students everywhere in 1966, managed to be both compliant and rebellious, anxious and flippant. Some wore a popular lapel button, "Mary Poppins Is a Junkie."

By now, Pamela's halo of fame from the Disney movie was fading. Students at Smith loved *The Hobbit, Peanuts,* and "books of spiritual realism," according to the owner of the The Quill student bookshop. His best-sellers were Gibran's *The Prophet,* the *Springs of Wisdom* series with their quotations from great philosophers, and "the philosophical nature books of Anne Morrow Lindbergh and Rachel Carson."[24]

An assistant professor in the English faculty, Elizabeth von Klemperer, heard that Pamela was hurt "because more of a place was not made for her. She was in an odd slot because she was a writer for children. At that time, children's literature was not the big thing it became later. I don't think her interests and the department's coincided. It was a sad chapter."[25]

When a new professor came to Smith, the students usually invited them to dinner or afternoon tea on Friday. The Lamont House women planned to ask Pamela to join them at the Mary Marguerite tea room one afternoon soon after her arrival. They were soon discouraged by gossip that she refused to go anywhere without a formal invitation, even to dinner in Lamont House. She made it clear quite quickly that she wanted the girls to come to her rather than vice versa.[26]

Some did, approaching her with caution. Late in September, two reporters from the college paper, the *Sophian,* were greeted with the usual warnings when she told them she could not discuss her current projects, as "writing was private, like having a baby." They stared at her bookshelves, noting a Latin dictionary near *Three Pillars of Zen.* She explained, "I'm preparing *Mary Poppins from A to Z* for Latin and hope very much to find the right translator while I am here either at Smith or Amherst." Then there was a more peculiar book, on gorillas— her favorite animal, she told the interviewers. Suddenly, she said, "I don't like pets...if somebody could make a very small cow to fit on my rug then I'd certainly have an animal pet." Why was the cow her favorite? Thinking of an ideal Pamela, and how she might like to be seen, she replied, "The cow is the most meditative of creatures, very quiet, very simple, highly curious and inquisitive and she looks beautiful. She has a beautiful coronet of horns like a duchess and she bears herself proudly and well. And she's so serene and independent, I love her." But gorillas? "You can never make a gorilla small enough to fit into a walnut shell and that's the only kind I could have with me."

This seemed like seriously weird stuff to the students, who nevertheless kept working doggedly through their list of questions. In one exchange worthy of Oscar Wilde, they asked, "Do you have a very unusual approach to life?" "Oh," said Pamela, "you don't approach life, you live life. You approach a railway station." Veering off on another tangent, the author intoned, "I'm very interested in that phrase, 'rapture in precision.' You can't have rapture without precision, or that's what I think and for me there's a kind of precision in rapture."[27]

The free-floating exchange between Pamela and her inquisitors continued on two parallel paths, never meeting. It had a slightly unhinged quality, the subject not so much a crone in a rocking chair dispensing wisdom, as a woman locked into herself. She might have engaged them by explaining her fascinating theory on the rapture to be found in precision, but instead sat back and waited for the students to reject her.

In the first of only two public appearances at Smith, she dutifully emerged in a suit, coat and pale leather gloves to sign books at a fund-raising fair, Sophia's Circus. The college had organized a Mary Poppins theme, with Poppins Popwiches, sold by three professors, Poppins Posies, and a stall called Spoonful of Sugar, manned by faculty wives who had prepared baked goods, Mary's Pops and ice cream.[28]

Press photos show a tireder, plumper and more solid figure than the one she presented at Radcliffe. Two days later, on October 7, she delivered a long lecture called "Myth, Fairy

Tale and Mary Poppins" at Sage Hall. A writer for the *Smith College Quarterly* thought that "after an hour's rambling about her childhood in Australia and the years she spent in Ireland working with W. B. Yeats and AE, she got to her myth, fairy tale and Mary Poppins. She didn't tie the subjects together, and the only thing I can remember clearly was her assertion that a writer doesn't create a character, he "summoned" him."[29]

Her ninety-minute talk was a dress rehearsal for a more significant lecture she was to give late in October at the Library of Congress in Washington. To celebrate National Children's Book Week, the library had asked Pamela to speak as the lecturer chosen that year by its Gertrude Clarke Whittall Poetry and Literature Fund. Her first lecture, on October 31, was called "Only Connect," her second, the next day, "Never Explain."

"Only Connect" meant several things to Pamela. She told her audience it was an attempt to link her skepticism with the desire for meaning, to find the human key to an inhuman world, to connect the individual with the community, the known to the unknown, the past to the present and both to the future. "Only Connect" was taken from E. M. Forster's novel *Howards End*. The phrase, she said, had become a kind of motto for her, one she would like on her gravestone.[30] The lecture was a long autobiographical statement, beginning with her romanticized childhood drenched in the Celtic Twilight, then moving on to AE and Yeats and how she was now enthralled by fairy tales which she saw as "minuscule reaffirmations of myth," not hocus pocus but old wives' tales. Naturally, she believed in old wives' tales. It was "the proper function of old wives to tell tales." Becoming a crone, she believed, was the last great hope of women. The lecture was given on Halloween, the night when the shadows came alive in *Mary Poppins in the Park,* and for Pamela that night, "the fairy tales are abroad...good fairies and demons."

Back at Smith, she felt duty bound to talk to the pesky students. They read on their notice boards that P. L. Travers would be "at home" in her Lamont House suite on Wednesdays at 8 P.M. Patricia Forster and four of her friends thought they might give it a try. Pamela greeted them in a kimono and slippers, ushering them into the living room. "Talk," she instructed. One student ventured a question about Mary Poppins. "No, no, no, not that kind of question. Surely you must be wondering about *life's* questions. That's what we should talk about." The five girls sat mute. She asked them about themselves. Forster told her she was an English major interested in teaching. This rekindled Pamela's insecurity about her formal education. One learns, she said, by thinking and listening not by jamming facts into one's head like so many little cod liver oil pills. Formal education stifled the imagination and, once the imagination was dead, so was the spirit.

Not many students went to the suite for a second lecture. Pamela had no understanding of why she was being left alone. In search of some male company, she agreed to an interview for Amherst University's Four College radio station WFCH and gave an encouraging interview to the *Amherst Record,* saying she welcomed students from all the neighboring institutions. "I love meeting people, faculty and students. I don't want to be left alone on a shelf like a Dresden china ornament. I like to have men come because their questions are so good and the girls become better when men are present."[31]

The gambit seemed to work, and through November she spent time at Amherst with Professor Peter Marshall of the Classics Department who had agreed to work on the Latin translation of *Mary Poppins from A to Z*. Her namesake Pamela, daughter of her agent Diarmuid Russell, also lived in Amherst with her husband Andrew Haigh. She charmed their friends and their children, but, said Pamela Haigh, "this was a public performance, the way lots of people give them. She saw herself as a performer. She had a theatrical flair. There was quite a difference between the private person and public persona. She was quite lonely and defensive, about her work. And she had no car, she was dependent on us to do the ferrying."[32]

One evening Pamela asked Francis Murphy, an associate professor in Smith College's English Department, to drive her to a party at Amherst. The house, down an unlit road, proved to be hard to find. Murphy thought she saw something on the road, stopped the car, found it was only a muffler, and threw it in a ditch. Instead of helping, Pamela told Murphy, "Well, do take care, I don't want to lose my driver." Remembering the detail of the evening thirty years later, Murphy thought Pamela could not "sort people out because she was intensely self-centered. She treated me as her driver yet I was an English professor. She expected a great deal. She thought that the students would come and ask what they could do for her. She wanted *Mary Poppins* translated into Latin because *Winnie-the-Pooh* had been, and she had asked me if there was a good Latinist—a really famous Latin scholar—to do this. She had big intellectual pretensions. There was a lot of Mary Poppins about her, that commanding air, but it didn't work that way in real life."[33]

On December 13, a few weeks before Pamela left Smith College, *Look* magazine published an article by Joseph Roddy, well known to Pamela's friend at Radcliffe, Deane Lord, who was also friendly with the *Look* editors. Headlined "A Visit with the Real Mary Poppins," the article featured a flattering photograph of Pamela and began with a word picture of a sophomore knocking on "P. L.'s door," announcing "I'm looking for peace of mind." It went on: "'Oh, that's a marvelous search,' P. L. says, 'but peace of mind is not for you my dear. Nobody young can have it.'" Roddy, who thought the Smith girls had a "dangerous radiance about their eyes" reported how the talk "leaps across centuries every night P. L. has open house." Roddy continued, "She wants, to be plain, more men around, because without them, girls will ask her how to write for children. 'How should I know? I don't write for children, I turn my back on them…My dear, I delude myself into thinking my books are grown-up books.'" Roddy wrote that, "In a moment, the Smith girls were talking about the life stages of women: nymph, mother, crone." Pamela was "a timeless, gentle lady coexisting in all three." She told him, "There is too much stress on ramming in knowledge. Education is thinking and listening." What a pity, she said, that she was treated at Smith "like a piece of Dresden china on a shelf…when I came, they said to me, 'All we want to do is touch the hem of your garment.'"[34]

That was really too much for the Smith women. Five planned to write to the editor to complain about the depiction of Smith students "wise beyond their years with dangerous radiance around their eyes" coming to this guru for peace of mind and tea. Later, Patricia Forster wrote in the *Smith College Quarterly* that "Miss Travers implies in the article she is leaving Smith because she wants more men around. I'm sure if she stepped beyond the confines of her private suite in Smith she would have found men almost every day of the week. One gets the impression from the article that Miss Travers is a witty, benign, delightful well-beloved lady who felt misunderstood at Smith. She claims we treated her like a piece of Dresden on a shelf. If that is true, it is because she made it clear that was what she wanted and expected."[35]

Two weeks after the *Look* piece, *The New York Times* published a kind of rebuttal that showed evidence of real digging by the reporter, Richard R. Lingeman. Just the same, he was not able to persuade the Pamela critics to come out in public. He quoted an "English professor" who said, "She's as touchy as hell. It's a mistake to say she's a beloved English writer." A "visiting scholar, known for his acidulous characterizations of fellow denizens of the academic jungle" said, "I absolutely refuse to talk about her. All I know is a lot of rumor, hearsay and gossip."

A "plump girl at Lamont House" remarked, "Miss Travers—we call her Miss Poppins—is really opinionated and just dismisses everything we say to her. She said you can just knock on the door and go in, but nobody respected her intellectually, so no one made the big effort." And a "pretty brunette" told the reporter, "Some students felt the college should have invited a more intellectual writer in residence. They don't respect her because she is a commercial success."

Lingeman thought her "penchant for privacy converted her into a sort of ogre lurking behind her door whose meals were brought in." One day a few students passing saw that hardly anything on the tray had been touched. They wrote a note, "Think of all the starving children in China!" Later, they learned that "Miss Travers suffered from stomach trouble and felt sorry." On the other hand, he had seen a happy Thanksgiving note pinned to the notice board asking the students to "Come and see me, I'm always at home, just knock on my door."[36]

By the time the article appeared, Pamela had left Smith forever and was soon to return to London. She had one last bit of business on the East Coast. Early that year, she suggested a Mary Poppins bronze statue be erected in Central Park. A letter to the Parks Commissioner of the City of New York, Thomas Hoving, brought a reply in March 1966 that when she came back to the United States next fall, he hoped she would be in touch about the statue. It would be "a lovely thing" for the park, "if the money can be found." That summer, Pamela had posed on tiptoe at Shawfield Street for sculptor T. B. Huxley-Jones, who prepared some pen-and-ink sketches of Mary Poppins looking more like Julie Andrews than a Mary Shepard drawing. In October, Thomas Hoving held a press conference to say his department would erect the statue. It had three pledges amounting to $4,500 but was calling for more contributions to cover the $10,000, the cost of a life-sized bronze of Mary Poppins. She would join Alice in Wonderland

and Hans Christian Andersen in the Conservatory Lake area of the park, near 72nd Street. He handed out copies of the sketch, but declined to name the three contributors.

In November, Pamela told *The New York Times* that the statue should not be a climbing statue like Alice. "Mary Poppins is not someone you climb on. Statues have their own kind of dignity too." The next month, she grumbled that the news on the statue had been given prematurely. It would not be near the statues of Alice and Hans Christian Andersen, as these were "gigantic works and I have never seen Mary Poppins as more than life size but rather less. I have always preferred the small and delicate to over large." Pamela stuck with the story, telling an academic researcher in the 1980s that "the park people" decided against the statue because "a non climbable statue would not blend in."[37]

But an internal Parks Department memo written in December showed the project failed through lack of interest. The only problem was, what should they do with the money? There was only $2,100 in the account. Of this, $2,000 had been contributed by Pamela. The remainder was made up of very small contributions from about thirty people. "This money with interest, if any, has to be returned to all these people, probably with a delicately drafted explanation. The money returned to Pamela Travers should be accompanied by an even more delicately drafted letter."[38]

Pamela was on her way to total obscurity, to the state of Anon which she always claimed she most desired.

15

Looking for Pamela Travers

In her old age, Pamela gravitated to the gurus of the New
Age. As the new hippies reveled in the Age of Aquarius,
she became their spiritual sister. Rather than settle into the
soothing tick tock of the rocking chair, Pamela traveled restlessly from guru to guru, seeking cure after cure, from the
Black Forest to Rome, from Switzerland to Ireland, California to New York—still in search of herself, even in her
seventies.

Euripides said that "the wisest men follow their own direction and listen to no prophet guiding them." But Pamela could
never quite discard her prophets. While she stayed faithful to

von Dürckheim, she also fell under the spell of the charismatic Indian guru, Krishnamurti. The late 1960s and the 1970s went by in a daze of meditation as she gazed at Buddhas and dabbled with Sufism.

Three demons drove Pamela now. The first was a fear of her own death. Although she had consistently lied about her age, she knew of course that she would soon be seventy. In an effort to preserve and glorify the public P. L. Travers— soon to be further elevated with an OBE and doctorate—she planned to sell her literary papers to a university and to donate a collection of Mary Poppins mementos to the New York Public Library. The second demon drove the private Pamela to sum up her life through spiritual disciplines. She hoped each of her gurus held the key to her secret self, the one that had fallen asleep in her childhood. As she wrote in *About the Sleeping Beauty,* if you don't waken it, life is meaningless. The theory that adult sleepers must wake to enlightenment was underlined by Ouspensky's and Gurdjieff's teaching, one she herself passed on to a Gurdjieff group which gathered in her home in the 1970s. Pamela once told the group the story of an angel who comes to all babies at birth and tells them the meaning of life. But sshhhh! they mustn't tell. The angel places a finger on the babies' mouths, which is why we all have that distinctive curve of the upper lip—what's left from the gentle pressure of the angel's finger. Most people forget the angel's message, but through diligent seeking, the meaning of life might be recalled.

None of this was much help in dealing with the third demon, physical distress, which attacked her in the abdomen, the very area she thought was her spiritual center. The pain was always compounded by worry over Camillus. It had been almost a decade since he learned of his adoption, yet Camillus had not rejected Pamela and had never gone looking for his family, unlike his sister Sheila, who went on a search for her real family and found them in 1964 by ringing all the Hones in the Dublin telephone directory. Camillus, whose real mother had died in 1963, retained the name Travers, and stayed on more or less friendly terms with Pamela. But his life, like that of his own father, was badly affected by drinking. It affected whatever job he turned to, from broking to working in a fashion business with a friend, Martin Harris.

Pamela tried to surrender herself to the idea that she had done everything possible for her son, and would hand him over to God. She never could. In March 1967, Pamela returned to the Salvadore Mundi Hospital where she wrote to a friend that she hoped the treatment would help. But, as this was a chronic condition, much of the cure was a case of mind over matter.[1] After Rome, she planned to go on to Todtmoos to see von Dürckheim for another week.

Pamela's old journalistic bogeyman—you are nothing without something in preparation or in print at all times—could not let her abandon her Shawfield Street studio. Several projects were on the boil. Still aiming for a posthumous halo, she offered her literary papers and AE's letters to Texas University (the asking price was $15,000). As well, there was the outline for a possible Broadway play of Mary Poppins, the final proofs to check for a Latin edition of *Mary Poppins from A to Z,* and, finally, a *Mary Poppins Story for Coloring* in 1968.[2]

There was something rather shameful about a children's coloring book. All along, she was thinking of something much more profound, the tale of an heroic, godlike monkey. During 1966, she had started work on a project which would be published five years later as *Friend Monkey*. At first glance, the novel is an overblown imitation of *Mary Poppins,* but it was designed to be a statement of her religious faith, a summing up of her childhood, and a symbol of her fascination with the legends of India, the birthplace of many fairy tales and myths.

Set in London in 1897, *Friend Monkey* tells how a little

monkey travels on board a ship to London. There, he is taken in by the family of poor-but-honest Alfred Linnet, a shipping company clerk at the Port of London. Linnet makes lists of goods as they're unloaded, the crates of tea, bags of sugar and spices and rolls of silk. This monkey is not just a piece of animal cargo, but a servant with a human soul who is so eager to help that wherever he goes he creates chaos from order— the reverse of Mary Poppins. The Linnet household has much in common with 17 Cherry Tree Lane. Mrs. Linnet, like Mrs. Banks, is vague and flustered. The Linnets have two children, with the boy, Edward, being the sensitive equivalent of Jane Banks. But while the Banks are reasonably well off, the Linnets are poor. Their benefactress is their elderly neighbor, Miss Brown Potter. The villain of the story appears to be Professor McWhirter, an animal fancier and collector, to whom Pamela gave a dreadful Scottish brogue—"Nay, he's a puir, low spirited creature more frightened ah don't doot than yersel."

Pamela admitted to the similarity of themes in *Friend Monkey* and *Mary Poppins*—"perhaps I am not very inventive." She conceded that Miss Brown Potter contained elements of Mary Poppins as well as the explorer Mary Kingsley, and Beatrix Potter, with whom she shared both her name and sheltered upbringing.[3]

Pamela never confessed that Miss Brown Potter was in fact another version of Aunt Ellie. While Ellie owned two dogs, Badger and Tinker, Miss Brown Potter has a badger called Tinker and a dog, Badger. Both Ellie and Miss Brown Potter wore black bonnets with flowers, velvet capes studded with jet and elastic-sided boots. They were both shy and lonely girls brought up by governesses. Both remembered watching their parents' parties, the swish of taffeta, and the tinkle of silver on china and glass against the background of a quartet playing *The Blue Danube*. Like Aunt Ellie, and Pamela herself, Miss Brown Potter was an inveterate traveler, and in her youth had dreamed of faraway places. She had even considered Australia. And while Aunt Ellie sheltered the Goff girls and Pamela adopted a little boy, Miss Brown Potter took into her household a deaf and dumb African boy called Stanley Livingston Fan. The whole of *Friend Monkey* is redolent with Pamela's past in Allora and Bowral and even acknowledges her true beginnings: Mr. Linnet is the alter ego of Pamela's grandfather, Henry Lyndon Bradish Goff, a London shipping agent.

As Pamela told the writer Shusha Guppy, "*Friend Monkey* is really the favorite of all my books because it is based on a Hindu myth of the monkey lord who loved so much that he created chaos wherever he went. If you read the *Ramayana* you will come across the story of Hanuman on which I built my version of that ancient myth."

In *Ramayana,* Hanuman was the servant of the high king, Rama, whom he helped in a battle with the demon king of Ceylon. When Rama was wounded, Hanuman knew that the only herb to heal the wounds was far away, in the Himalayas. He took one leap from Ceylon to the Himalayas, where he seized not just one herb but a whole mountain top of herbs. Hanuman was enshrined in India as a god of the people. Worshiped in his own temples, he was supposed to bestow the gift of long life.

Pamela had thought of the meaning of the *Ramayana* since AE had told her of the myths of India when they walked on the sand in Donegal. Now that she knew much more, from Zen Buddhism to the origins of the fairy tales, the monkey god meant even more. She had traced the fairy tales of Russia, Europe and Scandinavia back to their origins in India and Persia, and she wondered if the Brothers Grimm knew that all their princes had Rama as their "hidden name." Pamela knew also that the Indian god Vishnu had sent to earth nine avatars (a god in visible form), one being Rama, another Buddha, but that Vishnu had yet to send the tenth avatar, who would usher in a new world. This avatar would be a white horse, like the white horse who inspired *Mary Poppins* when Pamela told the story to her sisters by the fire in Bowral.

Ever since she looked for salvation in Dürckheim's prescription of Christianity and Buddhism, Hanuman had been her own personal myth. She was thrilled by his excessive love, the kind that "cannot wait to serve." There was something magical in the fact that he had no half measures, always overdoing things in his selflessness. But above all, Hanuman was for her the loving servant of God, just as she began to insist that Mary Poppins was, above all, a servant.[4]

Pamela had started to write *Friend Monkey* in her Chelsea studio when Gurdjieff friends asked her to look after a family of three Tibetans visiting London. Yes, they could stay in her studio, she said, privately irritated that her sanctuary would be occupied for weeks. Not only that, but she had to make them special meals complete with extra chilies, do their washing and even find an appropriate doctor when one became ill. When they left at last, she went back to her desk as a thirsty woman goes to water, to find her two-hundred-page *Friend Monkey* manuscript had disappeared. In line with her New Age beliefs, Pamela called in two dowsers, who went over the house with pendulums. They searched everywhere, even in hatboxes and luggage, in the bathroom, the garden, under the sofa. Nothing. Resigned at last to the possibility of it having been tossed out in the garbage, Pamela tried to forget the story of the monkey who came to serve.

In 1968 she returned to von Dürckheim's care in Todtmoos, this time working with him on a translation of his book *The Way of Transformation: Daily Life as a Spiritual Exercise.* She took notes of her dreams, her fears and resolutions, how she was rich but felt poor, how she might be a good mother to herself, how to build courage, confidence and patience, how to do something different each day, and get rid of "all that blocks inner life." Slowly Pamela began to rewrite *Friend Monkey*. The meditation had helped it return. By the time she moved on to Switzerland the same summer, a third draft came to her word for word as it was in the original.

She had taken a chalet for a month in the village of Saanen, near Gstaad, where every summer the Jesus-like figure of Krishnamurti enthralled his disciples at mass meetings. They gathered under the shelter of a big tent, these hundreds, their sad or anxious faces raised to the guru on high. Among them that year were Pamela, accompanied by Jessmin Howarth and her daughter Dushka, and another Gurdjieff friend from New York, Dorothea Dorling. The women saw in his face and bearing a god, with more gravitas than the Beatles' guru, the Maharishi, or the guru of the orange people, the Bhagwan Shree Rajneesh—altogether the perfect avatar of both Buddha and Jesus Christ.

With his fine, Roman nose, flowing aura of white hair, and his body wrapped in a red-bordered dhoti, Krishnamurti walked to his dais "surrounded by people but untouched by them." Then, as he sat on the platform, his presence reached out and drew his listeners in close. He imparted simple yet memorable messages—"Life is so rich, yet we go to it with empty hearts," "Life is strange, one needs infinite pliability," "Be supple mentally," "Be absolutely alert, make no effort."[5] For Pamela, Krishnamurti was a reincarnation of Gurdjieff. Each summer, she became part of his Saanen court.

He was four years older than Pamela, born in 1895 in south India. In labor, his mother uttered the words, "Rama, Rama, Anjaneya"—Anjaneya being another word for Hanuman. He was inducted into the Theosophical Society while still a boy. One of the society's leaders, the pederast Charles Webster Leadbetter, took a particular fancy to him, and began to investigate Krishnamurti's former lives, publishing the work as *The Lives of Alcyone,* a variation on Halcyon, the brightest star in the Pleiades. By the time he was eighteen, Krishnamurti had developed his own following. Like von Dürckheim and Pamela, he practiced yoga, meditating on an image of the Buddha known as Maitreya. He lived partly in the Californian haven Ojai, and relied on patronage of wealthy Europeans. Like Gurdjieff, he attracted artistic women—including Frieda Lawrence, who thought "the things Krishnamurti says are much like [D. H.] Lawrence."[6] Most of all, he appealed to rich women, many of them widowed, single or divorced and looking for a purpose in life. Krishnamurti, they understood, was celibate, which made him all the more attractive.

Krishnamurti showed no apparent signs of being a charlatan. Charming, gentle, courageous and compassionate, he gave all his attention to each disciple. He could be convincing publicly and privately that he wanted to help, to alleviate suffering, to heal. Yet, after he spoke at mass meetings, no one was quite clear about what he said. As the American writer Peter Washington wrote in *Madame Blavatsky's Baboon,* a book about gurus, this confusion could be a definition of charisma. Each person had used Krishnamurti as a mirror, to reflect his or her own inner state.

His friends and adherents included some of the best known writers, musicians and actors of the time. Among those who came to sit at his knee were Christopher Isherwood, Aldous Huxley, Luise Rainer, Anita Loos, Greta Garbo, Bertolt Brecht, Igor Stravinsky and Charlie Chaplin. His European patrons were Signora Vanda Scaravelli and his English representative, Miss Doris Pratt. From 1961, the year he first called the faithful to him at Saanen, until 1983, Krishnamurti stayed every July and part of August with Signora Scaravelli at her Chalet Tannegg in Gstaad. There, he was given a Mercedes, which he drove with skill around the mountainous roads. (He also loved to have his hair cut in Bond Street, and to wear custom-made suits from Huntsman at Savile Row.)

Two of his closest associates were his business manager, Desikacharya Rajagopal, and Rajagopal's American wife, Rosalind Williams. Rajagopal ran Krishnamurti Writings Inc., the organization responsible for the copyright, editing and publication of the guru's work. He also oversaw Krishnamurti's properties and doled out money, or withheld it, when Krishnamurti wanted land in Saanen and the United Kingdom. The relationship between these three represented a giant hypocrisy in Krishnamurti's life. From 1932, he had conducted a secret affair with Rosalind. When this was revealed to Rajagopal, the fallout led to painful legal battles between the two men. Krishnamurti accused his old friend of mismanaging funds and the feud finally led to a public denunciation by Krishnamurti of Rajagopal in Saanen in 1968 and the establishment of a new organization, the Krishnamurti Foundation, based at Brockwood Park in England. After years of litigation and cross claims, the legal cases were eventually settled. Krishnamurti died in 1986, with his official biographers skating over the truth about his life. The daughter of the Rajagopals revealed the details of the love affair in her book *Lives in the Shadow,* published in 1991.

If she had known that the messianic Krishnamurti hid an affair with his close friend's wife while he preached goodness, honesty and simplicity, Pamela might not have cared. After all, she had glossed over the shallowness in Gurdjieff. She came to him for his blessings and promises of insight and peace. His philosophical unguents counted far more than any weakness of character.

No stranger who saw Pamela in her last public appearances knew anything other than a sharpish, domineering woman, utterly confident and sure of her place. Yet all through the 1970s, the righteous, bumptious, public P. L. Travers masked an uncertain private woman still searching for reassurance. Age did not temper the search, which became even more intense when her brief decade of Disney fame almost faded away.

In 1970 she visited her friend Bettina Hurlimann in her country home at Uerikon in Switzerland, where she worked on a fourth draft of *Friend Monkey*. One night she pressed the manuscript into the hands of Hurlimann and went to bed at nine. Pamela was so desperate for approval, yet so self-involved, that she asked Hurlimann and her husband Martin to give their opinion next morning.[7]

Late in 1969, she had sent out a one-page prospectus promoting herself as "the author of *Mary Poppins* etc.," and a potential writer in residence at any university on the West Coast of America. Money was not an issue. She merely wanted to be comfortable on a campus where students could come and go and where she could work on her next book. Among those who received the prospectus was the administrator of the Blaisdell Institute for Advanced Study in World Cultures and Religions in Claremont, California, who passed it on to Scripps College, also in Claremont. (Scripps, a women's university, was named after its founder, Ellen B. Scripps, the half sister of newspaper chain proprietor Edward Wyllis Scripps.)

The president of Scripps, Mark Curtis, wrote to Pamela, offering her two months of the spring semester as writer in residence and lecturer in creative writing. He could also offer her the Clark lectureship, given each year to a distinguished woman, usually a writer. Pamela readily accepted, although she told Curtis her kind of writing could not be taught, as it had to "rise from the unconscious." She would be happy to give the Clark lecture, but wanted an audience far beyond just the

Scripps girls, suggesting young, old, male, female—a "melange." In a letter to the college's dean, Marjorie Downing, Pamela said she was thrilled to be coming to California. She had visited the state only twice, once to talk over her film script, and again for the first night of *Mary Poppins,* an occasion when "only a hero could refrain from weeping." She had once been told by a "necromancer" that California was the luckiest place in the world for her.

She arrived at Scripps on February 10, 1970, and two days later delivered a lecture called "In Search of the Hero—the continuing relevance of myth and fairy tale." Pamela spoke to the Scripps students as little as she could, leaving few memories behind when she left in early April. She told the dean in a letter she had been happy at Claremont, walking among camellias and magnolias, "pregnant with a book, and time in which to write it." The students, she assured Downing, would be good mothers and good women, not *good* women but good *women*. In the Scripps gardens she left cuttings of three roses: the Pamela Travers, the Sleeping Beauty and the Mary Poppins.[8]

During her weeks at Scripps, Pamela had finished *Friend Monkey*. When it was published the following year she was astonished to find her beloved monkey god torn to pieces by the critics. *The New York Times* sneered at *Friend Monkey*'s "tiresome stock characters, overdone writing, full of 'would be poetic' adjectives, and strained metaphors."[9] In February 1972, the *Horn Book Review* noted the "plethora of characters...of the flat comic variety" and the plot boiling over with incidents that were "ludicrous without being funny." Pamela sighed in a letter she wrote a few years later that "it was not accepted, alas—everyone wanted another *Mary Poppins*."[10] In fact, she told interviewers, the book was hardly on the shelves before the retailers sent the unsold stock back to the publishers. Pamela never accepted the rejection. She absolutely *knew* it was her best book, so proud of her work that near the end of 1972 she sent a copy to the Queen.[11]

New York remained her spiritual home. She decided to rent an apartment in a towering, anonymous block overlooking the East River at 1385 York Avenue. Here, in New York, the Welches once more enfolded her within their Gurdjieff group. Now enshrined as a crone who had once sat at the feet of Gurdjieff and Ouspensky, she lectured on the meaning of myth to men and women who had never met the two masters. Late in the spring of 1972, Pamela decided to donate some mementoes to the children's room of the New York Public Library. She collected all the little treasures—a Doulton plate, a toy horse, a doll, a hen—and a handful of other modest trinkets that had inspired chapters in the Mary Poppins books. The library, keen for publicity, announced that Pamela herself would be handing over the trinkets and speaking publicly at the ceremony. The media were invited. Feenie Ziner, writer and teacher, described the scene for *The New York Times* under the headline "Mary Poppins as a Zen Monk."

Pamela was "sixtyish and square, with a quantity of silver bracelets and a beautiful necklace of jade." No one approached. Ziner herself made a tentative opening gambit. "One of my students," she said, "has written a paper in which she describes Mary Poppins as a Zen monk. Would you care to comment?" "The gray head reared, the eyes narrowed. 'That is a very interesting idea. I should very much like to read the paper. Of course I shall not comment upon it or return it. Would you send it care of my publisher.'" Ziner was dismissed. The donation ceremony began. With formidable detachment, Pamela spoke of how, when she was dead, this humble collection would remain for children at the great library.

She looked down at the treasures of her lifetime, a plastic

Pegasus, a jointed wooden doll, quite without clothing, a flow-ered ceramic cat, a setting hen of translucent blue glass, and a Staffordshire lion. She glared at the librarian: "You had him listed as a dog!" The audience settled in when she spoke of her father, "whose prerogative it had been to bestow a name to each of her dolls." Later, she remembered how "when I was doing the film with George Disney—that is his name isn't it, George?—he kept insisting on a love affair between Mary Poppins and Bert. I had a terrible time with him." Once again, she explained that Mr. Banks was Mary's real opposite number. Pamela picked up a small glass paperweight enclosing the words "Home Sweet Home." "Some day," she said, "I might write a story about this paperweight because nowadays there are so few people—so few—who have that sense of home, a safe place, eternal, hidden in their hearts." She gazed deeply into the glass, "long enough for people to begin to wonder if she had come to the end of her speech, standing in front of the room, she was sinking out of sight. Could she not go on? Was she about to cry?" She seemed poised "on that tenth of an inch difference by which heaven and earth are set apart. Then slowly, her face lifted toward the light, as if an arrow had been released from deep within her. Transfigured with joy, she said, 'Maybe I'm writing it right now.'"[12] The actress in Pamela had emerged once again, the timing she knew so well, the thrill of holding the audience just one moment more.

Back in Switzerland in July, this time at the Hotel Olden Gstaad, the words of Krishnamurti were balm enough for her mind but her body was still in its same old knotted state. Her London doctor, Bernard Courtenay Mayers, said he would try to help, prescribing a mixture of phenobarbitone, bismuth sub-sitrate, kaolin and oil of peppermint.

All these years, the checks from Disney's Burbank studios kept rolling in, not just for the film but for spinoffs such as Disney arena productions in which Mary Poppins characters appeared. In 1970, Pamela and her lawyers had established the Cherry Tree Trust, a foundation that gave grants to children, using some of the profits from the movie. But the trust funds represented just a slice of the Disney money; the more the money flowed, the greater the tax burden became. Pamela's advisers knew that in Ireland writers lived virtually tax free, and suggested she might take up residence there. It seemed a brilliant idea, to maintain the apartment in New York but to live for a large part of the year in the country she had loved as a young woman. Pamela bought a house at 69 Upper Leeson Street, Dublin. But the promised land of her twenties—the city where she had fallen in love with AE and Yeats almost fifty years earlier—had vanished. It was a disaster, according to her friend Jenny Koralek, "because of course Ireland had changed. She used to ring me and say 'Find me some interesting people here or I'll die.'"[13]

In September 1972, she escaped to Brockwood Park, the Krishnamurti Foundation's center near Alresford in England, where she could talk to others in the same need of help or simply meditate in her own room. She tried to focus her mind, to "narrow down" her wishes and desires to one of two things. This, she told an interviewer, made "the channel deeper and gives more strength to it." All her writing effort, though, was placed in *About the Sleeping Beauty,* still unwritten, though brooding in her since Radcliffe College. In 1975, when the book was finally published by McGraw-Hill, Pamela began writing to the last of her Mr. Banks figures, a professor in Sweden.

Their long and intimate correspondence represented a kind of love affair—on paper alone. For three years, Pamela told her secrets to this Mr. Banks, as if dropping one veil after another. He was Staffan Bergsten, from the University of Uppsala, who, like many supplicants before him, begged Pamela for information on the meaning of *Mary Poppins.* He planned to write a thesis about "Poppins and myth." She was entranced.

Bergsten had thought much more deeply than any other man on the nanny and all her meanings. He had seen all the associations with Zen, Blake, Yeats and AE, as if he had read her mind. It was all immensely flattering, reassuring too. Pamela wrote to him first in February 1975. The aerograms that flew between Sweden and London over three years included ten long letters from her, followed by two final letters in the 1980s. In these, she asked Bergsten if he would send her copies of the original letters—not for her to destroy, but to form part of a collection of her personal papers that she sold eventually to the Mitchell Library in Sydney, Australia. The inclusion of these letters in the collection—freely available to any member of the public to read—appears to be irrefutable proof that she wanted her personal life revealed, despite many protestations that she was Anon personified and wanted to remain so.

In the first letter, she adopted her usual flattering tone, telling Bergsten that men and boys always asked her the best questions. She started with some standard responses, that she had not thought of Poppins as part of the Christian tradition but was always thinking of what children know and later forget. Bergsten's next move was to send her his book on the Swedish poet Osten Sjostrand. Pamela told him she would send him *Friend Monkey*, a book "very dear to my heart." But as much as she clung to Hanuman, her opus *Sleeping Beauty* was to be her ultimate statement, as she explained to the professor. Although she knew McGraw-Hill was keen on the manuscript, Pamela also modestly explained it away as a very small book which would cause not much of a stir.

The most revealing letters from Pamela followed the publication of *About the Sleeping Beauty* in 1975. The whole of the previous year had been spent in perfecting this book about the sleeper, her court and her fate. Nobody knew, not Bergsten certainly, or any reviewer, just how many ways the Sleeping

Beauty appealed to her, how she had thought for years of this woman who waits to be remembered. Repeating the lessons she had taken to heart from Ouspensky and Gurdjieff, she speculated on the drive in men and women to shake off their waking sleep, to see a higher reality, and to gain esoteric knowledge. What was it, she wanted to know, that at a certain moment fell asleep in everyone? Who lay hidden deep within us? Who would come at last to wake us—what aspect of ourselves?

Her book told five versions of the Sleeping Beauty story, including Grimms' and Perrault's, as well as her own version of the tale and an afterword. Pamela's tale, set in the court of a sultan, was heavy with symbolism, or what one academic later called "Jungian blather." When the prince stared at the princess, he knew himself to be at the center of the world and that in him, all men stood there, gazing at their heart's desire, or perhaps their innermost selves. The kiss was an earth-moving experience when the lovers "plumbed all height, all depth, and rose up strongly to the surface, back to the shores of time."[14] Yes, she told Bergsten in March 1976, "The Sleeping Beauty" was certainly erotic, like many of the fairy tales. That's why she placed in her version of the story a dove and a cat, the most strongly sexed bird and animal, and a lizard, which was a phallic symbol, like the spindle.

In her afterword to the book, she linked the sleeping princess with other famous sleepers in literature: Snow White, Brynhild, Charlemagne, King Arthur, Holga the Dane, Oisin of Ireland and a Hindu king. The sleep of the princess was a symbolic death of her entire court. When she woke, everyone else woke too, which reminded Pamela of the Grail Legend, where the whole court is out of sorts when the Fisher King is ill. (This prompted Bergsten to tell her that a book about the Grail Legend formed the kernel of T. S. Eliot's *The Waste Land*.)

The American reaction to *About the Sleeping Beauty* was

mostly negative, with the *Kirkus Reviews* attacking the afterword as "repetitious and windy...buried in self-infatuated blah."[15]

But when the book was published by Collins in England in 1977, the *Times Literary Supplement* praised it as a "brilliant success."[16] In both countries, the everyday reader who had been captured by the simple magic of *Mary Poppins* was lost in the maze. Who had the time or inclination now to follow these intricacies? This book had been one for the insiders. Or perhaps for Pamela alone, a woman talking to herself.

Early in 1976 Pamela decided to return to London, not just as a homing pigeon returning to the city she felt was her birthplace, but for practical reasons. She owned two houses, one in Shawfield Street in London and one in Upper Leeson Street in Dublin, but was paying rent in New York. As a British citizen, though a rich one, she lived in New York on an allowance of U.S. dollars. She worried that the dollars never went far enough. By summer, the York Avenue apartment was packed, Pamela ready to go, her coffee tables strewn with books, the living room stacked with cases. She confided in interviewers and friends alike of her nervousness, even timidity about this "great move" home.

In a letter to Bergsten, Pamela said she belonged in the United States, a nation that was always in renewal. Yet London would be a new beginning too, she told him, not really convinced. There might be another *Mary Poppins* in the wind, but she was not sure if such a story was "needed." Pamela felt she might have nothing left to say. In a desultory way, she had edited her essays and lectures, to make a book out of them. Two American publishers wanted that, she told Bergsten. She had taken to heart someone's flippant comment that she was not fulfilling her destiny if she was not writing. This had upset her. She denied it. No, one's destiny must be in something deeper than that. Destiny meant allowing oneself to dwell in what Keats called the "vale of soul making." She told Bergsten everyone wanted her to stay in the United States to lecture, but she had to go, even though, unlike Mary Poppins, parting was always to die a little. Pamela told him she must "hold hard to the parrot-head of my inner umbrella and go."[17]

At the end of June, Pamela flew to Ireland and then on to Scotland for a holiday before settling back into Shawfield Street in September. Though she had dismissed the thought with Bergsten, death really did seem close, so close she told Jenny Koralek she had come home to die. Later in the year, she began thinking just *where* she might die.

Camillus, now in his mid-thirties, had decided to marry. The days of raucous drinking and partying with his friend Martin Harris, with whom he worked at Martinique Fashions, were over. In June, he had written to his mother in New York about his plans. There would be no church wedding, he had booked the Chelsea Registry Office for his marriage to Frances on July 30 at 11 A.M., then on to lunch. This might be all he needed, at last, to stop the drinking which had led to so much heartache, including his treatment at the private hospital Tice-hurst, in East Sussex. Pamela must have prayed, too, that this was the end of the agony.

Soon after she arrived back in England, she was captivated by an article in the *Listener*. Its message was religious, suggesting that a sin truly repented is "unhappened." The promise filled her with sudden light. Pamela knew now, that was it, a thing or event could be *unhappened*! Not just in the head but in the whole person. This was quite in keeping with Gurdjieff's idea, which he had discussed with her, that one could "repair" the past. She gave Camillus a present, the bronze head sculpted of him as a boy by Gertrude Hermes. After a honeymoon in Ireland, Camillus and Frances moved into a house in Ifield Road, Fulham, next to Brompton cemetery, where Pamela liked to walk, thinking of her son, dreaming of the church-yard in Allora where she had read the gravestones for all the lost children.

By the end of the year, Pamela was certain that she had no life left in her, nor any will to live. She wrote to the deputy medical director of St. Christopher's Hospice, in Sydenham, asking for advice. He suggested they get in touch the follow-ing year. There was clearly no urgency as far as he was concerned.

Only one thing remained. She went up to the studio and started writing again. Up there, she found comfort in her touchstones. On one wall was a copy of a nineteenth-century Indian painting showing Hanuman carrying Shiva in his heart. On another wall, her Sengai scroll paintings depicted a willow almost breaking in the wind, six persimmons, a cock crowing to the morning and a little hen nearby. She gazed again on her ox-herding pictures, an allegorical series of paintings meant as a training guide for Chinese Buddhist monks. Alongside were her photos of Buddhas, including Maitreya. She liked the way the Buddha's raised hand said, "Silence, don't explain, it cannot be explained." On the terrace sat her small marble Buddha in the midst of camellias and a bay tree. In the kitchen, her col-lection of hens sat brooding on the dresser, and at the back door she lovingly tended her twenty varieties of herbs.[18]

One day, the postman brought a letter from her friend in New York, Dorothea Dorling. Would she write for Dorling's new magazine? In the winter of 1976, Dorling had begun a brave new venture, a quarterly journal she called *Parabola,* "The Mag-azine of Myth and Traditions." For Dorling and Pamela, the word *parabola* meant "getting back to the beginning." A parabola curved and came back to rest. In the same way, they thought, all the myths and fairy tales went back to the beginning; you could search as much as you liked, but you couldn't find where they started. Dorling had talked to Pamela about the project in New York, persuading her to become a founding editor. Many threads linked Dorling back to Gurdjieff. Her sister had been one of Gurdjieff's original disciples in Fontainebleau and she herself had met Gurdjieff in the United States in 1948. In the 1950s, Dorling left her husband, a rancher in Montana, and moved to New York, where she met Pamela. The two women collaborated on a book, *A Way of Working: The Spiritual Dimension of Craft,* which was partly a model for *Parabola* magazine.

When she started the magazine, Dorling was sixty-six. She had been convinced years earlier that the wisdom in traditional myths enlightened her own search for meaning. In her prospectus for *Parabola,* Dorling explained to potential advertisers and readers that each issue of the magazine would be devoted to one theme. *Parabola* was not an official organ of the Gurdjieff Foundation nor was it "limited, as to readers or writers, to members of our groups, but it must have a point of view and this must be consonant with Gurdjieff's teaching, not in order to give answers, but to orient a search for man's place in his world." The aim was to bring together "the greatest formulations we can find...of the ideas in the fourth way as it appears in all traditions." Was there a way, the prospectus wanted to know, of recovering the "sense of a sacred dimension in our existence"? The editors felt sure that sacred tradition could still speak to "the present need." *Parabola* would include articles on legends, myths and folk tales, on Sufi and Zen stories, by some of the best writers it could find.

The theme of the first issue was The Hero. The byline of P. L. Travers appeared in this winter 1976 number and for most subsequent issues. Good writers and wealthy women's money kept the whole risky venture afloat. Over the years, Isaac Bashevis Singer wrote on death, the Dalai Lama on obstacles, and Pamela spoke with Laurens van der Post on "dreams and seeing." Many others sympathetic to the fourth way were writers whose names could help sell subscriptions—Joseph Campbell, Italo Calvino, John Updike, Peter Brook, Robert Bly, Lincoln Kirstein, Dag Hammarskjold, Krishnamurti, Karlfried von Dürckheim, David Malouf and Prince Charles. Their subjects ranged from addiction to death, to healing, sacred dance, the sun and moon, theft, sadness, mask and metaphor, and ceremonies.

Pamela wrote for *Parabola* on being one's own hero, on the dreamtime, on a Sufi poet, on Zen koans, on going to a druids' ceremony for All Souls Day, on Stonehenge, Silbury and Avebury, on the great goddess, the simpleton, and the youngest brother. Her densely packed essays, all in mythological code, allowed only glimpses of the intimate, personal life of Pamela. Now and again she talked of her childhood; another time, of her anticipation of death as she walked in the Brompton cemetery thinking of Camillus preparing to be a father.[19]

Parabola's circulation was never high, but the magazine was still alive in 1999, its advertisements symbolizing the nervous nineties with offers of a bachelor's degree in "transpersonal psychology," books on the sexuality of the soul, catalogues from the Krishnamurti Foundation and fourth way books by Ouspensky, Bennett and Gurdjieff. For the truly diligent seeker, one company advertised "wilderness in the Rocky Mountains for the re-enchantment of ourselves, fathers and adult sons—therapists' journey."

Despite the Buddha on the Shawfield Street terrace and the philosophy of Zen in her spirit, Pamela had taken to heart von Dürckheim's advice, that the sure way to peace came with a balancing dose of Christianity. She took communion at the nearby Christ Church, an Anglican church in Chelsea, and, as she knelt on the pew, she told herself she was not merely kneeling before the cross, but offering herself up as an empty vessel, in a gesture of submission. To the parishioners of Chelsea she no doubt seemed a traditional upper-middle-class elderly lady, with a cut-glass accent, her clothes suitably conservative, despite the Navajo bangles and a tendency to wear slightly eccentric tent-shaped dresses ending with a flounce. The neighbors and fellow members of the congregation kept their distance at first—she had retained, even increased, her superior manner and the air of a snob, bred from an outsider's insecurity.

Pamela was overjoyed to learn she was to receive an OBE in the New Year's honors list of 1977, asking the Queen's private secretary, Sir Martin Charteris, whether she should wear a hat for the investiture. In a letter to Charteris, she explained that when she once met President Roosevelt, she had bought a hat for the occasion, but, Pamela knew, times had changed. Would a hat still be proper? She also wanted the Queen to know how moved she was by her Christmas speech, so regal and yet so full of feeling.[20]

Early in 1977, she returned to New York to lecture at the Cosmopolitan Club, the Jung Foundation and the St. John the Divine church, where she read from *The Fox at the Manger*. To her audience at the church, she seemed an eccentric figure in her gray lambskin coat and brown galoshes. From under her pink-toned plaid suit peeked a shimmer of silver, her arms still laden with the work of the Navajo.[21]

Back in London, a letter was waiting from Professor Bergsten, who had now moved in closer to his thesis subject. Would she tell him something more of herself, not just of Mary Poppins? In her longest and most emotional letter to Bergsten, in February 1977, she wrote of her father's drinking and her sense of shame about his death. She knew he was an alcoholic although her sisters denied it. What's more, she had always suffered from the drinking of men who were close to her.

In the next letter, the following month, she told Bergsten

she had no regrets about revealing so much. She still longed
for the United States. Her hopes for a new beginning in
England had come to nothing. In fact she was not even sure
why she had come back at all.[22]

Pamela collected her OBE at Buckingham Palace late in
March—not from the Queen, but from the less grand Duke
of Kent. To the media, she solemnly declared "I have accepted
it for Mary Poppins," but to Bergsten she confessed she was
still an ignoramus. The letters after her name could have been
given to an idiot.

In April 1977, Frances Travers gave birth to Katherine
Lyndon Travers. About six months later, Camillus's drinking
problem returned. Pamela's friends tried to console her, but
she seemed, now, more dogged and resigned than before,
steadfastly keeping to her schedule of talks, including a regular reading in New York each Christmas from *The Fox at the
Manger*. Pamela also maintained her own Gurdjieff group at
Shawfield Street, trying to impart her guru's principles to shy
and much younger adherents than herself.

The Bergsten connection was about to end, with the professor's publication in Stockholm in 1978 of his thesis, *Mary
Poppins and Myth*.[23] He sent Pamela a copy, inscribed to "the
mysterious P. L. Travers." Pamela was unhappy, she told him, to
see her name given in the first chapter as Pamela and not P. L.,
but not annoyed enough to cut off communication. She planned
to send him a thesis by an American woman on the Mary
Poppins books which compared them with the work of E.
Nesbit, "an honor for me." The student had insisted that all the
books were about growing up, losing all the things one knew
early in childhood, with Mary Poppins being the only one who
does not forget. Pamela saw this as a valid point of view.[24]

At last, she was to be given the prize she had yearned for
since her first books were published forty-five years before.
Not a literary acknowledgment, but a validation of her intel-

lect, at least. In May 1978, Chatham College in Pittsburgh, Pennsylvania, gave her an honorary doctorate degree in humane letters. Chatham was a small women's college with fewer than eight hundred students, itself seeking publicity by conferring honorary degrees. But Pamela seized on the doctorate with great pride, forever after insisting that she be called Doctor. Now that she had shed the honorific Miss (never Ms.), she dreamed again of her old love, Francis Macnamara. In the dream, he spoke to a circle of men around him: "That's Pamela, we must call her Doctor now." She wondered if *doctor* was a metaphor for some new feeling of his. In the dream, she met Francis's wife. This was the moment, she knew, to reveal their love. In other, more turbulent dreams, she had seen AE ill, in a swimming pool, and Gurdjieff, sad, dispirited. Pamela wrote a note to herself, almost a postscript to her life, that "all our days are as grass."

In July 1979 Jonathan Cott, a consulting editor of *Parabola*, came to her in a depressed state. She called him "my dear," this other young man in search of help. In a long interview for a book, *Pipers at the Gates of Dawn*, Cott drew out of Pamela the way in which she now dealt with her own inner turbulence. She told him to "accept everything that comes and make jewels of it." She did not mean to sound pious but "I feel like that, and that's what I call the hero nature, you can only be the hero of your own story if you accept it totally."

She played with the idea of Sufism, absorbed the poems of the Sufi poet Jalalu'ddin Rumi, meditated on "the great bowl of the abdomen," and lay awake thinking how Little Bo Peep had lost her sheep, but when she left them alone, they all came home. You must, she thought, leave a problem alone. Don't even look for its solution, and it will come home. "I know where I leave it alone, right in here two inches below the navel, the vital center, that's where everything goes and is allowed to simmer."

She took Cott on a tour of her home, noting AE's portrait of her reclining in the tree (she said AE was the "tutelary deity of the house"), the Japanese scrolls, and, in the hallway, a rocking horse that she had bought for the grandchildren but loved too much to give away. Here, in the rocking horse, were all the things she loved in one, the merry-go-round, the rocking chair, the Pegasus.

Early that year her sister Barbara Moriarty had died in Sydney, the little sister who had been so much prettier and had life so much easier, the sister who had hardly journeyed beyond one suburb for decades. Pamela left no record—in a poem, letter, or note of any kind—of her feelings about the death. Moya stayed on alone, in Mosman, turning to a neighbor for friendship and support.[25]

By now, Pamela had become more of a guru herself than a disciple. As Dr. Travers, the great lady who once knew Ouspensky and Gurdjieff, she was in demand as a counselor for the third- and fourth-generation Gurdjieffians. In May 1979, she spoke to a gathering on "Gurdjieff: a Universal Man." Her voice was deep but muffled, slightly slurred with age, breathless, in contrast to the cool, clear and crisp younger voices of her audience. She told them of her friendship with Ouspensky who advised her to "speak in other categories, think in other categories," and how she remembered thinking, "How could I think, with no scientific mind, of the fourth dimension?"

Dr. Travers asked for questions. There were none. After a long silence she said, "I was thinking, at least let me do no harm." Another long silence. Then, "We have talked a lot about Mr. Gurdjieff as man and teacher, not so much about his ideas, I wonder if anyone has anything to say?" Silence. She told them that in Paris, he sometimes gave talks but more often would call for questions. Deathly silence. At last, a woman asked meekly whether Gurdjieff spoke about reincarnation. Pamela crossly replied that she never heard him do so. She could only point to Ouspensky's book, *In Search of the Miraculous,* in which he talked of recurrence, that our lives go around and around on the same old track. Pamela explained that she did not want to be specific or absolute about anything. As she grew older, she knew less. In fact, if they knew Henry Moore's reclining women, studded with holes, she was very like that and getting "holier" every day. But she, too, found the idea of repairing the past essential.

The session ended with one of Pamela's favorite quotations from Ecclesiastes:

> or ever the silver cord be loosed, or the golden bowl
> be broken...then shall the dust return to the earth as
> it was: and the spirit shall return unto God who gave it.

Tiring, she told them that was that. "If things go too long, things devolve and people chatter and it's lost."

It was extraordinary that, at eighty, she kept up the pace. As she wrote to Jessmin Howarth in November 1979, she had lost her housekeeper of the last six years, had found no replacement and grew more exhausted every day trying to run the house, cook and work. A lecture the previous month had been a great success but a drain on her energy. Things were, in fact, ghastly. Even writing a letter in her studio, with her ear cocked for the doorbell, was a chore. She was struggling constantly to retreat to the "green pastures" of her mind.

Pamela kept the pressure on herself. Her only relief seemed to come from the support of younger members in her group, and the love she felt for her granddaughters. (Frances and Camillus had another baby in November 1979. She was given the Christian names of girls in the Goff and Morehead families, Cicely Jane.)

At Christmas 1980, her Gurdjieff group gathered to pray, and to sing the old English songs she remembered from her childhood: "Drink to Me Only with Thine Eyes," "Greensleeves," "A Frog He Would a Wooing Go," "Green Grow the Rushes, oh." Shawfield Street rang with their true, solemn voices, as they ended with the Twenty-third Psalm, followed by "God Be in My Head" and "Lord of the Dance."

I am the lord of the dance said he,
Dance, then, wherever you may be.

That year, Pamela rested at Chandenon, in Switzerland. She could not let go of the idea that Mary Poppins *must* come back, one more time.

16

Fear No More the Heat of the Sun

Swedish television crew called on Shawfield Street in 1991. Amazed to find Pamela Travers was still alive, the documentary team was excited by the possibility that she might reveal the origins of Mary Poppins. The reporter suggested Mary was, well, an ordinary name. "Ordinary, yes," said Pamela. Then she glanced upward, indicating heaven. But the name "Mary" could mean...And there was a pause. Pamela almost sighed, "It could mean...higher matters."

She spoke with great difficulty, as if through clenched teeth.

Her nose drooped sadly down, her tongue restlessly explored her lips and mouth. But her eyes remained intensely alive as she suggested her perfect nanny was related to the mother of God. Pamela assured the interviewer that "all the men fall in love" with Mary Poppins. "But she doesn't love them?" "Oh no!"

Even at ninety-one, Pamela maintained the facade of a mysterious yet playful woman. In truth, her cronedom represented a permanent state of nervous anxiety about her health, her publishers, her money, and her son. Her only daily company was a succession of housekeepers. Less often, she saw her Gurdjieff group and her grandchildren.

In her early eighties Pamela's energy had seemed undiminished, but a decade later her spirit and physical strength were all but extinguished. On a good day she could walk the distance of three lampposts in Shawfield Street, on a bad day, none. Occasionally she made it as far as the Kings Road, where she liked to talk to the punks, unafraid of their costumed aggression. Her watery blue eyes took in their hair, jelled into spikes of lime and raspberry, their chained necks, their safety-pinned noses. Pamela wondered why they dressed in that outlandish way. Perhaps their lives were so limited they had to do something desperate to make it all matter. They looked "lovely," she told them. *That* would bring them down a peg, take the sting out of their rebellion. The punks ignored her, or sneered "Ya wot?" But this old lady knew more than they could ever imagine. She even knew the words of "Strawberry Fields Forever," much cleverer than one of their subversive anthems. Not only that, but the crumpled shopper in the Kings Road was a multimillionaire whose agents and lawyers constantly reassured her of her wealth. She had over £1 million invested and another half million in current accounts. But the money was of no comfort to Pamela. She even worried about whether she had enough to pay the wages of her carers, professional women who were paid to nanny old women.

In her old age, Pamela wrote two more Mary Poppins books. Not only did they reflect her own isolation, but they both conveyed a sense of separation from a homeland. Pamela never returned to Australia, but she did go back in spirit, almost against her will, when her literary and personal papers were sold to Sydney's Mitchell Library.

Their long journey home had resumed in 1980, when she asked her literary agents, David Higham Associates, to send her a copy of the catalogue of her papers, which had been prepared a decade earlier. She was determined to get the summary of her life's work into a library this time. She also asked her New York law firm to see if Harvard had any interest in the papers. The lawyers thought not, suggesting Boston University or the University of Texas. Bruce Hunter at David Higham had not been very encouraging at all, telling her the market had gone rather flat for literary archives. The firm had already offered the collection to the antiquarian booksellers, the Toronto Public Library, Toronto University Library, McMaster Library, the University of Texas and Anthony Rota, with no success.

Eventually there was no more room at David Higham for the stacks of papers, which were then dispatched from the firm's upstairs offices in Golden Square, Soho, to the downstairs storerooms of Bernard Quaritch. The antiquarian bookseller eventually prepared them for sale. A typed letter offering the collection carried the asking price of seventy-five thousand Australian dollars. It is uncertain whether the promotional letter was actually sent, but it did indicate the plan of attack. Either Pamela or her agents now had Australia in mind.

"To the scholar of twentieth-century literature, the letters from AE to Miss Travers are a valuable and exciting find... there are over 160 letters here, many illustrated with his delightful drawings," the letter read. It also boasted of her childhood letters, early photos, and the recollections of Aunt Ellie, and suggested the papers on offer were the only ones

Pamela had kept. (In fact, her studio at home was stacked with letters, fragments of diaries, photographs and audiotapes.) As "the archive of an author of international fame, this collection would be of interest and value to many institutions in the world. To Australia, it is something more, the sum of the past of her best-known author, one whose life and work belong fairly and squarely in the history of Australia, a significant part of the country's heritage."

In 1980, at the time Pamela felt such a sense of urgency about selling her papers, she began work on a new Mary Poppins adventure. This fifth Poppins book, meant as a coda to her own life, turned out to be her favorite. She wrote an early draft of *Mary Poppins in Cherry Tree Lane* in the mountainous Valais district of Switzerland, at Chandolin, where she had begun to spend each summer as a guest of Bettina Hurlimann.

The idea behind the story, she once wrote, was the premise that "all that's lost is somewhere." This phrase first came to her as a song, and, like a catchy melody, she could not banish it from her mind. Everyone in *Mary Poppins in Cherry Tree Lane* is searching for something—everyone except Mary Poppins. The book has the air of a midsummer night's dream, in which all manner of herbs make a guest appearance as agents of witchcraft and healing. The time is midsummer's eve. The setting is a supper picnic in the herb garden of the park. All the familiar friends are there, the Park Keeper, Miss Lark, the Banks children, Mrs. Corry, Ellen and of course Mr. Banks.

The sun is reluctant to set, a common theme in Pamela's life, and, as the twilight lingers on, couples enter the park, two by two. Miss Lark is there, waiting for her love, who turns out to be a professor. She thinks he might have lost his way, but he meets her at last, just as Professor Bergsten had entered the life of Pamela. Next the Park Keeper seeks his own true love. He meets Ellen, spouting the wisdom of grandmothers. She tells him that if he walks backward, he might find his beloved. He does so, and stumbles into the herb garden where Mary Poppins and the Banks children are now partying with stars, including the constellations known as the Bear, Fox and Hare. Orion is there too, that giant hunter in the skies always chasing the Pleiades, and the heavenly twins Castor and Pollux.

Handsome, half-naked Orion in his lion skin makes the central speech of the book when he tells the earthlings that they have no room to spread their wings down here. On earth, everything was too close to something else. Houses leant against each other. Trees and bushes crowded together. Pennies and halfpennies clinked in pockets. Friends and neighbors were always at hand. Orion says, with a sense of regret, that on earth, there was always someone to talk to, someone to listen. He preferred silence, or perhaps the noise of the stars singing in the sky.

Mr. Banks arrives at the party, searching for a lost half crown. He looks in vain. The piece of silver has been taken back to the sky with Orion. Back in the heavens, Orion places it on his belt, to make a fourth star. Mr. Banks looks up to the sky, thrilled to discover that Orion's belt now has four stars instead of three. The scene was directly inspired by Pamela's life in Allora, but then *Mary Poppins in Cherry Tree Lane* contains a whole galaxy of memories from Allora and Bowral, from the sweet shop to her fear of the sun going down. Pamela told Staffan Bergsten in 1989 that she loved her new Mary Poppins book, in which everything came two by two like the earth and sky, or a man beside a woman.

Mary Shepard, now living alone in St. Johns Wood, used her own reflection in the mirror as a model for Mary Poppins, but this time the finished artwork showed a younger, rounder nanny, not the stern and bony Mary of the 1930s. It had been so long since Pamela and Shepard had settled on the Dutch doll look as they strolled in the London park. As well as her own image, Shepard consulted cartoons in the leather-bound volumes of her late husband's *Punch* magazine to remind her of the world of the 1930s.[1]

Pamela wrote to tell her U.S. publisher, Harcourt Brace Jovanovich, that it was her best ever Mary Poppins. Furthermore, her agents in both England and the United States were not only delighted with the book, but illuminated by it.[2] They may have been delighted, but Collins paid her an advance of only £1,500 before the book was published in Britain in 1982.

The bulk of Pamela's income had always come from the United States, but, almost two decades after the Disney movie, that looked like it was changing, too. Pamela had reached a critical point in her relationship with Harcourt Brace Jovanovich. First, she feared that the editor-in-chief of children's books had no interest in her work, but, more important, she believed that the whole company was running down its children's book department. When *Mary Poppins in Cherry Tree Lane* was sent to Harcourt early in 1981, the publisher rejected the book on the grounds that it was too obscure and too full of herbal and mythological references. Pamela was outraged. The whole American publishing edifice looked like it was tumbling down. Already, she claimed, another U.S. publisher, Viking, had made a botch of publishing one of her short stories which had first appeared in *Parabola*. She thought the presentation of the book—called *Two Pairs of Shoes* and published in 1980—was vulgar and its illustrations "atrocious."[3]

Even before the Harcourt rejection, Pamela had told her New York literary agents, Harold Ober Associates, that she dreaded the thought of giving her new Mary Poppins to the editor-in-chief of children's books, urging them to find someone else to deal with at Harcourt Brace. Perhaps they could convince another publisher to take over her entire output, or what she labeled her "oeuvre." Would they send her a list of all Harcourt's juvenile writers as she certainly did not want to be among a list of "has beens."

In January 1982 Harold Ober Associates sent the new book to Delacorte/Dell, hoping the publisher would bring all the Mary Poppins titles together under one imprint through its Dell paperback list. Earnings were going nowhere, as it was. By the end of 1982, the accountants had established that Pamela had earned only $7,000 that year in royalties from Harcourt's Voyager editions of the Mary Poppins books. Maybe a mass market reprinter, preferably Dell, could take over the titles, under license, and really get behind them.

Harcourt, which had sold at least 1.5 million copies of Mary Poppins books in hardback over the years, had always resisted publishing the books in mass market paperback editions. All along, the publisher had received 5 percent of the U.S. and Canadian earnings from the Disney movie, while Pamela's share ended up as 2.5 percent of worldwide earnings. So Harcourt had good reason to retain the hardcover rights, although the film had now run its course. But, at the time, Harcourt rejected Dell's offer of $100,000 for paperback rights, suggesting it might launch a major new marketing drive behind the Mary Poppins titles.

The underlying cause of tension between Pamela and Harcourt Brace Jovanovich went back to 1980, when the *Los Angeles Times* revealed that Mary Poppins had been removed from the San Francisco Library because of racist references in "Bad Tuesday," one of the adventures in the first Mary Poppins book. The library's director of children's services, politically correct, and no doubt with an eye to publicity, decided "the book treats minorities in ways that are derogatory, it's written from the old English view of the 'white man's burden.'" In the story, Mary Poppins and the children travel around the world with the aid of a magic compass. In the north, they encounter an Eskimo who rubs noses with them. His wife offers them hot whale blubber soup. On a South Seas island, a tiny, black, naked "piccaninny" sits on the knee of "a Negro lady" who speaks in an embarrassing approximation of a black American accent.

The chapter had already been changed in the 1960s when a friend of Pamela's, Dr. Francelia Butler, pointed out how embarrassed she had been by the passage when she read it aloud to black students in 1962. At that time, Pamela transformed the Negro lady into a "dark lady" while the piccaninny became a "tiny plum baby." The book was reprinted in 1971, but now Pamela felt cornered into changing the chapter entirely, not because she believed any minority was offended, but because if this book was refused to children, the whole series might be. She told friends she had her "bread and butter to think of." In 1981, Pamela rewrote "Bad Tuesday" to take the children to visit a polar bear (in the north), a hyacinth macaw (south), a panda bear (east) and dolphin (west.)

She had learned of all the fuss through friends, not from Harcourt. In her eyes, that meant the publisher had not defended her loudly enough. Harcourt reprinted the book, asking her to take a lower royalty on an edition of only five thousand copies. She agreed, provided the cover was printed in a different color and carried the words "revised edition."

In all Pamela's business dealings, her peremptory tone did not show any signs of her real weaknesses—her advanced age, bad health and the tensions which sparked these outbursts. Her strengths, combined with her vulnerability, were seen clearly at the time by Nancy Mills of the *Herald Tribune* who visited Shawfield Street in 1981 to talk about "Bad Tuesday."

Mills watched Pamela "slowly climbing the stairs to get to her studio…out of breath, settling her stout frame onto a sofa." Even so, Pamela seemed formidable. "She speaks slowly…her watery blue eyes looking firmly at the intruder." Pamela barked, "Who is a writer anyway? I just scribble." She refused to pose for a photo. Mills took note of a poster on the studio wall admonishing, "The Greatest of Sins is Wandering Thoughts. Watch!"

When her thoughts did wander, as they so often did, her mind returned to Camillus, to her own loneliness, and to her never-ending problems with her helpers. She thought often of the words of Walter de la Mare's, "look thy last on all things lovely every hour." In 1981, Camillus's marriage was about to fall apart. Frances had taken divorce proceedings against him, no longer able to bear his drinking. Pamela cared deeply about him still, and especially about her granddaughters, who hugged her with arms of iron. She didn't see them often; they lived so far away now, at Twickenham.

Alberta was now her housekeeper, forty-two years old, single. She read German philosophy and couldn't cook an egg. The house was meticulous, though, not a single speck of dust was allowed to blow into the front hall. Pamela had no energy to cook herself, but food was not her main problem anyway. What she needed so desperately, she thought, was someone to cherish her while she wrote, because when she was at work, Pamela felt her only surges of energy.

Frances told her late in 1981 that she had now decided against a divorce. Camillus had always swung from charming to impossible but always came back to charming again. Pamela was afraid to say too much.

Each summer, whether at Bettina Hurlimann's or the Hotel Plampras in Chandolin, she remained in constant touch with her agents, lawyers, friends, accountants. In the summer of 1981, Pamela asked David Higham to investigate Jules Fisher, a Broadway producer who wanted to stage a Mary Poppins musical. Fisher, who had produced the successful Broadway musical *Dancin'*, as well as *Lenny* (about Lenny Bruce) and *Beatlemania,* met Pamela in London in January 1982. They talked of possible writers for the book of the musical, perhaps Richard Wilbur, who had adapted *Tartuffe,* or Jay Presson Allen, who wrote *The Prime of Miss Jean Brodie*. In February, Fisher spoke to Stephen Sondheim. Fisher told Pamela Sondheim had always adored the books, and as an exercise, when he was beginning in the theatre, had attempted to write a musical version of *Mary Poppins*. The bad news was, Sondheim now wanted to produce something very American, contemporary and hard-edged. Mary Poppins was not it.

Again, the letters worried over the question of who owned what, how much they should all get, and which writers would be subtle but not obscure. The original Disney contract with Pamela was ambiguous, but it seemed she retained the rights to any live musical. She wanted Lord Goodman to write to Disney to assert that right. Fisher suggested more possible writers: Tim Rice, Peter Schaffer, David Storey, Tom Stoppard, Frederick Raphael, Jonathan Miller and Arthur Laurents. She in turn proposed Wally Shawn, who had written *My Dinner With Andre*, Alan Jay Lerner (she loved *My Fair Lady*), and Paul McCartney. "Now Paul can write a lyric, 'Strawberry Fields Forever,'" she told Fisher. She wasn't sure about his orchestration. But if he liked the books she could fire him with enthusiasm. Pamela hoped Vanessa Redgrave or Maggie Smith might play Mary Poppins.[4] By the summer of 1983, the Disney company advised it had no objections to the musical while Fisher was on the brink of offering Wally Shawn the job of writing the script.

At the same time, another Poppins proposition had come from Walt Disney Television, which wanted to produce thirteen episodes of a TV series. Pamela stalled; the musical should come first. But Disney, as usual, did not give up. Early in 1984, the company offered her $86,000 for an initial six one-hour TV episodes. If Disney went ahead and made thirteen episodes, as planned, her share for the rights and consulting fees would be close to $200,000. In February Ed Self, from Walt Disney Television in the United States, called on Pamela. She agreed and they celebrated with a couple of Jack Daniels. Next month, he told her that he wanted her to collaborate on the TV series with Max Shulman, a novelist and screenwriter who wrote *Rally Round the Flag Boys, The Tender Trap, House Calls* and the Dobie Gillis TV series.

For the remainder of the 1980s, the business and creative instincts of Pamela were in conflict, neither fully satisfied. Her last years and final deals were to fall into a jumble of frustrations. The Jules Fisher musical ran aground eventually, but took years to do so. The plan for Shawn to write the script fell through. Fisher proposed a treatment by Arthur Giron but Pamela insisted on Alan Jay Lerner. Fisher told her that finding a writer to adapt Poppins was a serious problem. Her own material was so clear that most established writers had turned the project down, unsure that they could add enough of themselves to make it worthwhile.[5] Pamela asked him to go back and try Rice and Lerner once more. Both declined. She never gave up hope for a musical, even writing into a will her desire to have such a project taken to completion.

Early in May 1987 Pamela's remaining sister, Moya, died in Sydney, at the Edina Nursing Home in Waverley. Although Pamela had set up a trust to pay income from some of her shares to Biddy and Moya, when Moya made her will she left almost her entire estate to a friend, Agnes Williams. Pamela's bequest was just ten thousand Australian dollars. She learned of the gift from Moya's lawyer who described the small, sad huddle of people at the Northern Suburbs Crematorium. He sent her the money in September, asking if she planned to make a claim under the Family Provision Act. But this was clearly out of the question. No judge of the New South Wales Supreme Court would take pity on the millionairess of Chelsea.

Her sister's death reinforced her determination to leave her life's work to an institution. At the end of 1987, Pamela wrote

again to her professor in Sweden. She hoped he wouldn't be
shocked into a heart attack, hearing from her again, after all
these years. But could he please send her copies of her letters
for her files? They would form part of her papers, which, she
told him, were being recatalogued.[6]

Bergsten was apprehensive about his correspondence ending
up in a file. It sounded suspiciously like the secret service.
Nevertheless, he took the risk.[7] Early in 1988 he sent her a
copy of each of her eleven letters to him. She bundled them
up for Bernard Quaritch to add to her collection, which was
finally sold in 1989 to the Mitchell Library in Sydney for
£20,000. Pamela had wanted much more than that amount.
She told Bergsten the papers had been sold to "some institute
in New South Wales."[8]

Although Pamela had promised the journalist Michele Field
in 1986 that she would never allow Disney to make a movie
sequel,[9] in January 1988 she agreed to Disney's latest proposal. The studio had at last decided to go ahead with a second
film, *Mary Poppins Comes Back,* and again Pamela was to receive
2.5 percent of the gross profits of the film. As an advance,
there would be $100,000 for the rights, and a further $25,000
for a treatment, to be shared by Pamela and her collaborator,
the English radio dramatist Brian Sibley.

Why did she change her mind? It may have been a case of
the old Disney charm at work again, or an illusion that even
now, she needed more money. Walt was dead, but Walt Disney
Productions' vice-president in charge of production, Martin
Kaplan, filled in as the flatterer, telling Pamela that her outline was both charming and extremely promising.[10]

The plot revolved around the imminent collapse of Mr.
Banks's bank, a perfect theme for the year after a disastrous
slide in stock markets all over the world. Just like the Queensland banks in the 1890s, Mr. Banks's bank was in severe
difficulties due to unwise investments. A rival firm wanted to

take it over, but Mr. Banks hoped to stave off the deal. But once again, the movie proposal ended with nothing resolved, and eventually Disney abandoned the project as too costly.

By now, Jules Fisher had spent at least $200,000 trying to make the musical happen. Each time he visited Shawfield Street he enjoyed the endless cups of tea and the Jack Daniels as he listened to Pamela tell him how Walt Disney personally "tricked" her over the movie. At last he seemed to have the right man for the script, Jules Feiffer, but Pamela was still not satisfied. By the end of 1988 Fisher's collaborator, Graciela Daniele, suggested they abandon a conventional musical in favor of a formless show using a "new vocabulary of dance/theatre." It would be a "world of images, a dance form with songs." Fisher outlined the suggestion to Pamela but confessed "perhaps we may not be the right people for this project." He was right. In the end, her demands overwhelmed him.[11]

So it proved with everyone. Only one person, she thought, could translate Poppins for the stage—herself. She was wrong. As Jules Fisher told her, her stories were perfect to read to children at bedtime. The theatre demanded drama to make people come back after intermission.

All the failed plans to adapt her books led her back to Mary for one last adventure. The hero of this slender book was the house next door to the Banks's home. Number 18 Cherry Tree Lane was a house of dreams, vacant for many years, boarded up, ripe for fantasy. Mr. Banks thought an astronomer lived there, a wise old man with a telescope in the attic, making sense of the universe. Michael Banks hoped a clown lived at number 18, while Jane Banks imagined the Sleeping Beauty inside, her finger still bloody from the prick of the spindle.

Mary Poppins and the House Next Door opened with the return of a crone, Mr. Banks's old governess, Euphemia Andrew, who this time brings with her a Jesus-like figure, Luti, a young boy with an angelic manner from the South Seas. His name means "Son of the Sun," and the greeting he smiled at all was, "Peace and blessings." Like Mary Poppins he is a servant, attending to Miss Andrew's querulous demands. He makes friends with the Banks children, never complaining of his lot, until he hears a voice calling him back to the South Pacific. It might be his grandmother, Keria, who likes to cast spells at her clay oven. With the help of Mary Poppins he visits the Man in the Moon then leaves for his journey home, using the clouds as stepping stones, clad only in a pink sarong made from Mary's scarf.

Mary Poppins is a more shadowy figure than before. The emphasis is on reconciliation, on objects and relationships broken and mended, on wise women, and the moon and the stars. Luti's homeland, a Pacific island, was close to Australia. With *Mary Poppins and the House Next Door,* Pamela had come full circle, to her own home in the Southern Hemisphere. Luti was a reincarnation of herself, the Little Black Boy of Blake's poem, who was born in the southern wild, just like Lyndon Goff, but who had been called away to London.

Pamela told Staffan Bergsten that she imagined Luti was born in the Gilbert and Ellice Islands (now Tuvalu). Her inspiration for Luti had come from the books of Arthur Grimble, the former administrator of the Gilbert and Ellice Islands, a colony administered by Britain. The islands, a string of low-lying coral atolls to the northeast of Australia, were dependent on Burns, Philp and Co. steamers from Australia for their supplies. One of Grimble's books, *A Pattern of Islands,* published in 1952, sold an astounding quarter of a million copies. It had sat on Pamela's bookshelves for decades. She remembered how Grimble explained that the islanders said "blessings and peace" and told Bergsten she turned the phrase around. Like Grimble's islanders, Luti had thought of the sun as his ancestor. Even Keria, the wise woman, had her basis in the women of *A Pattern of Islands* who conjured up spells by their clay ovens.

Pamela dedicated this last Mary Poppins book to Bruno, her only grandson, Bruno Henry Travers, born in 1985. The advance from Collins was only £4,000, barely enough to cover the wages she paid all her helpers, but again, America paid more. When the book was published in the United States, Delacorte Press paid her an advance of $24,000.

To each correspondent now, Pamela explained that the arthritis in her hands hurt too much for her to write or even to type. Her feet ached even more. She tried reflexology and faradic baths, and acupressure, all without much success. She shuffled about the house, hardly daring to walk down Shawfield Street. Was it rheumatoid arthritis? Courtenay Mayers assured her the pain was only a mild form of arthritis in her spine as well as her hands.

Pamela shut off the world. No more newspapers (she had liked the *Guardian*), no more walks to the Kings Road. She sat in her chair by the window. On the wall beside her was a wooden angel. In the hallway, the rocking horse still sat riderless. Mervyn, she called him, after Mervyn Peake, the author of *Gormenghast*. Her only writing now was for *Parabola*. A collection of those *Parabola* pieces was published as *What the Bee Knows*. It was her last book, published in March 1989 by Aquarian Press. All her old fans as well as all the new seekers for information about her life were urged to read *What the Bee Knows,* which she saw as a guide to her life's journey. The problem was, the book was written for insiders, a tight circle who had studied myth or followed the Work. To outsiders, everything about it was obscure, from the title which came from the old English adage, "Ask the wild bee what the Druids knew," to the cover illustration of a bee. This was no ordinary bumblebee, but, as she explained, a hieroglyphic bee which was the sign of the king of Lower Egypt, from the coffin of Mykerinos, 3633 B.C.

With superhuman effort, Pamela could still climb to the top of the house, up to her typewriter. Her papers were a jumble now, the desktop covered with dust and old rubber bands and carbon paper. On good days, she could type a little. In June 1989 she wrote a letter to Camillus. The tone was modest. If it was not too much trouble, she would like to let him know how to conduct her funeral. Pamela wanted to be buried in the courtyard at St. Luke's Church in Bovington, near Hemel Hempstead at Hertfordshire, where she gave the eulogy for Rosemary Nott. Here, after the funeral for Rosemary, she had bought a grave. They could take her there in her coffin the day after her funeral service at Christ Church, where she had been a regular parishioner and where her three grandchildren were christened.

He should let all the Gurdjieff people know of her death. It was the custom for the people in the Work to come and sit with the dead person for a while. They could do so in her bedroom, where she would be laid out on her bed, or perhaps in the sitting room. For the service, she wanted John Bunyan's hymn "He Who Would Valiant Be." The service could end with "God Be in My Head." Above all, she wanted her funeral to be festive, not dreary. Pamela had remembered that day in Paris so clearly, the sunny day when Gurdjieff died. She wanted music from the Gurdjieff years as well, music she had heard in the movement halls of London and Paris. If anyone felt moved to speak, well and good, otherwise someone might recite "Fear no more the heat of the sun" from Shakespeare's *Cymbeline*.

The Times would have to be told, but the death notice should not reveal any personal data, just "Pamela Lyndon Travers, eldest daughter of the late Robert and Margaret Goff." Camillus was not to reveal her age, nothing. She reminded him how much she valued anonymity. The more information was released, the more he could expect reporters buzzing around. In any case, the obituaries were bound to be full of nonsense.

Early in 1991, Pamela signed a will leaving specific bequests to the Gurdjieff Society, to Jessmin Howarth's daughter, Dushka, to her grandchildren, and to Camillus. Her trustees were to administer two funds for Camillus and Frances. She wished her death to be verified by the opening of a vein by Bernard Courtenay Mayers and her burial to be postponed for some time after her death so people could come and sit and watch with her. This time, she had left suggestions for her funeral with Adam Nott, making a special request that any obituary written about her should be as modest and reticent as possible.

Death felt close. Most days, Pamela thought she might be physically ill, and none of her old medicines helped. She had consulted a neurologist, two orthopedic surgeons, and a specialist at the foot hospital, but nothing could reassure her. From head to foot, Pamela was a walking compendium of worry. One doctor removed the warts from her face while another assured her that her feet were not really shrinking at all.

In 1992, she moved into a nursing home in Pimlico but returned after a few weeks to Shawfield Street, where the only option seemed to be to install a stair lift. As well, she ordered special orthopedic chairs and a series of noisy bells that would call the maids and housekeepers to her side. The bells might clang and *brrring* at any hour of the day or night, even at three in the morning.

Her caregivers were a succession of maids—Maria and Kay and Sheryl and Marli—but her main support was Patricia Feltham, a Gurdjieff friend who managed her business and personal affairs, even dealing with her lawyers.

In 1994, a reporter from *The New York Times* reminded her

how much she had looked forward to her rocking chair and to knowing all the answers. Pamela almost shouted back, "But here I am sitting in my chair and I don't think I'm going to know all the answers. I'm human." The next year, a journalist from the *Observer,* Nicci Gerrard, found Pamela talking in gulps, her crumpled body sitting by the window, her tongue rolling over swollen lips, her hands held carefully in her lap. She answered, "I have no gift for numbers" to Gerrard's questions "How long have you lived here?" "How old are you?" and "I hear you have many grandchildren, how many?" Again and again came the mantra, "My dear, you are asking the wrong questions, I have no gift for numbers."

All she could tell Gerrard, really, was how "I've been looking for an idea all my life. I know what it is and sometimes I come near to it, and that's all I will say." Did Gerrard know that there was something deeper than happiness? Happiness was like the weather. Yes, sometimes she was scared of death. After the interview, Pamela spoke to Gerrard on the phone. There was just once thing she wanted to add: happiness was not the same as being happy-go-lucky. "I have not said this before, but I have suffered a lot in my life. I will only share my suffering with my pillow."12

The reason for the interview was a last glimmer of hope for a Mary Poppins musical. In 1995, her agents had optioned the rights to the producers David Pugh and Cameron Mackintosh. There was, as yet, no script but plenty of hope; after all, Mackintosh was an impresario with some serious money behind him. Word had spread that Meryl Streep, Emma Thompson or Fiona Shaw might play Mary Poppins this time.

Pamela spent the last year of her life as a recluse in Shawfield Street. Sometimes she wrote a few lines to Camillus or her friends in a thin and wavery hand. Like the last letter of Aunt

Ellie, her words seemed to run off the page in a cobwebby shiver. In the summer of 1995 she wrote to "Darling Camillus," asking him to come and see her. She needed to talk to him; after all, she would be ninety-six in August.

Of all the little aches and pains in her fingers, joints, spine and stomach, it was her heels that hurt the most. Courtenay Mayers suggested sheepskin booties. She called the offices of Goodman Derrick. It was time to sign a new will. Her three trustees were all to be lawyers from Goodman Derrick. The three were to administer a discretionary trust of which Camillus and his children were the main beneficiaries. The Cherry Tree Foundation would be the other beneficiary of the trust. Pamela left £2000 to Bernard, $5,000 to Dushka Howarth, and her books and two paintings by AE to Camillus. Some of her silver jewelry was willed to Patricia Feltham while other friends would receive specific amounts from income from any future commercial production of Mary Poppins. One such beneficiary was AE's granddaughter, Pamela Jessup. The will was witnessed on February 9 by Pamela's housekeeper, Kay Ercolano, and a Danish woman from a nursing care agency, Pernille Boldt.

The will was oddly similar to Aunt Ellie's, almost as careful, almost as detailed, her life's treasures allocated like so many coffee spoons. Nothing for Mary Shepard, now in a nursing home. Nothing to come home to Australia. But then there was no one left there for her to remember.

Pamela died in April. The "cruellest month," T. S. Eliot called it, "mixing memory and desire, stirring dull roots with spring rain." In winter she had been cushioned inside, like her aching feet in the sheepskin booties, but now, with the first glimmer of spring, her body refused to go on. Two days before she died her friend Ben Haggarty saw her in what seemed a deep sleep. Her face, he thought, looked profoundly Celtic.

Camillus came to Shawfield Street on April 22, the day before she died. Pamela couldn't speak. He sat beside her and began to sing a lullaby, one which she had sung to him. "Do you want the moon to play with, and the stars to run away with?"

Patricia Feltham had her official *Times* obituary ready. She was first into print, her tribute closely following the biographical entry in the catalogue to Pamela's papers in the Mitchell Library. The others followed days later: a former publisher, Adrian House, in the *Guardian,* Susha Guppy in the *Independent,* Margalit Fox in *The New York Times* (who said Pamela's father was a sugar planter). The Disney organization placed ads in trade magazines. They showed Mickey Mouse in tears.

Her funeral was held on May Day, at Christ Church, as she had wanted. In one bloc sat the accountants and lawyers, black-suited, enigmatic. In another sat the Gurdjieffians. They had said their farewells already, sitting with Pamela's body as she had sat with Gurdjieff in the American Hospital in Paris. In their hands, they all held the order of service, its pale yellow cover printed with a picture of Mary Poppins flying up to the sky, her umbrella opened in her right hand, her carpetbag packed and ready for the heavens in her left hand.

It all happened as she had hoped, beginning with the hymn of St. Patrick, "I Bind unto Myself Today." Camillus spoke. He had chosen words that he loved from the Wisdom of Solomon, a book in the Apocrypha, which refers to the cosmic god Aeon. The reading began, "But the souls of the righteous are in the hand of God, and no torment will ever touch them." He ended with the lines that conjured up a hazy golden light, like the burning horizons of a Turner painting:

Having been disciplined a little
they will receive great good
because God tested them and
found them worthy of himself
like gold in the furnace he tried them

and like a sacrificial burnt offering
he accepted them
in the time of their visitation they
will shine forth
and will run like sparks through the stubble

The congregation all sang the Twenty-third Psalm. Then Patricia Feltham read the lines from *Cymbeline*:

Fear no more the heat of the sun
nor the furious winter's rages
thou thy worldly task has done
home art gone and ta'en thy wages
golden lads and girls all must,
as chimney sweepers come to dust.

Pamela had asked Ben Haggarty to give the eulogy. Haggarty was a storyteller and former actor who had read her first piece in *Parabola*, "The World of the Hero," and felt his life transformed. This was what she wanted most, one of those young men who had always asked the best questions to say the last words for her.

The choir sang "God Be in My Head," unaccompanied. The congregation rose to sing "He Who Would Valiant Be" and, as the coffin left the church, Pamela's Gurdjieff group sang, spontaneously, "Lord of the Dance." She, the dancer, had loved that song. Her body was cremated and her ashes placed in the churchyard garden of St. Mary the Virgin Church, overlooking the Thames at Twickenham. Pamela had said she wanted to be near her only family, the grave at Bovington long forgotten. All that marked the final resting place of Pamela, actress, writer, poet, was a plaque that read "Pamela Travers." No dates, no details. Within the church and its grounds lay the remains of the poet Alexander Pope.

In September, probate was granted on her estate of £2,044,078. Camillus, now divorced, came to live at Shaw-field Street. Cameron Mackintosh ran into trouble with Disney, as expected. He wanted his stage version of *Mary Poppins* to be completely different to the books and movie but thought it essential to have the best known songs from the Sherman brothers' score. The Disney people would not allow the songs to be used. It was stalemate once again.

Pamela once said that if ever her friends held a memorial ser-vice for her, she wanted some lines read from Blake's poem "Night," one of his series of poems called *Songs of Innocence*. It began:

> *The sun descending in the west*
> *The evening star does shine.*
> *The birds are silent in their nest,*
> *And I must seek for mine,*
> *The moon like a flower,*
> *In heaven's high bower,*
> *With silent delight*
> *Sits and smiles on the night.*

The words had carried her back to the night sky of Allora, to the moment when everything stood still at sunset, to the memory of the prickly grass digging into her bare shoulders, the lights shining from the house, her mother calling her in, "Lyndon, Lyndon..."

When she thought about who she really was, not Dr. P. L. Travers, but Helen Lyndon Goff, an Australian woman who had taken a circuitous journey of a hundred years, she knew the truth of the lines she often quoted from the American poet, Theodore Roethke: "You learn by going where you have to go." As she said, "You can't learn before you set out, can you? You go along the road, and you learn as you go."[13] Ouspensky had told her the spiritual quest was its own justification. He quoted T. S. Eliot: "To make an end is to make a beginning." So it proved to be for Pamela Travers.

She spent her life searching for Mr. Banks. She never found him. All the Mr. Bankses on the way, from Lawrence Campbell to Allan Wilkie to Frank Morton, to Yeats, Orage, AE, Ouspensky, Gurdjieff and Krishnamurti, helped Helen Lyndon Goff grow into Pamela Travers. But in the end, she found her own identity, masked though it might be, through her own long search, conducted alone. She was, as she always knew she would be, the hero of a story—her own.

Notes

PREFACE

1. Letter from Ted Hughes, undated, Mitchell Library, Sydney.
2. P. L. Travers, *About the Sleeping Beauty* (London: Collins, 1975).
3. Feenie Ziner, "Mary Poppins as a Zen Monk," *The New York Times,* May 7, 1972.
4. "A Remarkable Conversation About Sorrow," interview on June 23, 1965 by Janet Graham, *Ladies' Home Journal.*
5. Letter to Staffan Bergsten, February 19, 1977.
6. Michael Holroyd, interview by Nigel Farndale, *Daily Telegraph,* July 4, 1998.
7. The late wind that cools Sydney after a hot summer day.
8. Boston radio station interview, 1965.
9. "A Remarkable Conversation About Sorrow."
10. Ibid.
11. Ms. note written by P. L. Travers during World War II, Mitchell Library.
12. Salman Rushdie, interview by Nigel Williamson, *The Times,* April 3, 1999.
13. Jonathan Cott, *Pipers at the Gates of Dawn: The Wisdom of Children's Literature* (New York: Random House, 1983).

PROLOGUE TO PART 1

1. Lecture notes prepared by P. L. Travers, 1947/8, Mitchell Library, Sydney.

1. THE REAL MR. BANKS

1. P. L. Travers, *Johnny Delaney* (New York: Reynal & Hitchcock, 1944).
2. Interview by Robert Anton Wilson, *New Age Journal,* August 1984.
3. Shusha Guppy, *Looking Back: A Panoramic View of a Literary Age by the Grandes Dames of European Letters.* (New York: Simon & Schuster, 1993); letter to Staffan Bergsten, February 19, 1977.
4. Westpac archives.
5. The AJS bank continued under that name until 1906 when it was re-formed as the Australian Bank of Commerce. Eventually it became part of the Bank of New South Wales, then Westpac.
6. P. L. Travers, *Mary Poppins* (London: Gerard Howe, 1934).
7. Letter to Staffan Bergsten, February 19, 1977.
8. Helen Morehead's memoirs, Mitchell Library, Sydney.
9. David S. Macmillan, "R.A.A. Morehead" in *Australian Dictionary of Biography,* vol. 2 (Melbourne: Melbourne University Press; London/New York: Cambridge University Press, 1967).
10. P. L. Travers, *Aunt Sass* (New York: Reynal & Hitchcock, 1941).
11. Ross Fitzgerald, *From the Dreaming to 1915: A History of Queensland* (Queensland, Australia: University of Queensland Press, 1982).
12. Letter to Staffan Bergsten, February 19, 1977.
13. Article by P. L. Travers in *The New York Times,* October 20, 1962.
14. "Only Connect," speech to the Library of Congress, October 31, 1966.
15. Letter to Staffan Bergsten, February 19, 1977.
16. Letter from Travers Goff to Margaret Goff, Mitchell Library, Sydney.
17. Jonathan Cott, *Pipers at the Gates of Dawn: The Wisdom of Children's Literature* (New York: Random House, 1983).
18. "A Radical Innocence," *The New York Times,* May 9, 1965.
19. "A Remarkable Conversation About Sorrow," interview on June 23, 1965 by Janet Graham, *Ladies' Home Journal.*
20. "A Radical Innocence."
21. "A Radical Innocence"; "Only Connect"; interview by Michele Field, *Good Weekend,* January 25, 1986; Roy Newquist, *Conversations* (New York: Simon & Schuster, 1967); "A Remarkable Conversation About Sorrow."
22. Interview by Melinda Green, 1976; "The Primary World," *Parabola,* 1979; *Conversations*; "Only Connect"; "Joyful and Triumphant, Some Friends of Mary Poppins," *McCall's,* May 1966; "The Black Sheep," *The New York Times,* November 7, 1965; "A Remarkable Conversation About Sorrow"; "Looking Back," *The New Yorker,* October 20, 1962; interview by Robert Anton Wilson, *New Age Journal.*
23. "A Remarkable Conversation About Sorrow"; Cott, *Pipers at the Gates of Dawn;* "A Radical Innocence."
24. "The Primary World."

25. "Silver Lake, Golden Window," *Good Housekeeping*, April 1948.
26. Westpac archives.
27. Cicely Goff's birth certificate.
28. Travers, *Aunt Sass*. In this account of Helen Christina Morehead, she was called "Aunt Sass" or "Christina Saraset."

2. ELLIE AND ALLORA

1. P. L. Travers, *Aunt Sass* (New York: Reynal & Hitchcock, 1941).
2. "A Radical Innocence," *The New York Times*, May 9, 1965.
3. Letter from Travers Goff, August 5, 1905, Mitchell Library.
4. "Silver Lake, Golden Window," *Good Housekeeping*, April 1948.
5. "The Black Sheep," *The New York Times*, November 7, 1965.
6. Ms. note by P. L. Travers, Mitchell Library, Sydney.
7. "Meet the Creator of Mary Poppins," interview by Ian Woodward, *Women's Weekly*, 1975.
8. Ms. note by P. L. Travers at Shawfield Street, Chelsea.
9. *Good Housekeeping*, April 1948.
10. "Where will all the stories go?" *Parabola*, 1982.
11. Lecture notes prepared by P. L. Travers, 1947/8, Mitchell Library, Sydney.
12. "The Primary World," *Parabola*, 1979.
13. Letter to Staffan Bergsten, March, 20, 1977.
14. "Now Hail and Farewell," *Parabola*, 1985.
15. Boston radio station interview, 1965.
16. "A Remarkable Conversation About Sorrow," interview on June 23, 1965 by Janet Graham, *Ladies' Home Journal*.
17. "That Friend," *Good Housekeeping*, November 1950.
18. "A Radical Innocence."
19. Lecture notes prepared by P. L. Travers, 1947/8, Mitchell Library, Sydney.
20. Ms. note in Mitchell Library, Sydney.
21. Jonathan Cott, *Pipers at the Gates of Dawn: The Wisdom of Children's Literature* (New York: Random House, 1983).
22. Interview with Camillus Travers, 1997.
23. Cott, *Pipers at the Gates of Dawn*.
24. "Letter to a Learned Astrologer," *Parabola*, 1973.
25. "Fear No More the Heat of the Sun," *Parabola*, 1977.
26. "The Black Sheep."
27. "I Never Wrote for Children." *The New York Times*, July 2,1978.
28. Shusha Guppy, *Looking Back: A Panoramic View of a Literary Age by the Grandes Dames of European Letters*. (New York: Simon & Schuster, 1993).
29. "Now Hail and Farewell."
30. Cott, *Pipers at the Gates of Dawn*.
31. "A Remarkable Conversation About Sorrow."
32. "Threepenny Bit," article by P. L. Travers in ms. form, Mitchell Library, Sydney.
33. Interview by Melinda Green, 1976, typescript, Mitchell Library.

34. "Fear No More the Heat of the Sun."
35. Roy Newquist, *Conversations* (New York: Simon & Schuster, 1967).
36. Boston radio station interview, 1965.
37. "A Radical Innocence."
38. "Only Connect," speech to the Library of Congress, October 31, 1966.
39. "Letter to a Learned Astrologer."
40. Ms. note in Mitchell Library, Sydney.
41. P. L. Travers, *Johnny Delaney* (New York: Reynal & Hitchcock, 1944).
42. Letter to Dushka Howarth, November 1981.
43. Letter to Professor Staffan Bergsten, February 19, 1977.
44. "Threepenny Bit."
45. Letter to Staffan Bergsten, February 19, 1977.
46. Travers, *Aunt Sass.*

3. OLD ENGLAND IN AUSTRALIA

1. *The Triad,* September 10, 1923.
2. Ms. note in Mitchell Library, Sydney.
3. "Miss Quigley," *Parabola,* 1984.
4. Aunt Ellie's memoirs, Mitchell Library, Sydney.
5. Article in ms. form at Shawfield Street, Chelsea.
6. Shusha Guppy, *Looking Back: A Panoramic View of a Literary Age by the Grandes Dames of European Letters.* (New York: Simon & Schuster, 1993).
7. The concern over being the oldest child appears in many reminiscences, including "A Remarkable Conversation About Sorrow," interview on June 23, 1965 by Janet Graham, *Ladies' Home Journal.*
8. Letter to Staffan Bergsten, February 19, 1977.
9. "A Radical Innocence," *The New York Times,* May 9, 1965.
10. The account of her mother's distress and the tale of the white horse appear in "The Interviewer," *Parabola,* 1988, and in a letter to Staffan Bergsten, February 19, 1977.
11. Ibid.
12. P. L. Travers said twice she went to Normanhurst boarding school aged eleven. But as she consistently lowered her age, and as there is no record of her in the school's magazine before 1913, this seems unlikely. The pupil records of the school no longer exist. The school itself closed in 1941.
13. Ms. note in Mitchell Library, Sydney.
14. Sheena and Robert Coupe, *Speed the Plough: Ashfield 1788–1988* (Ashfield, Australia: Council of the Municipality of Ashfield, 1988).
15. Interview by Miss Arledge, undated, Mitchell Library, Sydney.
16. "Threepenny Bit," article by P. L. Travers in ms. form, Mitchell Library, Sydney.
17. Jonathan Cott, *Pipers at the Gates of Dawn: The Wisdom of Children's Literature* (New York: Random House, 1983).
18. Normanhurst School Magazine, issues 1913 through 1916, Mitchell Library, Sydney.

19. *Good Weekend,* January 25, 1986.
20. Roy Newquist, *Conversations* (New York: Simon & Schuster, 1967).
21. Rosemary Broomham, *First Light: 150 Years of Gas* (Sydney, Australia: Hale and Iremonger, 1987; Helen Rutledge, *My Grandfather's House* (Sydney, Doubleday, 1986).
22. Guppy, *Looking Back.*
23. P. L. Travers, "A Note on Cliques," Christchurch *Sun,* May 22, 1924.

4. THE CREATION OF PAMELA

1. Maryborough *Chronicle,* April 18, 1945.
2. P. L. Travers, *Shakespeare in the Antipodes*, unpublished ms., Mitchell Library.
3. Ibid.
4. Shusha Guppy, *Looking Back: A Panoramic View of a Literary Age by the Grandes Dames of European Letters.* (New York: Simon & Schuster, 1993).
5. *Australian Dictionary of Biography,* vol. 8 (Melbourne: Melbourne University Press; London/New York: Cambridge University Press, 1981).
6. *All the World's My Stage: The Reminiscences of a Shakespearean Actor Manager in Five Continents,* unpublished ms. in La Trobe Library, Melbourne.
7. Travers, *Shakespeare in the Antipodes.*
8. *The Triad,* April 11, 1921.
9. Travers, *Shakespeare in the Antipodes.*
10. Maryborough *Chronicle,* April 18, 1945.
11. Ibid.
12. *The Triad,* May 10, 1922.
13. *The Triad,* July 10, 1923.
14. *The Triad,* November 10, 1923.
15. Roy Newquist, *Conversations* (New York: Simon & Schuster, 1967) and Guppy, *Looking Back.*
16. Maryborough *Chronicle,* April 18, 1945.
17. Ms. note in Mitchell Library, Sydney.
18. P. L. Travers, *Aunt Sass* (New York: Reynal & Hitchcock, 1941).
19. *The Triad,* February 11, 1924.
20. *Australian Dictionary of Biography,* vol. 10, B. G. Andrews and Martha Rutledge, 1986.
21. *The Triad,* May 1923 to December 1924.
22. Newquist, *Conversations.*
23. "Only Connect," speech to the Library of Congress, October 31, 1966.
24. Travers, *Aunt Sass.*
25. "More Last Words: Pamela Passes London-ward," Christchurch *Sun,* March 13, 1924.
26. This book was never published.
27. *The Triad,* February 11, 1924.

5. FALLING INTO IRELAND

1. "Letter to a Learned Astrologer," *Parabola,* 1979.

2. "Song of Joyous Garnering," Christchurch *Sun,* March 21, 1924.
3. "Now Hail and Farewell," *Parabola,* 1985.
4. *Australian Women's Weekly,* December 28, 1966.
5. *The Triad,* August 11, 1924.
6. *McCall's,* May 1966.
7. Ibid.
8. Martin Green, *Children of the Sun: A Narrative of Decadence in England After 1918* (London: Constable, 1977).
9. Ibid.
10. David Thomson, *England in the Twentieth Century* (Baltimore: Penguin Books, 1965).
11. Ibid.
12. *The Triad,* July 10, 1924.
13. Autobiographical note, Shawfield Street, Chelsea; P. L. Travers, "The Death of AE, Irish Hero and Mystic" in *The Celtic Consciousness,* ed. Robert O'Driscoll (New York: Braziller, 1981).
14. "Only Connect," speech to the Library of Congress, October 31, 1966.
15. Letter from Simone Tery to AE, 1933, in the Denson Collection, National Library of Ireland.
16. R. F. Foster, *W.B. Yeats: A Life,* vol. 1, *The Apprentice Mage* (Oxford: Oxford University Press, 1997).
17. "Only Connect."
18. Oliver St John Gogarty, *As I Was Going Down Sackville Street* (New York: Reynal & Hitchcock, 1937).
19. Ibid.
20. John Eglinton, *A Memoir of AE* (London: Macmillan, 1937).
21. Ibid.
22. Henry Summerfield, *That Myriad Minded Man: A Biography of George Russell "AE," 1867–1935* (Gerrards Cross, UK: Colin Smythe Ltd, 1975).
23. Anthony Storr, *Feet of Clay: A Study of Gurus* (London: HarperCollins, 1996).
24. Richard Ellmann, *Yeats: The Man and the Masks* (New York: W. W. Norton, 1979).
25. Summerfield, *That Myriad Minded Man.*
26. AE [George William Russell], *The Candle of Vision* (London: Macmillan, 1918).
27. Hubert Butler, *Independent Spirit* (New York: Farrar, Straus & Giroux, 1996).
28. Summerfield, *That Myriad Minded Man.*
29. Kenneth R. Philp, *John Collier's Crusade for Indian Reform, 1920–1954* (Tucson: University of Arizona Press, 1977).
30. Butler, *Independent Spirit.*
31. Ms. note written by P. L. Travers, Mitchell Library, Sydney.
32. AE's letter to P. L. Travers, October 5, 1927.
33. Summerfield, *That Myriad Minded Man.*
34. Letter to Staffan Bergsten, February 19, 1977.
35. "The Death of AE."
36. "Only Connect."

37. Ibid.

38. "The Death of AE."

39. August 7, 1926.

40. "The Death of AE."

41. *Australian Women's Weekly,* interview by Bill Wilson, December 28, 1966.

42. Jonathan Cott, *Pipers at the Gates of Dawn: The Wisdom of Children's Literature* (New York: Random House, 1983).

43. Letter dated December 22, 1926.

44. Tape of Travers talking to students at Cambridge, Massachusetts, January 15, 1966.

45. The Christchurch *Sun,* October 23, 1926.

46. "Only Connect."

47. Letter to Leah Rose Bernstein, June 11, 1929, Denson Collection, National Library of Ireland.

48. Letter dated July 11, 1932, Denson Collection; letter to John Quinn, 1904; letter to Leah Rose Bernstein; letter to Yeats, July 11, 1932; Eglinton, *A Memoir of AE.*

49. Some of the description is from notes in the Denson Collection.

50. "The Death of AE"; Eglinton, *A Memoir of AE.*

51. Eglinton, *A Memoir of AE.*

52. Ruth Pitter's letter to Alan Denson, National Library of Ireland.

53. Ms. note, Mitchell Library, Sydney.

54. "Only Connect."

55. "The Death of AE."

56. Letter to P. L. Travers, January 6, 1928.

57. Ms. note written by P. L. Travers, Mitchell Library, Sydney.

6. LOVERS, GURUS AND THE GLIMMERING GIRL

1. Letter dated October 5, 1927.

2. Burnand was editor of *Punch* from 1880 to 1906. Frank E. Huggett, *Victorian England as Seen by Punch* (London: Sidgwick and Jackson, 1978).

3. Letter dated October 4, 1927.

4. Letter dated August 19, 1927.

5. P. L. Travers, "The Death of AE, Irish Hero and Mystic" in *The Celtic Consciousness,* ed. Robert O'Driscoll (New York: Braziller, 1981).

6. Audiotape recorded at Smith College, Northampton, Massachusetts, October 1966.

7. Shusha Guppy, *Looking Back: A Panoramic View of a Literary Age by the Grandes Dames of European Letters.* (New York: Simon & Schuster, 1993)

8. Letter to Professor Carens, August 3, 1978, Mitchell Library.

9. Travers's letter to a Mr. Hamilton, November 19, 1986.

10. Letter to P. L. Travers in Mitchell Library, writer's name not given.

11. Letter to Leah Rose Bernstein, August 28, 1928.

12. Letters in the Denson Collection at the National Library of Ireland. Leah Rose wrote to Alan Denson, the compiler of this collection of AE's letters:

"This was a beautiful romance. AE and I adopted each other, I as a model, he as my inspiration. We painted all day and talked all night. I regret now I didn't go to Ireland with him but I was young and modest and afraid."

13. Letter dated July 16, 1928.
14. *The Irish Statesman,* October 12, 1929.
15. *The Irish Statesman,* October 26, 1929.
16. "The Plane Tree," April 23, 1927.
17. "Prayer in a Field," February 25, 1928.
18. Patricia Demers, *P. L. Travers* (Boston: Twayne Publishers, 1991). The Canadian academic Patricia Demers includes a chapter on Travers's poetry of eroticism. Demers speculates that Travers was disappointed with various relationships, but has no evidence to prove there were any. She discusses the poems from a feminist point of view.
19. *The New Triad,* August 1927 to July 1928.
20. Letter to Professor Carens, August 1978.
21. Letter dated February 29, 1929.
22. Henry Summerfield, *That Myriad Minded Man: A Biography of George Russell "AE," 1867–1935* (Gerrards Cross, UK: Colin Smythe, 1975); and letter in the Denson Collection, National Library of Ireland.
23. Letter to Professor Carens.
24. Letter dated February 13, 1930.
25. Letter dated May 6, 1930.
26. Letter dated December 2, 1930.
27. Letters to Joseph O'Neill and P. L. Travers, October and November 1930.
28. Letter dated December 2, 1930.
29. Undated letter, 1931.
30. "Some Friends of Mary Poppins," *McCall's,* May 1966.
31. Interviews with Doris Vockins, 1997 and 1998.
32. Letter dated December 15, 1931.
33. Letter, undated, late 1931.
34. Letter, undated, late 1931.
35. Letter dated January 20, 1931.
36. Letter dated February 18, 1932.
37. Letter dated March 6, 1932.
38. Letter dated August 11, 1932.
39. Hubert Butler, *Independent Spirit* (New York: Farrar, Straus and Giroux, 1996).
40. Audiotape recorded at Harvard, November 9, 1965, Mitchell Library.
41. Letter dated October 7, 1933.
42. Ms. note, Shawfield Street, Chelsea.
43. Letter dated October 7, 1933.
44. Peter Washington, *Madame Blavatsky's Baboon* (London: Secker & Warburg, 1993).
45. P. D. Ouspensky, *In Search of the Miraculous* (New York: Harcourt Brace, 1949).

46. J. G. Bennett, *Witness* (London: Hodder and Stoughton, 1962); Anthony Storr, *Feet of Clay: A Study of Gurus* (London: HarperCollins, 1996).
47. A. R. Orage, *Essays and Critical Writings of Orage,* ed. Herbert Read and Denis Saurat (London: S. Nott, 1935).
48. James Moore, *Gurdjieff: The Anatomy of a Myth* (Shaftesbury, UK: Element Books, 1991).
49. Letters dated April 18 and 23, 1934.
50. Letter, undated, 1934.
51. Letter dated August, 1934.
52. Letters dated October 10 and December, 1934.

PROLOGUE TO PART 2

1. P. L. Travers, *Mary Poppins Comes Back* (London: L. Dickson & Thompson, 1935).

7. POPPINS AND PAMELA IN WONDERLAND

1. Speech to Smith College students, October 7, 1966.
2. Ibid.
3. Jonathan Cott, *Pipers at the Gates of Dawn: The Wisdom of Children's Literature* (New York: Random House, 1983); Patricia Demers, *P. L. Travers* (Boston: Twayne Publishers, 1991).
4. Ms. note, Shawfield Street, Chelsea.
5. Letter to Joyce Madden, October 1964, Illinois State University.
6. Letter to Staffan Bergsten, February 20, 1978.
7. Staffan Bergsten, *Mary Poppins and Myth* (Stockholm: Almqvist & Wiksell International, 1978).
8. June 1, 1928.
9. Jackie Wullschläger, *Inventing Wonderland* (London: Methuen, 1995).
10. Letter to Staffan Bergsten, February 19, 1977.
11. Speech at Radcliffe College, January 1966.
12. *The Art of Beatrix Potter* (London: Frederick Warne, 1955).
13. Milo Reeve [P. L. Travers], "The Hidden Child" *New English Weekly,* April 10, 1947.
14. *New Age Journal,* August 1984.
15. Speech at Radcliffe College, January 1966.
16. Ibid.
17. Letter to Joyce Madden, October 1964.
18. Ibid.
19. Letter to Staffan Bergsten, February 19, 1977.
20. Shusha Guppy, *Looking Back: A Panoramic View of a Literary Age by the Grandes Dames of European Letters.* (New York: Simon & Schuster, 1993).
21. Letter to Staffan Bergsten, February 19, 1977.
22. Letter to Joyce Madden, October 1964.
23. "Where Did She Come From?" *Saturday Evening Post,* November 7, 1964.
24. Interview by Melinda Green in ms. form, Mitchell Library.

25. *Sun Herald,* August 4, 1963.
26. "The Pen and the Hand," *Christian Science Monitor,* October 15, 1960.
27. Letter to Mary Shepard, March 3, 1962.
28. Speech given at Radcliffe College, January 1966.
29. Guppy, *Looking Back.*
30. Ian Woodward, "Meet the Creator of Mary Poppins," *Women's Weekly,* 1975; interview on Boston radio station, 1965.
31. *Christian Science Monitor,* October 15, 1980.
32. Ms. note in Mitchell Library.
33. "The Pooh Poppins Connection," *Hampstead and Highgate Express,* May 21, 1982.
34. Guppy, *Looking Back.*
35. *Christian Science Monitor,* October 15, 1980.
36. Shepard's unpublished autobiographical notes.
37. Speech given at Radcliffe College, January 15, 1966.
38. Radcliffe College, January 8, 1966.
39. Guppy, *Looking Back.*
40. Nicolette Devas, *Two Flamboyant Fathers* (London: Collins, 1966).
41. Augustus John, "Chiaroscuro," quoted in Devas, *Two Flamboyant Fathers.*
42. Oliver St John Gogarty, *It Isn't This Time of the Year at All! An Unpremeditated Autobiography* (London: MacGibbon and Kee, 1954).
43. Devas, *Two Flamboyant Fathers.*
44. Ibid.

8. A BEAUTIFUL NIGHT FOR A DEATH

1. Letter to Lesley, an Australian friend, October 23, 1935.
2. Letter dated January 2, 1935.
3. Kenneth R. Philp, *John Collier's Crusade for Indian Reform, 1920–1954* (Tucson: University of Arizona Press, 1977).
4. Letters to Joseph O'Neill, January 26, 1935 and to P. L. Travers, February 9 and 18, 1935.
5. Letter to Lesley.
6. Note written by P. L. Travers, 1942, Mitchell Library.
7. Letter dated May 22, 1935.
8. James Moore, *Gurdjieff: The Anatomy of a Myth* (Shaftesbury, UK: Element, 1991).
9. Letter to Lesley.
10. Letter dated July 4, 1935.
11. Letter to Lesley.
12. Henry Summerfield, *That Myriad Minded Man: A Biography of George Russell "AE," 1867–1935* (Gerrards Cross, UK: Colin Smythe, 1975) .
13. Rough of letter written by P. L. Travers, dictated by AE, Mitchell Library.
14. Letter from P. L. Travers to Professor Carens, 1978.
15. Notes by P. L. Travers in 1942; "The Death of AE, Irish Hero and Mystic"

in *The Celtic Consciousness,* ed. Robert O'Driscoll (New York: Braziller, 1981).

16. Letter to Lesley and typed notes of P. L. Travers.
17. Lecture given at Smith College, October 7, 1966.
18. Letter to Lesley.
19. Ibid.
20. Ibid.

9. THE CROSSING OF CAMILLUS

1. P. L. Travers, *Aunt Sass* (New York: Reynal & Hitchcock, 1941).
2. Patricia Demers, *P. L. Travers* (Boston: Twayne Publishers, 1991).
3. Interview with Doris Vockins, then seventy-six years old, October, 1997.
4. William Patrick Patterson, *The Ladies of the Rope: Gurdjieff's Special Left Bank Women's Group* (Fairfax, CA: Arete Communications, 1999).
5. Maryborough *Chronicle,* April 18, 1945.
6. Letter to Staffan Bergsten, March 20, 1977.
7. Interview with Doris Vockins.
8. Doris says she left because her parents moved to Dunstan's Cross, nearer the village of Mayfield. Pamela did not offer to drive Doris to and from work and the three miles from Mayfield to the cottage was too far for her to walk. Doris left without acrimony.
9. *New English Weekly,* November 16, 1939.
10. Interview with Joseph Hone, October 1997.
11. Joseph Hone, *Children of the Country: Coast to Coast Across Africa* (London: Hamish Hamilton, 1986).
12. Interview with Sally (Hone) Cooke-Smith, October 1997.
13. Interviews with Joseph Hone and Camillus Travers.
14. Interview with Joseph Hone.
15. Interview with Sally Cooke-Smith.
16. Interview with Camillus Travers.
17. *New English Weekly,* January 11 and August 15, 1940.
18. Interview with Andrew Firrell, October 1997.

10. THROUGH THE DOOR TO MABELTOWN

1. P. L. Travers, *I Go By Sea, I Go By Land* (London: Peter Davies, 1941).
2. Carlton Jackson, *Who Will Take Our Children?* (London: Methuen, 1985).
3. Travers's letter to a Mr. Hamilton, November 19, 1986.
4. *I Go by Sea, I Go by Land.*
5. Ibid.
6. "Letters from Another World," *New English Weekly,* January 2, 1941.
7. Ibid.
8. "The Big Family," Mitchell Library, written approximately 1950.
9. Interview by Melinda Green, 1976, typescript, Mitchell Library.
10. Letter to Staffan Bergsten, February 20, 1978.
11. Letter to Mr. Hamilton.

12. "A Remarkable Conversation About Sorrow," interview on June 23, 1965 by Janet Graham, *Ladies' Home Journal*.
13. Lecture at Radcliffe College, 1965.
14. Farewell evening, Radcliffe Graduate Center, February 1996.
15. Travers "at home," talking to students at Cambridge, January 15, 1966.
16. Transcript of an "at home," Radcliffe.
17. *The New York Times Book Review,* December 19, 1943.
18. Lecture on myth given at the home of the Welches, February 11, 1972.
19. P. L. Travers, "The Bear Under the Bed," *Harper's Bazaar,* June 1943.
20. Notes from a lecture, 1946/47, in ms. form, Mitchell Library.
21. "The Big Family."
22. Interview by Melinda Green.
23. "The Big Family."
24. Ibid.
25. Shusha Guppy, *Looking Back: A Panoramic View of a Literary Age by the Grandes Dames of European Letters.* (New York: Simon & Schuster, 1993); autobiographical notes at Shawfield Street.
26. Ms. note in Mitchell Library.
27. Letter, August 15, 1943.
28. John Eldridge, *Growing Up in Wartime Mayfield, 1939–45* (Books for Dillons Only, 1997).
29. Autobiographical notes in Shawfield Street, Chelsea.
30. Maryborough *Chronicle,* April 18, 1945.
31. Interviews by Professor Robert Young, University of New Mexico, and Grace Gorman, Ganado, Arizona, January 1997.
32. Autobiographical notes, Mitchell Library.
33. "At home" talk at Radcliffe, 1965.
34. "The Big Family."
35. Jonathan Cott, *Pipers at the Gates of Dawn: The Wisdom of Children's Literature* (New York: Random House, 1983).
36. "At home" talk at Radcliffe, 1965.
37. "Name and No Name," *Parabola,* 1982.
38. Interview by Miss Arledge in ms. form, Mitchell Library, Sydney.
39. "Name and No Name."
40. Lois Palken Rudnick, *Mabel Dodge Luhan: New Woman, New Worlds* (Albuquerque: University of New Mexico Press, 1984).
41. Ibid.
42. Patricia Leigh Brown, "Parnassus in Taos," *The New York Times,* January 16, 1997.
43. A comment made by photographer Ansel Adams.
44. Harry T. Moore, *The Priest of Love: A Life of D. H. Lawrence* (London: William Heinemann, 1974).
45. James Moore, *Gurdjieff: the Anatomy of a Myth* (Shaftesbury, UK: Element, 1991).
46. Notes written by Travers on November 7, 1944.

47. Farewell evening with Travers at Radcliffe College Graduate Center, February 1966.
48. Talk at Radcliffe College, November 9, 1965.
49. "The Big Family."
50. Ibid.
51. Ibid.
52. *New English Weekly*, September 27, 1945.
53. *I Go by Sea, I Go by Land* and Eldridge, *Growing Up in Wartime Mayfield*.
54. *New English Weekly*, September 27, 1945.

11. MONSIEUR BON BON SAYS AU REVOIR

1. *New English Weekly*, September 27, 1945.
2. Typewritten notes, Shawfield Street, Chelsea.
3. Letter dated April 11, 1946 from Joseph Hone to Travers.
4. Letter from Travers to Dushka Howarth, 1981.
5. Diary kept by Travers, 1948.
6. Comments to portrait painter at Westminster Nursing Home in the 1990s.
7. Ibid.
8. Ibid.
9. J. G. Bennett and Elizabeth Bennett, *Idiots in Paris: The Diaries of J. G. Bennett and Elizabeth Bennett, 1949* (York Beach, ME: Samuel Weiser, Inc., 1991).
10. Ibid.
11. Diary.
12. Ibid.
13. Ibid.
14. Travers's letter to Louise Welch, 1949.
15. Diary, November 1, 1949.
16. Letter to Louise Welch.
17. Diary and letter to Louise Welch.
18. Diary.

12. SHADOWPLAY

1. Letter to Eugene Reynal, about 1950.
2. Interview by Melinda Green, 1976.
3. "Some Friends of Mary Poppins," *McCall's*, May 1966.
4. Interview with Joseph Hone, 1977.
5. Letter to Mary Shepard, September 18, 1958.
6. Interview with Joseph Hone.

13. THE AMERICANIZATION OF MARY

1. Marc Elliott, *Walt Disney: Hollywood's Dark Prince* (Secaucus, NJ: Carol, 1993).
2. *New York Herald Tribune* magazine, September 20, 1964.
3. Letter to Mrs. Reitsma-Bakker dated December 10, 1965.
4. *New York Herald Tribune*, July 7, 1963.

5. Steven Watts, *The Magic Kingdom: Walt Disney and the American Way of Life* (Boston: Houghton Mifflin, 1997).
6. Ibid.
7. *Wisdom* magazine, 1959.
8. Watts, *The Magic Kingdom.*
9. Interview by Virginia Peterson, Boston TV station, 1965.
10. "Some Friends of Mary Poppins," *McCall's,* May 1966.
11. Ibid.
12. Letter to Dr. Dennison Morey dated January 1965.
13. Letter from Travers to "John," 1989.
14. Letter dated April 14, 1961.
15. Telegram from Disney to Travers at Sheraton East dated April 14, 1961.
16. Interview by Jenny Koralek, May 1996.
17. Letter, month not given, 1961.
18. Letter dated June 6, 1961.
19. Letter dated June 10, 1961.
20. Letter dated August 26, 1961.
21. Letter dated March 2, 1962.
22. Letter dated March 9, 1962.
23. Interview by Janet Graham, *Ladies' Home Journal,* June 1965.
24. *The New Yorker,* October 20, 1962.
25. *Julie Andrews, Back on Broadway,* a WNET/Thirteen production for BBC World-wide.
26. Robert Windeler, *Julie Andrews: A Biography* (London: W. H. Allen, 1982); *Julie Andrews, Back on Broadway.*
27. *New York Herald Tribune,* July 7, 1963 and letter to Mary Shepard dated March 22, 1966.
28. Windeler, *Julie Andrews.*
29. Ibid.
30. Interview by Virginia Peterson, Boston TV station, 1965.
31. Letter dated November, 21, 1962.
32. *New York Herald Tribune,* September 20, 1964.
33. Nora E. Taylor, "If I Had to Lose . . ." *Christian Science Monitor,* November 3, 1964.
34. Shusha Guppy, *Looking Back: A Panoramic View of a Literary Age by the Grandes Dames of European Letters.* (New York: Simon & Schuster, 1993)
35. Interview by Janet Graham, 1965.
36. Interview by Melinda Green, 1976.
37. *Parabola,* 1987.
38. Letter dated February 11, 1964.
39. Letter to the UK publisher Collins dated August 18, 1964.
40. Ibid.
41. Letter dated August 12, 1964.
42. Letter to Collins, August 18, 1964.
43. Letter to Collins dated September 1, 1964.

44. Ibid.
45. Letter dated August 31.
46. Letter dated September 1, 1964.
47. Letter dated September 2, 1964.
48. Interview by Janet Graham, 1965.
49. Letter to M. Bryden from Travers at Whitman Hall, Radcliffe, 1965.
50. Ibid.
51. Richard Schikel, *Walt Disney* (London: Weidenfeld and Nicolson, 1968).
52. Letter to Joyce Madden, October 1964.
53. Letter to Dorothy Bart dated February 13, 1965.
54. Interview on June 23, 1965.
55. Letter to Mr. Fadiman, 1968.
56. Interview by Melinda Green, 1976.
57. *Trade News,* December 12, 1964.
58. Letter dated January 21, 1965.
59. Letter to Dr. Morey dated January 28, 1965.
60. *Saturday Review,* November 7, 1964.
61. *Chicago's American,* November 5, 1964.
62. The interview took place on June 23, 1965. Dozens of pages of transcript were sent to *Ladies' Home Journal,* which eventually published a short version of the interview in 1967.

PROLOGUE TO PART 3

1. Boston radio station interview, 1965.

14. A CRONE AMONG THE SLEEPING BEAUTIES

1. *The New York Times,* December 25, 1966 and Marina Warner, *From the Beast to the Blond: On Fairy Tales and Their Tellers* (London: Chatto & Windus, 1994).
2. Letter dated February 11, 1965.
3. Letter dated August 29, 1965.
4. Interview with Anthony Oettinger, January 1997.
5. Issue dated December 5, 1965.
6. "At home" recordings in January 1966, part of which appeared in the Radcliffe journal *The Island,* March 1966.
7. Ibid.
8. Ibid.
9. Interview by Paula Budlong Cronin, *Radcliffe Quarterly,* February 1966.
10. "Only Connect," speech to the Library of Congress, October 31, 1966.
11. Ibid.
12. *Boston Globe,* October 10, 1965.
13. Interview with Paula Cronin, January 1997.
14. *Christian Science Monitor,* November 16, 1965.
15. Boston Forum, WNAC, January 4, 1966.
16. *Homes and Gardens* (UK), January 1966.
17. Boston radio station interview, 1965.

18. Interview in January 1997 with Francis Murphy, formerly associate professor of the English faculty of Smith College, who said that Travers wrote to the office of the president, Thomas C. Mendenhall, seeking residency and that he then asked the English department if they would have her.

19. *The New Yorker*, October 20, 1962.

20. November 17, 1965.

21. Letter dated September 30, 1966.

22. Letter dated June 5, 1966.

23. "A Letter from Smith College," December 1971.

24. *The New York Times*, December 25, 1966.

25. Interview with Elizabeth von Klemperer, January 1997.

26. Article by Patricia Foster, *Smith College Quarterly*, February 1967.

27. *The Sophian*, October 6, 1966.

28. Ibid.

29. *Smith College Quarterly*.

30. Amherst's Four College radio interview November 8, 1966 and *Amherst Record*, November 15, 1966.

31. *Amherst Record*, November 10, 1966.

32. Interview with Pamela Russell Haigh, now Pamela Jessup, January 1997.

33. Interview with Francis Murphy, January 1997.

34. *Look*, December 13, 1966.

35. *Smith College Quarterly*, February 1967.

36. *The New York Times*, December 25, 1966.

37. Patricia Demers, *P. L. Travers* (Boston: Twayne Publishers, 1991).

38. Memo dated December 13, 1967.

15. LOOKING FOR PAMELA TRAVERS

1. Letter to Margaret McElderry dated March 31, 1967.

2. P. L. Travers, *Mary Poppins ab A to Z*, trans. into Latin by G. M. Lyne (New York: Harcourt Brace, 1968); book was dedicated to Arnold Abraham Goodman; translator is an Englishman, Maxwell Lyne, not the American professor from Amherst.

3. Shusha Guppy, *Looking Back: A Panoramic View of a Literary Age by the Grandes Dames of European Letters.* (New York: Simon & Schuster, 1993) and letters to Staffan Bergsten, January and March, 1976.

4. *The New York Times*, January 14, 1977; letters to Staffan Bergsten, January and September, 1976.

5. Pupul Jayakar, *Krishnamurti: A Biography* (San Francisco: Harper and Row, 1986).

6. Radha Rajagopal Sloss, *Lives in the Shadow with J. Krishnamurti* (London: Bloomsbury, 1991).

7. Bettina Hürlimann, *Seven Houses: My Life with Books*, trans. Anthea Bell (London: The Bodley Head, 1976).

8. Letters from Travers to Marjorie Downing, April 1, 1970 and from the rose grower Dr. Dennison Morey to Scripps College, February 12, 1970.

9. *The New York Times,* November 7, 1971.

10. Letter to Staffan Bergsten dated February 14, 1975.

11. Letter from William Heseltine dated September 15, 1972.

12. *The New York Times,* May 7, 1972.

13. Interview with Jenny Koralek, May 1996.

14. Patricia Demers, *P. L. Travers* (Boston: Twayne Publishers, 1991).

15. Ibid.

16. *The Times Literary Supplement,* December 2, 1977.

17. Letters dated March 8, April 21 and May 14, 1976.

18. Jonathan Cott, *Pipers at the Gates of Dawn: The Wisdom of Children's Literature* (New York: Random House, 1983), and letters to Bergsten, various dates.

19. *Parabola* essays, 1976 to 1979.

20. Letter dated December 27, 1976.

21. *The New York Times,* January 3, 1977.

22. Letter dated March 20, 1977.

23. Staffan Bergsten, *Mary Poppins and Myth* (Stockholm: Almqvist and Wiksell International, 1978).

24. Letter dated February 20, 1978.

25. Barbara Moriarty died on January 11, 1979.

16. FEAR NO MORE THE HEAT OF THE SUN

1. "The Pooh Poppins Connection," *Hampstead and Highgate Express,* May 21, 1982.

2. Letter to U.S. publisher Harcourt Brace Jovanovich dated February 21, 1981.

3. Letter to Barbara Lucas at Harcourt Brace Jovanovich dated February 25, 1981.

4. Letter to Jules Fisher dated August 17, 1982.

5. Letter from Jules Fisher dated April 27, 1984.

6. Letter to Staffan Bergsten dated December 9, 1987.

7. Letter from Staffan Bergsten dated December, 21, 1987.

8. Letter to Staffan Bergsten, May 1989.

9. Articles in *Good Weekend,* January 25, 1986, and *Publishers Weekly,* March 21, 1986.

10. Letter from Martin Kaplan dated March 8, 1988.

11. Interview with Jules Fisher, September 1998, and letter from Jules Fisher dated December 28, 1988. Graciela Daniele went on to choreograph the Woody Allen movies *Mighty Aphrodite* and *Everyone Says I Love You.*

12. Interview in *The Observer,* March 1995.

13. Jonathan Cott, *Pipers at the Gates of Dawn: The Wisdom of Children's Literature* (New York: Random House, 1983).

Bibliography

Ackroyd, Peter. *T. S. Eliot*. London: Hamish Hamilton, 1984.

Anderson, Margaret C. *The Unknowable Gurdjieff*. London: Routledge & Keegan Paul, 1962.

Bennett, J. G., and Elizabeth Bennett. *Idiots in Paris: The Diaries of J. G. Bennett and Elizabeth Bennett, 1949*. York Beach, ME: Samuel Weiser Inc., 1991.

Bennett, J. G. *Witness: The Story of a Search*. London: Hodder & Stoughton, 1962.

Bergsten, Staffan. *Mary Poppins and Myth*. Stockholm: Almqvist and Wiksell International, 1978.

Bettelheim, Bruno. *The Uses of Enchantment: The Meaning and Importance of Fairy Tales*. London: Thames & Hudson, 1976.

Blake, William. *The Complete Poems*. London: Penguin, 1977.

Butler, Hubert. *Independent Spirit: Essays*. New York: Farrar, Straus & Giroux, 1996.

Cooper, J. C., ed. *Brewer's Book of Myth and Legend*. London: Cassell, 1992.

Demers, Patricia. *P. L. Travers*. Boston: Twayne Publishers, 1991.

Dhu, Corbie [Bert Munro Sims], ed. *Allora's Past: The Early History of the Allora District, Darling Downs, Queensland. Incorporating Forgotten Tales*. Queensland, Australia: Allora Bicentennial Committee, 1987.

Eldridge, John. *Growing Up in Wartime Mayfield, 1939–45*. Books for Dillons Only, 1997.

Eliot, T. S. *The Waste Land and Other Poems*. London: Faber and Faber, 1940.

Eliot, Marc. *Walt Disney: Hollywood's Dark Prince*. Secaucus, NJ: Carol, 1993.

Ellmann, Richard. *Yeats: The Man and the Masks*. New York: W.W. Norton, 1979.

Foster, R. F. *W. B. Yeats: A Life*. Oxford: Oxford University Press, 1997.

Fuchs, John. *Forty Years After Gurdjieff: A Guide to Practical Work*. Denver, CO: Gurdjieff Group of Denver, 1994.

Grant, Michael, and John Haze. *Who's Who in Classical Mythology*. London: Weidenfeld & Nicolson, 1973.

Green, Martin. *Children of the Sun: A Narrative of Decadence in England After 1918*. London: Constable, 1977.

Grimble, Sir Arthur. *A Pattern of Islands*. London: John Murray, 1952.

Guppy, Shusha. *Looking Back: A Panoramic View of a Literary Age by the Grandes Dames of European Letters*. New York: Simon & Schuster, 1993.

Hürlimann, Bettina. *Seven Houses: My Life with Books*. Translated by Anthea Bell. London: The Bodley Head, 1976.

Igoe, Vivien. *A Literary Guide to Dublin: Literary Associations and Anecdotes*. London: Methuen, 1994.

Jackson, Carlton. *Who Will Take Our Children? The Story of the Evacuation in Britain 1939–1945*. London: Methuen, 1985.

Jayakar, Pupul. *Krishnamurti: A Biography*. San Francisco: Harper & Row, 1986.

Lane, Margaret. *The Tale of Beatrix Potter: A Biography*. London: Warne, 1946.

Lucas, Robert. *Frieda von Richthofen: Ihe Leben mit D. H. Lawrence*. Munich: Kindler Verlag, 1972.

Maddox, Brenda. *The Married Man: A Life of D. H. Lawrence*. London: Sinclair-Stevenson, 1994.

Maltin, Leonard. *The Disney Films*. New York: Crown, 1973.

Maryborough, Wide Bay and Burnett Historical Society. *A History of Maryborough, 1842–1976*. Queensland, Australia, 1976.

Moore, Harry T. *The Priest of Love: A Life of D. H. Lawrence*. London: William Heinemann, 1974.

Moore, James. *Gurdjieff: The Anatomy of a Myth*. Shaftesbury, UK: Element, 1991.

Page, Susanne, and Jake Page. *Navajo*. New York: Harry N. Abrams, 1995.

Patterson, William Patrick. *The Ladies of the Rope: Gurdjieff's Special Left Bank Women's Group*. Fairfax, CA: Arete Communications, 1999.

Peters, Fritz. *Gurdjieff Remembered*. London: Victor Gollanz, 1965.

Rudnick, Lois Palken. *Mabel Dodge Luhan: New Woman, New Worlds*. Albuquerque: University of New Mexico Press, 1984.

Rutledge, Helen. *My Grandfather's House*. Sydney: Doubleday, 1986.

Schickel, Richard. *Walt Disney*. London: Weidenfeld & Nicolson, 1968.

Sloss, Radha Rajagopal. *Lives in the Shadow with J. Krishnamurti*. London: Bloomsbury, 1991.

Storr, Anthony. *Feet of Clay: A Study of Gurus*. London: HarperCollins, 1996.

Summerfield, Henry. *That Myriad Minded Man: A Biography of George Russell "AE," 1867–1935*. Gerrards Cross, UK: Collins Smythe, 1975.

Thompson, David. *England in the Twentieth Century, 1914–63*. Baltimore: Penguin Books, 1965.

Travers, P. L., "Gurdjieff" in *Man, Myth and Magic: An Illustrated Encyclopedia of the Supernatural*. Edited by Richard Cavendish. London: Purnell for BPC, 1970–1972.

Warner, Marina. *From the Beast to the Blonde: On Fairy Tales and Their Tellers*. London: Chatto & Windus, 1994.

Washington, Peter. *Madame Blavatsky's Baboon: Theosophy and the Emergence of the Western Guru*. London: Secker & Warburg, 1993.

Watts, Steven. *The Magic Kingdom: Walt Disney and the American Way of Life*. Boston: Houghton Mifflin, 1997.

Windeler, Robert. *Julie Andrews: A Biography*. London: W. H. Allen, 1982.

Wullschlager, Jackie. *Inventing Wonderland: The Lives and Fantasies of Lewis Carroll, Edward Lear, J. M. Barrie, Kenneth Grahame, and A. A. Milne*. London: Methuen, 1995.

Yeats, W. B. *The Poems*. London: Dent, 1990.

Published Books by P. L. Travers

Moscow Excursion. New York: Reynal & Hitchcock, 1934.

Mary Poppins. London: Gerald Howe, 1934.

Mary Poppins Comes Back. London: L. Dickson & Thompson, 1935.

I Go by Sea, I Go by Land. London: Peter Davies, 1941.

Aunt Sass. New York: Reynal & Hitchcock, 1941.

Ah Wong. New York: Reynal & Hitchcock, 1943.

Johnny Delaney. New York: Reynal & Hitchcock, 1944.

Mary Poppins Opens the Door. London: Peter Davies, 1944.

Mary Poppins in the Park. London: Peter Davies, 1952.

Mary Poppins from A to Z. London: Collins, 1963.

The Fox at the Manger. London: Collins, 1963.

Friend Monkey, London: Collins, 1972.

About the Sleeping Beauty. London: Collins, 1975.

Mary Poppins in the Kitchen: A Cookery Book with a Story. New York & London: Harcourt Brace Jovanovich, 1975.

Two Pairs of Shoes. New York: Viking Press, 1980.

Mary Poppins in Cherry Tree Lane. London: Collins, 1982.

Mary Poppins and the House Next Door. New York: Delacorte Press, 1989.

What the Bee Knows: Reflections on Myth and Symbol. Wellingborough, UK: Aquarian Press, 1989.

Acknowledgments

Many people helped and supported me in the research and writing of this book but my greatest thanks go to P. L. Travers's son, Camillus Travers, for allowing me access to the studio of his late mother, for his generosity with his time, and for his willingness to share his memories about his mother and his own life.

Three women have been vital in the decade it took for the book to develop from an idea to reality. Michele Field, who interviewed Travers in the mid-1980s, suggested a biography to me in 1990. Five years later, Alison Pressley enthused me once again and, through the long process to publication, has been a wonderful ally and friend. And through all the ups and downs, Lyn Tranter kept me laughing and kept me going.

To the librarians of the Mitchell Library of the State Library of New South Wales, my deepest thanks, particularly to Louise Anemaat, who catalogued Travers's papers, to the manuscript librarian Paul Brunton, and to Rosemary Block, curator of oral history.

In Wellington, New Zealand, Rachel Lawson and Nicholas Lawson researched the Christchurch *Sun*. Their findings added immeasurably to research work already done by Dr. F. W. Nielsen Wright on Travers's journalism in New Zealand.

In the United Kingdom and the United States, my thanks to Mary Shepard's agent, Kathy Jakeman, for her generosity and kindness; to Ann Orage for her detailed work on Jessie Orage's diaries; to George William Russell's granddaughter, Pamela Jessup; to Camillus Travers's brother, Joseph Hone, his sister, Sheila Martin, and his aunt, Sally Cooke Smith, for many very helpful memories about the Hone family.

To Doris Vockins (now Doris Bruce), Lucy Firrell and Andew Firrell in Mayfield, Sussex, thank you for the afternoons in the sun at Pound Cottage and your unstinting help.

My thanks also to Ellen Dooling Draper, Penelope Fitzgerald, Jules Fisher, Robert Gray, Dushka Howarth, Minette Hunt, Joy McEntee, Sir Cameron Mackintosh, Maureen J. Russell, Michael Theis, Frances White, the Maryborough Historical Society, the Allora Historical Society, Jane Knowles, archivist at Radcliffe College, the archivists at Smith College, Scripps College and Chatham College, the librarians at the National Library of Dublin, the British Library, the U.S. National Archives, the U.S. National Library, the City of New York Parks and Recreation department, the public affairs office of the U.S. Library of Congress, and the staff of *Parabola* magazine, New York.

Thanks also to Faber and Faber and to the Trustees of the Eliot Estate for permission to reproduce the quotation from "Little Gidding" by T. S. Eliot.

Thank you Victor, Lucy and Annie Carroll for accompanying me on "the Pamela hunt" through the United States, Ireland and the United Kingdom and for adding to the pleasure of traveling with a purpose.

Index

Illustration Sources

Page 1: The Travers family collection

Page 2 (*top*): Photographed by Valerie Lawson, 1996; (*bottom*): The Travers family collection

Page 3 (*top and bottom left*): State Library of New South Wales; (*bottom right*): *Green Room* magazine

Page 4: The Travers Collection in the Mitchell Library, Sydney

Page 5 (*top and bottom right*): The Travers family collection; (*bottom left*): Photographed by Valerie Lawson, 1997

Pages 6 and 7: Illustrations from the Mary Poppins books by Mary Shepard, reproduced courtesy of N. E. Middleton Artists' Agency

Page 8 (*top left*): Hulton Getty; (*top right and bottom*): The Travers family collection

Page 9: The Travers family collection

Page 10: © Earl Thiesen/LOOK magazine, reproduced by permission

Page 11 (*top left*): © Earl Thiesen/LOOK magazine, reproduced by permission; (*top right*): *Modern Woman* magazine, January 1965; (*bottom right*): *Everybody's*, November 11, 1964; (*bottom left*): The Travers Collection in the Mitchell Library, Sydney

Pages 12 and 13: The Travers Collection in the Mitchell Library, Sydney

Page 14 (*top and lower right*): The Travers Collection in the Mitchell Library, Sydney; (*lower left*): *The Australian Women's Weekly*, December 28, 1966

Page 15 (*top*): *The Drapers' Record;* (*bottom*): The Travers Collection in the Mitchell Library, Sydney

Page 16 (*top*): The Travers family collection; (*middle*): © LOOK magazine; (*bottom*): © Jane Bown 1995, reproduced by permission